Understanding the Social Economy and the Third Sector

UNDERSTANDING THE SOCIAL ECONOMY AND THE THIRD SECTOR

2nd Edition

Simon Bridge, Brendan Murtagh & Ken O'Neill

contents

PART II   THE NATURE OF THE SOCIAL ECONOMY

figures, tables, illustrations and cases

figures

tables

illustrations

cases

preface

This is a book about the social economy and that section of the economy which is now often referred to as the third sector: a name which is intended to distinguish it from the public and private sectors. For many people the most important part of the third sector is the social economy, often because it seems to be the part which offers the most economic and social benefit. Some people refer to this area, or to parts of it, as the voluntary sector or the community sector, and there are other concepts associated with it such as social capital.

However, although these and other associated terms are now in relatively wide use, there is no general agreement about what they mean, and there seems to be little clarity about how they are linked. As a result, for those now working in this field, especially when they are new to it, there can be considerable confusion about what is involved. While there has been a third sector in an economy for as long as there have been the two other sectors, much of the language about it is only now developing, and, often with government encouragement, a new industry is evolving to promote and support it.

The aim

The aim of this book is to help make sense of this field by summarising, in an objective framework, what is known about these and similar issues and by indicating some of the main perspectives on them. The book therefore tries to present an overview of the key concepts, to explore the relevance today of the third sector and its components, to explore the varied meanings and definitions of these components including in particular the social economy, and to highlight some of the current key issues in the field, how they are being addressed, and some of their future implications.

Who should read this book

This book is targeted at policy-makers and staff of social enterprise support organisations, at students of the third sector at universities and business schools, at researchers and teaching staff, at social entrepreneurs and those working in the sector, and at funders and potential funders of third sector organisations. It provides a foundation text for those who are studying this sector and want a perspective appropriate both for those who might want to engage in it and for those who might want to work with, but not necessarily in, it. It has been written in the UK but it also refers to developments in other countries, and much of its content should be relevant elsewhere, where people, for whatever reason, wish to know more about the third sector and its context. It seeks to present them with a sound introduction to the key concepts and issues as a grounding for understanding and work in this area and as a starting point for further explorations of more specialised aspects.

The second edition

In this second edition we have endeavoured to update our reporting on the social economy and the third sector. We have also tried to focus more on the social economy and less on the wider third sector.

We have altered the layout slightly. In particular, we have added a new fifth chapter in which we consider the different paradigms of, and aspirations for, the social economy and what they might mean for its future. This replaces and amplifies the material which was in the Afterword. Other significant changes include:

Part I has been restructured to describe the social economy by considering its past, its present, and its future. Chapter 2 has been redrafted to describe economic evolution and the history of that part of an economy which is neither public nor private. Chapter 3 presents a picture of various aspects of the current position, including for instance Big Society, and Chapter 4 follows that with more detail on definitions and differing interpretations. Chapter 5 has then been added, incorporating much that was in Chapter 10.

Part II has been updated throughout – and the chapters renumbered after the addition of the new Chapter 5. For instance, information on Community Development Finance Institutions (CDFIs) and the Big Society Bank has been added to Chapter 7, a vitamin analogy for social capital has been added to Chapter 8, and policy updates to Chapter 9. Chapter 10 now concludes the book by looking at the impact of the social economy and includes a critique of some of the estimates which have been offered to indicate the scale of the sector.

Thank you

In our work in writing this book we have been conscious of many people who have helped and encouraged us, and others who have been tolerant of the time we have devoted to this instead of to other tasks. There are too many to name here but we owe them all considerable thanks.

Simon Bridge
Brendan Murtagh
Ken O'Neill
Belfast, April 2013

1

why address the social economy?

contents:

- introduction
- interest in the social economy and the third sector
- the appeal and benefits of the social economy
- the agenda of this book

Key concepts

This chapter covers:

- the emergence of interest in the social economy, its scale, and why it might have been overlooked in the past;
- the concept of the third sector and how it relates to the social economy;
- the range of benefits which, it is claimed, the social economy has the potential to deliver;
- the agenda, and layout, of this book.

Learning objectives

By the end of this chapter the reader should:

- understand why interest in the social economy is now growing;
- understand the concept of the social economy, why it might not have been widely recognised in the past, and why interest in it is now growing;
- understand the concept of the third sector and how it links to the social economy;
- appreciate the range of benefits that might be provided by this sector.

Introduction

This book is about an area of organised human activity which has often been overlooked but is now receiving greater recognition. It is an area which has both social and economic impact and is often referred to as the social economy. This, it has been said, 'constitutes a significant movement worldwide'[1] and has become 'a prominent field of public policy innovation, directly linking social policy and economic development'.[2] This link with social policy is often associated with the concept of social capital which the social economy is said to use and to build in the same way that many businesses use and build financial capital. But, although the social economy has been linked to social policy in this way, it is not in the public sector and, despite its links to economic development, it is not in the private sector either (although see the suggestions of Bjerke and Karlsson summarised in Chapter 5). It is therefore said to be, or to form a significant part of, the third sector of an economy. But what exactly are the social economy and the third sector, what is social capital and why is it relevant, why are these issues now of interest, and what is being achieved? These are the types of questions to which this book attempts to provide some answers. Much written material about these subjects tends to be academic, disparate, partial, and/or scattered, so this book attempts to bring key aspects of it together to provide a general introduction for those seeking to learn about it – or a starting point for those who might wish to delve deeper.

If economies are about apportioning resources and if, as has been suggested, the two main means for apportioning resources are the market and the state, what is the role of the social economy? Markets are linked to the private sector and the state to the public sector, so what then is the third sector to which reference is sometimes made, and what has it got to do with the social economy?

Traditional economics sometimes appears to ignore the social economy, apparently seeing no role for it in a modern system. Thus, a recently published book called *Modern Economics* includes the following statement about what is in a mixed economy:

> It is convenient to distinguish between the 'private sector' and the 'public sector'. The former consists of those firms which are privately owned. The latter includes government departments, local authorities, and public bodies such as the Environment

Agency. All are distinguished by the fact that their capital is publicly owned and their policies can be influenced through the ultimate supply of funds by the government. [3]

Thus it seemed to many that, based on the market and the state as the two main means of apportioning resources, the two key parts of an economy were the private and public sectors. Indeed, about 50 or so years ago, the two main options for society appeared to be private sector led, market-based capitalist economies of the sort apparently exemplified by the USA or public sector, state-controlled Marxist/socialist economies of the sort to which the USSR apparently aspired. However, while communist societies sought to abolish the private sector, capitalist societies still saw the need for some state input – recognising, for instance, that there were some things, like defence, which the private sector could not deliver satisfactorily. Also the state was needed to police and balance what might otherwise be the unrestrained power of private sector business.

Marx had seen the dangers of unrestrained capitalist power, but his ideas for a solution led, under communism, to the state takeover of all business. Thus, in those economies, the public sector became all powerful but with no separate monitoring or regulatory force. History, it would seem, has subsequently shown that such forms of unrestrained state power have not worked well. Therefore, to many observers, the 'capitalist' system seemed, on balance, to be better able to deliver a rising standard of living, and, around 50 years ago, it seemed that economic development was, and would continue to be, driven by big businesses which could maximise the advantages to be gained from economies of scale. However, John Kenneth Galbraith spoke then of the economic future as 'big business' balanced by 'big labor' and 'big government'. [4] Thus, just as a monopolistic state sector had not worked in communist systems, Galbraith was pointing out the danger of too much monopolistic power accruing to the big businesses which had come to dominate the private sector. But Galbraith was not just suggesting a balance of power between the private and public sectors: 'big business' and 'big government'. He also included 'big labor', and the views of 'big labor' are often voiced by labour unions, which, it is generally acknowledged, belong in neither the public nor the private sectors.

It is relevant, therefore, to ask whether it is sensible to divide an economy just into the private and public sectors, as suggested by the above quote from *Modern Economics*. A division into sectors implies that clear boundaries can be identified between the sectors, and recognising just two sectors suggests that between them they include all the relevant components. Is the reality not that there is a spectrum of different organisations, some of which may clearly be private sector as usually defined and some clearly public sector but with a variety of organisations lying between them and elsewhere? In a spectrum there are gradations of change with no sharp distinguishing features between different areas: for instance in the light spectrum between say what is clearly red and what is clearly yellow.

Even in the most capitalist of societies there are generally many organisations which do not seem to fit into the private sector yet which are not part of the public sector – and Table 1.1 lists just a few of them. Their capital is not privately owned and, although they may trade, they exist for a social purpose rather than to make money for their owners yet neither are they state/public bodies and so do not belong in either sector. Nevertheless, they have an economic impact and are part of the economy because they spend money, because many of them employ people, and, in some cases, because they generate income by trading. In the past it seems that the dilemma of where they belong in an economy may, to some extent, have been avoided by ignoring them, but now that their impact is being highlighted, that is less easy to do.

Table 1.1 Organisations and activities not in the public or private sectors

Amateur dramatic clubs	Mountain rescue services
Building preservation trusts	National Trust
Co-operatives	Oxfam
Donkey sanctuaries	Professional associations
Enterprise agencies	Quakers
Foundations	Rotary clubs
Golf clubs	Scouts
Hospices	Trade unions
Independent schools	University colleges
St John Ambulance	Voluntary Service Overseas
Knights of St Columbanus	Women's Institutes
Lifeboat service	Youth clubs

Note: The organisations and activities in this table are all part of the economy because they trade, buy things, and/or employ people. However, if the economy is thought only to consist of the private sector, in which organisations trade in order to make profits for their owners, and the public sector, in which organisations use public funding to deliver government services for the benefit of those who need them, then where do these organisations belong? (See also Table 3.1 for an expanded list.)

All of the organisations listed in Table 1.1 have to generate enough income to sustain themselves, but their purpose is not fundamentally concerned with making money. Some of these organisations, such as churches, have been around for a very long time, longer than any private sector businesses, but they have not been widely thought of as comprising a specific sector, possibly, as noted earlier, because of the lack of language with which to make that distinction. Now the words needed are starting to appear, and the terms 'social economy' and 'social enterprise' are often used to refer to this sector, or this portion of the spectrum, and to the organisations within it. However there are, as yet, no agreed standard definitions of these terms, and some consider that not all the organisations listed are social enterprises, or are in the social economy. Therefore, reference is increasingly being made to the 'third sector', to which, it is assumed, all such organisations will belong.

Interest in the social economy and the third sector

Although, as indicated above, for a long time traditional economics seemed largely to ignore the social economy, its importance is now being recognised, at least in government circles (as Case 1.1 suggests). This interest in the social economy and its various ramifications has arisen, however, not because the social enterprises in it are necessarily new types of organisation or are engaging in any new areas of activity, but because there is a new expectation of the potential of this sector of the economy to address some of the problems in, or of, society. Despite this potential, and despite the history of some of the organisations which might now be considered to be in the social economy, it was, until recently, often overlooked in economic analysis, at least in the UK, and there are a number of probable reasons for this:

- *It has been a very disparate area.* The social economy does not have a clear homogeneity, as is indicated by the differing definitions of it (see Chapter 4) and the variety of social enterprises and other organisations within it.

- *There was no agreed vocabulary with which to discuss it.* It is hard to discuss a subject without having agreed words in common with which to refer to it.

- *There was little information about it.* Many social enterprises have been created, operated, and closed without leaving clear records of their presence. They have not been officially categorised, and the statistical information on them which has been collected has been fragmentary and incomplete.

- *Attention has been focused either on the public or on the private sector, or on the comparison between them.* The socialist economic systems of formerly 'communist' countries focused on the public sector, and their failure was seen by many to demonstrate the superiority of capitalism and of the private sector. At the same time, in countries such as the US and the UK, which actually had mixed economies, there was an emerging political emphasis on the supposed efficiency of the private sector and its economic development potential. There was an emphasis therefore on enterprise and markets, and a desire, where possible, to transfer activity from the public to the private sector under the banner of privatisation. All this has tended to highlight the economic value of the private sector, and to contrast it with many parts of the public sector and, as a result, to overshadow other areas which were in neither the public sector nor the private sector.

- *Social economy organisations rarely make the headlines.* Almost all social enterprises and other organisations of which the social economy is comprised are relatively small, and few of them receive much publicity, whether for good or bad reasons. It has been the larger private sector organisations which, because of their successes or spectacular failures, have featured in the headlines, often because of the large amounts of money involved. Similarly, large public sector organisations, such as government departments, have also featured in press stories, again often because they have lost money or otherwise been shown to impact on a large scale. In contrast, many social enterprises, because they are small, have not been seen as worthy of individual attention, even when they too have had successes and failures.

However, recently, interest in the social economy has grown, as the perception of the benefits and the economic contribution of the area of activity has widened. This is not unlike the rise of interest in small businesses which occurred in the 1980s. There always had been small businesses since businesses began but it was not until the end of the 1970s, when Birch published the results of his research into employment in the US, that significant interest in them as a distinct sector of business began to develop. The second half of the 1970s was a time of rising unemployment, and so when Birch concluded that it was those small firms employing up to 100 people which had, in the 1970s, created over 80 per cent of the net new jobs,[5] governments took notice. Not least because of that link to employment creation, small businesses became the subject of much attention and many new programmes. Since the link was highlighted, small businesses have arguably become the most researched and supported part of the business spectrum. Some key dates in the emergence of interest in the social economy have been outlined in Table 1.2.

Indications of the scale and impact of the sector

It was not that social economy organisations had not employed people before the end of the twentieth century, but just that the totality of their economic contribution, and

Table 1.2 Some key dates

Emergence of the co-operative movement in the UK	1880s
Possible first use of the term 'social capital' in the US	1916
First European Conference of Co-operatives, Mutuals and Associations	1978
Establishment of Social Economy Unit within EU DGXXIII	1989
Establishment of the Social Exclusion Unit to help the UK government reduce social exclusion	1997
OECD report on social enterprises	1999
Social Enterprise Unit set up within the UK Department of Trade and Industry	2001
UK Prime Minister Blair hosts a social enterprise breakfast at 10 Downing Street	2002
UK Department of Trade and Industry publishes *Social Enterprise: A Strategy for Success*	2002
The publication in Scotland of the Scottish Executive's social economy review	2003
Launch of the *Social Enterprise Journal*, the first journal dedicated to social enterprise	2005
New Office of the Third Sector formed within the UK government's Cabinet Office	2006
Publication by the Office of the Third Sector of the *Social Enterprise Action Plan: Scaling New Heights*	2006
Publication by the UK government of *The Future Role of the Third Sector in Social and Economic Regeneration: Final Report* to provide 'a vision of how the state and the third sector working together . . . can bring about real change' and the announcement of an investment of over £500 million 'to make this vision a reality'[6]	2007
The Office of the Third Sector was renamed the Office for Civil Society (OCS) under the coalition government	2010
UK government announcement of a new fund aimed at enabling public sector workers to create mutuals to take over the running of services	2010
Launch in the UK of Big Society Capital as a £600 million social investment wholesaler to invest in organisations that lend money to charities and social enterprises	2012
Public Services (Social Value) Act requires public authorities in the UK to have regard to economic, social, and environmental well-being when awarding public service contracts	2012

particularly of their employment impact, had not been recognised. However, in 2005, it was claimed that in the UK social enterprises generated about £18 billion in annual turnover and employed more than 775,000 people.[7] In 2012, it was suggested that these may have been underestimates and that in England there were more than 1.1 million full-time equivalent employees in the sector, equating to over 5 per cent of the workforce.[8] In the European Union, the European Commission estimated that by 2007 approximately 10 million people were employed in the social economy, that co-operatives had a total of 78 million members, and that at least 109 million Europeans were insured with mutual insurers.[9] (See Chapter 10 for a fuller critique and exposition of UK statistics and international comparisons.)

The social economy is not the biggest sector of the economy but it is nevertheless a significant sector in many countries. In addition, the social economy appears to be able to provide not just jobs and economic activity but jobs in deprived areas and with associated social benefits. It appears to be able to respond to opportunities to establish economic activity where the private sector could, or would, not operate. As Amin et al. have suggested,[10] as well as this ability to avail of 'market opportunities' to address needs not met by the public and private sectors, there were other expectations of the social economy:

• It had a potential role in building social capital, which was seen as an ability and capacity to enhance economic efficiency and collective engagement.
• It helped to build participatory democracy.
• It supported a counterculture of survival and transformation on the margins of capitalism.

These are among the reasons why the social economy, or the third sector if that terminology is used, matters and why there is interest in it. It is why in the UK the Prime Minister described it, in his introduction to the report on the future role of the third sector in social and economic regeneration, as being 'at the heart of society'.[11]

Issues of terminology

Although, as indicated here, there is now considerable interest in the social economy and/or the third sector, noticeably in government and research circles, there is no single clear definition of what the social economy is. The third sector is easier to define as it is generally taken to refer to that area of the economy encompassing those organisations which are in neither the public nor the private sectors. The term 'third sector' is thus inclusive – including all those organisations not in the other two sectors. However, the term 'social economy' is different as it is often used in a way which excludes those organisations which do not fit within a particular definition – even if they might nevertheless be considered to be in the third sector. Nevertheless, those exclusions are often ignored and the term social economy is used synonymously with the term third sector, although that is not always the case.

The term social economy itself apparently entered the English language only in the late 1980s and early 1990s, having been taken from the French term *l'économie sociale*, and it is generally used to refer to a set of organisations with social purposes which neither are in the public sector nor have the profit-realising objective that typifies the private sector, although they do generate at least some of their income from providing goods or services. Such organisations are often called social enterprises and reference is made to the social entrepreneurs who have created them and to the social entrepreneurship that is demonstrated in their creation. Associated with them, community enterprise and community business are also referred to alongside the voluntary and community sector, and sometimes other terminology is used as well (see Table 1.3). This variety of terms may be a reflection of the interest in the subject although the terms are not only varied but are also varyingly defined – and occasionally the subject of disagreement. (These issues are explored further in Chapter 4.)

The appeal and benefits of the social economy

The above explanation might be summarised as the suggestion that, as well as the public and private sectors, there is in an economy a 'third sector', which includes a wide variety of organisations established for social and other purposes, such as the pursuit of artistic,

Table 1.3 Some current terminology in this field

Association	Non-profit
Charity	Not-for-profit
Citizen entrepreneur	Not-for-profit-distribution
Community business	Social economy
Community enterprise	Social economy business
Community interest company	Social economy enterprise
Citizen sector	Social enterprise
Community sector	Social entrepreneur
Company limited by guarantee	Social entrepreneurship
Co-operative	Third sector
Foundation	Voluntary organisation

sporting, environmental, ethical, or cultural objectives. Sometimes referred to as the social economy, or at least said to include the social economy, this sector has the potential to provide a variety of contributions, the recognition and appeal of which explain why interest in it has grown. It is relevant in this introduction to try to list and summarise some of the main benefits claimed for it, although the proclaimed benefits can depend on the perspective from which the sector is viewed, and, in any case, it is not claimed that all organisations in the third sector provide all these benefits.

The provision of goods and services which are free from excessive private sector profit-taking

Some people see the social economy as an alternative to the private sector for the provision of some goods and/or services. In the belief that often the private sector is subject to excessive capitalistic monopoly profits and restrictions, they think that social economy organisations will provide a more equitable or fairer allocation of returns. Thus, for instance, fair trade organisations try to pay Third World producers a fair price and co-operative distributors also try to reduce the potential for excessive middleman profiteering.

The provision of services and social benefits which the public sector does not provide adequately

Social economy organisations often attempt to meet basic needs and to improve people's lives. In the past, hospitals were often in the third sector before there was a public health service, and hospices often still are. Third sector organisations have for a long time been active in the education field, and some still run 'specialist' schools such as faith schools and integrated schools.

Social economy organisations may see the need to act to improve things before governments do, and, currently, that is particularly noticeable in the area of the environment. Schools and hospitals are also examples of initiatives which were pioneered in the third sector and only later taken over by the public sector once they were shown to be addressing a clear need. Social economy organisations are also active in areas such as arts, culture, and sports, which people welcome but which often do not offer enough financial return to attract private sector investment. And, of course, while religion has in the past been closely aligned with the state in many countries, and might have been considered to have been part of the public sector, it would now generally be considered to be in the third sector.

A means for addressing some problems of the welfare state

An extension of the above benefits is the potential the social economy is seen by some to have to complement public service delivery by addressing some needs without the drawbacks which had become apparent in the welfare state system of public sector provision. Amin et al. suggest a number of reasons why the principle of a universal welfare state was, towards the end of the twentieth century, being reconsidered. These include the following:

- Economic growth was faltering and so the employment prospects of the more excluded were reducing.
- Tax revenues were threatened and objections were being raised to the use of tax revenues for universal welfare and income redistribution.
- The welfare state was seen as a choiceless option and more people wanted choice.
- Political parties were starting to reject the idea of the all-providing state and suggested that it fostered a culture of dependency and entitlement. [12]

For reasons such as these, the social economy has been seen sometimes as having the potential to provide more efficient and more effective delivery of public services.

The provision of jobs for people who might not otherwise be employed

While the private and public sectors also provide employment, the third sector often provides jobs for people who might not find employment easily in either of the other two sectors. Jamie Oliver's Fifteen Foundation deliberately recruits unemployed young people to train for jobs in its restaurants in order to give them a start which they might not otherwise have got. Other social enterprises deliberately try to employ people from disadvantaged areas or people with particular disabilities. Many of these organisations would be categorised as intermediate labour market (ILM) organisations and often access national and European funding for such initiatives.

The fostering of enterprise and innovation

The social economy is thought to help foster new and better ways of doing things, particularly in more marginalised areas. The evidence for this is said to be seen in a positive correlation between the strength of social enterprises and that of the local mainstream economy, [13] although such a correlation does not indicate what of this is cause and what is effect. It is thus recognised that many individuals wish to display their entrepreneurial abilities through projects with a social purpose. and the third sector can foster such entrepreneurship.

The promotion of environmental sustainability, or ethical operations

Whereas some social enterprises are formed specifically to deliver environmental benefits, others at least try to operate in environmentally sustainable ways or to promote ethical behaviour. A building preservation trust, for instance, may have been formed specifically to restore a particular building, but it will often try to do so in a way which causes a minimum of consequential environmental damage. Although social enterprises often struggle financially, and so do not want to pay more than absolutely necessary for a good or service, they are not institutionally bound always to select the lowest-cost route and they are often closer to those who might be most affected by their actions. For instance, as already mentioned, fair trade organisations deliberately try to pay an above-market price for their supplies, where the market price is thought to be unfairly low.

The creation of social capital and social cohesion

It has been suggested that social capital is an essential, but often overlooked, prerequisite for success in an enterprising venture, whichever sector it is in. It has also been suggested that it is a lack of social capital that explains why the provision of financial capital, through grants, has often not been enough, on its own, to help ventures in deprived areas. Thus the idea that social enterprises can generate social capital, in parallel with the way that financial ventures can generate financial capital, and that social capital can also help to develop social cohesion, is seen as indicating another important benefit which they have to offer. (For more on this, see Chapter 8.)

Other development help

As well as building social capital, it is also argued that the social economy, and other third sector organisations, can offer services to the local economy or help local developments in other ways. The provision of start-up workspace, work preparation training for unemployed people, and childcare provision are all activities often undertaken by social enterprises, which can, in turn, benefit other businesses in that area.

The ability to reach parts that other initiatives cannot reach

As well as the provision of both economic and social benefits, there is another feature of at least part of the social economy which is often of interest to governments, and that is its geographic dimension. As their name suggests, community businesses are linked to communities, and, although that can refer to an 'interest'-based community, it is usually a place-based concept at least in terms of the employment and other benefits provided by the organisations concerned, and it is the locality focus typical of some social enterprises that is 'the thread that connects them to disadvantaged neighbourhoods'.[14] Governments have noted that many social enterprises and/or community businesses have been established in areas of need, and it has been said that the major objectives of social enterprises are to provide goods and services which the market or public sector is either unwilling or unable to provide, to develop skills, to create employment, and to foster pathways to integration for socially excluded people.[15]

There are several aspects of the social economy which, to some extent at least, have been thought to have an impact on deprivation. As a result, as one analysis suggests:

> It is becoming seen as a holistic solution for social exclusion in a number of ways. First, by encouraging collective self help, confidence and capacity building, and nurturing the collective values of the economy via socially useful production. Second, by humanising the economy via an emphasis upon autonomy, associated values, and organising the economy at a 'human' scale. Third, by enhancing democracy and participation via a decentralisation of policy to local communities and places. Fourth, by bringing about a greater degree of systemic coherence to the local economy via the

local production and consumption of goods and services. Fifth, by acknowledging the relationships between economy, environment, politics, and society.[16]

There has therefore been a tendency to see social enterprise as capable of reaching the parts that other initiatives cannot reach. It is as if it might be a sort of magic bullet for targeting social exclusion and reducing deprivation.

A mechanism for a counterculture

As previous points suggest, there can be a strong political dimension to some of the bene-fits claimed for the social economy, or at least for some of its components. For some, the social economy offers an alternative to high and/or increasing state expenditure on social services. Others claim that it can provide components of a counterculture to respond to some of the drawbacks of capitalism. Graefe suggests that the social economy was 'once advanced by social democratic and radical academics as a core element of an alternative to neoliberalism',[17] and according to Amin et al.:

> There is a long utopian tradition in favour of the organisation of society around needs, self-autonomy, and social and ecological balance. This utopian view reacts against the capitalist emphasis on individual greed, profit and market value rather than social need. As Fordism slid into crisis, this counter culture gained momentum . . . (and) some intel-lectuals even argued that 'the end of work' after Fordism offered a major opportunity to shift social organisation in this direction.[18]

Summary – the significance of the social economy

Twenty-five years ago, such a list of benefits might have looked a little strange, not because they did not exist, but because few realised that they did exist. Now there is a wider appre-ciation of the appeal of the social economy and a wider recognition of the benefits it pro-vides. As a result, there is increasing interest in the sector, not just for its social impact and its economic contribution but also, as seen in the different perspectives on its potential, for its political significance. There is thus an increasing appreciation of its potential:

> We need to recognise anew . . . the importance of the one to one, face to face, not impersonal but personal care, the support from families, neighbourhoods and volun-tary organisations that are often the difference between success and failure and the support that demonstrates both the limits of markets and the limits of state action.

> So in future I want . . . a new compact that elevates the third sector as partner, not as . . . a cut price alternative to government, but government fulfilling its responsibilities to fund services and fully valuing the contribution the voluntary sector can make.[19]

The agenda of this book

If the wording of the above list of benefits suggests that some of what is claimed about the social economy, and about its links and effects, might be more supposition than proven fact, it is intentional. Because the interest in the sector is relatively new, because there has not yet been an enormous amount of research into it (compared to, say, the small business sector), and because it seems to suit some people's agenda but not others', there still appears sometimes to be an element of politics, wishful thinking, and controversy in what is said about it. There is disagreement, for instance, about definitions of the social economy, and there are disputes about what should and should not be considered to be a social enterprise and what constitutes a 'community' in a community enterprise.

In any emerging field of study, it takes time for information gained to be analysed, and, despite considerable discussion and research, that information is not always converted into relevant and shared knowledge. Like the example of small businesses already mentioned, when interest in such a field grows, it is not always based on good knowledge, and areas of ignorance will remain. There will be a variety of approaches, alternative theories and opinions, and differing vocabularies. In such an evolving field, it can be hard to find a general introduction to help newcomers to make sense of the debate and to serve as a starting point for further exploration. This book is an attempt to do that.

The evolution and role of the social economy

Because there is such a jumble of definitions and of facts, supposition, and wishful thinking, Part I tries to map out how the social economy has evolved, what its current position appears to be, and how it is perceived. It starts, in Chapter 2, with a look at the history of the social economy, exploring the way in which it might have evolved into its current form.

Chapter 3 looks at the present state of the social economy and at various aspects of its current position. Because of the variety of different views which are held about the sector, Chapter 4 examines the variations in terminology, definitions, and interpretations that have been advanced and/or applied and may therefore be encountered in writing about it.

Finally, in this part, Chapter 5 looks at some different perspectives on the sector and at what they might imply for its future.

The nature of the social economy

Part II then looks at some concepts and issues in more detail in describing the nature of the sector, because it looks at how things behave, how they relate to other things, and how they might therefore be influenced. Chapter 6 examines the characteristics of social economy organisations including their legal structures, aims, methods, and management, and Chapter 7 considers their funding and includes a critique of sources of finance from micro-level support to venture capital, including the role of social business angels and other funding mechanisms.

A key area of potential linkages is explored in Chapter 8, which explores the concept of social capital and the evolution of some of the theories about it and how it might be linked to a wider socio-political concern for the health of civic society. Governments, and other stakeholders, are often interested in influencing and promoting the development of the third sector, so Chapter 9 explores the main issues associated with attempts to advance the social economy including both why this is attempted and the methods that have been used to affect the social economy. At the end of this part, Chapter 10 reviews the impact the sector is supposed to have and the evidence for that impact.

///

Key Points of Chapter 1
- The social economy has a long history but has, until recently, received relatively little economic attention.
- The language with which to describe the social economy and its components has been limited, but is now starting to evolve.
- Organisations which belong in neither the public nor the private sector of an economy are considered to form a third sector. The social economy can be variously considered to be either a part of this 'third sector' or synonymous with it.

- Interest in the social economy is now growing because it appears that:
  a) Its size and impact are economically significant.
  b) It, or parts of it, can provide benefits such as the following:
     - providing goods and services which are free from excessive private sector profit-taking;
     - providing some services and social benefits which the public sector does not adequately provide;
     - providing jobs for people who might not otherwise be employed;
     - fostering enterprise and innovation;
     - assisting environmental sustainability and ethical business; and
     - creating social capital and fostering social cohesion.
  c) It can provide these benefits for areas and parts of the system that other sectors cannot reach. In particular, it is supposed that it can help to reduce social exclusion and counter deprivation.

Case 1.1 | Official interest in the social economy

One way of documenting official interest in the social economy is by listing initiatives which sought to recognise and/or help it. Here are some of them:

- In October 2001, the UK government launched the Social Enterprise Unit within the (then) Department of Trade and Industry (now the Department for Business, Innovation and Skills – BIS). In May 2006, this was brought together with the Active Communities Unit in the Home Office to form a new Office of the Third Sector, the creation of which reflected 'the government's recognition of the value, influence and importance of the third sector'.[20]
- Also in October 2001, the European Commission established a Social Economy Unit in Directorate General (DG) XXIII.
- In 2002 a book about the social economy introduced it in this way:

  > Until the 1990s the term social economy hardly featured in English speaking academic and policy discourse, while older terms such as 'third sector', 'non-profit activity', 'community business' or 'voluntary organisation' captured something more modest. They described activity on the margins of a mainstream with primarily a welfare function... They were not seen as part of the economy (as they were not motivated by job generation, entrepreneurship, meeting consumer demand, or producing profit), nor were they seen as political (promoting citizenship, or empowerment). Their role was to see to the welfare of the marginalised.[21]

- In 2003, the Scottish Executive published 'A Review of the Scottish Executive's Policies to Promote the Social Economy', which set out 'the Government's vision for the social economy... and the strategic priorities necessary to help the social economy realise its full potential'.[22]
- In 2006, Invest NI, the Northern Ireland government's business development agency, announced a two-year programme of support for the social economy sector.
- In 2011, The Department for Social Justice and Local Government of the Welsh Assembly Government commissioned an independent review of funded support for

social enterprise development in Wales. The review's aim was 'to assess the suitability of the current core funding arrangements in supporting the growth and development of Social Enterprise'.[23]

- In 2011, in Northern Ireland, the Enterprise Minister released the findings of a report into the social economy sector, a report which 'sought to determine the sector's potential to contribute to the economic regeneration of our communities, and to establish the best mechanism to take this work forward'.[24]

- In 2011, the UK Secretary of State for Business said at a conference: 'What is it about social enterprise which attracts three ministers and the leader of the Opposition to your event?...I think the sector is big and growing...I think it is also important in terms of the Government agenda.'[25]

Questions, Exercises, Essay, and Discussion Topics

1. Many colleges were founded and endowed to provide education. They have to secure enough income from their endowments and the services they provide to maintain their operations. They do not remit profit to individuals and they reuse any surpluses to enhance their activities. Are they social enterprises?

2. Does the language currently available provide clarity or cause confusion about the social economy and the third sector?

3. If the social economy and/or the third sector are so beneficial, why have they been overlooked for so long?

4. What might a government hope to get from its support for the social economy?

5. What would life be like without the third sector?

Suggestions for further reading

A. Amin, A. Cameron and R. Hudson, *Placing the Social Economy* (London: Routledge, 2002).

J. Pearce, *Social Enterprise in Anytown* (London: Calouste Gulbenkian Foundation, 2003).

R. Ridley-Duff and M. Bull, *Understanding Social Enterprise: Theory and Practice* (London: Sage Publications, 2011).

References

1. A. Molloy, C. McFeely and E. Connolly, *Building a Social Economy for the New Millennium* (Derry: Guildhall Press/NICDA Social Economy Agency, 1999), p. 5.

2. P. Graefe, 'The social economy and the state: Linking ambitions with institutions in Québec, Canada', *Policy and Politics*, Vol. 30, No. 2 (Bristol, UK: The Policy Press, 2002), p. 247.

3. J. Harvey, *Modern Economics* (Basingstoke: Macmillan, 1998), p. 22.

4. J. K. Galbraith, *American Capitalism: The Concept of Countervailing Power* (Boston: Houghton Mifflin Co., 1956).

5. For more on this, see Chapter 1 of S. Bridge, K. O'Neill and S. Cromie, *Understanding Enterprise, Entrepreneurship and Small Business* (Basingstoke: Palgrave Macmillan, 2003).

6. HM Treasury/Cabinet Office, *The Future Role of the Third Sector in Social and Economic Regeneration: Final Report*, HM Treasury, July 2007.

7. Taken from the draft speech to have been given by Barry Gardiner, Minister for Competitiveness in DTI, at the BLU/SBS seminar on Passion, Entrepreneurship and the Rebirth of Local Economies with Dr Ernesto Sirolli in London on 10 November 2005.

8. The Third Sector bulletin, www.thirdsector.co.uk (accessed 12 June 2012).

9. http://europe.eu.int/comm/enterpriSocial Economy/ (accessed 2007).

10. A. Amin, R. Hudson and A. Cameron, *Placing the Social Economy* (London: Routledge, 2002), pp. 6–8.

11. HM Treasury/Cabinet Office, *The Future Role of the Third Sector in Social and Economic Regeneration: Final Report*, HM Treasury, July 2007.

12. A. Amin, R. Hudson and A. Cameron, *Placing the Social Economy* (London: Routledge, 2002), p. 5.

13. Ibid., p. 119.

14. D. Smallbone, M. Evans, I. Ekanem and S. Butters, *Researching Social Enterprise* (Sheffield: Small Business Service, Research Report RR004/01, July 2001), p. 5.

15. Department of Environment, Transport and the Regions, *Community Enterprise: Good Practice Guide* (London: DETR, 1999).

16. A. Amin, R. Hudson and A. Cameron, *Placing the Social Economy* (London: Routledge, 2002), pp. 19, 20.

17. P. Graefe, 'The social economy and the state: Linking ambitions with institutions in Québec: Canada', *Politics and Policy*, Vol. 30, No. 2 (2002), p. 248.

18. A. Amin, R. Hudson and A. Cameron, *Placing the Social Economy* (London: Routledge, 2002), p. 8.

19. From Gordon Brown's speech, as Chancellor of the Exchequer, to the Labour Party conference in 2006.

20. Letter (undated) issued by the Cabinet Office after the relevant reshuffle to explain the changes.

21. A. Amin, A. Cameron and R. Hudson, *Placing the Social Economy* (London: Routledge, 2002), p. 2.

22. On www.scotland.gov.uk/Topics/People/ Voluntary-Issues (accessed 11 July 2006).

23. Welsh Assembly Government, Research Summary No. 03/2011, www.cymru.gov.uk (accessed 7 February 2013).

24. www.northernireland.gov.uk/index/media-centre/ news-departments/news-deti/achive-deti-september-2011 (accessed 7 February 2013).

25. Dr Vince Cable, MP, speaking at the Voice 11 conference, London, 30 March 2011.

Part I

The Evolution and Role of the Social Economy

Part I of this book presents summaries of what has been said about the past, present, and future of social economy. It tries to map out the main concepts associated with, and the relationships between, the social economy and the third sector, and between the third sector and the rest of the economy. In effect, it tries to describe the 'geography' of the field by indicating what is in it, where it is positioned, and where it might be going.

It starts, in Chapter 2, with an overall look at the history of the social economy sector. This chapter explores the economic evolution and the history of that part of an economy which is neither public nor private. It considers the way the different sectors in an economy might have evolved and the key components and concepts associated with them. It looks at the way in which they have been presented and contrasts the way they have been defined and/or described by different stakeholders in, or observers of, the sector.

Chapter 3 then looks at the present state of the social economy and at various aspects of its current position. It considers the variety of labels which have been applied to the sector and its components and explores the range of organisations which operate within it.

Following that, Chapter 4 looks in more detail at some of the terminology and definitions applied to the social economy and other parts of the third sector. It considers various contentions on what should, or should not, be included within the social economy. It explores the things which those organisations included in it have in common, and what is said to distinguish them from the rest of the third sector.

In the final chapter of Part I, Chapter 5 builds on current views of the sector by exploring new ideas and developments in and around the social economy. It also suggests that it may be time to change some of the assumptions that have been made about it.

2

the evolution of the social economy

contents:

- introduction
- the evolution of an economy
- the public and private sectors – and other activity
- the emergence of the social economy
- mapping an economy
- conclusion

Key concepts

This chapter covers:

- the way that, following the agricultural revolution, economies have evolved with three sectors;
- the lack, for a long time, of an agreed language to describe the third of those sectors;
- the emergence of the term social economy and its relationship to that third sector;
- the lack of clear distinct boundaries distinguishing these sectors and the existence of hybrid organisations with a mix of characteristics from different sectors.

Learning objectives

By the end of this chapter the reader should:

- understand how different economic sectors have evolved;
- understand how the concept of the social economy has emerged;
- appreciate the difficulty of considering such concepts without a clearly defined language for them;
- appreciate that the range of different sorts of organisation is more like a spectrum than clearly differentiated and separated categories.

Introduction

Chapter 1 introduces the concept that within most economies, as well as the traditionally recognised public and private sectors – with which many may be familiar – there are also parts which belong in neither of those two sectors. Those parts which are neither public nor private are now sometimes referred to as the social economy or the third sector. However, as Chapter 1 indicates, that vocabulary is of relatively recent origin. Before that, without appropriate words, it was difficult to distinguish, and thus to discuss, this third area.

This chapter therefore looks at how the different sectors of economic activity may have evolved and at how the distinctions between them may have arisen. That provides a context in which the social economy/third sector and the rest of an economy can be considered in more detail.

The evolution of an economy

Economics has been defined as 'the study of how people allocate their limited resources to provide for their wants',[1] and an economy is the system within which people do that allocation. But when did the different sectors of an economy evolve? It would seem that, in the early stages of their existence as a distinct species, human beings were all nomadic hunter-gatherers moving around in family bands in search of food. They worked directly to use their resources, such as their time and skills, to provide the food, shelter, warmth, and other things that they wanted. This work was probably undertaken on an 'all for one and one for all' basis and, while it might be supposed that individuals would vary in their relative ability to undertake different tasks, there would have been little specialisation and all organised activity must have happened within the family context. Trying to draw distinctions in that situation between public and private sector work would have been meaningless.

Recent observations of surviving hunter-gatherer societies indicate that, although occasionally more food may be obtained than can be consumed in the short term, such surpluses are of little use as freshly picked berries or freshly killed meat cannot be stored and/or protected for any length of time either as an investment for the future or for exchange with others. Probably because food procured by some members of the group could not be put aside to trade for the work of others, it is also found that in such societies there were few or no full-time specialists. Almost everyone engaged in all the work of the society.

The first big change or, in Toffler's term, wave[2] in economic evolution was the advent of farming. Although observation has also shown that hunter-gatherers may have needed to work for fewer hours a day than farmers, nevertheless farming may have become necessary to support greater population densities. With the change from hunter-gathering to agriculture, societies became more settled, surpluses could be stored (for instance grain in grain stores or live animals in fields) and guarded, and non-food-producing specialists began to emerge, including eventually rulers and bureaucrats. Families may have grouped together as tribes, and agriculture led to larger, denser, and stratified societies,[3] but the kinship basis for groups may have persisted with no significant human organisation existing outside the extended family or tribe. That must have continued as long as tribal society survived, and, for instance, even when Christianity first came to Ireland, it was established on a clan basis, although its missionaries, such as Patrick, would have known of the continental model in which bishops, rather than local civic leaders, had the overall authority for church functions. The concept of a wider permanent power than that of clan leaders was however lacking and without it bishops could not function. However, one feature which has survived from those times, it is suggested, is the traditional Irish *meitheal* (lit. 'working party') system of mutual support among farmers, especially at harvest time, which was therefore an early system of co-operative working.[4]

Eventually, even tribes grouped together as larger units, and, once the superior authority of kings and other rulers became established, it meant that some activity of, or for, government clearly took place outside the family. This activity of government could be considered to be work to provide for some of society's needs which was undertaken separately from the work of providing goods, such as food, for consumption. It is here that the beginnings of distinct public sector activity might be found. Today the heart of the public sector is the civil service, and the origins of the British Civil Service, it has been suggested, lie in the court servants that followed the Saxon kings of England from one resting place to another[5] – although it might be argued that they were more personal servants of the monarch than true servants of the public.

Another feature of agriculturally based societies was the emergence of craft working and craft workers which led eventually to the establishment of specialised businesses. Many of these would have been family businesses but there were also examples of non-family organisations engaging in trading – for instance monasteries which produced goods such as beverages for their own consumption and then sold surpluses to others. Once such ventures grew bigger than the family, or had a regular surplus to trade, they too might be distinguished as a separate economic activity. Case 2.1 presents the example on one English company which can trace its origins back as far as 1189, and later others sought legal recognition and/or permission for their activities. The East India Company is an early example of one such business clearly being established with a separate legal identity as it derived its powers from a Royal Charter of 1599. Consequently, at that stage, a distinction could clearly be made between that economic activity outside the family which was organised for private gain and that which was organised for, or by, the state, even if some of our current terminology for these activities had not yet been established.

A snapshot of the economy of England at the end of the seventeenth century can be gained from the work of Gregory King, who was at one time Secretary to the Commissioners for Public Accounts and who produced an estimate for the population and wealth of England in 1688 (which is summarised in Table 2.1). It is interesting to note that his main unit for this accounting was the family.

Gregory King does not distinguish between agricultural and non-agricultural labour – which would have been difficult at the time as the 'putting out' system in textiles and other manufacturing sectors distributed industrial work for the underemployed agricultural population to undertake in their homes. Nevertheless, perhaps half of the employed population earned their living in agriculture or at least had an attachment to the land, and this proportion would have been much higher in all other countries in Europe except the Netherlands. However, the subsistence sector of the economy appeared to be very small, with only a tiny proportion of the population growing and consuming their own food. It would also appear that government expenditure was no more than 5 per cent of national income.[6]

The figures in Table 2.1 show England before the Industrial Revolution but they do indicate that, while at that time traces of family-based subsistence agriculture remained, many people already worked off the land, mostly for someone else, in what would now be considered to be the private sector. Only a small proportion worked for the government, in what would now be called the public sector, and much of that public employment would have been in the armed services. The Industrial Revolution, however, caused a huge redeployment from agriculture into industry, and by 1801 only about 36 per cent of the labour force was employed in agriculture, from which about one-third of the national income was then directly derived. By 1851 that proportion had reduced to about 20 per cent and by 1901 they were only six to seven per cent.[7] Over the same period, from 1801 to 1901, the proportion of the labour force employed in industry, mining, and construction rose from 30 to 46 per cent. In the meantime, the proportion working in trade and transport had risen from 11 to 22 per cent but the number employed in public services and the professions stayed the same at about 23 per cent.

As well as agriculture being family based, so too was much of early manufacturing, and it was usually financed by reinvestment of profits. However, during the nineteenth century, more and more businesses became incorporated and subject to a wider ownership. For instance in 1809 only one brewery was listed by the Stock Exchange but by 1900 there were 200.[8] That does not mean that all the family businesses had disappeared but it does indicate that working for the family had ceased to be the norm for a lot of people.

Table 2.1 Gregory King's picture of the English economy in 1688

Rank	Families	Individuals	Total income
Lords, knights, and gentlemen	16,600	153,000	£6,286,000
Professional classes (Church, Navy, Army, office-holders)	55,000	308,000	£5,280,000
Merchants, traders, and shopkeepers	50,000	696,000	£4,200,000
Artisans and handicraftsmen	60,000	240,000	£2,400,000
Freeholders and farmers	330,000	1,730,000	£16,960,000
Labouring and out-servants	364,000	1,275,000	£5,460,000
Cottagers and paupers	400,000	1,300,000	£2,600,000
Others (common soldiers, common seamen, vagrants)	85,000	250,000	£1,550,000

Source: Based on P. Mathias, *The First Industrial Nation: An Economic History of Britain 1700–1914* (London: Methuen, 1983), table II, p. 24

The public and private sectors – and other activity

It is clear that, by 1900, in the more developed economies most people worked outside the family, and that much of this employment, and much economic activity, took place in the private sector with the other significant source of employment apparently being the public services. It seems reasonable therefore to suggest that, between the eighth- and ninth-century Saxon kings and the eighteenth- and the nineteenth-century Industrial Revolution, the economy of places like England changed from one in which the vast majority of people provided for their wants through family-based agriculture to one in which there were distinct private and public sectors. The private sector matched wants with resources through markets which covered labour as well as goods and services, and the public sector, which also employed people in the labour market, used taxation income to provide for other wants.

But at the same time as many aspects of economic activity could be separated into distinct public and private sectors, other organisations were also being established outside the family which were run neither for the state nor for private gain. Altruistic charity or other socially beneficial activity, carried out neither for direct personal gain nor because of threat or compulsion, must have taken place from a very early stage, and establishing permanent sustainable organisations for this might have started with temples and churches. Later, more secular organisations may have emerged. The Romans had colleges for craftsmen, and guilds appeared in Germanic regions as early as the ninth century. The Middle Ages could be said to have had a rich associative life with many countries having forms of corporation, often organised on the basis of trades or professions, which provided reciprocal mutual support and charity. In England and in much of Western Europe, in medieval times, schools and hospitals were generally run or controlled by the Church. Later, other, secular organisations were founded for such purposes although finding a suitable procedure for creating them officially was not always easy (see Case 2.2). These early schools, universities, and hospitals were not state run but, unlike trading companies, they were not established for private monetary gain either, although possibly they did confer on their founders or benefactors gains in conscience, prestige or even favour. (For a well-placed courtier, becoming a benefactor of a college which the monarch was founding might even have had an element of compulsion.) Such activities do not seem to have appeared on the economic 'radar', however, and, even today, economic histories and textbooks often focus largely on the private sector with some reference to the contribution of the public sector.

As well as such involvement of philanthropic individuals and groups in providing for those less well off than themselves, there were also organisations designed to provide their members with mutual benefit. This was particularly noticeable in countries like the UK when, in the late nineteenth century, the co-operative movement emerged. By the middle of the twentieth century, though, the economies of many developed countries were based on what has been called 'Fordism'.[9] This involved a combination of large businesses producing relatively cheap goods through the economies of scale of mass production, and employing many people for whom they provided jobs for life, together with a welfare state providing many public services funded by the tax revenues from the private sector. By this stage, in many countries, the state had taken over responsibility for many social services such as health and education and most hospitals and schools were in the public sector. Thus there might have seemed to be little need for the services of other organisations and no role, therefore, for a third sector social economy.

However many other areas of activities, such as charity and religion, which were neither public nor private sector had not been taken over by the state. They, together with co-operatives and similar organisations in a number of European countries, continued to exist outside the two acknowledged sectors, except possibly in 'communist' countries, where the public sector took over almost everything. Also, towards the end of the twentieth century, Fordism had become vulnerable to challenges such as rising energy prices, competition from industries in low-wage economies and new technologies. Private sector jobs were being lost while, at the same time, strains were becoming apparent in the bureaucracy of mass state provision of many public services. By the end of the century the ability of the public and private sectors between them to provide for society's needs was thus being questioned, and when the potential contribution of the other sector became apparent, it looked appealing.

The sectors of an economy

Economics may be about allocating resources to address wants, but that has become a very varied activity. In early society all provision for wants was done solely within the family, but now, not only is some of it done by the private sector and some by the public sector of an economy, but some is also done by a range of organisations which belong to neither of those sectors.

The private sector

In most economies the market has a key role to play in the allocation of resources to meet wants. In such a 'market economy', the allocation of resources is done based on the price consumers are willing to pay, with purchasers/consumers seeking to pay low prices, other things being equal, and the owner/producer of the goods or services seeking to get as large a reward as possible for their use. This system balances supply and demand and rewards efficiency but is not good for delivering community services such as policing and justice or ensuring that everyone has a basic provision. It also does not address well third-party effects such as pollution.

Nevertheless, so many wants are addressed through the market that economic analysis has often concentrated primarily on private sector activity. Private sector organisations are characterised as being owned not by the state but by private individuals or groups of individuals and making profit for their owners by trading in the marketplace. Such organisations vary enormously in size and scope as the private sector encompasses the following:

- multinational companies;
- larger businesses (established as companies limited by shares);
- smaller businesses (small and medium-sized enterprises – SMEs), including micro businesses, some of which may be companies and some partnerships or sole traders;
- crime and the black economy. (Crime is an economic activity and is carried out almost entirely for the financial, or other asset, gain of individuals. It may be illegal, but it is still private sector activity.)

The public sector

Using the state, as opposed to the market, as a basis for allocating goods and/or services does have some advantages. For instance state provision can ensure that resources are allocated where they are needed, rather than just where they can be paid for. Things like education, medical care, policing, and defence come into this category and are therefore better paid for through taxes than a market. However such systems are bad at matching supply and demand or at providing a very wide range of consumer goods.

An alternative to a market economy is a 'command economy' in which the production, distribution and pricing of goods and services are decided centrally by an all-powerful planning authority. A 'command economy' is a public sector economy because the government provides the 'all-powerful' planning authority. Even in mixed economies, public sector organisations are financed mainly, if not wholly, from the public purse, which is usually derived from taxes. These organisations endeavour to execute government policy and provide services to meet wants in furtherance of that policy. Like private sector organisations, public sector organisations also exist at different levels:

- At an international level there are organisations such as the UN, WTO, and the EU.
- At the level below that, there are national and regional governments and their departments, agencies, and executives, with the latter including military forces, police services, health services, and education systems.
- Then there are local authorities and the activities for which they are responsible, including, possibly, roads, libraries, waste disposal, and tourism promotion.
- And there may be community councils and similar bodies.

The remainder

Most economies are neither purely market economies nor purely command economies. Even in the most capitalist of economies some services, such as defence, are provided on a command basis, and even in communist command economies some individuals still did jobs for each other, even if it was unofficial and discouraged. Most economies are officially mixed economies in which consumer goods are generally provided by the private sector, so decisions on what to produce are directly linked to demand, while services such as defence, policing and justice, and basic health and education are centrally provided, together with overall controls on matters like pollution.

Nevertheless, the short summary of economic evolution given earlier indicated that in the economies of most societies, in addition to the state (or public) sector and the business (or private) sector, there were a number of other activities. These have included the work of those organisations founded for benevolent purposes and the remnants of the original, family-based economies, which were not considered to be in either of the two recognised sectors. For the purposes of this book, it is not necessary to establish exactly when distinct public and private sectors emerged, but just that they, and the distinction between them, did emerge, and that, even when this did happen, there were already some established activities with an economic impact which fitted into neither of those two categories.

Table 1.1 lists just some of the sorts of organisation which fall into neither the public nor the private sector. They range from near–private sector organisations such as co-operatives, some of which do distribute profits to their members (and might therefore be considered really to belong in the private sector), to near–public sector organisations such as hospices and care centres, which deliver services to people on the basis of need and which can be paid for by public funds (and which many people might feel should be undertaken by the public sector itself).

In between those extremes there is a wide range of organisations established by individuals, not by governments, but set up for the purpose of supplying things that people need or want rather than for making money. Charitable organisations clearly come into this category but so too do many other clubs and societies set up to service the requirements of their members. They may not all trade, but, if they employ people or otherwise buy things, they have an economic impact. They are therefore part of the economy but not part of either of the two sectors of the economy described above. In consequence, together they are sometimes referred to as the third sector and some (or sometimes all) of them, more specifically, as the social economy.

The limitations of language

'The limits of my language', said Wittgenstein, 'mean the limits of my world', and the language we use colours the way we think and filters the way we see things. For a long time we have had a language of business which has affected the way we think of business and the private sector. Indeed it would seem that it was actually a private sector business, the East India Company mentioned earlier, which introduced to the English language the term 'civil servant', a term which we now think of as referring to the archetypal public sector employee. At one time people who worked for companies were referred to as company servants, and, therefore, when the East India Company wished to distinguish between the soldiers and the administrators who helped it to control much of India, it called the former its military servants and the latter its civil servants. (The East India Company could therefore be said to have had private sector civil servants!) The introduction of this terminology from India into England has been attributed to Macaulay's essays on Clive and Warren Hastings which were published in 1840 and 1841.[10]

When we consider the variety of organisations that contribute to our economy, we have tended to use economic language to describe them. Except in very socialist economies, we have recognised that there are separate private and public sectors and we have referred to those organisations which are not public sector organisations as businesses. We think of businesses typically as relatively large limited companies established with the aim of making profits for their owners. We may acknowledge that some businesses are small, even very small, and many businesses are partnerships or sole traders, rather than limited companies, but we still think that all of them are generally 'in it for the money'. In doing so, those businesses sell goods or services to customers who pay for them. For most or all of us that is what the private sector is about.

In contrast, the public sector is there to carry out the operations of government. It is there to formulate, facilitate and give effect to government policies and decisions. It has clients and/or consumers of its services but they are not customers as they do not generally pay for all of those services, except indirectly through taxes. The public sector is not there to make money but is paid instead from the public purse to carry out its duties. (If public servants were to accept money from members of the public for services which ought to be free, that might constitute bribery and, in effect, be the illegal introduction of private sector practices into the public arena.)

We can also recognise that there is another sector of the economy but, without a common language for it, it has not been as easy to discuss it. The term 'third sector' has been introduced as an all-encompassing term for those economic activities not included in the other two sectors but some prefer the term 'social economy' for at least some of these activities which have a number of variously specified features in common. However, this lack of an accepted terminology for the sector, together with a failure to appreciate its merits, has undoubtedly contributed to the lack of attention paid to it. Now, however, terms for it are emerging, although they are not always applied in consistent ways. They are discussed below and in the next two chapters.

The emergence of the social economy

When did the concept of the social economy first emerge? Moulaert and Ailenei[11] have described how the term *économie sociale* became accepted after it was first used in 1830 by the French economist Charles Dunoyer. They suggest that the emergence of the social economy as a specific concept, in France and at that time, was the result of institutionalisation and a theoretical assessment of practical experiences – and those practical experiences were of a variety of organisations formed by groups of people to address needs where neither the market nor the state would or could help.

Those experiences might be said to have had their roots in aspects of Egyptian, Greek, and Roman life and later in the guilds that appeared in north-west Europe in medieval times. This was the case in other parts of the world also, including medieval Byzantium, Muslim countries, and India, in which 'associations' were formed in order to organise and protect communities of interest. Moulaert and Ailenei quote several authors who contend that the social economy has a history of emergence and re-emergence linked to a series of economic and social crises. Many of the guilds and other associations, they suggest, were created to provide assistance, mutual support, and charity in the uncertain times of the early middle ages. The changes later brought about by the Industrial Revolution led to a decline in craft co-operatives and created renewed interests in 'utopian socialism' and the values of co-operation and mutual support. The French Revolution, it has been argued, fostered political equality but not material equality, and because material inequalities remained, mutual support organisations (*mutuelles*) appeared in the middle of the nineteenth century. In the last quarter of that century, agricultural and savings co-operatives were formed in response to the needs of small producers affected by increasing accumulation and the economic power of the bigger businesses thus created. In France, it might be said, republican ideals generated distinctive interests in associations as a buffer between individuals and the state, whereas in England, ideas around communitarianism strongly influenced the co-operative movement.

Based on an assessment of such experiences, in particular in France, the concept of *l'économie sociale* came to be seen as encompassing the co-operatives, *mutuelles*, and associations mentioned above (and foundations were added later – prompting the acronym CMAFs). As mentioned earlier in this chapter, when the private and public sectors evolved as separate parts of an economy, there was still a wide range of activities which belonged in neither of those two sectors, and so they are said to be in the third sector. That approach to the third sector defines it as including everything not in the other two sectors. The approach to the social economy described above is different as it is based on including only certain categories of organisations which have a number of shared characteristics. However, today, according to Moulaert and Ailenei:

> The social economy represents a wide family of initiatives and organisational forms – i.e. a hybridisation of market, non-market (redistribution) and non-monetary (reciprocity) economies showing that the economy is not limited to the market, but includes the principles of redistribution and reciprocity.[12]

In the UK much of this activity was referred to as civic society and, at the beginning of the twentieth century, it was relied on in many instances for income and welfare security which the state was not then providing. However, this voluntary provision was uneven and unpredictable, and one consequence of the economic changes later that century, together with the emergence of the welfare state funded by tax revenues from increasing prosperity, was that many welfare functions were taken over by the state. As a result, 'civil society came to be seen as the area of self-help, associational activity and social life, not that of economic activity or preparation for it'. [13]

Although the social economy may have been first conceptualised in the nineteenth century, there have been crises since then which have further stimulated its development. In the twentieth century, the economic collapse of 1929–1932 led to the formation of consumption co-operatives for food and housing, [14] and further initiatives in 1970s' Europe have been seen, on the one hand, to be a reaction to the crises in the mass production system and, on the other hand, to be a response to the overburdening of the welfare state. [15] Indeed Amin et al. trace the most recent interest in the social economy to the end of full employment and the crisis in welfare provision which started in the 1970s. This 'post-Fordist' environment, they suggest, was characterised by:

- rising global energy prices;
- rising imports from low-wage countries and flexibly organised new economies;
- wage drift and sustained opposition from organised labour;
- decreasing return on sunk capital;
- growth of new technologies and organised principles no longer dependent on economies of scale;
- falling demand for mass-produced goods and the rise of customised consumption;
- waning support for mass representative democracy; and
- strains on government to provide expensive welfare services and the rise of new right market ideas on the management of the relationship between the state and the economy. [16]

Teague points out that, in this context, governments and policy-makers have sought too much from the sector by combining its roles in business incubation, social repair, and welfare delivery. [17] However, this latest crisis of state management, Amin et al. suggest, simultaneously renewed interest in the potential of the social economy as a place of work and provider of welfare services. For instance, the European Commission established its Social Economy Unit, within DGXXIII, in 1989, and the importance of the social economy was formally recognised by the European Union in its 1994 white paper on 'Growth, Competitiveness and Employment'. This paper indicated that the EU saw the 'third sector' as a potentially important contributor to the growth of employment and as means of avoiding dual labour markets, twin-speed societies, and urban segregation.

Towards the end of the twentieth century, cracks had appeared in the welfare state. It often seemed to be hampered by its associated bureaucracy, it appeared sometimes to encourage dependency instead of enterprise, and it appeared to be unable to reach some areas of social exclusion such as persistent long-term unemployment. In these circumstances, the potential of the social economy seemed again to be attractive, in particular its economic contribution including employment and its supposed ability to reach those social parts that other initiatives cannot reach. For whatever reason, by the end of the 1990s attention was being paid to the social economy in the EU (see Illustration 2.1) and in many of the EU member states, including the UK (see Chapter 9), and it would seem that this re-emergence of the social economy as a subject of interest can be linked to economic and social change resulting, at least in Western Europe, from the late-twentieth-century 'post-Fordist' changes to manufacturing strength and the welfare state environment. Thus, from different shades of political opinion, the social economy is, in many quarters, now attracting considerable attention.

Illustration 2.1 European recognition

In the late 1980s, the Economic and Social Committee of the European Commission commissioned research into the social economy sector which led in 1989 to the establishment of the Social Economy Unit within DG XXIII. Following that move, the Commission gave increasing recognition to problems such as social exclusion and the potential of the social economy to address them, and 'the concept of the "third system", was adopted as a formal policy strategy . . . although it was deliberately vaguely specified, so that it can explicitly subsume a variety of different terms with broadly the same meaning': [18]

> Third system, third sector, social economy, community development, local development and employment initiatives, local and territorial pacts for employment, endogenous local development, sustainable economy . . . the abundance of terms used to describe a group of innovative phenomena shows the current froth around a set of largely unknown realities. [19]

However, although the realities were described as 'unknown', the Commission nevertheless attempted to define the organisations in the 'third system':

> These organisations aim to find solutions rather then [*sic*] to place themselves in a new market sector;

> They often refer to factors such as social solidarity, democratic organisations or the primacy of the individual over capital;

> These organisations are *often the result of public/private partnerships and have a close relationship with their local communities;*

> The market is not their sole source of income with organisations securing public subsidies, donations or loans – they often have very *mixed income;*

> Specific attention is often given to *disadvantaged* people by these organisations;

> These organisations are often small-scale structures often with larger numbers of non-active associates or unpaid *volunteers.*

> Finally, the most important factor which justifies the growing interest in this type of initiative naturally concerns their close relationship to the development of new types of jobs, mainly linked to satisfying new personal and collective needs which neither the public not the market can currently meet. [20]

(emphases in the original)

Mapping an economy

If the social economy is essentially co-operatives, mutuals, associations, and foundations (CMAFs) and the third sector all that is not in the public and private sectors, how does the concept of the social economy relate to a wider concept of the third sector and how do both of them relate to the public and private sectors within the totality of an economy?

To illustrate these relationships, a number of diagrams have been produced, which are, in effect, attempts to 'map' the subject. But such maps, like geographical maps, are not themselves real, but are intended to inform us about the reality by illustrating some of its features. In particular, they try to show how those features are positioned relative to each other.

One approach is that of Billis, who suggests that within an economy 'ideal type models' can be constructed for the private and public sectors using five core structural elements, which can then be used to identify the principles distinctly applicable to the third sector (see Table 2.2).

Billis further suggests that hybrids of organisations result when organisations develop characteristics that are found across the sectors (i.e. across the columns in Table 2.2). Table 2.3 presents examples of some of these hybrids.

Then there are continuum models in which it is suggested that there is a continuum between the private sector on the one hand and the government or the public sector on

Table 2.2 Ideal type sectors and accountability

Core elements	Private sector principles	Public sector principles	Third sector principles
1. Ownership	Shareholders	Citizens	Members
2. Governance	Share ownership size	Public elections	Private elections
3. Operational priorities	Market forces and individual choice	Public service and collective choice	Commitment about distinctive mission
4. Distinctive human resources	Paid employees in managerially controlled *Firm*	Paid public servants in legally backed *Bureau*	Members and volunteers in *Association*
5. Distinctive other resources	Sales, fees	Taxes	Dues, donations, and legacies

Source: D. Billis, 'Towards a theory of hybrid organisations', in D. Billis (Ed.) *Hybrid Organisations and the Third Sector: Challenges for Practice, Theory and Policy* (Basingstoke: Palgrave Macmillan, 2010), p. 55, reproduced with permission of Palgrave Macmillan

Table 2.3 Examples of hybrid organisations

Public–Third Hybrids	Quangos (quasi-autonomous non-governmental organisations), non-departmental public bodies (NDPBs) or 'local public spending bodies', e.g. great national museums and the BBC
Public–Private Hybrids	Nationalised industries such as the former British Rail, coal industry, British Leyland
Public–Private–Third Hybrids	Not for profit 'public bodies', such as housing associations, government audited, profit orientated with social mission.
Private–Public Hybrids	Public private partnerships (PPPs)
Private–Third Hybrids	Social enterprises, e.g. John Lewis
Private–Public–Third Hybrids	Private business with shareholders whose businesses heavily rely on government monitoring and give donations of funds through charitable partners, e.g. the National Lottery/Camelot
Third–Public Hybrid	Associations orientated towards government and using paid staff to deliver what we have called public services, and/or local government has its representatives on the management committee of the voluntary organization
Third–Private Hybrids	Charitable structures which have successful business spin-offs, e.g. museums and museum shops, charity shops
Third–Private–Public Hybrids	Volunteer organisational structure that was heavily dependent on government funding becomes service provider to government, e.g. relationship counselling, charity recruiting staff, and holding contracts with NHS/government

Source: Based on D. Billis, 'Sectors, Hybrids and Public Policy: The Voluntary Sector in Context' (draft), Paper presented at the ARNOVA 2003 Conference

the other hand. An example of this approach comes from Social Enterprise London and is shown in Figure 2.1.

In Figure 2.1 the term 'socially responsible businesses' is used. Others have made a distinction between socially responsible activity – described as that 'which pursues a financial return on capital, traditionally understood, but within a framework of social and environmental standards' – and socially directed activity, which 'pursues a return on capital where this is more widely defined to integrate social and environmental outcomes'. Socially responsible activity is the realm of most corporate responsibility agenda whereas socially directed activity covers much of 'the work of non-profit organisations and "social enterprises" which generate a degree of earned income in pursuit of a social return'.[21]

An attempt to provide a map of the whole of an economy was made by Pearce and it is shown in Figure 2.2. It indicates not just the third sector (or system, as he calls it) and its components, including the portion he suggests is in the social economy, but also where the boundaries are between it and the first two sectors: the public and private systems/sectors.

The position of the social economy

Of these maps or models, Figure 2.2 is the only one which explicitly identifies and includes the social economy. Chapter 1 introduced the term 'the social economy', its origins are outlined earlier in this chapter, and Figure 2.2 suggests that it is an important part of the third sector but is not all of it. Most definitions of it are not broad enough to include all the organisations which are in neither the private nor the public sector, but some commentators, nevertheless, use the terms 'social economy' and 'third sector' synonymously. The varying interpretations of the social economy are explored further in Chapter 4 but, because of them, it is difficult to place it precisely in a map of an economy, since its position depends on which definition is being used. This confusion highlights a dilemma in attempts to delineate this area. Should everything not in either the public or the private sector be considered, by definition, to be in the third sector? Or should the third sector be defined by common characteristics, which some of its component organisations share, although that would still leave out some organisations, which could thus form a fourth sector?

Social enterprise in a wider context				
Private sector	Socially responsible businesses	Social enterprise	Charity & voluntary sector	Government
Enterprises ~ income from sales			Grants & donations	Taxes
Private goals	Social goals			Political goals
Private ownership		Social ownership		Public ownership

Figure 2.1 The context of social enterprise
Source: Social Enterprise London, *Introducing Social Enterprise* (2001)

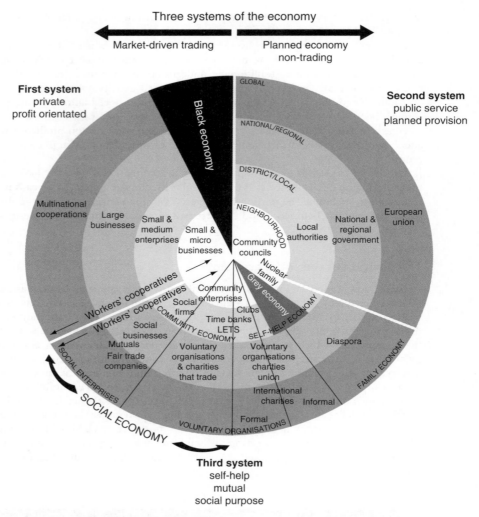

Figure 2.2 The three systems of an economy
Source: J. Pearce, *Social Enterprise in Anytown* (London: Calouste Gulbenkian Foundation, 2003), p. 25

Clear boundaries are not real

As the various continuum models recognise, the boundaries between sectors are never really going to be clear because the sectors themselves are, at least at their margins, rather fuzzy concepts. It might be convenient to consider similar activities as a category but the boundaries indicated between categories are not precise division points. The lines shown on diagrams between the sectors, and between different categories within sectors, are rather like contour lines drawn on a map: they help to indicate where land is rising or falling but you will not find them on the ground. The reality is that different types of economic activity are more like different colours in a spectrum: you can distinguish the main area of one colour from other areas of different colours but in between they blend into each other so there are no precise boundaries where one colour clearly ends and another begins. Also a colour which, for instance, may appear to be a shade of red when contrasted with pale orange may itself appear to be orange when placed beside dark red. (Some of these reservations are recognised in the portrayal in Figure 5.2.)

Uncertain areas

Because there is a spectrum of organisations, rather than everything being in discrete separate groupings, and because of the fuzzy nature of the concepts being considered, there are often areas of uncertainty where it is not clear to which sector an activity should belong. The public and private sectors of an economy may be defined more or less exclusively as they include only those activities which meet certain criteria, and so often is the social economy, although definitions of it are very varied. In contrast, the third sector is usually defined inclusively in that it encompasses all economic activity not included in either of the other two sectors. Nevertheless, there are hybrid organisations (see Table 2.3), other borderline cases (such as those highlighted in Illustration 2.2), and some commonly misplaced organisations (see Illustration 2.3).

Illustration 2.2 Some borderline organisations

- *Sole traders and small partnerships.* It might be thought that one-person businesses run by people operating as sole traders would be considered to be very small private sector businesses run for the profit of the sole trader. But probably very few people who work as sole traders always allocate their time in the way which best maximises their personal financial return, and the same might also apply to owner-managers of small businesses and to small partnerships. For a sole trader there is no distinction between wages and profits, and many small business owners, while wanting to earn enough money to maintain their lifestyle, will also sometimes do things either free or cheaply for other people or organisations which, for whatever reason, they wish to support. Thus, in their operations, the owners of many small businesses may sometimes behave like social entrepreneurs.
- *Worker co-operatives.* A business might be established as a worker co-operative if its founders wished it to function on co-operative principles applying any surplus for the benefit of the founding community. Yet the format of a worker co-operative can allow it to distribute its surplus to its worker members, who are, therefore, in a similar position as shareholders in a private sector business taking personal financial returns from the business's profits.

Illustration 2.3 Some misplaced organisations

Three organisations whose activities would place them in a different sector from that which their form might indicate:

A company limited by guarantee which was really in the public sector!

It might be thought that companies limited by guarantee are archetypical third sector organisations. They are not usually considered to be in the public sector because public sector organisations are usually created by statute and are not bound by company law, and they are not in the private sector because private sector organisations can distribute profits as dividends, which companies limited by guarantee cannot. However, in Northern Ireland, the Local Enterprise Development Unit (LEDU) was established in 1972 as a company limited by guarantee but it was set up by the Northern Ireland government as its small business agency. It was entirely funded by the Northern Ireland government, which also approved its plans and budgets and appointed its members. In effect, the government also decided who it should appoint as directors and as chairman, with the implied threat that its funding would be withdrawn if it did not comply. Also its Chief Executive had to answer to the Permanent Secretary for the use of the government funding, which was its sole source of income, even though there were times when the Chief Executive was not a director and so could not sign the annual accounts. In practice, if not in theory, LEDU was part of the public sector.

A company limited by shares which was really a social enterprise!

The well-known ice-cream-maker Ben and Jerry's was started as a company limited by shares so that the local community could share in its ownership. That might suggest that it was a private sector business. In all other ways, though, it was a social enterprise as it sought not to maximise the financial return to its shareholders, but to operate ethically for the benefit of the local community. However, when Unilever offered to buy it, and so move it into the private sector, a majority of the shareholders decided to sell their shares to Unilever even though this was contrary to the wishes of the founders.

A public sector organisation which is really a trade association!

The Livestock and Meat Commission for Northern Ireland was founded by statute and is funded by a statutory levy on businesses in the livestock and meat industry. Thus it is considered to be in the public sector. Nevertheless, it acts on behalf of the meat-producing and meat-processing businesses in its industry, very like a trade association would act for its members, although, for the latter, membership and associated subscriptions would be voluntary.

Conclusion

Human behaviour does not evolve in neatly separated areas of action, and economic activity is no exception. This chapter describes how three broad areas of economic activity can now be distinguished, although one of them has historically received less recognition than the others. In their core areas, the three sectors are clearly different from each other. While they may all help to address human needs, they do that in different ways, being influenced by different mechanisms, obtaining their income from different sources, and responding to different underpinning governance principles. However, while it is often useful to recognise and understand such differences among the three areas, they do not have distinct borders and, at the margins, there is overlap or scope for organisations to be classified in more than one sector. Therefore, it is in this context that the social economy and the third sector, described in more detail in the next chapter, need to be understood.

Key Points of Chapter 2

- Following the agricultural revolution, three economic sectors have evolved:
    - the private sector – which allocates resources to needs based on market forces;
    - the public sector – which directs where resources should be applied to address needs;
    - a third sector – which is neither of the above.

- However the third sector has received little recognition, possibly because, without a common language for it, it has been hard to discuss it.
- One term which has emerged, from French sources, is the social economy, which includes many organisations in the third sector. Thus it is sometimes used synonymously with the third sector.
- However, there are no clear distinct boundaries separating any of the sectors but instead there is a range of different organisations, some of which might be described as hybrids as they appear to share some characteristics with more than one sectors.

Case 2.1 | The oldest company in the UK

'The Company and Fraternity of Free Fishermen and Dredgermen of Faversham' was in existence in 1189, if not earlier. It was a 'labour corporation', or trade collective, the profits of which were shared in proportion to the amount of work put in by each individual member. To become a 'freeman' of the Company, applicants had to serve a seven-year apprenticeship and be married.

There was good money to be earned from oysters and it is recorded that in the eighteenth century ships from the Netherlands queued to load oysters for the Dutch ports. However, by the beginning of the twentieth century, pollution from sewage was beginning to take its toll and in 1903 the oyster beds were declared unfit for use. In 1908 the company was desperate and brought a High Court action against the Council. The Company won and the Council was forced to build a proper sewage treatment plant.

Despite this, as a trade collective, the Company never regained its vitality and in 1930 it was re-established as a conventional limited company in which the former freemen became shareholders. Although the oyster grounds were subsequently let to a neighbouring fishery, they failed after some harsh winters in the 1950s and 1960s. The Company, though, is still in existence and lets the grounds as moorings or for use by wildfowlers. On the strength of its existence in 1189, it claims to be the oldest company in the UK.

Source: Based on information on www.faversham.org (accessed 29 April 2007)

Case 2.2 | Establishing an early social enterprise

On 24 May 1514, Henry VIII granted John Dowman a licence to found, in the parish church of Pocklington, a Guild which, according to its original patent, would among other things be able to hold lands with a yearly value of £13 6s 8d and to 'find from time to time one man fitted, and sufficiently learned in grammar, to instruct and educate all and singular scholars who resort to the town of Pocklington for the aforesaid purpose of receiving education'. Pocklington, which was mentioned in the *Domesday Book*, was then one of the significant market towns in Yorkshire, and, at that time, most towns of importance boasted a school. Nearby there was an ancient school at York, where teaching was recorded in the early eighth century, and Beverley School had also been in existence for a long time as its records were apparently consulted in 1304 to settle a dispute about 'a very ancient custom'. Those old schools were ecclesiastical, for Medieval England had entrusted its education to the Church. However, by the thirteenth century, schools were being founded which were secular both in their purpose and in their government, and, in default of any precedent for creating a special governing body, the roundabout procedure of founding a guild was discovered as a means by which to provide lay governors for such schools. As a result of this foundation early in the fifteenth century, Pocklington then had its own grammar school like York, Beverly, Howden, Hemingborough, and Hull.

John Dowman (also sometimes known as Dolman) had been a lawyer and churchman of some eminence. He was made a Bachelor of Canon and Doctor of Civil Law by Cambridge University and was Prebend first of Sarum, then of St Paul's and finally of Lichfield Cathedral. When St John's College was founded in Cambridge in 1511 by Bishop Fisher, acting as executor to Lady Margaret Beaufort (the mother of Henry VII), the executors lodged for a time with Dr Dowman, possibly to seek his legal advice. Certainly he made two significant benefactions to St John's College and linked the school he founded to the College by, for instance, obliging the Guild officers to consult the College about the appointment of a schoolmaster.

However, John Dowman's school did not always have an easy existence. In 1547 Henry VIII died and was succeeded by his nine-year-old son Edward VI. Edward's ministers followed a reformation policy and, by the Chantries Act of 1547, abolished all the religious guilds and confiscated their property, although the colleges of Oxford and Cambridge were exempted from its provisions. Some provision was made for the temporary continuance of the Guild schools, usually by setting aside a small part of their property to provide maintenance. The result was that some schools disappeared while others survived somehow on a meagre allowance. Pocklington School, however, escaped in an odd way. When he founded it, John Dowman had intended to endow it with some of his property but this was not done. Therefore, when the Guild was abolished, Thomas Dowman, who was the son of John Dowman's first cousin and his heir, offered the property again. He petitioned the Parliament and, in 1551, obtained a private Act of Parliament establishing the Free School of Pocklington. It then flourished, except for occasional lapses, until near the end of the seventeenth century, but then had a century and a half of relative decline, although it did educate William Wilberforce from 1771 to 1776. It was resuscitated in the middle of the nineteenth century by a headmaster who was recorded as having 'rescued' the school from 'the scandalous neglect prior to his appointment'. A Victorian inspector reported that 'the one great want of such a town as Pocklington is one good school which is on a sufficiently large basis to admit the boy who is going to university side by side with the boy who will leave earlier, and which knows how to do full justice to the requirements of both'. He did, however, also criticise it for 'partaking too much of the character of a private school'.

At the start of the twenty-first century, the school John Dowman founded still survives in Pocklington as a public school. (NB: The title 'public' for what would now be seen to be a private, fee-taking school is a legacy of the time of the school's foundation when there were no state schools and places in it were open to the public, whereas entry to some other schools was more limited.)

Source: Based on P. C. Sands and C. M. Haworth, *A History of Pocklington School, East Yorkshire 1514–1950* (London and Hull: A Brown & Sons, circa 1951)

Questions, Exercises, Essay, and Discussion Topics

1. Which came first: the public, the private, or the third sector? Discuss.

2. Into which of the three sectors (public, private, and third) would you place the following and why:

   Sole traders?
   Worker co-operatives?
   The BBC?
   Family economy activity?
   Grey economy activity?

3. 'Originally economic activity was neither private sector nor public sector. Thus it must have been in the third sector.' Discuss.

4. Is it possible, on a two-dimensional map, to illustrate all the variants of economic activity?

5. 'The issues which are important in understanding why a business behaves as it does are not the legal form it has taken and where it might formally be placed on a map of the economy, but are the aspirations, intentions, and behaviour of its founder(s) and/or owners/members.' Discuss this in the light of Illustrations 2.2 and 2.3 and Cases 2.1 and 2.2.

Suggestions for further reading

A. Amin, A. Cameron and R. Hudson, *Placing the Social Economy* (London: Routledge, 2002).

D. Billis. (Ed), *Hybrid Organisations and the Third Sector: Challenges for Practice, Theory and Policy* (Basingstoke: Palgrave Macmillan, 2010).

F. Martin and M. Thompson, *Social Enterprise* (Basingstoke: Palgrave Macmillan, 2010).

References

1. J. Harvey, *Modern Economics* (Basingstoke: Macmillan, 1998), p. 7.

2. A. Toffler, *The Third Wave* (London: Collins, 1980).

3. For further discussion of such implications of farming, see J. Diamond, *Guns, Germs and Steel* (London: Vintage, 1998), pp. 85–104.

4. A. Molloy, C. McFeely and E. Connolly, *Building a Social Economy for the New Millennium* (Derry: Guildhall Press/NICDA Social Economy Agency, 1999), p. 7.

5. P. Hennessy, *Whitehall* (London: Fontana Press, 1990), p. 18.

6. P. Mathias, *The First Industrial Nation: An Economic History of Britain 1700–1914* (London: Methuen, 1983), pp. 24–9.

7. Ibid., p. 308.

8. Ibid., pp. 352–3.

9. See A. Amin, A. Cameron and R. Hudson, *Placing the Social Economy* (London: Routledge, 2002), pp. 2–3.

10. P. Hennessy, *Whitehall* (London: Fontana Press, 1990), p. 18.

11. F. Moulaert and O. Ailenei, 'Social economy, third sector and solidarity relations: A conceptual synthesis from history to present', *Urban Studies*, Vol. 42, No. 11 (2005), pp. 2037–53.

12. Ibid., p. 2044.

13. A. Amin, R. Hudson and A. Cameron, *Placing the Social Economy* (London: Routledge, 2002), p. 3.

14. F. Moulaert and O. Ailenei, 'Social economy, third sector and solidarity relations: A conceptual synthesis from history to present', *Urban Studies*, Vol. 42, No. 11 (2005), p. 2041.

15. Ibid., pp. 2037–53.

16. A. Amin, A. Cameron and R. Hudson, *Placing the Social Economy* (London: Routledge, 2002), pp. 3–4.

17. P. Teague, 'Developing the social economy in Ireland?', *International Journal of Urban and Regional Research*, Vol. 31, No. 1 (2007), pp. 91–108.

18. Commission of the European Communities, *The Third System and Employment: A First Reflection* (Brussels: European Commission, 1998), p. 4 – quoted by A. Amin, R. Hudson and A. Cameron, *Placing the Social Economy* (London: Routledge, 2002), p. 21.

19. Ibid.

20. Ibid.

21. Based on S. Foster, E. Mayo and J. Nicholls, *Social Return on Investment: Concept Paper* (London: New Economic Foundation, 2002); and D. Aeron-Thomas, J. Nicholls, S. Foster and A. Westall, *Social Return on Investment: Valuing what matters* (London: New Economic Foundation, 2004).

3

current perceptions of the social economy and the third sector

contents:

- introduction
- what is in the third sector?
- a variety of labels
- the social economy
- other sub-sectors
- the fourth sector
- conclusion

Key concepts

This chapter covers:

- the range of organisations included in the third sector;
- the variety of labels sometimes used for this sector – or parts of it;
- the concept of the social economy and what it might include;
- different views on the role of the social economy;
- other possible sub-sectors;
- indications of the scale of the social economy.

Learning objectives

By the end of this chapter the reader should:

- be aware of the range of activities ascribed to the third sector;
- appreciate different ways in which the sector, or parts of it, can be labelled;
- understand the concept of the social economy and what it might include;
- be aware of some of the different roles sometime ascribed to the social economy;
- be aware of the other possible sub-sectors;
- appreciate the size of the social economy.

Introduction

Chapter 2 shows how, as the private and public sectors of the economy evolved as distinct fields of economic activity, other organisations were created which contributed to the economy but which belonged to neither of those two sectors. Sometimes therefore labelled the 'third sector', these organisations have often been overlooked in traditional economics. Nevertheless, there is a wide range of activities which come into this category, and this chapter considers current views on this sector, and in particular on those activities considered to be in the social economy.

What is in the third sector?

Illustration 3.1 A sector attempt to define what it is

The NCVO (National Council for Voluntary Organisations) has embarked on research designed to answer the unanswerable question: what exactly is the third sector?

The idea came about because the research team responsible for producing the umbrella body's UK Voluntary Sector Almanac struggles to decide which organisations to include.

'There is plenty of research about the sector, but definitions vary, so it's hard to compare findings', said Oliver Reichardt, one of the almanac's authors. 'It's important the sector takes the lead on this, otherwise somebody else will. The Government chose the term third sector, and lots of people are unhappy with it.'

Reichardt said the NCVO was consulting widely over the issue and it could take up to two years to finalise a definition.

If it proves impossible to reach agreement across the sector, he said, the NCVO will probably drop the project altogether.

Whatever the outcome of the research, sector organisations will no doubt continue to ponder their true identity for a while yet.

Source: www.thirdsector.co.uk/News/DailyBulletin/741663 (accessed 3 October 2007)

Table 3.1 is an expansion of Table 1.1 but still lists only a few of the organisations and categories of organisation which have an economic impact but which would not generally be considered to belong in either the private or the public sector. The range of organisations in this sector is also indicated in Table 3.2, which lists the main classification categories recommended by the United Nations.

Some activities with an economic impact are generally associated with only one sector of the economy. For instance, stock exchange activity is associated with the private sector, government activity with the public sector, and religious activity, except in theocracies, with the third sector. Some activities, however, can be found in more than one of these sectors, and there are some which can, at least in the UK, be found in all three. The following are examples:

Sport: Sport, when it is done in schools, takes place in a public sector context. Most sports clubs are in the third sector. However, professional coaching is often delivered for private gain and many major football clubs are also clearly private sector organisations.

Business support: There are government-established business support agencies which are in the public sector. Chambers of Commerce and other organisations such as the Institute of Directors are third sector organisations which deliver business support. Much business support is, however, bought from private sector consultancies.

Table 3.1 Third sector activities: an indicative list

Amateur dramatic clubs	Intermediary funding bodies
Arts and culture organisations	St John Ambulance
Associations*	Knights of St Columbanus
Building preservation trusts	LETS
Business schools	Lifeboat services
Chambers of Commerce	Medical charities
Charities	Mosques
Churches	Mountain rescue services
Community enterprises	Mutuals*
Community health care bodies	Rotary clubs
Co-operatives*	Political parties
Credit unions	Professional bodies
Donkey sanctuaries	Social clubs
Enterprise agencies	Social housing schemes
Fair trade companies	Sports clubs
Faith schools	Synagogues
Family activity (DIY, vegetable gardens, etc.)	Temples
Famine relief agencies	Time banks
Foundations*	Trades unions
Freemasons	Universities and university colleges
Golf clubs	Voluntary organisations
Hospices	Women's Institute
Housing associations	Worker co-operatives

*Associations, co-operatives, mutuals (and foundations) are the categories of organisation included in the classification *Économie sociale* in some EU member states. Descriptions of them are provided in Chapter 4

Housing: There is private sector housing provided for sale or rent to make a profit for its builders/owners. There is public sector housing (such as 'council housing' in the UK) which is provided as a public service. There is also social housing provided by housing associations whose board members are volunteers and whose surpluses must be reinvested in housing activities.

Education: Much education is provided by the public sector. However, some independent schools and colleges are third sector bodies, and some forms of education, such as private tuition, is provided on a for-profit basis.

Health care: Like education, health care can be provided by all three sectors. In the UK much health care is provided in the public sector by the National Health Service (NHS). However, there is also a significant provision of supplementary care by third sector bodies such as community health care organisations and St John Ambulance. In addition, some people pay for private sector treatment, possibly because it is quicker or is not available from the NHS.

Forestry: In Britain, environmental charities now own a significant amount of the forested land, as Table 3.3 shows.

Table 3.2 The main groups of non-profit organisations

The *UN Handbook on Non-Profit Institutions in the System of National Accounts* recommends the International Classification of Non-Profit Organisations (ICNPO) system. It includes 12 major activity groups:
• Culture and recreation • Education and research • Health • Social services • Environment • Development and housing • Law, advocacy, and politics • Philanthropic intermediaries and voluntarism promotion • International activities • Religious congregations and associations • Business, professional associations, unions • Not elsewhere classified

Source: www.un.org (accessed 15 August 2007)

Table 3.3 Ownership of forests in England

In 1998, the ownership of forests in England was split between the following:	
Ownership category	**Per cent of forested land**
Personal sector (individuals and families)	47
Business sector (for profit)	15
Forestry Commission (public sector)	22
Other public sector including local authorities	9
Charities (often for conservation purposes)	7
Community ownership, common land, and unidentified	1

Source: Forestry Commission, *National Inventory of Woodland and Trees – England* (Edinburgh: Forestry Commission, 2001) p. 28

A variety of labels

Illustration 3.2 A view from the USA

The third sector (is) a label for organizations in the economy that are neither traditional for-profit businesses nor government agencies . . . Neither capitalist nor public, the *third sector* is the third element in the mixed economy of the United States. It consists largely of private organizations that act in the economic arena but that exist to provide specific goods and services to their members or constituents. These organizations act neither to enrich 'owners' nor to provide high income for top executives. Some are used to protect entrenched interests, and others are used to do social good.

Non-profit organizations fall into two broad categories: some serve only their members, and others perform a broad array of public services. The first group includes social clubs, political parties, labor unions, business associations and cooperatives.

The third sector is a pastiche – a collection of organizations that are usually defined by their *not* being of the larger two sectors but that are otherwise varied in nature.

Source: C. Gunn, *Third-Sector Development: Making Up for the Market* (New York: Cornell University, 2004), pp. vii, 1, 6

Although this book tends to refer to the third sector of the economy as the 'third sector', others have given it different labels, including the 'non-profit sector', the 'voluntary sector', the 'voluntary and community sector', the 'social economy', and the 'social enterprise sector' (and it has also been referred to as the third system[1] and the third way).[2] Behind this varied nomenclature, it would seem that there have been two broad approaches to definitions about, in, or for the third sector and its components:

- *Exclusive.* One approach is more narrow and focused. It seeks to delineate a set of organisations which share certain characteristics, even if those characteristics are quite widely held, and to exclude others which do not. What is included in such a definition is likely to be relatively homogeneous. Definitions of the social economy, of social enterprise, or of other components of the third sector are generally of this sort.
- *Inclusive.* The other approach is broader and more embracing. It seeks to include, rather than to exclude, and to integrate, rather than to separate. What it includes may therefore be quite heterogeneous. Definitions of the third sector itself generally fall into this category (see Table 3.4 for some of the categories of organisation which would be included in the third sector in this way).

Definitions of the second, inclusive, sort will tend to be of a higher level and thus similar and compatible as they will all seek to include more or less the same things. In contrast, definitions of the first sort can differ and even be incompatible because they can differ on the characteristics they wish to include and those they wish to exclude. Such differences can arise because definitions are developed for different reasons and because, in any newly developing field of interest, there tends to be an initial proliferation of variations before any common trend or agreed approach has had time to emerge. The result is that, when it comes to things like social enterprises, social businesses, social economy enterprises (SEEs), and community enterprises, there is a plethora of definitions, some overlapping, some disagreeing, some traditional, some fashionable, and some serving special purposes or reflecting differing agenda. For some of these expressions and labels, therefore, there is a spectrum of possible meanings and plenty of potential for miscommunication if the meanings intended by the different parties involved in any particular discussion or situation are not made clear.

Table 3.4 Categories of third sector organisations and activity

A list of categories of organisations, or of activity, that might be considered to operate wholly, or at least in part, within the third sector, might include the following:

- The social economy (including co-operatives, mutuals, associations, and foundations), social enterprises, and social economy enterprises
- The voluntary sector
- The community sector/economy and community enterprises
- The family economy
- The self-help economy
- Civic organisations
- Funding intermediaries
- Member service organisations including clubs, trades unions, business and professional bodies, and political organisations
- Mutual benefit and co-operative organisations, including credit unions, worker co-operatives, consumer co-operatives, and agricultural co-operatives
- Charities
- The grey economy (but not the black economy, unless the crime is not for personal enrichment – as in the case of Robin Hood?)
- And others such as those sole traders and small businesses who contribute to their community and who take 'a reward for work done' rather than always seeking to maximise personal profit?

If the third sector of the economy is defined as encompassing those activities with an economic impact which are in neither the private nor the public sectors, that is a definition which includes all the activities listed in Table 3.1 and is an inclusive one. It emphasises the only feature which all such organisations have in common, which is that they belong in neither of the two other sectors. In the list in Table 3.1 there are many different bodies, some of which have a number of similarities but some of which are very different.

In this field, other, more exclusive categories have been suggested, based on a number of shared characteristics. The definitions advanced for these categories are exclusive definitions and they may be suggested in order to focus on the particular category being defined but they do have the additional effect of indicating sub-sectors within the overall ambit of the third sector. Such is the real or apparent extent of some of these other categorisations that they are sometimes seen either as alternative labels for the third sector or at least as being so distinctive and/or important as to constitute a third sector in their own right. In that case, because they are exclusive categorisations which do not include some organisations which are not in the public or private sectors, they suggest that, in theory at least, there must be a fourth sector for those excluded categories.

Table 3.5 lists some of the labels given either to the whole sector or to specific sub-categories within it. Some of the terms have been used only to refer to the overall sector

Table 3.5 Labels for the 'third sector', or for large parts of it

third sector, third system, third way

non-profit, not-for-profit, or not-for-profit-distribution sector

social economy, social enterprise sector

voluntary sector, voluntary and community sector, community

sector, community enterprise, community economy

self-help economy, family economy

organised civil society

and some clearly refer to significant sub-sectors within that overall sector. Nevertheless, many of the terms not only have at some time been used more or less interchangeably with one or more of the others but also have sometimes been used to refer to a sub-sector and sometimes to the sector overall. The result is that this is often an area in which the terminology can be confusing as there is no accepted standard practice, as the following examples illustrate (italics added) (and see also Illustration 3.3):

> In 2003, the voluntary, third or non-profit sector occupies centre stage in public policy discussions in the UK.[3]

> In what might be called the 'community era' we talked of community action, *community enterprise, and community business.* Today, in the contemporary 'social era', we are more likely to talk of social entrepreneurs, *social enterprise and social business.* Is there some serious significance in this shift in vocabulary from community to social? Does it matter?[4]

> *Social economy* refers to a *third sector* in economics between the private sector . . . and the public sector.[5]

> The *non-profit sector,* usually in the hands of the *Third Sector,* is no longer seen as a residual and poor cousin to the state or the market.[6]

> I want a new compact that elevates the *third sector* as partner, not as . . . a cut price alternative to government – but government fulfilling its responsibilities to fund services, and fully valuing the contribution the *voluntary sector* can make.[7]

> Economies may be considered to have three sectors:
>
> - The business private sector, which is privately owned and profit motivated.
> - The public sector which is owned by the state and provides services in the public interest.
> - The *social economy*, that embraces a wide range of community, voluntary and not-for-profit activities . . . The *third sector can* be broken down into three sub-sectors: *the community sector, the voluntary sector and the social enterprise sector.*[8]

It is of course possible, as the last quote above illustrates, to see many of these labels, such as the social economy, the voluntary sector, and the community sector, as referring to specific sub-sectors within the third sector. John Pearce, in the diagram of the three sectors reproduced in Figure 2.2, has indicated that within the third sector there are a number of sub-sectors or sub-groupings including the social economy, the community economy, the self-help economy, and the family economy – and of these the main one is the social economy.

Illustration 3.3 An EMES view

The EMES European Research Network was formed in 1996 to study the emergence of social enterprises in Europe and build up a European corpus of understanding of 'third sector' issues. The EMES focus areas include social enterprise, the non-profit sector, and the third sector but it does not appear to insist that these are clearly separate categories.

For instance, among the comments made on its website or in publications arising from its work and listed on its website are the following:

> The term 'third sector' is often used because it appears as a neutral term, free of an *a priori* link with any theoretical or ideological tradition. This, however, implies that the same word, 'third sector', can have different meanings.[9]

[The] third sector ... is often called the 'non-profit sector' or the 'social economy'. [10]

There is no universally accepted definition of the non-profit sector. However [it suggests] the non-profit sector consists of organisations with the following characteristics:

a) they are formal, ie they have a certain degree of institutionalisation ...
b) they are private, ie distinct from both the state and those organisations issuing directly from public authorities.
c) they are independent ...
d) they cannot distribute profits to either their members or their administrators ...
e) they must involve some level of voluntary participation ... [11]

In today's terms, the social economy gathers enterprises of the co-operative movements, mutual benefit and insurance societies, foundations and all other types of non-profit organizations which all share some principles making them correspond to the 'third sector' of modern economies. [12]

The social economy

The social economy is often the focus of attention for many people interested in the non-private and non-public sector of the economy and there have been many attempts to define it. According to one source:

The social economy constitutes a broad range of activities and practices which have the potential to provide opportunities for local people and communities to engage in all stages of the process of local economic regeneration and job creation, from the identification of basic needs to the operationalisation of initiatives. The sector covers the economic potential and activities of the self-help and co-operative movements, i.e. initiatives which aim to satisfy the social and economic needs of local communities and their members. The sector includes co-operatives; self-help projects; credit unions; housing associations; partnerships; community enterprises and businesses. [13]

This and many other definitions are exclusive definitions which do not include all the organisations covered by inclusive third sector definitions. (For instance, a Canadian study specifically states that 'the non-profit and voluntary sector ... is considerably larger than the social economy'.) [14] Nevertheless, the term 'social economy' is sometimes used as a label for the third sector, presumably on the basis that those organisations it does not include are assumed to be relatively insignificant or that what it does include is relatively so important and homogeneous as to constitute the sector in its own right. Although the labels 'voluntary' and/or 'community sector' are also on occasion used in the same way, the social economy is so often given such prominence that it is given more detailed consideration in Chapter 4, in particular in the way it is frequently defined in terms of the sort of organisations within it.

The social enterprise sector

A term associated with the social economy is the 'social enterprise sector', which is also discussed in Chapter 4. Some sources, for instance Pearce in Figure 2.2, present the social enterprise sector as a significant component of the social economy. Others seem to use the term almost as a label for the whole of social economy. For instance, in the foreword to the UK government's *Social Enterprise: a strategy for success*, Tony Blair, who was then Prime Minister, states that when he hosted a social enterprise breakfast at No. 10, he met 'people from every part of the social economy'. [15] The social enterprise action plan later produced by the UK Cabinet Office's Office of the Third Sector states that 'Britain's social enterprise sector is one of the most successful and vibrant in the world'. [16] However, while the action plan refers frequently to social enterprise and social enterprises, it does not use the term 'social economy' but does refer occasionally to the social enterprise sector and to the third sector. The latter, it indicates, embraces social enterprises together with voluntary and community organisations, charities, mutuals, and co-operatives.

What is the social economy?

'The social economy', it has been said, 'is an imprecise term – but in general can be thought of as those organisations who [*sic*] are independent of the state and provide services, goods and trade for a social purpose and are not profit distributing.' [17] Nevertheless, there are, between some different stakeholders, deep theoretical and policy differences as to what constitutes the social economy and what its ultimate political purpose is. [18] The classification *économie sociale* used in some EU member states has specifically included three categories of organisation – associations, co-operatives, and mutuals – and was expanded in the early 1990s to include foundations also. However, as an earlier quotation indicates, at least in UK government circles, the social economy is defined only very loosely in terms of some characteristics of the organisations within it. The European Commission also does not formally define the social economy but, presumably based on the *économie sociale* classification, has indicated that:

> The so-called social economy, including co-operatives, mutual societies, non-profit associations, foundations and social enterprises provides a wide range of products and services across Europe, and generates millions of jobs. [19]

Also, that

> The importance to the European economy of co-operatives, mutual societies, associations, foundations and social enterprises (which together are sometimes referred to as the Social Economy) is now receiving greater recognition. [20]

The latter reference adds that

> The social economy is found in almost all economic sectors. Cooperatives are particularly prominent in certain fields, such as banking, crafts, agricultural production and retailing. Mutual societies are predominately active in the insurance and mortgage sectors, whilst associations and foundations figure strongly in the provision of health and welfare services, sports and recreation, culture, environmental regeneration, humanitarian rights, development aid, consumer rights, education, training and research. Some Social Economy bodies work in competitive markets while others work close to the public sector. Cooperatives, for example, which are formed on the basis of fulfilling the interests of their members (producers or consumers) play an important role in several markets and contribute to effective competition. [21]

In the UK, the Industrial Common Ownership Movement (ICOM), the federal organisation of UK co-operatives, has argued that the social economy sector should be thought of as a continuum in an approach similar to the French *économie sociale*, [22] and Molloy et al. presented this diagrammatically, as shown in Figure 3.1.

The approach in Figure 3.1 presents the social economy as a sector encompassing a range of organisations, with agencies positioned in different places in the range depending on their economic rationale and constitutional status. Cooper [23] defined the social economy as areas of activity that overlapped between the private, public, and voluntary

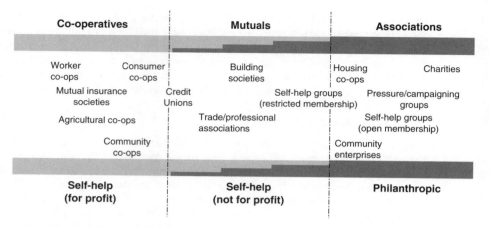

Figure 3.1 Traditional components of the social economy
Source: A. Molloy, C. McFeely and E. Connolly, *Building a Social Economy for the New Millennium* (Derry: Guildhall Press, 1999), p. 12

sectors and saw it as flexible but characterised by a number of a common features. These are shown in Table 3.6.

Another approach is that of Sattar and Mayo,[24] who suggest that the social economy can be described using three 'I's:

- *Identity* covering those for whom there is a convergence of interest and sense of identity as a social economy distinct from other sectors of the economy;
- *Institutions* covering the three main institutional categories of co-operatives, mutuals, and voluntary associations; and
- *Intention* covering economic activities pursued with a social or ethical intention.

Models of Social Enterprise

Ridley-Duff and Bull[25] suggest that social enterprise can be seen in a spectrum of activity between the traditional areas of for-profit and non-profit embracing corporations practising social responsibility, socially responsible business, non-profits funded (mainly)

Table 3.6 Common features of the social economy

Values	Characteristics	Organisations	Activities
Democratic Collective Co-operative Mutual Sustainable Equitable and open	Economically active Mutually supportive Community or common ownership Community benefit Common use/ distribution of surplus Community based	Co-operatives Community businesses Charitable trading LETS Credit unions Community-based development trusts Ethical banks/community finance schemes Industrial and provident societies	Creating and managing workspace Developing property Training Job creation schemes Providing local services Running commercial services Providing social housing Providing low-cost personal loans

Source: Based on M. Cooper, 'The development of the third sector in Bristol', *Local Economy*, Vol. 14, No. 4 (1999), pp. 348–349

by trading activity and non-profits with some income-generating activity. They add that it is counterproductive to debate in which of these areas organisations have the greater claim to be social enterprises and cite criticisms of restrictive definitions. However, they also present a cross-sectional view incorporating all three sectors (see Figure 3.2) in which they suggest that the ideal type of social enterprise is the multi-stakeholder model (see also Table 3.7).

A number of other writers have been concerned about the relationship among sectors in defining the social economy and also see value in a concept centred on the expression of connections between the state, the market, households, and the access that third sector organisations have to the grant economy:

> The social economy is a hybrid. It cuts across the four sub-economies: the market, the state, the grant economy, and the household. Each of these sectors has its own logics and rhythms, its own means of obtaining resources, its own structures of control and allocation, and its own rules and customs for the distribution of its outputs. But the parts of these economies which we term the social economy are united by their four goals, by the importance given to ethics and their multiple threads of reciprocity. Their production ranges from the micro scale of domestic care in the household to the universal services of a national welfare state. Although analytically distinct from the private market, it includes social enterprises engaging in the market, as well as some of the activities of private companies that have primarily social goals [26]

The diagram in Figure 3.3 shows that the social economy happens in and across all sectors – in this case including the household sector. This produces six interfaces: the first three are between the state and the other three sub-economies. Central to these interfaces is the way finance crosses the borders: inwards in forms of taxation and fees, outwards in form of grants, procurement, and investment. Regulation, fiscal, and legal controls also influence the level of innovation, with for example Community Interest Companies (CICs) reflecting innovation in company law. The fourth interface is between the private

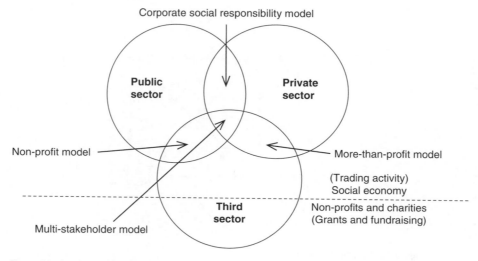

Figure 3.2 A composite theory: the triangle of social enterprise
Source: R. Ridley-Duff and M. Bull, *Understanding Theory and Practice* (London: Sage, 2011), p. 75

Table 3.7 A typology of social enterprises

Type A Non-profit model	
In the boundary areas of the public and third sectors. Shares a 'public' interest outlook and hostility to private sector ownership and equity finance	Social enterprise as a 'non-profit' organisation: obtains grants and/or contracts from public sector bodies and other third sector organisations, structured to prevent profit and asset transfers except to other non-profit organisations
Type B Corporate social responsibility model	
In the boundary areas of the public and private sectors. Suspicious of the third sector as a viable partner in service delivery and economic development	Social enterprises as a corporate social responsibility project: environmental, ethical, or fair trade business; 'for-profit' employee-owned business; public/private joint venture or partnership with social aims
Type C More-than-profit model	
In the boundary areas of the private and third sectors. Antipathy to the state (central government) as a vehicle for meeting the needs of disadvantaged groups, and realistic about the state's capacity to oppress minorities	Social enterprise as a 'more-than-profit' organisation: single- or dual-stakeholder co-operative, charity trading arm, membership society, or association, or a thrust that generates surpluses from trading to increase social investment
Type D Multi-stakeholder model (ideal type)	
At the overlap of all sectors. It replaces public, private, and third sector competition with a democratic multi-stakeholder model. All interests in a supply chain are acknowledged to break down barriers to social change	Social enterprise as a multi-stakeholder enterprise, new co-operatives, charities, voluntary organisations, or co-owned businesses using direct and representative democracy to achieve equitable distribution of social and economic benefits

Source: R. Ridley-Duff and M. Bull, *Understanding Theory and Practice* (London: Sage, 2011), pp. 75–6

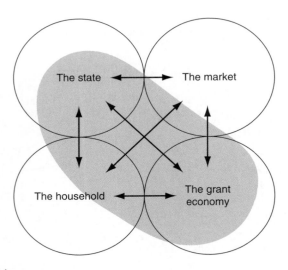

Figure 3.3 The social economy
Source: R. Murray, J. Caulier-Grice and G. Mulgan, *The Open Book of Social Innovation* (London: The Young Foundation, 2010), p. 143

market and grant economy and includes corporate sponsorship, corporate social responsibility, and peer mentoring. There are also emergent forms of collaborative working among private companies.

The fifth and sixth interfaces shown in Figure 3.3 constitute the household economy's relations with the other three sub-economies. At the interface between the household and the private market, there are examples of alliances that have been built around climate change, especially through reducing energy consumption, home insulation, and more sustainable modes of power, especially from renewables. There are also two relations between households and the grant economy through donations, volunteering, and more formally via Time Banking and reciprocal exchange schemes such as Local Enterprise Trading Schemes/Systems (LETS).

Paradigm differences: What is the social economy's role?

Basing descriptions of the social economy on objective assessments of what is in it, as this chapter has tried to do, might appear to be logical, but it is not the sequence that often appears to be followed. Instead, assessments of what is considered to be in the social economy are, in effect, based on definitions subjectively derived from the function that it is thought, expected, or hoped that the social economy will serve.

One of the reasons advanced for the lack of a single, generally accepted, definition of the social economy is that it is due, at last in part, to the various different traditions and policy emphasis that exist. Amin et al., for instance, have identified 'considerable international differences in the ways in which the social economy and its relationship to market, state and civil society are envisioned'. In the United States, they suggest, which, compared to many European countries, has a weak welfare state playing a largely residual role, the sector is shaped by 'bottom-up' community development processes fronted by a voluntary sector now only loosely connected with political activism. In Western Europe, the tendency towards a withdrawal of state funding has encouraged stronger community economic development and enterprise linked to an expanded role for the third sector more generally. France could be seen perhaps as the paradigmatic model of a state-supported social economy in which the social enterprise has been accorded a specific legal status. But within Europe there are significant variations between a French–German–Belgian tradition of strong social economy providers recognised and regulated by national governments and a weaker Mediterranean model where formal recognition and development of a social economy distinct from strong charities is, at best, embryonic. The Anglo-Saxon model, which has a particular emphasis on tackling social exclusion, has become strongly spatialised and, in the UK, has been closely connected to what were New Labour's ideas of building a Third Way between the market and the public sector. Amin et al. also find potential in Nordic interpretations of the social economy, as there the presence of large public sectors and comparatively strong welfare systems creates the conditions for the social economy to play a strong role in the progressive politics of redistribution. [27]

The different roles that social enterprises in these different traditions have played, or are expected to play, not only lead to different definitions reflecting those different roles but also lead some people to focus on the social economy and some on social enterprises. Peter Lloyd, for instance, has identified two very different schools of thought, one of which he identifies as of a US/UK approach and the other as of a European approach. The European approach, he suggests, is a social economy approach which does not hold back from offering a challenge to the post-1980s' hegemony of liberal market forces as the only grand narrative and takes a whole society perspective instead of just a business-focused one. In contrast, the US/UK approach is a social enterprise approach as it starts with the enterprises of which the social economy is composed, and defines them as businesses operating in a market context but using surpluses to achieve social objectives. Lloyd suggests that this difference reflects a fundamental difference in paradigm between a European political economy approach and the narrow market-based approach arising from Anglo-Saxon neoliberal traditions. [28]

Graefe has suggested that the situation presents three potential economic development scenarios in late welfare state countries. The first is a neoliberal one, where the marketplace is pre-eminent and where the social elements of the economy are pushed aside, and the second involves a return to traditional social democratic forms based on reconstructing the welfare state. However, neither of these, he suggests, is either likely or practicable, leaving a third option to connect market and non-market components of the modern economy:

> It is in this context that the social economy finds its full expression: as part of renewed social democratic strategy that includes work-time reduction, greater workplace participation, and the provision of services that meet new demands and needs. On the one hand, the social economy can meet new needs by mobilising resources latent within communities, and by building new solidarities. On the other hand, this social provision bypasses the Taylorist welfare state and is based on more participatory forms of organisation and decision making. More broadly, as economic success increasingly comes to rely on extra-economic resources (such as social capital), strategic spaces are opened for a vision of development that integrates social priorities at every stage. [29]

The different definitions officially advanced largely follow the different roles officially assigned to the social economy, and, it is suggested, the argument over the role of the social economy can, at times, be reduced to three broad choices:

- An economic/entrepreneurship approach, which sees social economy organisations as 'businesses' that can assist community regeneration and puts an emphasis on their financial sustainability. Social enterprises will function, it is believed, where the private sector will not, or at least not until some pump-priming has been done by the sector to make it attractive for private interests. It could be argued that in the UK the (former) Department of Trade and Industry (DTI) perspective on the sector held this view but that subsequently it was softened with the relocation of the Social Enterprise Unit to the Cabinet Office.
- A socio-economic policy approach, which sees the sector as 'patching up' the inadequacies of the welfare state, while still confining it to a marginal role in the economy. The sector should confine itself to 'the parts that government cannot (or will not) reach' and thus it is characterised as a 'low-cost provider', supplementing rather than complementing the welfare state.
- A political/ideological approach which envisages a social economy sector significantly strong to lever institutional change and to promote more democratic structures and citizen participation in decision-making.

Typically, an emphasis on the first, or on the second, of these roles will lead to a focus on social enterprises and to definitions of them which emphasise their business attributes. The third one, however, leads to a focus on the social economy and to definitions which emphasise the democratic nature of its components. For instance, the first and second might be associated with the US/UK approach, which, Lloyd suggests, has, in the UK, produced the (then) DTI definition of a social enterprise, which is as follows:

> A business with primarily social objectives whose surpluses are principally reinvested for that purpose in the business or in the community, rather than being driven by the need to maximise profit for shareholders and owners. [30]

The third is closer to the European approach, which Lloyd illustrates with a definition from Laville, for whom social enterprises are:

> Enterprises initiated by groups of citizens who seek to provide an expanded range of services and more openness to the community – they place a high value on independence and economic risk taking. [31]

This difference in approach, it would appear, can be seen not just across countries but also among different stakeholders. Policy-makers, it has been suggested, generally want to fund social enterprises whereas practitioners often want to develop a social economy.

The lack of a clear generally accepted terminology for the social economy may reflect not just different national paradigms but also changes in perception, and of language, over time. Within the UK, it has been suggested, the vocabulary shift, from 'community businesses' to 'social enterprises' (and now to 'third sector' or 'civil society'?), might reflect a pragmatic change in the emphasis, in the management, and perhaps in the values of the sector. Factors such as the poor experience of some Scottish community business projects in the early 1990s, the political impact of Thatcherite ideas on market efficiency and performance, and the appeal of high-performing entrepreneurs might all have had an impact. The community and co-operative organisations created at local level had been seen by some as part of a process of seeking different economic forms as an alternative to the dominant system but now, according to Pearce:

> Much contemporary debate on social enterprise tends . . . to be satisfied to identify sectors within the twenty-first century mainstream economy where it is considered appropriate for social enterprises to operate. That means taking on tasks which governments are insisting the public sector should no longer fulfil but in which the private sector has no interest because they are not really profitable. Social enterprises thus become the problem fixers.

> There is a danger therefore of social enterprises being boxed into that corner of the economy which deals only with the most disadvantaged in the poorest areas mopping up the problems of society as cheaply as possible by using voluntary and work-for-the-dole labour. In this scenario, the social economy would continue to be no more than the prop which underpins the 'real' economy – very much the third sector, subservient to the public and to the private, pre-eminent sector. Not a third system and no longer an agent for change. [32]

Other sub-sectors

In seeking to identify economic sectors and sub-sectors, there are a number of possible bases for distinguishing between different organisations and activities including the following:

- *Legal form.* In the UK many organisations in the third sector have been formed as companies limited by guarantee. However, examples can be found of companies limited by guarantee which are, *de facto* if not *de jure*, public sector organisations (see the example of LEDU in Illustration 2.3).
- *Purpose and/or potential benefit.* Organisations in this field have been established for a variety of purposes and they can provide a variety of benefits, which are not always the

same as their original purposes. An example of a potential benefit which can be particularly attractive to governments is the ability to combat social and economic exclusion, even though that might not be the main reason for starting the activities in question.

- *Size.* Just as in the public and private sectors, third sector organisations can range in size from large and/or international in their coverage to very small and/or local, although at the smallest level it could be hard to draw a clear distinction between a one-person private sole trader and a one-person third sector organisation.
- *Extent of volunteering.* The use of volunteer directors and/or staff is an important aspect of many third sector organisations.
- *Democratic participation.* Many organisations in the third sector have been established to represent or serve particular communities. However, there are differences in the extent to which those communities can or do influence the organisations concerned.
- *Degree of independence from the state.* While it might be thought that all third sector organisations would be independent of the state because they are not in the public sector, there are degrees of this independence. In particular, those organisations which are heavily dependent on state funding, whether that is through grants, annual subventions, or purchase of services, will be limited in their freedom of action to some extent.
- *Social impact.* The type and extent of social impact of organisations in this sector will be closely linked to their purpose and/or benefits.
- *Economic impact.* The type and extent of the economic impact of the different organisations in this sector of the economy varies substantially.
- *Sources of income.* The sources of income for third sector organisations include 'trading' income earned from the provision of goods and services, grants and donations, and other sources such as investments and membership fees. Not all the organisations in this sector trade, but some do, and in this they are to a greater or lesser extent close to the private sector. (However, see also Illustration 3.4.)

Illustration 3.4 Trading: What is so special about it?

A number of definitions of social enterprises indicate that they derive at least some of their income from trading but why does the trading element seem to be so crucial? If Pocklington School (see Case 2.2) in its early years depended entirely on benefactions and endowments for its income, does that mean that it was not a social enterprise? Did anything fundamentally change when it began to charge fees and 'traded', and today, as a fee-charging 'public' school, is it a social enterprise, even if there is now adequate alternative provision for education in the public sector?

If an organisation with a social purpose receives an endowment and invests it to provide an income to fund its activities, that might not be considered by some to be trading. But the organisation in which the endowment is invested might be a trading organisation and the profits it remits to the investing organisation would be used for a social purpose. Between the investor and the recipient of the investment there are therefore both trading and social purposes, but which organisation, if either, would be the social enterprise?

Pearce, in producing the map of the sectors reproduced in Figure 2.2, used the dimensions of size and proximity to either the public or the private sector to show how different types of organisation might be positioned relative to one another on a two-dimensional 'map' of the third sector. Other dimensions will produce different spreads. However, in trying to understand the third sector, it is probably more relevant to look not at how organisations might in theory be categorised but at how they are in practice categorised, and in particular at the most common categorisations which are probably those variously given the labels 'voluntary', 'community', and 'social', each of which is examined below.

The voluntary sector

Jeremy Kendall, in the introduction to his book *The Voluntary Sector*, states that 'In 2003, the voluntary, third or non-profit sector occupies centre stage in public policy discussions in the UK.'[33] This clearly suggests that, in that context, the label 'voluntary sector' can be applied to the whole of the third sector of the economy. Later in the book, though, Kendall introduces three definitions of the voluntary sector for use when making international comparisons, but which are less all-embracing. He starts with the 'Broad Nonprofit Sector' (BNS), which includes 'all entities which are formal organisations having an institutionalized character; constitutionally independent of the state and self-governing, non-profit-distributing; and involve some degree of volunteerism'. This, he says, 'is a definition which has been reached through a process of consensus-building within (an international) framework, is relevant for international comparisons, while representing a relatively inclusive definition compared to traditional UK usage'.[34]

Kendal's 'default' definition of the voluntary sector includes 'organizations which are formal, non-profit-distributing, constitutionally independent of the state, self-governing and benefiting from voluntarism'.[35] These groups, he suggests, can be seen as comprising a 'Broad Voluntary Sector' (BVS),[36] which includes all organisations in the BNS other than political parties and religious congregations. He then also introduces a definition for the Narrow Voluntary Sector (NVS) which includes all organizations in the BVS, less organizations not traditionally thought of as being part of the voluntary sector in the UK. This is primarily because they are seen as effectively being part of the state despite their constitutional status, and/or because they are not thought to be sufficiently altruistic or public-benefit oriented. Excluded on this basis are all universities, schools, sports and social clubs, and trades union and business associations.[37]

Another definition of the voluntary sector is that provided by the UK's National Council for Voluntary Organisations (NCVO), which aims to 'give voice and support to voluntary and community organisations'.[38] It refers sometimes to the voluntary and community sector and sometimes just to the voluntary sector which it has described as including 'those organisations that are: formal (they have a constitution); independent of government and self-governing; not for profit; and operate with a meaningful degree of volunteer involvement. Examples include housing associations, large charities, large community associations, national campaign organisation etc.'[39]

By remarks such as 'as the boundaries between the public, private and voluntary sectors become increasingly blurred',[40] the NCVO suggests that it might also see the voluntary sector as itself comprising the third sector rather than as just one component of it. Nevertheless, these voluntary sector definitions, even the broadest ones, leave out some of the organisations listed in Table 3.1, such as some co-operatives, fair trade companies, and business schools which may not have a meaningful degree of volunteer involvement. Therefore, if the voluntary sector is to be considered to be the third sector, these definitions imply either that any organisation without volunteers is in the private or public sector, or that there is still a fourth sector.

Moreover, as Kendall indicates, the language has been changing and, while some people use the recently favoured terms, others still use older terms, and this can lead to confusion. For instance, he acknowledges that 'other language – viz., voluntary and community sector, organized civil society, social economy, third sector or system, and so on – has apparently gained currency in recent years', but he explains that the voluntary sector definitions to which he refers were earlier 'used to conduct statistical mapping, so to change language while leaving the coverage unaltered would be confusing' and that 'the shift in language has largely been an elite-led process, and has not really been adopted on the ground'. 'Certainly', he says, 'in conducting fieldwork... "voluntary sector" was the single most commonly utilised collective noun, usually implicitly deploying our narrow definition.'[41] (NB: A further term more recently introduced is big society – see Case 3.1.)

Another aspect of the definitions indicated above is that they indicate that voluntary sector organisations are independent of government or the state. Yet the trend in countries like the UK to contract out public services to voluntary sector bodies may have the effect of compromising this traditional identity. Volunteering has also been a key characteristic associated with voluntary organisations but an element of volunteer input is a feature of some organisations not normally viewed as being in the voluntary sector, but which would come under the category of 'associations', such as trade unions, schools with elected governors, housing associations, professional associations, employers' organisations, and political parties.

The community sector

John Pearce (e.g. in Figure 2.2) uses the term 'community economy', which he sees as overlapping, but not being coincident with, voluntary organisations. He indicates that the community economy is that part of the social economy 'at neighbourhood and district levels where there is a strong sense of local affiliation' and is comprised of social enterprises which are 'closely linked to their particular locality'.[42] He acknowledges, however, that some definitions of community enterprise have also included those social enterprises 'serving communities of interest' which are not based on geography.

As well as 'community sector' and 'community economy', the term 'community business' has also been used, for instance in the Community Business Scheme, which ran in Glasgow in the 1980s and which was described as the largest social enterprise development programme in the UK. Under the scheme, 'community businesses' were given up to 7 years' funding, after which they were expected to have become financially independent and community-owned businesses. Although the scheme was extended to cover most of Scotland, the greatest level of activity was in Glasgow, where several hundred 'community businesses' were established before it was wound up.[43]

Hayton, who commented on this scheme, suggested that a community business was:

> a trading organisation which, through the sale of goods or services, aims to become self-sustaining. Through its activities it creates jobs for those living in particular areas: ones generally characterised by high levels of unemployment and other symptoms of multiple deprivation. Residents of these areas are members of the business, and thus own and control it, although they do not necessarily work in it. Directors are elected from the membership and there is usually provision to co-opt non-executive directors. Trading profits are either reinvested or are spent on projects of benefit to the local community.[44]

Based on these characteristics, he found that many of the enterprises established were not actually community businesses. The 'businesses', he reported, fell into the following four groups:

- Community businesses owned and controlled by local residents with a remit to create jobs for local people by setting up commercially viable trading organisations.
- Enterprises that were essentially conventional private sector companies with ownership and control vested in those who owned the company rather than the wider community.

- 'Businesses' that were Urban Programme-funded projects that had been set up to run for the duration of the grant.
- 'Businesses' whose objective was to create a service for a community rather than jobs. Effectively these were voluntary sector projects which, after an initial period of public subsidy, were able to survive as they relied upon unpaid labour. They had no intention of becoming commercially viable.[45]

Although many enterprises which were called community businesses might today be referred to as social enterprises, nevertheless the definition given earlier by Hayton does emphasise the relationship between the business and the community it serves. It is that relationship which, for many people, makes a business a community business, but there can be different degrees of community involvement as Illustration 3.5 describes.

Pearce suggests (see Figure 2.2) that community economy organisations are generally small, being comparable in size to SMEs and micro businesses in the private economy, while other social economy organisations can be larger. He makes a distinction, therefore, between community enterprises, which have a distinctly local quality, and social enterprises, which are not bound to place and can have regional, national, and even international reach. This distinction is set out in Table 3.8.

Table 3.8 Community and social economy

Community enterprises	Social enterprises
Community ownership company	Building society
Community-based housing association	Charity trading arm
Community benefit corporation	Consumer retail society
Community business	Credit union
Community co-operative	Fair trade company
Community credit union	Housing association
Community development corporation	Intermediate labour market
Community development finance initiative	Marketing co-operative
Community housing trust	Mutual co-operative society
Community interest company	Public interest company
Community trading organisation	Social business
Community trust	Social firm
Employee-ownership business	Workers' co-operative
Housing co-operative	
(Local) development trust	
Local Exchange Trading Scheme	
Neighbourhood co-operative	
Neighbourhood enterprise	
Social co-operative	
Social firm	
Time bank	
Voluntary enterprise	
Workers' co-operative	
Neighbourhood, Local, District	**Regional, National, International**

Source: J. Pearce, *Social Enterprise in Anytown* (London: Calouste Gulbenkian Foundation, 2003), p. 29

However, Pearce detects a shift in the vocabulary of what was the community development field, behind which it is possible to discern three strands of changing thought:

- a shift from an emphasis on collective action to that on entrepreneurialism;
- a shift from an emphasis on ownership and accountability to a focus on what the organisation delivers; and
- a shift from a political perspective to one emphasising a more technical approach aimed at getting the job done. [46]

One aspect of this changing vocabulary, suggests Peace, is that whereas 'in what might be called the "community era" we talked of community action, community enterprise and community business. Today, in the contemporary "social era," we are more likely to talk of social entrepreneurs, social enterprise and social business.' [47]

Illustration 3.5 The degree of local community influence in community businesses

The following observations on the degree of community involvement in so-called 'community enterprises' were made in 1991:

> There are many differing views on who should run community ventures. One way to look at the problem is to classify the available choices by the degree to which residents of a community exert influence over the project or enterprise . . . At one end of the scale (community provision) members of the local community play no part whatsoever. At the other end (community control) local residents are encouraged to become members of the venture and in this way exercise complete ownership and control.

Community Provision
The project is controlled by a board which is either appointed directly, or heavily influenced, by the main funders, which will be composed almost entirely of business or professional people and is only accountable to the funders. The project will be run on the basis that the board know what is needed in the area. Also, any assets will normally revert to the funders when the lifetime of the project is complete.

Community consultation
The project is controlled by an appointed or self-selected board or committee. The main funders influence the choice of controlling group, which tends to be composed almost entirely of business or professional people. The controlling group attach some importance to consulting the community and do this through public meetings, questionnaires, or more informal contacts. Attempts may be made to distribute progress reports to the community, but there is no effective system of accountability to the community. The community has no claim on the assets whether during the lifetime of the project or on dissolution.

Community co-option
Some local residents are intentionally co-opted onto a self-selected board or committee but form only a small (and often non-vocal) minority. However, because there are local representatives on the board/committee, it tends not to undertake consultation or establish an effective process for accountability. The community again has no claim on the assets either during the lifetime of the project or on dissolution.

Community management
Local residents are encouraged to take over the management of the project. The board or committee must operate, however, within the budget provided and adhere to the guidelines laid down by the funders. While there is a budget, there are usually no assets involved.

Community representation*

While local residents are not members of the enterprise, care is taken to ensure that the controlling board/committee is clearly representative of a cross section of local interests, groups, and estates. People with helpful specific skills are invited to join and there is a strong desire to implement some effective system of accountability to the local community for whom the assets are held 'in trust'.

Community control

Local residents are encouraged to become members of the enterprise, and the members directly elect the board/committee on a one-person, one-vote basis. There is direct accountability, and powers of co-option allow people with specific skills to become members of the board/committee. The assets are controlled by the members.

Issues raised

These observations suggest that the actual degree of community influence in a project may depend on the balance struck between any conflicting wishes of the funders and the community. Funders may seek to impose conditions on the use of their money and, as customers who are prepared to pay for what they want, they are entitled to seek to impose their own conditions, especially when they relate to the responsible use of that money. If the conditions proposed are too onerous, then the group concerned has the options of seeking to renegotiate them or to refuse the deal on offer.

Note: *This, it is suggested, is often the most appropriate structure for enterprises in areas where there is little history of direct community involvement or where the nature of the project is too general to attract local membership.
Source: Based on an article by P. Nicholls, 'Who Should Run Community Enterprise?', in *Newsview*, Issue 2, which was published by Community Business Northern Ireland in November 1991

The fourth sector

If the third sector of an economy is defined inclusively as encompassing all those activities with an economic impact which are not included in either the public or the private sector, then there will be no fourth sector. If, though, the third sector is defined exclusively as comprising only those organisations which share most or all of a set of common characteristics, then it is likely that there will be some things not included – which might then be presumed to be in the fourth sector.

Indeed, the term 'fourth sector' is occasionally used. 'For some it is used to identify a segment for co-operatives, for others it points to a "household" sector.'[48] Similar to the 'household sector' concept, Wikipedia suggests that the fourth sector is sometimes considered to be 'the informal sector, where informal exchanges take place between family and friends'.[49]

Conclusion

It is clear that the terminology used when talking about this area of an economy frequently does not help as there is no universally agreed set of definitions. Instead, there is a variety of different terms, and many of those terms can themselves have a variety of meanings so that it is often not immediately clear, when different people use different terms, whether they mean the same thing, or separate things, or whether one of the things referred to might be a subset of the other. For instance, terms like 'the social economy', 'the voluntary sector', and 'the community sector' might be used as labels for what is considered to be the third sector of the economy, or they might be used to refer to different or overlapping sub-sectors within the third sector. Care is thus required.

Care is particularly necessary when dealing with those different definitions or inter-pretations which are based on, or promoted by, differing political or economic views. Some commentators have sought to avoid tight definitions in order not to offend others by excluding organisations they favour. Other proponents might be suspected of propos-ing very specific definitions in order to exclude organisations of which they disapprove or because they suit the causes they wish to promote. And, of course, as in many areas of society, fashions change and what it was at one time popular to promote can later lose favour. It is for reasons such as these that seeking to define the third sector and its components can be controversial.

///

Key Points of Chapter 3

* Because the third sector, as often defined, includes all those organisations with an eco-nomic impact which are in neither the public not the private sectors, it includes a wide variety of different activities.
* Although this sector may have been overlooked at least in part because of a lack of the vocabulary with which to describe it, there is now a wide variety of labels which have been, and are, applied to it or to parts of it.
* The term social economy came from the French term *économie sociale* and is usually defined as including organisations such as co-operatives, mutuals, associations, and foundations, and thus excluding other organisations. As such it is a key part of the third sector, although sometimes the term is used to refer to all of that sector.
* Other terms used for the social economy, or for parts of the third sector, include the voluntary sector, the community sector, civil society, and even big society.

///

Case 3.1 | Big Society

Its origins

Big Society was a key idea in the UK Conservative Party's 2010 election manifesto and, following the election, David Cameron, then the Prime Minister, relaunched it in July in a speech at Liverpool, which had been selected as one of its 'vanguard areas'. The rationale for the Big Society initiative, and the sources of its name, was that it was intended to counter the increasing tendency towards 'big government' by taking power away from politicians and instead putting it into people's hands: 'a transfer of power from Whitehall to local communities'.[50]

Before this, when the 'New Labour' government came to power in 1997, it had enthusiastically taken up the concept of the 'third way' between the state and corporate sectors, which 'represents a renewal of social democracy or centre-left politics, and pro-poses that civil society – the social economy – is a valuable, but underutilised resource for society, both as a necessary countervailing power between state and market, but also as a source of welfare provision'.[51] This, it has been suggested, delicately redefined the role of the state – no longer a source of universal welfare, the state's new role is to enable citizens to take responsibility for their own welfare through equality of opportunity.[52]

The centralized, top-down organisation of the welfare state had fostered a culture of dependency, and thus what was now required was a shift towards co-production of services.[53] Thus the emerging policy agenda for decentralisation, coupled with David Cameron's ideas of a 'Big Society', are supposed to have provided new opportunities for the transfer of traditional welfare state functions to the community and voluntary sector. [54]

Its agenda

The Big Society agenda was described as having three pillars or parts:

- *Community empowerment.* Decreasing the power of Whitehall and bringing decision-making much closer to the people.
- *Opening up public services.* Reforming and opening up public service to enable charities, social enterprises, and employee-owned co-operatives to compete to offer people high-quality services.
- *Encouraging social action.* Encouraging and enabling people to play a more active part in society. [55]

Its reception

However, the Big Society idea has had a mixed reception and progress was said in January 2013 to have been 'glacially slow'. [56] Although it was described as 'a loose and rather baggy concept (it was suggested that) few would dispute its fundamental premise: that in the years ahead government will be able to do less and society in all its forms will have to do more'. [57] Another source acknowledged that 'there are strong, sensible ideas at the heart of the Big Society vision' but pointed out that it went 'hand in hand with deep cuts in public spending... [which] are only feasible alongside a strategy for shifting responsibility away from the state'. [58]

Thus it was suspected by some that its primary purpose was not to provide for more community empowerment but instead was to camouflage, soften, or even justify social service budget cuts. As the Archbishop of Canterbury put it: ' "Big Society" rhetoric is all too readily heard by many as aspirational waffle designed to conceal a deeply damaging withdrawal of the state from its responsibilities to the most vulnerable.' [59] At the time of writing, over two years after its launch, there still seems to be little evidence of any impact it might be having on government policies.

Questions, Exercises, Essay, and Discussion Topics

1. How many different third sector organisations can you think of beginning with each letter of the alphabet?
2. If the social economy and the third sector are not the same thing, what are the differences?
3. What distinguishes co-operatives, mutuals, associations, and foundations from each other and from the rest of the third sector?
4. Ideally what role should the social economy play in a modern economy?
5. Is there a difference between the voluntary sector and the community sector?
6. Is there a future for the Big Society agenda?

Suggestions for further reading

D. Billis (Ed.) *Hybrid Organizations and the Third Sector: Challenges for Practice, Theory and Policy* (Basingstoke: Palgrave Macmillan, 2010).

A. Amin, A. Cameron and R. Hudson, *Placing the Social Economy* (London: Routledge, 2002).

J. Pearce, *Social Enterprise in Anytown* (London: Calouste Gulbenkian Foundation, 2003).
EMES European Research Network – www.emes.net.

References

1. For instance, EU DG V pilot action 'Third System and Employment', and reports produced for it, 1999.
2. For instance, 'A Third Way between state and market', Amin, A., A. Cameron and R. Hudson, *Placing the Social Economy* (London: Routledge, 2002), p. 11.
3. J. Kendall, *The Voluntary Sector* (London: Routledge, 2003), p. 1.
4. J. Pearce, *Social Enterprise in Anytown* (London: Calouste Gulbenkian Foundation, 2003), p. 66.
5. From the Wikipedia entry on social economy (www.wikipedia.org, accessed July 2006).
6. A. Amin, A. Cameron and R. Hudson, *Placing the Social Economy* (London: Routledge, 2002), p. vii.
7. From the speech of Gordon Brown, Chancellor of the Exchequer, to the Labour Party Conference on 25 September 2006.
8. www.wikipedia.org/wiki/Social_Economy (accessed 7 December 2006).
9. www.emes.net/about-us/focus-areas/the-third-sector (accessed 20 April 2013).
10. J. Defourny, 'From third sector to social enterprise', in C. Borzaga and J. Defourny (Eds), *The Emergence of Social Enterprise* (London: Routledge. 2001), p. 1.
11. www.emes.net/about-us/focus-areas/the-non-profit-sector (accessed 20 April 2013).
12. www.emes.net/about-us/focus-areas/social-economy (accessed 20 April 2013).
13. A. Molloy, C. McFeely and E. Connolly, *Building a Social Economy for the New Millennium* (Derry: Guildhall Press/NICDA Social Economy Agency, 1999), p. 11.
14. *What We Need to Know About the Social Economy: A Guide for Policy Research* (Canada: Policy Research Institute, July 2005), p. 4.
15. *Social Enterprise: a strategy for success*, Department of Trade and Industry, 2002.
16. Cabinet Office: Office of the Third Sector, *Social enterprise action plan: Scaling new heights* (London: HM Government, 2006), p. 3.
17. Policy Action Team 3, HM Treasury, *Enterprise and Social Exclusion*, 1999 (www.hm-treasury.gov.uk/docs/1999/pat3.html, accessed 1 March 2000), paragraph 5.2.
18. E. Hunt, 'The normative foundations of social theory: An essay on the criteria defining social economics',

Review of Social Economy, Vol. LXIII, No. 3 (2006), pp. 423–448.
19. http://ec.europa.eu/enterprise/entrepreneurship/social_economy.htm (accessed 3 August 2007).
20. http://ec.europa.eu/enterprise/entrepreneurship/coop/index.htm (accessed 3 August 2007).
21. Ibid.
22. Guide to Co-operative and Community Business Legal Structures (London: IOCM, 1999).
23. M. Cooper, 'The development of the third sector in Bristol', *Local Economy*, Vol. 14, No. 4 (1999), pp.348–359.
24. D. Sattar and E. Mayo, *Growth Areas of the UK Social Economy* (London: UK Social Investment Forum, 1998).
25. R. Ridley-Duff and M. Bull, *Understanding Theory and Practice* (London: Sage, 2011).
26. R. Murray, J. Caulier-Grice and G. Mulgan, *The Open Book of Social Innovation* (London: The Young Foundation, 2010), p. 142.
27. A. Amin, Cameron and R. Hudson, *Placing the Social Economy* (London: Routledge, 2002), pp. 9–11.
28. P. Lloyd, in CU2 Contested Cities – Urban Universities (Eds) *Rethinking the Social Economy* (Belfast: The Queen's University Belfast, 2006), pp. 9–18.
29. P. Graefe, 'The social economy and the state: Linking ambitions with institutions in Quebec, Canada', *Politics and Policy*, Vol. 30, No. 2 (2002), p. 250.
30. Department of Trade and Industry (DTI), *Social Enterprise: a strategy for success* (London: Department of Trade and Industry, 2002), p. 14.
31. P. Lloyd, in CU2 Contested Cities – Urban Universities (Eds) *Rethinking the Social Economy* (Belfast: The Queen's University Belfast, 2006), p. 14.
32. J. Pearce, *Social Enterprise in Anytown* (London: Calouste Gulbenkian Foundation, 2003), pp. 69–70.
33. J. Kendall, *The Voluntary Sector* (London: Routledge, 2003), p. 1.
34. Ibid., p. 21.
35. Ibid., p. 6.
36. Ibid.
37. Ibid., p. 21.
38. www.ncvo-org.uk (accessed 8 December 2006).
39. www.wikipedia.org/wiki/Social_Economy (accessed 7 November 2006).

40. 'A Manifesto for Voluntary Action', www.ncvo-org.uk (accessed 8 December 2006).

41. J. Kendall, *The Voluntary Sector* (London: Routledge, 2003), p. 6.

42. J. Pearce, *Social Enterprise in Anytown* (London: Calouste Gulbenkian Foundation, 2003), pp. 28–29.

43. As reported in A. Amin, Cameron and R. Hudson, *Placing the Social Economy* (London: Routledge, 2002), p. 63.

44. K. Hayton, 'Scottish community business: An idea that has had its day', *Policy and Politics*, Vol. 28, No. 2 (2000), p. 195.

45. Ibid., p. 196.

46. Based on J. Pearce, *Social Enterprise in Anytown* (London: Calouste Gulbenkian Foundation, 2003), p. 66.

47. J. Pearce, *Social Enterprise in Anytown* (London: Calouste Gulbenkian Foundation, 2003), p. 66.

48. C. Gunn, *Third Sector Development: Making up for the Market* (New York: Cornell University Press, 2004), p. 189.

49. www.wikipedia.org/wiki/Social_Economy (accessed 7 November 2006).

50. Rt Hon Hugo Swire MP, 'Speech to UK Preservation Trusts Conference' (Belfast, 14 October 2011).

51. G. Seyfang, 'Harnessing the potential of the social economy? Time banks and UK public policy', *International Journal of Sociology and Social Policy*, Vol. 26, No. 9, p. 432.

52. G. Seyfang, 'With a little help from my friends. Evaluating time banks as a tool for community self-help', *Local Economy*, Vol. 18, No. 3 (2003), pp. 257–264.

53. D. Boyle and M. Harris, *The Challenge of Co-Production* (London: new economics foundation, 2009).

54. G Seyfang, *The New Economics of Sustainable Consumption: Seeds of Change* (Palgrave Macmillan: New York, 2009), p. 67.

55. Based on www.cabinetoffice.gov.uk/content/big-society-overview (accessed 11 November 2012) and Rt Hon Hugo Swire MP, 'Speech to UK Preservation Trusts Conference' (Belfast, 14 October 2011).

56. Sir Stephen Bubb, head of the Association of Chief Executives of Voluntary Organisations, as reported by the BBC (www.bbc.co,uk/news/uk-politics-20931121, accessed 7 February 2013).

57. The Young Foundation, 'Investing in *Social Growth*, Can the Big Society be more than a slogan?', September 2010, www.youngfoundation.org (accessed 6 June 2012).

58. A. Coote, *Cutting it: The 'Big Society' and the new austerity* (London: new economics foundation, 2010), p. 2.

59. R. Williams, *Faith in the Public Square* (London: Bloomsbury, 2012), p. 266.

4

social enterprise and the main components of the social economy

contents:

- introduction
- social enterprises
- other components of the social economy
- social entrepreneurship
- conclusion

Key concepts

This chapter covers:

- the way that the social economy is sometimes defined in terms of its components, which variously are said to include co-operatives, mutuals, associations, foundations, and social enterprises;
- the variety of ways in which social enterprises have been defined, and how little some of the definitions have in common;
- different international and ideological interpretations of the social economy and the role of social enterprises in the delivery of public services;
- the main components that make up the social economy;
- the link to social entrepreneurship.

Learning objectives

By the end of this chapter the reader should:

- understand the way that the social economy is often defined by means of its supposed components;
- appreciate the variety of ways in which social enterprises, which are a key component, have been defined, and the extent to which these definitions differ;
- appreciate the different political interpretations of the social economy from those who see it in the context of the reform of public services to those who see it as an alternative to global capitalism;
- understand the nature of the other components, including co-operatives, mutuals, associations, and foundations.
- appreciate the role of social entrepreneurship in providing innovation and empowering leadership.

Introduction

As Chapter 3 explains, the social economy has been the focus of attention for many people who are interested in the wider aspects of the economy beyond just the private and public sectors. As it also explains, the social economy is a term which can be used to refer either to a distinct and very significant part of the third sector of an economy or to a part of the economy which is itself sufficiently prominent to be considered to be the third sector. In either case it is thought by many people to be very important both economically and socially.

The social economy is usually defined in terms of the organisations said to be within it – an approach which serves to include some organisations but which excludes others. The organisations which are included in it have been grouped into a number of subsets or categories, and it was around three of these categories in particular – co-operatives, mutuals, and associations – that the concept of the social economy seems first to have been formulated. Because it was recognised that they shared a number of characteristics but did not fit into either the public or the private sector of an economy, these organisations were considered to be a third section of the economy and were, in French, referred to as *l'économie sociale*, from which the English term 'the social economy' was derived (as described in Chapter 2).

Because the social economy is often thus defined by the sort of organisations it includes, that in turn focuses attention on those organisations and the ways in which they have been defined. This chapter therefore explores the concept of the social economy further by examining some of these components and comparing some of the different definitions applied to them. It also highlights competing ideological definitions of the sector especially between pro-market and business-orientated approaches and those more concerned with developing alternatives to the capitalist economy and resistance to globalisation.[1]

Do the different definitions matter?

Chapter 3 and this chapter refer to a range of different definitions, both of the social economy and of some of its supposed components. However, it can be argued that these differences are not important because most people working in the area understand broadly what the social economy is and do not need to define it more precisely. Also, most people starting or running a social economy organisation are far more concerned with how well their organisation is performing than with how it might be categorised by bureaucratic or academic rules and principles.

Nevertheless, the definitions do matter to some people and they are worth considering for a number of reasons:

- *Consistent research.* Definitions matter to researchers in this field because they need to use clear definitions for what they are researching if they are to get consistent results and they need to know whether their definitions are the same as those used by other researchers to see if their results are suitable for comparison. Researchers, though, are also attracted to definitions which make measurement easy. Thus, a UK-wide survey of social enterprises, conducted for the Small Business Service, did not claim to describe the total population of social enterprises according to any of the usual definitions but instead focused just on those organisations registered as industrial and provident societies or as companies limited by guarantee (but excluding those companies in standard industry classifications deemed unlikely to include much social enterprise activity).[2]
- *Measuring the scale or impact of the sector.* Measuring the scale or impact of the social economy, or of a sub-sector of it, may be an example of research but it has a particular relevance to areas such as government policy because the bigger the impact of a sector appears to be, the more governments tend to be interested in it. Definitions therefore matter both because it is argued that the sector was not measured in the past as there was no agreed definition of it and because, when it is measured, the wider the definition used the bigger the impact that will be recorded.
- *Targeted policy.* If policy-makers are considering support for a sector or sub-sector, they will need to define what they wish to help with that support.
- *Fair and consistent disbursement of support.* The application of support policy can involve the provision of advice and information, grant or loan schemes, or tax incentives or concessions. If so, the people who are tasked with providing the advice, awarding the grants or loans, or approving the tax incentives or concessions need to able to decide, on a fair and consistent basis, which organisations would be eligible for that support and which would not be eligible.
- *The choice of legal form for organisations.* One consequence of limiting support to tightly defined sectors is that organisations may select, or change, their legal form in order to try to qualify for such support.
- *Politics or ideology.* Operators in, or advocates of, particular sections of the third sector sometimes wish to advance those specific sections for political or ideological reasons, and different definitions are likely to reflect different perceived roles that those sections are expected to perform (see also section 'Paradigm differences' in Chapter 3). For some the desire to provide better public services in more efficient ways should

characterise the social economy whilst for others a more radical approach sees the social economy as an arena of political activity and a way of resisting the privatisation of public goods and services.[3] As Wikipedia's entry on the social economy says, under the sub-heading of 'Controversy':

> Defining the limits of the social economy is made especially difficult by the 'moving sands' of the political and economic context. Consequently organisations may be 'part in, part out', 'in this year, out the next' or moving within the social economy's various sub-sectors.

> There is no single right or wrong definition of the social economy. Many commentators and reports have consciously avoided trying to introduce a tight definition for fear of causing more problems than they solve.[4]

- *The different definitions exist.* Whether they matter or not, the different definitions do exist, and it is therefore helpful to those who may come across them to know that they exist and to know that different labels can sometimes be given to the same thing, and that the same label can sometimes be given to different things. Without that sort of understanding, writings about the sector can appear to be very confusing.
- *The differences can be illuminating.* The differences between the different definitions can help to highlight key aspects of some of the organisations in the third sector.

Components of the social economy

Chapter 3 presents a number of different descriptions of the social economy often based on the sort of organisations said to be within it – followed by some definitions which largely follow the different roles assigned to it. This chapter continues that exposition by examining some of the main components supposed to be in the social economy and, where relevant, the different ways in which they are defined.

Social enterprises

It might be supposed that the social economy would consist primarily of social enterprises and it has been suggested that the gradual emergence, over the last 20 years or so, of social enterprises, and of the term 'social enterprise', is due to factors such as:

- 'The decline of state involvement in the planned provision of services in society; and conceptualisation of the "market".
- The focus of a culture that emphasises self-reliance and personal responsibility and the rise of entrepreneurship more generally.
- Changes in funding opportunities within the community, voluntary and non-profit (social) sectors – specifically the move from grant-giving to contract/competitive tendering and the devolution, deregulation and privatisation of welfare states globally'.[5]
- The financial and fiscal crises and the need to innovate more creatively in the design and delivery of public services.[6]

However, there are different interpretations of what social enterprises are. For instance the different models of the social economy summarised in Chapter 3 seem to treat them differently. The European approach, at least according to the EU's version, indicates that the social economy includes co-operatives, mutual societies, associations, and foundations, and social enterprises – and the ILO has also suggested that the social economy is a concept which embraces organisations, 'in particular co-operatives, mutual benefit societies, associations, foundations and social enterprises, which have the specific feature of producing goods, services and knowledge while pursuing both economic and social aims'.[7] Thus by specifying social enterprises alongside co-operatives, mutual societies, associations, and foundations, these formulations suggest that organisations in the latter categories, while being at the core of the social economy, are not themselves social enterprises.

Thus, as Kerlin points out, the EMES European Research Network stresses the positioning of social enterprise 'at the crossroads of market, public policies and civil society',[8] whereas, in contrast, the US tendency is 'to define social enterprises mainly as non-profit organisations more oriented towards the market and developing "earned income strategies" as a response to "increased competition for public subsidies and limits to private grants from foundations"'.[9] So, as indicated in Illustration 4.1, in the US the social economy has a stronger link with philanthropy, entrepreneurs, and market-based responses, whereas in the EU the emphasis is on collectivism, democratic forms of governance, and a more broadly based understanding of the social economy.[10]

Illustration 4.1 Different international perspectives on social enterprise

EU-style social enterprise	US-style social entrepreneurship
• Collective action	• Individual action
• Labour movement or government responses to social issues	• Entrepreneurial (market) responses to social issues
• Incremental building of social capital and assets	• Fast effective achievement of social outcomes
• Solidarity and mutuality	• Champions and change agents
• Accommodation of stakeholders	• Adherence to a vision
• Democracy (bottom-up governance)	• Philanthropy (top-down governance)
• Social economy	• Any sector

Source: R. Ridley-Duff and M. Bull, *Understanding Social Enterprise: Theory and Practice* (London: Sage, 2011) p. 60

The US/UK approach, however, in effect starts with social enterprises and seems to imply that the social economy amounts to the sum of all the social enterprises within it, which suggests that co-operatives, mutual societies, associations, and foundations are social enterprises because they are in the social economy. One way of avoiding the issue of whether social enterprises include co-operatives, mutual societies, associations, and foundations is to talk instead about 'social economy enterprises' as a generic term. The European Commission, for instance, under the heading of 'Social Economy Enterprises', indicates that there are certain common characteristics shared by what it then calls social economy entities:

• Their primary purpose is not to obtain a return on capital. They are, by nature, part of a stakeholder economy, whose enterprises are created by and for those with common needs, and accountable to those they are meant to serve.
• They are generally managed in accordance with the principle of 'one member, one vote'.
• They are flexible and innovative – social economy enterprises are being created to meet changing social and economic circumstances.
• Most are based on voluntary participation, membership, and commitment.[11]

This approach to defining not the social economy itself but some or all of its components is common. Those components have been variously labelled 'social enterprises', 'social economy enterprises' (SEEs), 'social economy entities', 'social economy organisations', and/or 'community enterprises' or 'businesses', and it is upon definitions of them that many approaches to the social economy are founded. The European research network, EMES, has, for instance, proposed a definition of social enterprise which is based on four economic and five social criteria (see Illustration 4.2) and which can provide a useful framework for differentiating definitions of social enterprise across Europe.

Illustration 4.2 The EMES-proposed definition of social enterprise

Economic criteria

1) Continuous activity of the production and/or sale of goods and services (rather than predominantly advisory or grant-giving functions).
2) A high level of autonomy: social enterprises are created voluntarily by groups of citizens and are managed by them, and not directly or indirectly by public authorities or private companies, even if they may benefit from grants and donations. Their shareholders have the right to participate ('voice') and to leave the organisation ('exit').
3) A significant economic risk: the financial viability of social enterprises depends on the efforts of their members, who have the responsibility of ensuring adequate financial resources, unlike most public institutions.
4) Social enterprises' activities require a minimum number of paid workers, although, like traditional non-profit organisations, social enterprises may combine financial and non-financial resources, voluntary and paid work.

Social criteria

5) An explicit aim of community benefit: one of the principal aims of social enterprises is to serve the community or a specific group of people. To the same end, they also promote a sense of social responsibility at local level.
6) Citizen initiative: social enterprises are the result of collective dynamics involving people belonging to a community or to a group that shares a certain need or aim. They must maintain this dimension in one form or another.
7) Decision-making not based on capital ownership: this generally means the principle of 'one member, one vote', or at least a voting power not based on capital shares. Although capital owners in social enterprises play an important role, decision-making rights are shared with the other stakeholders.
8) Participatory character, involving those affected by the activity: the users of social enterprises' services are represented and participate in their structures. In many cases one of the objectives is to strengthen democracy at local level through economic activity.
9) Limited distribution of profit: social enterprises include organisations that totally prohibit profit distribution as well as organisations such as co-operatives, which may distribute their profit only to a limited degree, thus avoiding profit-maximising behaviour.

Source: EMES (2001), *The Emergence of Social Enterprises in Europe*, Brussels: EMES; http://www.emes.net

Ridley-Duff and Bull[12] express the social economy at its simplest as a relationship between the three traditional sectors of the state, the market, and civil society but point out that it predates the formation of the capital or public economies. In their extensive analysis of the theoretical foundations of the 'sector', they highlight the contested and competing interpretations of its role and function:

> In one case, social enterprises form *within* the third sector at the point where the non-profit and cooperative sectors influence each other. In the other cases, social

enterprises are believed to form at the *boundaries* of the third sector where it is influenced by interactions with the private and public sectors (i.e. in public owned organisations, or voluntary organisations contracting to deliver public services). [13]

This distinction between instrumental and relationship approaches is also reflected in different understandings of social enterprises and their relationship to the ethic of community support and the pursuit of profit. Defourny and Nyssens[14] identify the fundamental tension between the non-profit school comprised of charities and voluntary organisations and more-than-profit school based on trading via co-operatives and mutuals. The former emphasise internal democratic control where members have a stake in management and governance and the latter an external orientation with regard to beneficiaries. This builds on the analytical framework developed by Pearce, whose 'map' of the three systems in an economy is reproduced in Figure 2.2, and who also suggests that there are six defining characteristics of a social enterprise (italics in original):

- Having a *social purpose or purposes*;
- Achieving the social purposes by, at least in part, *engaging in trade* in the market place;
- *Not distributing profits* to individuals;
- Holding assets and wealth *in trust for community benefit*;
- *Democratically* involving members of its constituency in the governance of the organisation; and
- Being independent organisations *accountable* to a defined constituency and to the wider community. [15]

Other definitions of social enterprises include the following:

- *UK government definition*: 'A social enterprise is a business with primarily social objectives whose surpluses are principally reinvested for that purpose in the business or in the community, rather than being driven by the need to maximise profit for shareholders and owners.' [16]
- *SBS definition*: The UK's former Small Business Service (SBS) (now subsumed into the Department for Business, Innovation and Skills (BIS)) stated that 'Social enterprises are competitive businesses, owned and trading for a social purpose. They seek to succeed as businesses by establishing a market share and making a profit. Social enterprises combine the need to be successful businesses with social aims. They emphasise the long-term benefits for employees, consumers and the community.' [17]
- *OECD definition*: 'Any private activity conducted in the public interest, organised with an entrepreneurial strategy but whose main purpose is not the maximisation of profit but the attainment of certain economic and social goals, and which has a capacity for bringing innovative solutions to the problems of social exclusion and unemployment.' [18]

Comparing definitions

Using a set of criteria based mainly on the EMES proposal, Table 4.1 presents a comparison of some of the definitions of social enterprises, or social economy component organisations, given above. This comparison suggests that, even for the limited number of definitions chosen, there is little that they all agree is an essential criterion except that of having a social purpose. Even the reinvestment of profits is not always an absolute requirement as both the (then) DTI and EMES definitions allow some profit distribution, the OECD definition does not disallow it, and some other definitions clearly include those co-operatives which distribute profits to their members. However, the definitions, in general, do suggest that there are some coherent traits, values, and organisational formats

Table 4.1 A comparison of definitions of social enterprises or social economy component organisations

Criteria	Source of definition							
	DTI	EMES	European Network for Economic Self-Help	European Commission	Laville	OECD	Pearce	SBS
Social purpose	Primarily social objectives	An explicit aim of community benefit	Seeks to tackle specific social aims	Created by and for those with common needs	An expanded range of services	Organised for certain economic and social goals	Has a social purpose or purposes	Owned and trading for a social purpose
Community		Involves people of a community with shared needs			More openness to the community			
Democracy		Decisions not based on capital ownership		Generally managed in accordance with the principle of 'one member, one vote'			Democratically involves members of its constituency in its governance	
Participation and account-ability		Users are represented and participate in governance	Structures encourage full participation of members	Mostly based on voluntary participation and are accountable to those they are meant to serve	Initiated by groups of citizens		Accountable to defined constituency and wider community	
Profits	Surpluses principally reinvested for the social objectives	Limited distribution of profits	All surplus profits reinvested in the enterprise or used to tackle its aims	Primary purpose is not to retain a return on capital		The main purpose is not profit maximisation	Does not distribute profits to individuals	For the benefit of employees, consumers and the community

Table 4.1 (Continued)

Criteria	Source of definition							
	DTI	EMES	European Network for Economic Self-Help	European Commission	Laville	OECD	Pearce	SBS
Trading		Continuous activity for the production/sale of goods/services	Tackle aims by engaging in economic and trading activity				Engages in trade (at least in part)	Seeks to succeed by establishing a market share and making a profit
Autonomy		A high level of autonomy			A high value put on independence		Is an independent organisation	
Risk		Viability depends on members' efforts			A high value put on economic risk-taking			
Employment		A minimum number of paid workers						
Assets			Assets held in trust for the benefit of those addressed by the aims				Holds assets in trust for community benefit	
Others			Encourages mutual co-operation with others in the local economy	Flexible and innovative – created to meet changing social and economic circumstances		Capacity for innovative solutions to social exclusion and unemployment		

which mark out social enterprises, and the social economy of which they are a significant part, as a distinctive economic, social, and cultural sphere of activity.

Other approaches and definitions

Another way of thinking about social enterprises is to look at their areas of work. Pearce identifies four main activity areas, which include the following: [19]

- local development and regeneration such as the management of workspace units, training programmes, business support, physical development and environmental work, and housing provision;
- working for the state, which involves the delivery of state services and asset transfer of local resources such as playgrounds or community facilities although, as we show later, this raises important concerns about the sector providing cheap alternatives to welfare provision;
- providing services to the community such as local retraining, a community café, or a second-hand store; and
- market-driven businesses that look like organisations in the first sector and which emphasise their profitability as well as their social mission.

Pearce also highlights the diversity of the sector which embraces both small and very large businesses such as the Co-operative Bank, large housing associations, and, in the UK, a growing credit union sector. Some enterprises are staffed entirely by voluntary staff whilst others have large workforces of paid employees. Similarly, a large number are dependent on grant aid or regular fund-raising whilst others can be financially self-sustaining, and the relationship amongst these types of income streams can vary over time. Linked to this, social enterprises tend to be people rather than profit centred although, as noted in Chapter 6, this is a constant tension in the operation of social enterprises and community businesses. A number of initiatives in the social economy demonstrate the value of alternative economic models including informal trading schemes and time banks, whilst others apply more formal business models to deliver social gain.

There is, in the other definitions of social enterprises given in Illustration 4.3, a shared concern for a social purpose and collective ownership, but combined with a business mode of operation. Profits are made but recycled within the organisation and not paid as a dividend for private gain. There are, however, subtle differences between the different definitions, and the list emphasises the plurality of definitions with community businesses being more closely linked to area-based regeneration specifically and to 'locality' more generally. Some attach priority to training and job creation although the definitions highlight the interchangeability of terms and concepts. This approach also underscores the tripartite functional distinction between the enterprise focus, social objectives, and democratic local ownership.

Illustration 4.3 Other definitions of social enterprises

Other definitions of social enterprises, collected by Pearce, include the following:

- Social enterprises:
  Are not-for-profit organisations.
  Seek to meet social aims by engaging in economic and trading activities.
  Have legal structures which ensure that all assets and accumulated wealth are not in the ownership of individuals but are held in trust and for the benefit of those persons and/or areas that are the intended beneficiaries of the enterprise's social aims.

Have organisational structures in which full participation of members is encouraged on a co-operative basis with equal rights accorded to all members.[20]

- ... organisations who [*sic*] are independent of the state and provide services, goods and trade for a social purpose and are non-profit-distributing.[21]
- Social enterprises are competitive businesses, owned and trading for a social purpose. (They) have three common characteristics:

Enterprise orientation – [are] directly involved in producing goods or providing services to a market ... seek to be viable trading concerns, making an operating surplus.
Have explicit social aims ... have ethical values ... are accountable to their members and the wider community for their social, environmental and economic impact.
Social ownership – are autonomous organisations with governance and ownership structures based on participation by stakeholder groups ... profits are distributed as profit-sharing to stakeholders or used for the benefit of the community.[22]

- Social enterprises try to make a profit, but they operate on a not-for-personal-profit basis, applying any surplus they create to furthering their social objectives. They put people first and, through their economic activities, seek to deliver employment opportunities and other social, environmental, or community benefits.[23]

Further definitions are as follows:

- Social Economy Enterprises are community owner/co-operative businesses, trading for economic and social purposes. They seek to succeed as businesses by establishing a market share and making a profit. They combine the need to be financially successful businesses with social objectives. They emphasise the long-term benefits for employees, consumers and the community.[24]
- The term 'social economy organisations' is occasionally used to include SEEs and other organisations in the social economy that carry out other activities, such as the provision of advice to governments and services to SEEs.[25]
- Social economy enterprises are organisations democratically governed by their members or the stakeholders they serve that use a combination of market (sales revenue and paid labour) and non-market (government funding, private philanthropy and volunteer labour) resources to produce and deliver goods and services in the market place based on a combination of the common interests of members and concern about the well-being of others. They are citizen-led, community-based organisations that deliver goods and services locally, sometimes as part of a network of similar organisations that provide financial, strategic and technical support.[26]
- SEEs are businesses that trade in the marketplace in order to fulfil economic and social aims. They bring people and communities together for indigenous economic development and social benefit. They have three common characteristics:

Enterprise Focused. They are directly involved in the production of goods and the provision of services to a market. They seek to be viable trading concerns, making a surplus from trading.
Social Aims. They have explicit social aims such as job creation, training and the provision of local services. They have ethical values including a commitment to local capacity building. They are accountable to their members and the wider community for their social, environmental and economic impact.
Local Ownership. They are autonomous organisation with a governance and ownership structure based on participation by stakeholder groups (users or clients, local community groups, and so on) or by trustees. Profits are distributed as profit sharing to stakeholders or used for the benefit of the community.[27]

- Social Enterprise = (social improvement and verification) + (competition and innovation).[28]

And some definitions of a community enterprise or business are as follows:

- A community enterprise is a non-profit-making organisation which is controlled and run by local people in the community. It is sustainable in the sense that it manages to raise enough funds through its activities or through fundraising in order to make ends meet financially. [29]
- A community business is a sustainable commercial enterprise which is owned and controlled by the local community. It aims to create jobs and related training opportunities and to encourage local economic activity. Profits are used to create more jobs and businesses and to generate wealth for the benefit of the community. [30]
- Community enterprise organisations working for sustainable regeneration in their community through a mix of economic, environmental, cultural, and social activities. They are independent, not-for-private-profit organisations, locally accountable and committed to involving local people in the process of regeneration. [31]
- A community co-operative is a multifunctional business run for local benefit and directly owned and controlled by the community in which it operates. Some of its activities may be social in character, but it must make a profit overall. [32]

Other components of the social economy

As well as social enterprises, the EU description of the social economy specifically includes co-operatives, mutuals, associations, and foundations. There are also other categories of organisation and enterprise which can be included such as local exchange trading schemes (LETS) and intermediate labour markets (ILMs). These categories, and some sorts of organisation within them, are therefore considered here.

Co-operatives

Co-operatives are democratic shareholding organisations run for and by their members on the basis of one member, one vote, rather than on capital shareholding, and have a range of social purposes, which may include increased control by people working in the enterprise, equal opportunities, and ethical trading. Members may be employees in a worker co-operative, savers and borrowers in a credit union, tenants in a housing co-operative, businesses in a marketing co-operative, or customers in a consumer co-operative (see Illustration 4.4).

Illustration 4.4 The core values of co-operatives

The International Co-operative Alliance has articulated the core values of co-operatives as a set of seven principles:

1st Principle: Voluntary and Open Membership
Co-operatives are voluntary organisations, open to all persons able to use their services and willing to accept the responsibilities of membership, without gender, social, racial, political, or religious discrimination.

2nd Principle: Democratic Member Control
Co-operatives are democratic organisations controlled by their members, who actively participate in setting their policies and making decisions. Men and women serving as elected representatives are accountable to the membership. In primary co-operatives members have equal voting rights (one member, one vote) and co-operatives at other levels are also organised in a democratic manner.

3rd Principle: Member Economic Participation

Members contribute equitably to, and democratically control, the capital of their co-operative. At least part of that capital is usually the common property of the co-operative. Members usually receive limited compensation, if any, on capital subscribed as a condition of membership. Members allocate surpluses for any or all of the following purposes: developing their co-operative, possibly by setting up reserves, part of which at least would be indivisible; benefiting members in proportion to their transactions with the co-operative; and supporting other activities approved by the membership.

4th Principle: Autonomy and Independence

Co-operatives are autonomous, self-help organisations controlled by their members. If they enter into agreements with other organisations, including governments, or raise capital from external sources, they do so on terms that ensure democratic control by their members and maintain their co-operative autonomy.

5th Principle: Education, Training, and Information

Co-operatives provide education and training for their members, elected representatives, managers and employees so they can contribute effectively to the development of their co-operatives. They inform the general public – particularly young people and opinion leaders – about the nature and benefits of co-operation.

6th Principle: Co-operation among Co-operatives

Co-operatives serve their members most effectively and strengthen the co-operative movement by working together through local, regional, national, and international structures.

7th Principle: Concern for Community

Co-operatives work for the sustainable development of their communities through policies approved by their members.

Source: International Co-operative Alliance (1994), 'Draft Statement on Cooperative Identity', Geneva, ICA

The International Co-operative Alliance, to which many co-operatives belong, states that:

> A co-operative is an autonomous association of persons united voluntarily to meet their common economic, social and cultural needs and aspirations through a jointly owned and democratically-controlled enterprise.[33]

Consumer and producer co-operatives

Broadly there are two major classes of co-operatives: those which are consumer or user led, in which the consumer is the primary stakeholder; and those which are producer or supplier or employee led, where whoever produces the goods or services is the primary stakeholder. Retail co-operatives fall within the first category, whilst agricultural co-operatives and worker co-operatives fall into the second group.

Service and care co-operatives

In a study for the UK Co-operative Council (UKCC), the Industrial Common Ownership Movement (ICOM) pointed out that there were a number of interlinked policy and funding changes that were increasing the importance of co-operatives in the delivery of core services. These included:

- the withdrawal of the state from key areas of welfare;
- the promotion of the third sector in the delivery of social programmes;

- a return to community ownership and consumerist management principles; and
- greater reliance on self-help in the processes of industrial change in advanced Western societies. [34]

There is an interesting structural variation within care co-operatives that highlighted the complexity of the constitutional and financial profile of the sector. In the agency co-operative model, carers are self-employed and pay the co-operative a commission for centralised services such as administration and locating work (a form of employment agency). In the worker co-operative (or 'principle' model), where the co-operative itself employs its members to deliver the service, the carers are employees of the co-operative. Each one has different implications for VAT, income tax, national insurance contributions, and the corporate financial growth of the sector.

Credit unions

Credit unions are co-operative financial institutions that are owned and controlled by their members and operate on a number of principles which include the following:

- Only people who are credit union members can borrow.
- Loans will be made for prudential productive purposes.
- A person's desire to repay will be considered more important than the ability to repay.

Credit unions are sometimes categorised as co-operatives and sometimes as mutuals. They are mutual organisations in that they exist for their members and, in the UK, they are not incorporated under co-operative legislation. However, they are defined by HM Treasury as 'co-operative organisations' (which encourage their members to save regularly and enable them to borrow at lower interest rates than those normally charged by other financial institutions). [35]

Credit unions in the UK are registered and regulated by the Registry of Friendly Societies under the Industrial and Provident Societies Acts of 1965–1968 and the Credit Union Act of 1979. The objectives of credit unions as defined by the 1979 Act are as follows:

- the promotion of thrift among the members by the accumulation of savings;
- the creation of sources of credit for the benefit of members at a fair and reasonable rate of interest;
- the use and control of members' savings for their mutual benefit; and
- the training and education of the members in the wise use of money and in the management of their financial affairs.

In 2012 there appeared to be just over 400 credit unions in the UK, regulated by the Financial Services Authority. It might have been expected that they would have found favour with many people following the UK's run of banking scandals, but it seems that they have yet to take off in the way they have in countries such as Ireland, the US, and Australia.

Mutuals

Mutuals are organisations, mainly in financial services, such as insurance mutuals, health mutuals, and building societies, which are formed to provide benefits for their members. They were important before the advent of the welfare state, enabling people, for instance, to protect themselves against adversity with mutual insurance schemes. Building societies and mutual insurance companies are the major mutuals which still exist, although this is changing as many building societies become banks in the drive to find new markets and capital. Co-operatives and mutuals are very similar structurally, having a common ancestry in the village and trade-friendly societies of the past.

Mutuals exist for the benefit of their members and are non-profit-making organisations as any surplus they make is returned to their members. Mutual societies were historically formed to overcome social or economic injustice confronting the poorer members of communities and for the purpose of trying to improve their members' lives. Friendly societies, which are mutual organisations, were originally formed to help poorer people save for funeral expenses and witnessed considerable growth following the Industrial Revolution in the nineteenth century. In the absence of a welfare state or social protection systems, friendly societies were used by people to save, to build retirement capital, or as a form of insurance against illness or an inability to work. At their peak in 1945, they provided for the needs of 8.75 million private subscribers in the UK through 18,000 branches of societies. [36]

Many mutuals have operated in the life insurance sector with profits being rebated to the clients in the form of dividend distributions or reduced future premiums rather than as a financial profit to investors. However, without shareholders, mutual companies lacked access to equity markets to grow, and financial deregulation in both the US and the UK led many large insurance companies and building societies to de-mutualise and to offer shares to current policyholders as a replacement for their stake in the company.

Associations

Associations are organisations which operate within a set of rules but are normally unincorporated. In the UK being unincorporated means that they are not incorporated as companies but do often have some other form of registration, which means that they can exist as a legal entity. [37] In the UK many voluntary sector organisations have been associations but there are also associations which might not be considered to be in the voluntary sector, such as trade unions, trust hospitals, schools with elected governors, housing associations, professional associations, employers' organisations, and political parties. As with other subsets of the social economy, associations vary in their size, sectoral coverage, and purpose.

Housing associations

Within the UK one of the most active manifestations of social economy associations is the housing association sector. This movement stemmed from the rise in homelessness in the 1960s and the perceived need for a new rented sector to fill the gap left by the decline in private renting. Since the early 1990s, housing associations have been the main providers of new social rented housing in England, primarily as homes for rent for disadvantaged groups such as homeless, elderly and disabled people, young single people, low-income families, and members of minority groups, but also low-cost home ownership housing, mainly through shared ownership schemes. Housing associations vary greatly in size, ethos, and tenant group, and new development schemes are financed by both public subsidy and private borrowing.

Since the 1988 Housing Act, housing associations have had to rely more heavily on private sector loan finance and this has caused tensions especially with matters such as development costs and the need to service the interest charges on private sector finance.

Partly in response to this vulnerability and partly to deepen their remit, many associations have ventured into new 'business areas' such as care services, especially for older people, community development, and training.

Among the characteristics of housing associations which they share with many other social economy organisations are the following:

- They have a 'mixed' funding capability and can match government grants with resources raised by the private sector.
- They have traditionally targeted excluded and marginal groups but some of them have developed mainstream roles especially in the management of stock transferred from local authorities.
- Most are governed by management committees rather than by elected representatives or local councils.
- They are registered charities.
- They have originated from a combination of charitable and entrepreneurial back-grounds rather than past involvement in municipal socialism.
- Many of them have a strong local orientation offering decentralised and sensitive management of geographic communities or communities of interest.

As the 1990s progressed, more emphasis was placed on the role of local authorities as strategic *enablers* not involved in the operational delivery of policies, including social housing.[38] Large Scale Voluntary Stock Transfer enabled tenants to have their houses managed by different landlords, which in particular benefited existing and new housing associations. Malpass[39] pointed out that in 1992 the housing association sector in Great Britain consisted of 733,000 dwellings but that it grew quickly as a result of both investment and stock transfer, and by 2002 it had more than doubled in size, reaching around 1.7 million units. The creation of about 200 new Registered Social Landlords has added to both the stock and the size and capacity of the largest associations. The Labour government supported stock transfer, which grew steadily after their election in 1997. However, many commentators feel that the transfer of housing has failed to deliver the levels of involvement aspired by those actively in the process, and that in some cases local authorities retained strong control over community-based housing organisations.[40] Moreover, others pointed out that this approach was less about developing the social economics of housing and more about rolling back the welfare state and the 'dem<unclear>u</unclear>nicipalization' of social housing.[41] Gibb made a crucial point in asserting that part of the problem has been that stock transfer to community level tends to treat the challenge of regeneration in relative isolation from wider economic dynamics.[42] Mooney and Poole thus argued that for transfer to be successful it should be less about simply managing the stock and more about the centrality of housing as a regenerator in the most disadvantaged areas of the UK.[43]

It is also interesting to note that, although associations are often considered to be archetypical components of the social economy and therefore clearly to belong in the third sector, in Northern Ireland, in compliance with Section 75 of the Northern Ireland Act 1998, housing associations have been officially designated as public authorities along with public sector bodies such as civil service departments.

Charities

Some may suggest that charities are not part of the social economy, but Figure 3.1 suggests that charities could be considered as a subset of the social economy within associations.

Some of the better-known charities such as, in the UK, Oxfam, Barnardo's, and the RSPCA, are philanthropic rather than self-help, and are clearly neither co-operatives nor mutuals. However, charities as a whole are a much broader group.

In the UK being a charity is not a distinct form of legal existence (but see Table 6.1 – Charitable Incorporated Organisation). Any organisation can apply for charitable status provided its purposes or aims are for public benefit, and thus many organisations which would otherwise fall under one or more of the definitions of social enterprise are also registered as charities. Before the Charities Act 2006, charities had to have objects which fell within one or more of the four broad categories of the relief of poverty, the advancement of education, the promotion of religion, and other purposes beneficial to the community which were recognised as charitable. The Charities Act 2006, which applies in England and Wales, specifically included public benefit in the definition of a charitable purpose but introduced a more extensive list of charitable purposes. This list came into effect on 1 April 2008 and includes:

a. the prevention or relief of poverty;
b. the advancement of education;
c. the advancement of religion;
d. the advancement of health or the saving of lives;
e. the advancement of citizenship or community development;
f. the advancement of the arts, culture, heritage, or science;
g. the advancement of amateur sport;
h. the advancement of human rights, conflict resolution or reconciliation or the promotion of religious or racial harmony or equality and diversity;
i. the advancement of environmental protection or improvement;
j. the relief of those in need, by reason of youth, age, ill-health, disability, financial hardship, or other disadvantage;
k. the advancement of animal welfare;
l. the promotion of the efficiency of the armed forces of the Crown, or of the efficiency of the police, fire and rescue services or ambulance services;
m. other purposes currently recognised as charitable and any new charitable purposes which are similar to another charitable purpose. [44]

Organisations with such purposes do not have to register as charities but may find that, on balance, it is advantageous to do so. Being a registered charity can help an organisation to attract volunteer help and it can help fund-raising because it can reassure potential donors. At least in the UK it also allows the charity to recover the income tax paid on 'gift aid' and can also have other tax advantages as it provides relief from a number of other taxes. There are disadvantages such as the limits it places on certain forms of political and campaigning activity and the extent on which charities can trade. Charities do not have to have a particular legal form and can be either incorporated bodies, such as companies and industrial and provident societies, or unincorporated bodies such as clubs and friendly societies.

The more famous charities might be thought to concentrate on things such as the relief of poor, sick, older or destitute people; or animals but, at least in the UK, many other organisations are charities including many housing associations, religious bodies, building preservation trusts, think tanks, educational organisations, arts bodies, and medical research establishments – to list but a few. Many areas within the third sector can therefore, if suitably presented, be accepted as charitable, and charities are not found only within a limited part of the third sector spectrum (see also Chapter 6).

Foundations

According to a communication from the European Commission on promoting the role of voluntary organisations and foundations, the latter, like voluntary organisations, undertake a wide range of activities but are legally a more homogeneous group and are essentially for public benefit, whereas voluntary organisations can be essentially for private benefit. For the purposes of the communication, foundations are described as:

> bodies with their own source of funds which they spend according to their own judgement on projects or activities of public benefit. They are entirely independent of government or other public authorities and are run by independent management boards or trustees.[45]

Foundations have been a long-established format for philanthropic giving as the example of the Carnegie Trust fund (see in Case 4.1) demonstrates. From an American perspective, Gunn[46] describes foundations as private entities given special non-profit status for their charitable or philanthropic distribution of money. They have investment portfolios which are used to generate a profit from money put into trust for the wider public or specified beneficiary groups. Because they rely on the stock market, the performance of foundations and the profits they yield for redistribution vary considerably. Large American foundations set up by millionaire business philanthropists such as Ford, Kellogg, and Gates have seen the value of their investment rise and fall as the market ebbed and flowed throughout the unpredictable late 1990s. Gunn points out that in 1998 the top one per cent of foundations controlled 60 per cent of all foundation assets.[47] Other entities in the non-profit sector include corporate foundations and community foundations. The former are used by large corporations to help even out the distribution (and tax benefits) of their charitable giving over years of relative high and low income. (In the US, corporations get the same tax relief as individuals for their gifts to foundations.) Case 4.1 includes a description of development trusts in the UK which are examples of community foundations.

Intermediate labour markets and transitional employment programmes

An intermediate labour market (ILM) has been defined as 'a diverse range of initiatives that typically provide temporary waged employment in a genuine work environment with continuous support to assist the transition to work'[48] and their principal characteristics have been identified as follows (and see Illustration 4.5):

* The main aim is to give those removed from the labour market a bridge back to the world of work by improving participants' general employability.
* The core feature is paid work on a temporary contract (often up to 12 months), together with training, personal development and job search activities.
* In order to limit the risk of replacing 'real' jobs, the work is in additional economic activities, ideally of community benefit.
* Projects and programmes rely on packages of funding from various sources including New Deal, the European Social Fund (ESF) and local regeneration funding.[49]

Illustration 4.5 Intermediate labour markets in the UK

Finn and Simmonds surveyed ILM initiatives in the UK and highlighted their labour market and regeneration potential. The overall average for job outcomes across all the ILMs surveyed was 43 per cent. This average, however, disguised a wide range of job outcome rates. For example, the average for non–New Deal ILMs was 67 per cent, and this may partially reflect the relatively higher employability of some recruits. In addition,

- The survey showed that in 2003 the turnover of ILMs had increased by almost 120 per cent since 2000, and the number of ILM jobs had increased to just over 7000. In total, there was an estimated minimum of 8700 ILM jobs in the UK.
- The duration of ILM jobs was mostly between 26 and 52 weeks, and the average length of stay varied from 65 to 75 per cent of the contract length, suggesting that around 12,000 people passed through ILMs in 2002–2003.
- This growth had mostly come from local partners and local organisations identifying ILMs as a tool to improve job outcomes and achieve regeneration and social objectives. At the national level there had been no specific actions by government to stimulate the growth of ILMs, but neither had it sought to restrict their development.
- The motivation and ability to start and maintain an ILM came mainly from local conditions and local capacity although the availability of European funding and the flexibility of New Deal had enabled this increase.
- The majority of ILMs were based on New Deal 18–24 and 25+ age ranges, and all of the larger ILMs were based on New Deal. A large majority of ILMs were with less than 100 jobs, but there were a few very large area-based ILMs, where there was a central organisation which co-ordinated, enabled, or directly funded local ILMs within the wider area.
- The largest single funding source was European funds.

Source: Based on D. Finn and D. Simmonds, *Intermediate Labour Market in Britain and on International Review of Transitional Employment Programmes* (London: Department of Work and Pensions, 2003), p. 57

A distinction is drawn between ILMs and Transitional Employment Programmes. The latter emerged in the US and the UK as a new generation of initiatives aimed at tackling long-term unemployed and hard-to-reach people in the labour market. However, unlike traditional job creation programmes:

TEPs (Transitional Employment Programmes) typically target the hardest to place unemployed and combine short periods of paid work experience with additional support and job placement services aimed at getting participants into regular jobs. TEPs also make more extensive use of private sector job placements but unlike conventional employment subsidies the goal of the programme is to offer temporary, relevant and realistic work, rather than a contract of employment and continuing employment with a particular employer.[50]

Community trading schemes

The new economics foundation (nef)[51] has drawn attention to the emergence of non-monetised, reciprocal training of time, services, and virtual currencies as an alternative to the private or state markets as a way of exchanging goods and services. These are often represented as local currencies which can be divided into two broad strands: those based on value, and those based on labour time.[52] Globally, there are three major community currency systems in operation: Local Exchange Trading Schemes (LETS), HOURS systems, and time banks.[53]

LETS monies typically mirror the value of the national currency, and members arrange and negotiate exchanges with one another, reporting transactions to the system accountant.[54] Members receive monthly statements of their accounts, which typically have credit and debit limits in order to prevent 'freeloading' and 'hoarding'. Approximately 300 LETS schemes operate in the UK today, involving an estimated 22,000 people and a turnover equivalent to £1.4 million annually.[55] However, Seyfang points out that LETS activity peaked in the mid-1990s and a significant proportion of LETS are restricted by low trading volumes and high administration costs.

Edgar Cahn[56] developed the concept of time dollars in 1983 in response to eroding social values and rising inequality, and the first time banks were mostly intra-generational, agency-based 'service credit banking' programmes in the US that recruited older people in a scheme to help them remain independent as they aged.[57] There is no hierarchy of value for services – one hour equals one time credit.

Time banks have become a popular tool among local authorities in the UK in order to generate community self-help and promote social inclusion in deprived areas by converting unpaid time into a commodity through mutual volunteering.[58] In the UK there are 103 established time banks in operation and 133 in development.[59] The number of participants has doubled to 16,563, and the number of hours traded has increased by 50 per cent to over 900,000.[60] Time banks operate with six core principles:

> recognizing people as assets and that everyone has skills to share; redefining work to include the unpaid 'core economy' of work in the neighbourhood and community; nurturing reciprocity and exchange rather than dependency; growing social capital; encouraging learning and skills sharing; involving people in decision-making.[61]

Time banking can occur in three contexts: the person-to-person model, which is the most common approach in the UK, person-to-agency model, and agency-to-agency. Person-to-person services can be set up in a variety of ways:

- An independent, stand-alone local organisation run as a self-help group, a co-operative, not-for-profit organisation or charity.
- A two way service run by statutory agencies utilising existing staff time and resources in collaboration with local residents in a defined community.
- A two way service run by a third sector organisation or social enterprise as one of many services they provide for the local community.
- A service commissioned by local statutory and voluntary agencies in response to identified needs – communities of interest.
- Small local neighbourhood time banks run and shaped by neighbours.[62]

There are a number of key differences between LETS and time banks. First, whilst LETS are proposed as alternative economic models that strengthen the local economy and promote informal employment, time banks are socially oriented volunteering initiatives that provide services associated with informal support networks that are not valued in the traditional market economy.[63] Second, LETS currencies tend to emulate the national currency and members negotiate amongst themselves to decide on the price of a service, whilst time banks operate on a principle of equality where one hour of service costs one credit, irrespective of the type of service, and a central broker (usually paid) arranges all exchanges. Third, unlike time credits, LETS currencies have not been declared exempt from tax and benefit calculations, which limits participation from the unemployed. Finally, LETS tend to be managed by volunteers while time banks necessitate more investment for a drop-in office and staff that will arrange exchanges and recruit members.

Illustration 4.6 Some problems in recognising the value of social economy activity

LETS involve the exchange of the outputs of work but without the exchange of real money. They do not provide formal paid jobs and do not therefore show up on the employment 'radar'. They are an example of social economy activity which does not register in formal measures of an economy, such as GDP and employment, and this raises problems in recognising the scope of the social economy sector because the formal economy does not recognise the economic value of community activity:

> It recognises only cash, trade and employment as economic, not life support systems and natural assets.[64]

In an understandable desire to use public resources efficiently, many official initiatives in disadvantaged areas have focused on specific issues such as unemployment and tried to set targets which were both specific and measurable.[65] That might lead, however, to a focus on identified symptoms and on specific and measurable interventions to address them, rather than on uncertain causes and on holistic but less measurable cures. Initiatives which, for example, seek to address unemployment as an identified problem will not recognise the value of organisations such as LETS because their outputs do not register in official measurements and do not include formal employment.

Chanan is critical of approaches that rely too much on jobs because they ignore the monetary value of other sectors of the economy and because spatial development goes beyond employment generation. She has pointed out that an emphasis on employment objectives has sometimes held back community involvement because, even in disadvantaged areas, the unemployed are a minority of the population. Moreover, employment often absorbs a large proportion of the local development budget, and the broad involvement of disadvantaged localities needs the participation of a cross section of the population, not just the unemployed.[66] She concludes that 'in order to fully come into its own, the social economy must liberate itself from the short-term politico-economic equation of social policy with employment policy'.[67]

Community asset transfer

Accompanying the UK government's Big Society (see Case 3.1) was a concern for local control, devolved decision-making, and the operation of public services by social enterprises. There has been 'community right to buy' in Scotland since 2004[68] but the Localism Act (2011) for England and Wales emphasised the potential of transferring publically owned, usually local authority assets, to local groups (at nil or nominal value). The Institute for Public Policy Research (IPPR) use the Development Trust Association definition of asset transfer as:

> Local communities' ability to acquire land and buildings, either at market value or at a discount, in order to deliver services that meet local needs. It is seen as one way in which local authorities (in particular) can support the development of social economy organisations, and thereby meet their wider strategies for renewal and improved delivery of local services.[69]

IPPR also point out that there is a considerable difference in the concept with some projects involving simply a right to use the asset while others transfer the legal title, permitting the organisation to earn an income from its use.

In an extensive review of asset transfer in the UK, Aiken et al.[70] distinguish between three types of transfer projects:

- Stewards – small, mainly volunteer-run groups with a single, long-standing asset (usually a building) used largely for hiring out to local community groups and residents. Such groups had a low income and rarely employed staff. One feature of the survey findings was the high proportion of very small rural organisations operating with few, if any staff.

- Community developers – medium-sized organisations, often with a range of assets, involved in local service delivery and local partnerships. These organisations normally had paid staff and a mix of sources of income.
- Entrepreneurs – organisations running larger, more professionally styled social enterprises. While still community based they have a mix of assets for social and commercial purposes and a business model. These organisations were more likely to have capital-intensive assets. [71]

Aiken et al. point out that without the right conditions in place, asset ownership and management can struggle to achieve benefits, especially for community groups. A clearer understanding is needed of the risks and costs involved in asset control, as assets can become liabilities that undermine the social purpose of many groups. Similarly, they point out that community organisations need to strike a balance between achieving financial sustainability and delivering community benefit. The opportunities for generating income to sustain the project financially vary considerably and new skills are required to manage assets effectively. For success, public authorities need to be supportive, strong governance should be in place to manage the project, and the asset should be in good physical condition. However, the benefits of effective asset transfer and management are considerable:

> The benefits of community control of assets included: a heightened sense of identity; greater financial viability; improved levels of activity and access to services; increased opportunities for training, jobs and business development; a better physical environment; and enhanced credibility with local authorities and outside agencies. These benefits contributed to a 'social good' of local wellbeing. [72]

The recent drive to promote asset transfer in the UK began with the Quirk Review and its resultant report, *Making Assets Work*, published in May 2007, which explored the barriers and incentives affecting the transfer of public assets to community management and ownership. Following the review, the Labour government set up the specialist Asset Transfer Unit, the Advancing Assets Programme operated by Locality, and a £30 million Community Assets Programme delivered by the Big Lottery Fund. Building on this, the Localism Act brought in:

- The General Power of Competence which gives local authorities the freedom to act in the interests of voters, not dissimilar to the 'power of wellbeing' proposed for Community Planning in the new councils;
- The Community Right to Challenge which gives local authorities and community groups an interest in taking over a local service or facilities; and
- The Community Right to Buy which will require local authorities to maintain a list of assets of community value which groups and individuals will be able to buy for a community use. [73]

Social entrepreneurship

If social enterprises are a key part of the social economy, where do social entrepreneurs fit in? Kickul and Lyons [74] examine social entrepreneurship and highlight the different views on defining entrepreneurship and associated disagreement on whether it depends primarily on generic traits or learned skills – and thus on the long-standing argument about whether entrepreneurs, social or otherwise, are born or can be created. However, they suggest, social entrepreneurs share common characteristics in that they actively seek out opportunities to innovate in order to add value to the lives of their customers. They pursue a strategy of growth in order to expand their business's market reach and profits. They are strategic in the way they manage their enterprises, and they ably build networks among their investors, suppliers and customers in order to achieve their business goals. [75]

Mawson identifies an important tension between democratic forms of inclusive governance and allowing 'leaders to lead [as] there is a natural geography of power'. [76]

Bornstein and Davis argue that social entrepreneurship also changes over time and recognised three distinct phases of development. Phase 1 was about identifying people, celebrating their success and support; Phase 2 emphasised organisational support and saw the performance of individual entrepreneurs linked to organisational efficacies; and Phase 3 is more concerned with social innovation, networking, and scaling entrepreneurial activities across enterprises, sectors, and the globe. [77]

Kickul and Lyons highlight the role of social entrepreneurs in introducing creativity and innovation and draw on a range of sources to identify seven types of innovation:

- the creation of new products or services.
- a new process for producing or delivering an existing product, service, programme, or project.
- delivering an existing product service, programme, or project to a new or previously underserved market.
- utilising a new source of labour or other production inputs.
- implementing a new organisational or industrial structure.
- implementing new ways of engaging 'customers' or target beneficiaries.
- the utilisation of new funding models. [78]

Praszkier and Nowak have identified five pivotal dimensions that form the skeleton around which the concept of social entrepreneurship seems to be constructed: social mission, social innovation, social change, entrepreneurial spirit, and personality. [79] Effective social entrepreneurs, they suggest, need vibrant networks to create the type of radical change implied in social innovation and these both produce and are reproduced by social capital. Overall, they suggest, social entrepreneurs are leaders, albeit providing a new kind of leadership, and they set out the approaches used by social entrepreneurs in building up their empowering leadership – see Table 4.2. As both Bornstein and Davis as well as Praszkier and Nowak have indicated, social entrepreneurship is linked to social innovation, which is considered further in a section of Chapter 5.

Conclusion

Because the social economy is often defined through its components, this chapter has reviewed efforts to define those components. Especially in the case of social enterprises, there is a lack of agreement among the various definitions, and even confusion over whether the other components sometimes listed, such as co-operatives, mutuals, associations and foundations are themselves social enterprises or something else distinct from them.

This lack of clear agreement on these components means that defining the social economy through its components still leaves areas of uncertainty. This is consistent with the different sectors of the economy being like different areas of a spectrum without

Table 4.2 Components of empowering leadership

Area	Practices
Social empathy	Understand the latent capacities of groups
	Revealing the dreams, frustrations, and aims of groups
	Identifying sectors or areas where groups could cooperate
Empowering groups	Facilitating change within and between groups
	Celebrating and rewarding success
	Democratic, rather than top-down, methods of learning and skills development
Modifying parameters	Building trust, optimism, and hope as a basis for change rather than confronting problems head-on
Identifying the best starting point	Brining innovation and fresh thinking to stubborn problems
	Managing conflict, resistance, and interval struggles

Source: Based on R. Praszkier and A. Nowak, *Social Entrepreneurship: Theory and Practice* (Cambridge: Cambridge University Press, 2012), pp. 149–50.

clear boundaries – rather than being separate activities with clear distinct divisions between them.

Nevertheless there are common traits, values, and organisational formats which are generally agreed to mark out the social economy as a distinctive economic, social, and cultural sphere of activity. Collective ownership, non-profit distribution, democratic governance arrangements, the inclusion of multiple stakeholders in planning and control, a clear social benefit, but with recognisable systems of trade and exchange relations, are some of the recurring themes in the social economy sphere. Although there is a lack of common agreement over just what is, or is not, thus included, it is these generally agreed characteristics and the relationships amongst them which are explored in greater detail in the second part of this book.

Key Points of Chapter 4

- The social economy is sometimes defined in terms of its components, which variously are said to include co-operatives, mutuals, associations, foundations, and social enterprises.
- Sometimes all those components are said to be social enterprises and sometimes they are seen as being distinct from the others.
- Social enterprises have been defined in a variety of different ways, with little that the various definitions agree on except a social purpose.
- The other components, including co-operatives, mutuals, associations, and foundations as well as a variety of other possible categories, also have their various definitions, and sometimes a number of sub-components.
- In at least some cases, such as social enterprises, there is no commonly accepted definition for the components of the social economy. Defining the social economy through its components thus still leaves areas of uncertainty, consistent with the different sectors being different areas of a spectrum rather than having clear distinct boundaries.
- Social enterprises are often the creation of social entrepreneurs, who provide things like innovation and empowering leadership.

Case 4.1 | Examples of some social enterprises

A mutual

The Communication Workers Friendly Society (CWFS) was founded in 1895 by the Postman's Federation to provide assistance to its members during illness or death. It was originally known as the Mutual Benefit Society. As the Society expanded, it changed its name to the Union of Communication Workers Insurance Society (UCWIS) and was run as part of the Union of Communication Workers (now CWU). With the introduction of the 1992 Friendly Society Act and changes to financial regulations, CWFS became an independent organisation which operated separately from the Communication Workers Union (CWU) and was responsible for its own decision-making. In 2005 CWFS was run by a Board of Directors, consisting of nine elected members of the Society and the Society provides affordable financial products with an ethos of mutuality and friendliness. It encouraged savings and accepted much lower premiums from savers than mainstream insurance companies.

According to CWFS:

> 'A mutual, mutual organisation, or mutual society is an organization (which is often, but not always, a company or business) based on the principle of mutuality. Unlike a true cooperative, members usually do not contribute to the capital of the company by direct investment, but derive their right to profits and votes through their customer relationship. A mutual exists with the purpose of raising funds, from its membership or customers, which can then be used to provide common services to all members of the organization or society. A mutual is therefore owned by, and run for the benefit of, its members – it has no external shareholders to pay in the form of dividends, and as such does not usually seek to maximise and make large profits or capital gains. Mutuals exist for the members to benefit from the services they provide. Profits made will usually be re-invested in the mutual for the benefit of the members, although some profit may also be necessary in the case of mutuals to sustain or grow the organisation, and to make sure it remains safe and secure.'[80]

At the end of 2005, CWFS had more than 27,000 members and total assets of over £110 million. CWFS provided a range of products with the benefit of having deductions made directly from pay, including Life & Savings Plan, Sickness Benefit Scheme, and Children's Savings Plan. As a friendly society providing financial advice and services, CWFS was authorised and regulated by the Financial Services Authority (FSA). In 2011, however, CWFS merged into the bigger Forester Life. This involved transferring its engagements into Forester Life and Forester Life continuing to provide the same services with any assets over and above the amount required to cover these liabilities being ring-fenced for the exclusive benefit of CWFS's with-profits policy holders.

Source: Based on information from http://www.cwfs.co.uk/societies.aspx (accessed 2007) and www.foresters.com (accessed 4 June 2013)

A trust

In 1901 Andrew Carnegie sold his massive steel business in Pittsburgh, US, for $480m in order to establish a series of trusts, many of which are operational still today. The Carnegie United Kingdom Trust was founded in 1913 and incorporated by Royal Charter in 1917. Its purpose was 'For the improvement of the well-being of the masses of the people of Great Britain and Ireland, by such means as ... the Trustees may, from time to time, select as best fitted from age to age for securing these purposes, remembering rather new needs are constantly arising as the masses advance ... ' The Trust's early work still leaves an imprint in Victorian cities, especially in the creation of community libraries that continued until the implementation of the Public Libraries Act 1947. The Trust also funded projects such as village halls, social services programmes, and youth projects. The Trust's current strategic plan, for 2011–2015, focuses on the three themes of people and place, enterprise and society, and knowledge and culture.

Sources: R. Lamont-Brown, *Carnegie*, Annex I (Stroud: Sutton Publishing Limited, 2005) and www.carnegieuktrust.org.uk/publications/2011/strategic-plan-2-11-15 (accessed 7 February 2013)

Development trusts

Development trusts are community organisations created to enable sustainable development in their areas. They use self-help, trading for social purpose, and ownership of buildings and land, to bring about long-term social, economic, and environmental benefits in their communities. Development trusts are a part of the community enterprise movement, and their profits are used to create community wealth that has a lasting impact on the renewal and improvement of an area.

Development trusts are organisations that are: engaged in the economic, environmental, and social regeneration of a defined area; independent, aiming for self-sufficiency and not for private profit; community based, owned, and managed; and actively involved in partnerships and alliances between the community, voluntary, private, and public sectors. They come in many different shapes and sizes and are involved in a wide range of activities, services, and facilities to the communities they serve. These include managed workspace; business support; childcare; cafes and restaurants; affordable housing; delivery of public sector contracts; training and education; community shops; festivals; employment services; renewable energy; consultancy; advice and guidance; community newsletters; parks and gardens; sports facilities; and transport.

Source: http://locality.org.uk/members/development-trusts/ (accessed November 2012)

Intermediate labour markets

The following is an indication of the variety of ILM approaches across Europe and the way in which they are applied in local settings.[81]

Glasgow Works was started in 1994 to engage long-term unemployed people in work and training on projects with a local social benefit, delivered as a partnership between the state, the private sector, and specialist voluntary sector organisations.

Rotterdam Works was started in 1989 from a jobs pool which targeted older people, the unskilled, and migrants, and at the time of reporting about 3200 jobs were created.

Atlantis is a Berlin-based not-for-profit company that links the production of ecologically orientated goods and services with ecologically oriented training and jobs. Four hundred jobs were created.

The *Wise Group* in Glasgow has been described as one of the biggest and best-known social economy projects in UK.[82] The Group, which comprises a series of not-for-profit businesses, was started in the early 1980s and its core businesses include Heatwise, which concentrates on home insulation and heating systems and home security and safety, and Landwise, which concentrates on environmental upgrading. The Wise

Group carries out its activity by recruiting, training, and managing a workforce drawn from the long-term unemployed. An evaluation[83] highlighted its distinctive approach in linking training to real job opportunities. Welfare payments are topped up during training in order to deliver the following benefits:

- It gives people a period of employment in their own right.
- It keeps them in contact with the habits of work.
- It improves their skills to keep them closer to the labour market.
- It prevents them dropping into unemployability.

Questions, Exercises, Essay, and Discussion Topics

1. Why is the search to define the social economy so difficult?
2. To what extent do definitions of social enterprises reflect political viewpoints?
3. What do you regard as the critical characteristics of social enterprises?
4. The social economy 'is about social justice, participatory practice, and equality. It is concerned with developing alternatives to public and private markets and enabling communities to take greater control over their economic and social lives.' Would all social economy stakeholders agree? – Discuss.
5. Is there an alternative name for the social economy which would better reflect the nature of the organisations in it?

Suggestions for further reading

J. Pearce, *Social Enterprise in Anytown* (London: Calouste Gulbenkian Foundation, 2003).

M. Price, *Social Enterprise: What it is and why it matters* (Vale of Glamorgan: Fflan Ltd, 2009).

R. Ridley-Duff and M. Bull, *Understanding Social Enterprise: Theory and Practice* (London: Sage, 2011).

References

1. A. Nicholls, 'Postscript: The legitimacy of social entrepreneurship: Reflexive isomorphism in a pre-paradigmatic field', in B. Gidron and Y. Hasenfeld (Eds) *Social Enterprises: An Organisational Perspective* (Basingstoke: Palgrave Macmillan, 2012), pp. 222–49.
2. IFF Research Ltd, *A Survey of Social Enterprise Across the UK,* research report prepared for the Small Business Service (SBS), July 2005.
3. See for example M. Edwards, *Small Change: Why Business Won't Save the World* (San Francisco: Berrett-Koehler, 2010).
4. wikipedia.org/wiki/Social_Economy (accessed 7 November 2006).
5. M. Bull, 'Challenging tensions: critical, theoretical and empirical perspectives on social enterprise', *International Journal of Entrepreneurial Behaviour & Research,* Vol. 14, No. 5 (2008) pp. 268–275.
6. M. Harris and D. Albury, *The Innovation Imperative: Why Radical Innovation Is Needed to Reinvent Public Services for the Recession and Beyond* (London: NESTA, 2009).
7. International Labour Office (ILO), *Regional Conference of Social Economy: Africa's Response to the Global Crisis,* October 2009.
8. For instance in the title of M. Nyssens (Ed.), *Social Enterprise: At the Crossroads of Market, Public Policies and Civil Society* (London: Routledge, 2006).

9. J. Kerlin, *Social Enterprise: A Global Comparison* (Medford, MA: Tufts University Press, 2009), p. xiii.

10. R. Ridley-Duff and M. Bull, *Understanding Theory and Practice* (London, Sage, 2011).

11. http://ec.europa.eu/enterprise/entrepreneurship/coop/index.htm, accessed 28 March 2007.

12. R. Ridley-Duff and M. Bull, *Understanding Social Enterprise: Theory and Practice* (London: Sage, 2011).

13. Ibid., p. 33.

14. J. Defourny and M. Nyssens, 'Defining social enterprises', In M. Nyssens (Ed.) *Social Enterprise: At the Crossroads of Market* (London: Routledge, 2006), pp. 3–26.

15. J. Pearce, *Social Enterprise in Anytown* (London: Calouste Gulbenkian Foundation, 2003), pp. 31–2.

16. Cabinet Office/Office of the Third Sector, *Social Enterprise Action Plan: Scaling New Heights* (London: Cabinet Office, 2006), p. 10.

17. Reported as being available on the SBS website in 2001 by D. Smallbone, M. Evans, I. Ekanem and S. Butters, *Researching Social Enterprise* (Sheffield: Small Business Service, Research Report RR004/01, July 2001), p. 14.

18. Organisation for Economic Co-operation and Development (OECD), *Social Enterprises* (Paris: OECD, 1999), p. 10.

19. J. Pearce, *Social Enterprise in Anytown* (London: Calouste Gulbenkian Foundation, 2003), pp. 51–5.

20. The Conscise Project, *Key Concepts, Measures and Indicators* (London: Conscise Project, Middlesex University , 2000).

21. Policy Action Team 3, *Enterprise and Social Exclusion, Report of the National Strategy for Neighbourhood Renewal: Policy Action Team 3* (London: HM Treasury, 1999).

22. Social Enterprise Coalition, *Introducing Social Enterprise* (London: Social Enterprise Coalition, 2001).

23. Social Economy Consortium, *Opening the Gateway to Birmingham's Social Economy* (Birmingham: Social Economy Consortium, 2001).

24. Social Economy Agency, *Defining and Explaining Social Economy Structures, Briefing paper for Assembly Members* (Derry: Social Economy Agency, Northern Ireland, 2001), p. 2.

25. Policy Research Initiative, *What We Need to Know About the Social Economy: A Guide for Policy Research* (Canadian Government: Policy Research Initiative, 2005), p. 2.

26. Ibid., p. 11.

27. From Social Economy Agency, *Defining and Explaining Social Economy Structures, Briefing paper*

for Assembly Members (Derry: Social Economy Agency, Northern Ireland, 2001).

28. L. Black and J. Nicholls, *There's No Business Like Social Business: How to be Socially Enterprising* (Liverpool: The Cat's Pyjamas, 2004) p. 16.

29. Voluntary Action Lochaber, *All You Ever Wanted to Know about Community Enterprises* (Lochaber: Voluntary Action Lochaber, 2002).

30. *Definition of Community Business* (West Calder: Community Business Scotland, 1991), as quoted in J. Pearce, *Social Enterprise in Anytown* (London: Calouste Gulbenkian Foundation, 2003), p. 33.

31. Development Trusts Association, *Annual Report 2000* (London: DTA, 2000).

32. Highlands and Islands Development Board, *Community Co-operatives* (Highlands and Islands Development Board, 1977), as quoted in J. Pearce, *Social Enterprise in Anytown* (London: Calouste Gulbenkian Foundation, 2003), p. 33.

33. International Co-operative Alliance, *Draft Statement on Cooperative Identity* (Geneva: ICA, 1994), p. 1.

34. Based on UKCC, *Co-operating in Care. A Study of Care Co-operatives* (London: ICOM, 1998).

35. HM Treasury (HMT), *Credit Unions the Future Taskforce Report* (London: HMT, 1999), p. 7.

36. http://en.wikipedia.org/wiki/Mutual_organization, accessed 16 August 2007.

37. For instance, in Northern Ireland, the Fold Housing Association is not a company but is registered under the Industrial and Provident Societies Act (NI) 1969. However, its sister organisation in the Republic of Ireland, Fold Ireland, is a 'not-for-profit company formed by guarantee of the members and without a shareholding' (see www.foldireland.ie, accessed 27 April 2007).

38. A. Holmans, M. Stephens and S. Fitzpatrick, 'Housing policy in England since 1975', *Housing Studies*, Vol. 22, No. 2 (2007), pp. 147–62.

39. P. Malpass, *Housing and the Welfare State* (Basingstoke: Palgrave Macmillan, 2005).

40. M. McKee, 'Community ownership in Glasgow: The devolution of ownership and control, or a centralising process?', *European Journal of Housing Policy*, Vol. 7, No. 3 (2007), pp. 319–36.

41. P. Malpass and L. Cairncross, *Building on the Past: Visions of Housing Futures* (Bristol: The Policy Press, 2006).

42. K. Gibb, 'Transferring Glasgow's council housing: Financial, urban and housing policy implications', *European Journal of Housing Policy*, Vol. 3, No. 1 (2003), pp. 89–114.

43. G. Mooney and L. Poole, 'Marginalised voices: Resisting the privatisation of council housing',

Glasgow, *Local Economy*, Vol. 20, No. 1 (2005), pp. 27–39.

44. *Charities and Public Benefit: Summary Guidance for Charity Trustees*, www.charitycommission.gov.uk (accessed 19 April 2008).

45. Communication from the Commission on Promoting the Role of Voluntary Organisations and Foundations in Europe on http://ec.europa.eu/enterprise/library/bib-social-economy/orgfd-en.pdf (accessed 27 April 2007).

46. C. Gunn, *Third Sector Development* (New York: Cornell University Press, 2004).

47. Ibid., p. 28.

48. D. Finn and D. Simmonds, *Intermediate Labour Market in Britain and on International Review of Transitional Employment Programmes* (London: Department of Work and Pensions, 2003), p. 4.

49. B. Marshall and R. Macfarlane, *The Intermediate Labour Market: A Tool for Tackling Long-Term Unemployment* (York: Joseph Rowntree Foundation, 2000).

50. D. Finn and D. Simmonds, *Intermediate Labour Market in Britain and on International Review of Transitional Employment Programmes*, 2003, p. 4.

51. New Economics Foundation (nef), *The New Wealth of Time* (London: nef, 2008).

52. *D. Grover,* 'Would local currencies make a good local economic development policy tool? The case of Ithaca Hours', *Environment and Planning C: Government and Policy*, Vol. 24 (2006), pp. 719–37.

53. E. Collom, 'Engagement of the elderly in time banking: the potential for social capital generation in an ageing society', *Journal of Aging and Social Policy*, Vol. 20, No. 4 (2008), pp. 414–46.

54. G. Seyfang, *The New economics of sustainable consumption: seeds of change*, (New York: Palgrave Macmillan, 2009) p. 146.

55. Ibid., p. 149.

56. E. S. Cahn, *No more throw-away people: the co-production imperative*, 2nd ed. (Washington, DC: Essential Books, 2000).

57. E. Collom, 'Engagement of the elderly in time banking: the potential for social capital generation in an ageing society', *Journal of Aging and Social Policy*, Vol. 20, No. 4 (2008).

58. G. Seyfang, 'Time banks: rewarding community self-help in the inner city?', *Community Development Journal*, Vol. 39, No. 1 (2004), pp. 62–71.

59. Timebanking UK, *People Can* (London: Timebanking UK, 2011).

60. New economics foundation (nef), *The New Wealth of Time* (London: nef, 2008).

61. G. Seyfang, *The New Economics of Sustainable Consumption: Seeds of Change* (New York: Palgrave Macmillan, 2009), p. 250.

62. TimeBanking UK (TBUK), *The Time of Our Lives: Time Banking for Neighbourhood Renewal and Community Capacity Building* (London: TBUK, 2011).

63. G. Seyfang, 'Time banks: rewarding community self-help in the inner city?', *Community Development Journal*, Vol. 39, No. 1 (2004).

64. G. Chanan, 'Employment policy and social economy: promise and misconceptions', *Local Economy*, Vol. 14, No. 4 (1999), p. 361.

65. *The Green Book* recommends that 'Targets should be SMART: i.e. Specific, Measurable, Achievable, Relevant and Time-bound' (HM Treasury, *The Green Book: Appraisal and Evaluation in Central Government*, London: The Stationery Office, 2003).

66. G. Chanan, 'Employment policy and social economy: Promise and misconceptions', *Local Economy*, Vol. 14, No. 4 (1999), p. 365.

67. Ibid., p. 367.

68. H. Holmes, *Providing Opportunities for Rural Communities in Scotland: The Community Right to Buy in Scotland* (York: JRF, 2010).

69. IPPR, *Community Asset Transfer: Overcoming Challenges of Governance and Accountability* (London: Adventure Capital Fund, 2006), p. 6.

70. M. Aiken, B. Cairns, M. Taylor and R. Moran, *Community Organisations Controlling Assets: A Better Understanding* (York: Joseph Rowntree Foundation, 2011).

71. Ibid., p. 6.

72. Ibid., p. 7.

73. S. Hostick-Boakye and M. Hothi, *Grow Your Own: How Local Authorities Can Assist Social Enterprises* (London: The Young Foundation, 2011).

74. J. Kickul and T. Lyons, *Understanding Social Entrepreneurship: The Relentless Pursuit of Mission in an Ever Changing World* (London: Routledge, 2012).

75. Ibid., p. 15.

76. A. Mawson, *The Social Entrepreneur: Making Communities Work* (London: Atlantic Books, 2008), p. 167.

77. D. Bornstein and S. Davis, *Social Entrepreneurship: What Everyone Needs to Know* (Oxford: Oxford University Press, 2010).

78. J. Kickul and T. Lyons, *Understanding Social Entrepreneurship: The Relentless Pursuit of Mission in an Ever Changing World* (London: Routledge, 2012), pp. 45–6.

79. R. Praszkier and A. Nowak, *Social Entrepreneurship: Theory and Practice* (Cambridge: Cambridge University Press, 2012), p. 15.

80. http://www.cwfs.co.uk/societies.aspx (accessed 2007).

81. A. McGregor, Z. Ferguson, I. Fitzpatrick, M. McConnachie and K. Richmond, *Bridging the Jobs Gap: An Evaluation of the Wise Group and the Intermediate Labour Market* (York: Joseph Rowntree Foundation, 1997).

82. A. Amin, A. Cameron and R. Hudson, *Placing the Social Economy* (London: Routledge, 2002), p. 35.

83. A. McGregor, Z. Ferguson, I. Fitzpatrick, M. McConnachie and K. Richmond, *Bridging the Jobs Gap: An Evaluation of the Wise Group and the Intermediate Labour Market* (York: Joseph Rowntree Foundation, 1997).

5

present and future perspectives

contents:

Key concepts

This chapter considers issues potentially relevant to the future of the sector. It covers:

- the more traditional views about what the role of social economy should be;
- some new developments in and about the sector which could change those views;
- other perspectives of the third sector which could also challenge some conventional views about it;
- the main internal and external factors that might influence the future of the third sector;
- a critical analysis of some of the assumptions underpinning the conventional wisdom in this area;
- the need to see the sector not as self-contained but as part of a more flexible set of economic relationships and dependencies.

Learning objectives

By the end of this chapter the reader should:

- understand the key traditional views on the role of the third sector and/or the social economy;
- appreciate the nature of some of the new developments in and about the sector;
- appreciate some of the other perspectives which might be relevant;
- appreciate some of the internal and external factors that might influence the future of the sector;
- understand why it might be appropriate to reassess some of the assumptions underlying conventional wisdom about the sector;
- understand the dynamic and interdependent nature of the sector.

Introduction

Chapter 2 looks at the evolution to date of three economic sectors, including the third sector encompassing the social economy. Chapter 3 then describes the current position of the social economy as a focus of attention for many people and Chapter 4 explores the concept of the social economy further by examining various definitions of it. After thus looking at the past and present of the sector, this chapter considers its future.

Predicting the future may be an art, but it is not a science. When attempts are made to try to apply a scientific approach to predictions, it is generally through attempts, in a supposedly scientific way, to extrapolate from present movement by a process of identifying the current trend and estimating what should happen should it continue. However, experience shows that reality rarely follows such extrapolations for long and that, rather than an inevitable progression, sooner or later there will be discontinuity and turbulence. In the case of the social economy, this approach is further complicated because there is more than one school of thought about what the present trend is.

Therefore, this chapter does not try to predict the future of the social economy and the third sector. Instead, it presents some of the factors likely to be relevant to the future of the sector and to any assessment of it.

Three traditional approaches

It is suggested above that a factor hindering extrapolation-based predictions about the future of the social economy is a lack of agreement on what is the present trend for the sector – and this may be exacerbated by the conflicting and/or provocative views advanced, on occasion, by particular people and/or organisations who appear, in effect, to be vying to establish their claim to provide the definitive perspective on a particular aspect or part of this sector. However, the summary of the arguments presented in Chapter 3, for instance, suggests that there are three broad choices, about the nature of the sector and therefore what its direction might be:

- An economic/entrepreneurship approach, which sees social economy organisations as 'businesses' that can function where the private sector will not operate, or needs 'pump-priming' measures before operations are likely to be sufficiently profitable.
- A socio-economic policy approach, which sees the sector as a low-cost provider patching up the inadequacies of the welfare state but confining itself to the parts that government cannot (or will not) reach.
- A political/ideological approach which envisages a social economy sector strong enough to lever institutional change and to promote more democratic structures and greater citizen participation in decision-making.

Underlying these choices, it is suggested, are two different traditions and/or political viewpoints. First there is what has been identified as a US/UK or neoliberal approach, which sees capitalism, the market, and private sector solutions as the logical and most efficient way of organising much economic activity. This leads to pressure to deregulate the market, privatise public services, dismantle welfare, and drive down public spending. In this situation, the third sector, and especially the social economy, is seen by some as a vehicle to challenge and/or replace public sector inefficiency and a potential replacement for much public sector provision because it brings an element of market discipline to its work.

The second approach, sometimes labelled a European view, sees danger in an unrestrained private sector and views the social economy as an alternative to the excesses of unrestrained capitalism and thus a means with which to challenge the post-1980s' lauding of liberal market forces as the only practical option. For instance, Borzaga and Tortia[1] suggest that, in explanations of the emergence of social economy forms of enterprise in market conditions, the approach mainly linked to Hansmann stands out. His theory, they suggest, explains the birth and development of a significant number of co-operatives and non-profit organisations when there are market failures and suggests that their role is supposed to lessen when markets become more competitive and failures become less frequent. That approach tends to present the social economy as an alternative, or at least as a supplement, to the private sector. As Lloyd quotes, 'Is the social economy predominantly seen as the basis for a radical grand narrative or a more limited "toolkit" to fix the social problems that arise out of the return to increasingly unfettered market forces?'[2] But, as Lloyd also acknowledges, the social economy has been seen as a 'service gap filler' and as a tool in providing policy solutions (that) came from attempts to address three long-standing but always changing problems:

- a rising demand for social, personal and community services;
- a need to find ways to meet these demands while constraining levels of direct state expenditure and rates of taxation; and
- the persistence of spatially localised pockets of deprivation where these service gaps are extreme regardless of the economic cycle.[3]

However, it can be argued that both of the approaches just described essentially see the economy as having two main sectors in which the scope for a third sector is either as a haven for dissenters or in alliance with, or as replacement for, one of the main sectors – rather like the role of a third party in a two-party political system. Thus the third sector and particularly the social economy are seen as having the potential to provide an alternative to at least parts of either the public or the private sector. The social economy is seen by some as more market driven than the public sector and thus as better able to deliver a range of public services, or is seen by others as more equitable than the private sector and thus as a preferable vehicle for much economic activity.

It can of course be pointed out that the third sector is not going to take over from the public or the private sector. All three sectors have always been there, and have coexisted, since separate economic sectors first became distinguishable. With the exception of tribal and communist economies, human society generally seems to have had mixed economies which incorporate all three sectors. Thus, there is a third approach which suggests that three sectors are needed if society is to function well and that the economy of such a society is like a three-legged stool which cannot work properly if one of its legs is missing. This scenario, it is suggested, is consistent with the third choice above in which the social economy sector is envisaged to be strong enough to lever change on its own. This view of the importance of having all three sectors is also supported by Taylor's suggestion that there are three main sources of power (see Illustration 5.1), which indicates that each of the sectors has different strengths to contribute.

Illustration 5.1 Why people do things – and the sources of power that indicates

There are three main reasons why we do things:

- Because we do what we're told to do.
- Because we do what everyone else is doing (ie it's the socially acceptable thing to do*).
- Because we do what we want to do.

*We systematically overestimate the degree to which we think that what we do is the result of personal choice.

This suggests that there are three sources of influence on what people do: hierarchical power, social solidarity and individual aspiration. Effective organisations and solutions combine all three sources of power but they also have to manage the tensions between them. When organisations have only one source of power they can be very dangerous, because that power is then unconstrained. No sector of the economy has a monopoly of any of the sources of power, but also no sector is typically good at all of them:

- The public sector is typically good at hierarchical power and not bad at social solidarity – but it is very bad at facilitating individual aspiration.
- The private sector is typically also good at hierarchical power and can be quite good facilitating individual aspiration – but it is weak on social solidarity.
- The social economy is not very good at hierarchical power – but it can do social solidarity and even facilitate individual aspiration.

Thus, it is in society's interest that organisations in any sector should seek to use more than one source of power. Also society as a whole is likely to benefit from having all three sectors because that is the best way of having all three sources of power.

Source: based on M. Taylor, 'The power to act: A new angle on our toughest problems', RSA Chief Executive's Annual Lecture (London, 12 September 2012) and presentation to Bryson Charitable Group Annual Conference (Belfast, 26 September 2012)

These three choices or approaches present organisations in the third sector (and especially the social economy) with both ethical and market challenges. Do they risk co-option by participating in the forecast changes, for instance replacing the state in the delivery of social care, or do they resist and create alternatives to the market economy by strengthening community ownership of assets and resources? Powell[4] is in no doubt about the importance of these tensions, the choices open to NGOs, and the whole purpose of civic society in Western states:

> Civil society offers a new social policy agenda because it opens up the state to citizen participation. It has the potential to democratise the welfare state so that it becomes more responsive to the needs of the citizen, in an era that requires social policy to address both economic equality and cultural difference. The debate about civil society is not simply about the defence of the Western state. It is about the creation of a new model of governance and participation for the welfare state.

The pressures on the social economy are thus complex and there is clear interdependency between the future of the private, public, and social economies. The performance of one is intimately bound up in the others, and it is not possible to understand restructuring in the social sector without approaching globalisation, privatisation, and the future of welfare.

Some new developments

The three choices or approaches outlined above stem from relatively well-established views and issues but there are also new developments which could change traditional/current perspectives on the social economy. Those summarised here are also indicated in other chapters but this selection indicates the range of their possible implications.

Hybrids – breaking down traditional boundaries

Alter suggests that the social enterprise can be seen as a new institutional animal – part business and part social – which combines a mix of social values and goals with commercial business practices and breaks down traditional boundaries between the non-profit and private sectors.[5] Thus, she indicates, there is a spectrum of hybrid organisations from the traditional non-profit, through non-profit with income-generating activities, then social enterprise, socially responsible business, and corporation practising social responsibility to the traditional for-profit.

Others, however, indicate that social enterprises are fully part of the third sector but that there are hybrids between it and the other sectors. Chapter 2 includes a summary of some of the work by Billis on hybrids: 'organisations which possess "significant" characteristics of more than one sector (public, private, and third)'.[6] Table 2.3, for instance, identifies examples of nine different types of hybrid arising from different combinations of sector characteristics. After examining various aspects of hybridity and whether it is 'eroding the unique qualities of the different sectors',[7] Billis suggests that the broad processes of change reveal a number of possibilities for the sector including erosion, emigration, infiltration, revitalisation, conception, and termination (of some organisations). He concludes by suggesting that the debate about the future of the third sector needs to be set within 'a broader and more complex context of a number of processes of change'.[8]

Conscious capitalism

Billis's hybrid organisations display the characteristics of more than one sector, and the composite theory presented by Ridley-Duff and Bull, and illustrated in Figure 3.2, suggests that there are areas where the sectors overlap and thus where organisations can actually belong in more than one sector. However, both these suggestions refer to organisations which are acknowledged in some way to be the result of sector mixtures. In contrast, conscious capitalism appears to have originated in one sector, the private sector, but nevertheless might be considered to be part of a paradigm change which increasingly recognizes that businesses are not divided into private sector businesses whose primary pursuit is profit and third sector businesses with social, environmental, and/or ethical aims. Conscious capitalism, it has been suggested, comes from 'a realization that business is a form of human social activity which is likely to be more sustainable in the longer term if it pursues both profit and wider benefits and seeks to satisfy all its stakeholders including, but not limited to, its financial backers'[9] and which appeals to multiple sources of influence (see Case 5.1). Such a paradigm has echoes in Kay's comment that often 'the most profitable businesses are not the most profit oriented'.[10] 'Recognizing that would change a lot of perceptions, such as the view sometimes held that all entrepreneurs are only interested in building their own wealth at the expense of others'[11] (also, see Illustration 5.2).

Illustration 5.2 Facebook's social mission

There was considerable interest in the initial public offering of Facebook shares in 2012. For this the stock was valued at $38 a share, pricing the company at $104 billion and highlighting its position as one of the stellar ICT company performers, although that share price was not then sustained.

Yet it is reported that one of the documents in Facebook's IPO prospectus which accompanied the offering was a letter from Mark Zuckerberg, Facebook's founder, in which he indicated that Facebook was not originally created to be a company but to accomplish the social mission of helping people connect to people. Further the letter suggested that he still cared more for Facebook's social mission than its business and that its business side existed primarily to support its product development.

Thus it would seem that, even at what some might see as the apex of private sector entrepreneurship, social aims can still predominate.

Source: www.businessinsider.com/facebook-stock-letter-shareholders   (accessed   21 January 2012)

Social innovation

According to Murray et al. in 2010, social innovation, which they define as 'new ideas (products, services and models) that simultaneously meet social needs and create social relationships or collaborations', moved to centre stage in the first decade of this century.[12] Nicholls and Murdock quote the OECD as indicating that:

> Social innovation is distinct from economic innovation because it is not about introducing new types of production or exploiting new markets in itself but is about satisfying new needs not provided by the market (even if markets intervene later) or creating new, more satisfactory ways of insertion in terms of giving people a place and a role in production.[13]

Nicholls and Murdock suggest that social innovation can be seen as a 'sixth wave' of macro-level change, after the other five waves of modern macro innovation (shown in Table 5.1). They suggest that it has the potential to be as disruptive and influential as the technological-economic waves that went before. However, they propose that 'social innovation often goes further and attempts to disrupt and reconfigure systems themselves via changes to their internal institutional logics, norms and traditions'.[14]

Table 5.1 The five waves of modern macro innovation

The Industrial Revolution (1771–1829)
The Age of Steam and Railways (1829–1875)
The Age of Steel, Electricity, and Heavy Engineering (1875–1909)
The Age of Oil, the Automobile, and Mass Production (1909–1971)
The Age of Information and Telecommunications (1971–)

Source: A. Nicholls and A. Murdock, 'The Nature of Social Innovation', in A. Nicholls and A. Murdock (Eds), *Social Innovation: Blurring Boundaries to Reconfigure Markets* (Basingstoke: Palgrave Macmillan, 2012) p.1

Kerlin highlights the importance of context for social innovation, and for social enterprise, by contrasting developments in the different contexts of 'village'-level societies associated with African and South-East Asian countries, 'post-authoritarian' countries such as those of Eastern Europe and Latin America, the 'welfare states' of Western Europe, and the 'laissez-faire' approach typified by the United States.[15] Thus, she indicates that different forms and activities of social enterprise emerge in response to different environmental factors.

However, it has been suggested, 'social innovation is never neutral but always politically and socially constructed'.[16] Nicholls and Murdock identify three levels of social innovation: incremental, which addresses identified market failures and focuses on products and services; institutional, which tries to reconfigure existing market structures and patterns to create new social value; and disruptive. Disruptive social innovation, they suggest:

> aims squarely at systems change from the start and is the realm of social movements and self-consciously 'political' actors, groups and networks aiming to change power relations, alter social hierarchies and reframe issues to the benefit of otherwise disenfranchised groups.[17]

Attempts to convert parts of the public sector to social enterprise

As well as government policies designed to advance and support the social economy and the third sector (see Chapter 9), there have also been examples of initiatives which specifically attempt to move some public sector provision into the social economy. This has taken more than one form:

- Some public sector work has, in effect, been subcontracted to the social economy – by a process of seeking tenders to do the work in question. However, at least in the UK, there have also been complaints from those in the sector that conditions attached to such tenders often disadvantage social enterprises, for instance by not recognising social value and by requiring evidence of significant reserves or of considerable prior experience of large contracts.
- Some efforts have been made to spin out social economy organisations from the public sector. For instance in 2012, with support from the UK government's Mutuals Support Programme, the Cleveland Fire Brigade announced that it planned to become a mutual and had launched a community interest company to sell services to local businesses to subsidise its public work[18] – see also the case of primary care trusts in Illustration 5.3.
- In some cases, stipulations are made that a new or replacement service must be delivered by social enterprises. An example of this is given in a report that regulations had been laid before parliament requiring new Healthwatch organisations, designed to champion the rights of health service users, to be social enterprises.[19]

Illustration 5.3 The public sector by another name?

In 2007, some charity leaders were reported to be alarmed that public bodies were setting up social enterprises to bid for contracts against smaller, local voluntary organisations.

The context of this was that the UK government had stated that it wished to see the third sector win more contracts to deliver public services and that, within the UK, the Department of Health has given a number of public sector organisations 'pathfinder' status, which provided funding to set up social enterprises to 'lead the way in delivering innovative community services in health and social care'. It appeared that the UK government was content to see public bodies spin off their service-providing arms and become established in the third sector as social enterprises, some as community interest companies (CICs). However, others had reservations about 'a new breed of voluntary sector behemoths with their roots in the health sector' and 'being dominated by quasi-governmental, monolithic bodies that are rife within a public sector culture'.

As reported also in Chapter 9, the 'Right to Request Programme' forms part of the Department of Health's wider programme 'Transforming Community Services'. The Right to Request Programme supports primary care trust (PCT) staff to join together and leave the NHS, 'spinning out' to form social enterprises. These become independent bodies, delivering services previously delivered in-house, under contract to the PCT. However, the National Audit Office has warned that 'there are many risks to be managed if the Department is to get value for money from the £900 million contracts awarded to social enterprises. The Department needs to reassess its approach, when contracting with social enterprises, of not requiring efficiencies over and above what would have been achieved if the services had remained within the Department.'

While the Department of Health argues that PCTs should divest themselves of their provider arms to ensure that commissioning and service provision are clearly divided (to demonstrate the fairness and transparency of the commissioning process), others have contended that such state-created new organisations are 'no substitute for the genuine engagement with the local community, choice, innovation and wider wellbeing that the third sector can deliver'.

Sources: Based on http://www.thirdsector.co.uk/news (accessed 14 August 2007) and www.nao.org.uk/report/establishing-social-enterprises-under-the-right-to-request-programme-2/ (accessed 30 March 2013)

Conclusion

These issues, undoubtedly, will be clearer looking back from a future perspective than from a present appreciation, which, inevitably, will be somewhat limited in its viewpoint, biased, and ignorant of a future of currently unforeseen developments.

Other perspectives

As well as the new developments, outlined above, which might have an impact on the future of the sector, there are other perspectives which challenge conventional views on where the sector is or where it might be heading. The following are some of them.

The perspective of the people behind a venture

The sector divisions described in the earlier chapters are based on considering the organisations concerned and the purpose of the activity in which they engage. Yet those organisations and their activities are merely the concrete manifestations of the aspirations of the people responsible for starting and running them. It is rather like the way that the mushrooms seen and picked are only the above-ground fruiting parts of the underground mycelia which actually constitute fungi.

Observers have pointed out that, in small business research, the emphasis has often been on the enterprise or business created, taking it as the primary unit of analysis. This is not least because it is relatively easy to research businesses as they have a legal existence, and data on their activities – including their start-up, operation, and, eventually, closure – can be obtained from official records and are the subject of required reports. Nevertheless, it has been shown that it can be much more revealing to look instead at the entrepreneur (or entrepreneurs) behind a business. For instance, traditional business-based data will not reveal habitual entrepreneurship, in which one entrepreneur starts several businesses either serially or in parallel, and neither will that reflect an owner's motivations, yet both these factors can be crucial to an understanding of what happens in a business. [20] Similarly, much of the analysis referred to in this book focuses on third sector organisations and organisational activity rather than on the people who create and operate those organisations.

If economics is concerned with how people provide for their wants, then it has to be realised that different people have different wants and that realising them can result in very different activities. Maslow's hierarchy of needs suggests that if people are very hungry, then their main want will be to satisfy that hunger. Once lower-order needs such as hunger and shelter are satisfied, higher-order needs come into play. At the top of Maslow's hierarchy is self-actualisation, and here especially different people want to do very different things. Some try to express themselves in art, some in conspicuous consumption, some in learning and discovery, and some through helping others. Many of these wants are not primarily about money and are registered in economic accounts only when money is used as a vehicle through which some or all of the wants might be realised.

People therefore start economic activities, or take up employment, for reasons which may be concerned more with self-actualisation than with personal financial enrichment. The forms those activities take, or the sort of jobs people seek, are related to, and evolve from, those reasons. People do not start activities to be in a particular economic sector; they start activities to meet the needs they perceive, whether that is a need for personal wealth, for the satisfaction of achieving something new, for helping other people, or for a mixture of these. It is not necessarily the case that people work in the private sector if they want to make money, in the public sector if they want to exercise power, or in the third sector if they want to help others. Where the activity they chose fits into an economic system is something others decide later and is based on arbitrary constructs which do not necessarily reflect the value of the relevant activity to the people concerned. Similarly, the choice of which legal form a particular organisation should take is limited by the forms known to be available, none of which may be ideally suited to the founder's purpose.

As noted above, people's objectives are varied, and many people have more than one objective, but realising them involves work. Therefore, different people will work in different ways, and sometimes in more than one way in order to achieve different objectives. A politician seeking power may work as an elected representative and find himself or herself in a parliament, which is a public sector organisation. A committed lay member of a church may work for a private sector business during the day to earn enough for the material wants of his or her family, but in the evenings or at weekends may get more satisfaction working on a voluntary basis for the church, which is a third sector organisation. A billionaire, having made a lot of money by starting and growing a successful private sector business, may then decide to put most of that money into a third sector foundation and concentrate on running that to support other worthy causes. It is also clear that the desire of people to do something, and the realisation of that desire through working in a variety of different ways, came long before the resultant activity was classified into different economic sectors. Those sector boundaries, and any sub-sector boundaries, do not therefore constrain what people want to do, and neither do the sectors necessarily reflect the ways in which people want to work.

Although the fruiting bodies of a fungus are the visible things sometimes called mushrooms, they are by no means the whole of the fungus. Similarly, the organisations actually created are not the totality of the aspirations of their founders. Instead, the legally constituted bodies, the existence and activities of which can be reported and recorded, are the result of the interaction of a number of factors including:

- the visions, aspirations, ideas, and ambitions of their founders;
- the selection by those founders of methods of operating to realise their purposes;
- the choice by those founders, from the options perceived to be available, of which legal form to use to give their organisations a legal existence.

However, just as the mushroom is the visible part of the fungus and is thus the part which is used to identify and classify it, it is the registered legal existence of organisations which is relatively easy to measure and record, and so organisational classifications are often based on that. Also, just as an underground fungus will often produce more than one above-ground mushroom, so too a founder's purpose may be realised in more than one business. This is recognised in the concept of the habitual entrepreneur. So a fuller picture may be gained not from looking at the legal entity but from considering all the relevant factors behind it, as suggested in Figure 5.1. This approach also suggests that, if the label 'social entrepreneur' is applied to someone who starts and/or develops a social economy business, that label is based on the nature of business that is realised and not on the entrepreneur's motivations. An entrepreneur with the same or very similar motivations might instead, or in addition, start a business which is judged to be in the private sector, and in that case he or she would not be described as a social entrepreneur.

The foundation of some social enterprises may be encouraged, not because of the enterprise of a founder, but because social enterprise solutions seem to be prescribed by a political agenda. As a result, these ventures may lack the enterprising attributes and resources, such as personal drive and opportunity identification, which are necessary for the success of the enterprise and lack the community links which are necessary for the social side. Amin et al. looked at the social economies in Glasgow and Middlesbrough, where local authorities were to varying extents involved in trying to run parts of the

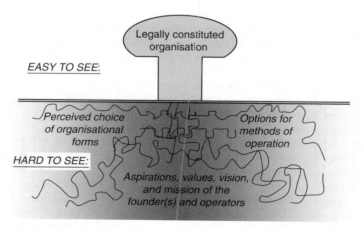

Figure 5.1 What is behind the activity?

social economy, and concluded that social enterprise solutions can be so prescribed by the agenda of the local authorities that they are simply not possible or relevant in some places. They point out that 'given the UK government's insistence on the greater use of self-help regeneration strategies for the poorest communities, including the greater development of social economy organisations, it may be advocating a solution that relies on the existence of those features of local political, economic, and social life that . . . the most excluded people and places most significantly lack'. [21] Thus, the enterprises resulting from such strategies may be labelled social enterprises but they differ from other social enterprises in that they lack the personal drive of a social entrepreneur. In such cases, the label social enterprise does not make this critical distinction.

A perspective outside mainstream economics

In his book *Trust*, Fukuyama suggests that, 'although economic activity is inextricably linked with social and political life, there is a mistaken tendency, encouraged by contemporary economic discourse, to regard the economy as a facet of life with its own laws, separate from the rest of society'. [22] If economic activity is considered from a perspective informed by classical economics, it might be seen as a separate area of human activity subject to its own particular modes and rationales of behaviour. The laws of economics are universal, it is suggested, and the motivation behind them is the pursuit of 'utility'. The basic definition of that utility has been linked to the pursuit of pleasure, or the avoidance of pain, but utility-maximising behaviour is essentially selfish and is often related to money. The label 'capitalism' for the dominant economic system further encourages us to see the provision of capital for financial return as a fundamental driver of the system, and often the key elements in an economic analysis are the firm and the profit it makes.

From that perspective, the social economy and/or the third sector might appear to be in a peripheral area, not in the mainstream and not essential to an economic system. As Fukuyama has commented, 'the very change in the name of the discipline from "political economy" to "economics" between the eighteenth and late nineteenth centuries reflects the narrowing of the model of human behaviour at its core'. [23] But economic activity can also be viewed as an aspect of a wider pattern of human interactions. As Fukuyama has also pointed out, 'Adam Smith well understood (that) economic life is deeply embedded in social life' [24] and it is therefore relevant to look at economic activity from a social perspective not as separate from other activity but as an integral part of human interaction. Looked at in that way, the third sector is no less central than other aspects of an economy. After all, those areas of activity referred to as the social economy and the third sector have existed for as long as distinguishable public and private sector activity.

If economics is solely, or at least mainly, about the financial return for effort, then organisations in the third sector, and the social economy within it, are deviant, because they do not necessarily seek to maximise their financial return. If, however, economics is about human effort for utility, and with a much wider interpretation of utility than is sometimes applied, then the social economy and the rest of the third sector are equally valid forms of economic effort. Economics does not just have to be about the pursuit of financial return. An understanding of economics has been used, for instance, to inform our understanding of relationships between other forms of life which do not use money. The application of economic approaches to ecological studies are to be found, for example, in works such as *Economics in Nature – Social Dilemmas, Mate Choices and Biological Markets*, [25] yet we do not think of those relationships which appear to follow economic laws as separate from other areas of biological activity. For Karl Popper, these complexities can be best understood in the differences between clocks and clouds (Illustration 5.4). The problem with economic analysis is that it attempts to reduce relations to a set of rational rules and procedures but the social economy is embedded in a more complex set of forces, relationships, and outcomes. The cloud analogy more satisfactorily captures the conceptual realties of the economy, the logics of the different sectors, and how they depend on one another.

Illustration 5.4 Clouds not clocks – looking at links, not components

It was Galbraith who coined the phrase 'conventional wisdom' and according to him:

> To a very large extent, of course, we associate truth with convenience – with what most closely accords with self-interest and personal well-being or promises best to avoid awkward effort or unwelcome dislocation of life. We also find highly acceptable what contributes most to self-esteem . . . But perhaps most important of all, people approve most of what they best understand . . . Economic and social behavior are complex, and to comprehend their character is mentally tiring. Therefore we adhere, as though to a raft, to those ideas which represent our understanding.[26]

One feature of our conventional economic wisdom seems to be the assumption that the behaviour of economies can be understood by examining their component sectors: in the way that clocks can be understood by examining their separate parts to see how they work. But there are many things, such as clouds, which cannot be understood in this way, because, although real, they are amorphous and constantly changing. This analogy was suggested by the Austro-British philosopher Sir Karl Popper. 'My clouds', he said, 'are intended to represent physical systems which, like gases, are highly irregular, disorderly, and more or less unpredictable', whereas clocks are 'intended to represent physical systems which are regular, orderly, and highly predictable in their behaviour'.[27]

Newton's laws appeared successfully to apply a clock-like approach to understanding and predicting the motions of the planets. Since then, Popper suggested, it has become a fundamental belief of Western science that all clouds are really clocks because, if examined closely enough, all things can be found to be comprised ultimately of predictable components such as atoms and even subatomic particles. But, said Popper, this is not the case: Einstein showed that there were inaccuracies even in Newton's laws, and Heisenberg, with his uncertainty principle, reintroduced indeterminism. Thus, instead of thinking that all clouds are basically clocks, we should instead recognise that, to at least some extent, all clocks are essentially clouds.

Economies are about people, as behavioural economics recognises, and, in talking about the behaviour of people, Earls makes a relevant distinction between the complex and the complicated:

> Here is an important lesson: mass behaviour is inherently complex because it is based on the interaction of individual agents. But we try to understand it as if it were complicated (i.e. reducible to individual component parts). This is why we find it difficult to understand mass behaviour.[28]

In this sense, clocks are complicated, but not complex, because they are reducible to individual components, Has this clock-like search for predictable components influenced our economic thinking? In looking at economies have we been tempted to think of the public, private, and third sectors as component sectors which each need to be understood separately, and similarly the different organisations within them? Thus we have tried to look for, to identify, to define, and to seek predictability in the component parts instead of considering how the system works as a whole. If, instead, we were to recognise that economies are complex and might therefore be clouds, then we might recognise that to understand their behaviour we need to look at the links between the apparently separate independent components that lead them to act together in concert, with each being influenced to a considerable extent by the behaviour of the others.

The perspective of civil society and big society – a citizen sector?

> The *Civil Society Almanac* is an indispensable guide to the sector. It gives an essential overview of where civil society organisations get their money from, how they spend it and how the sector is changing.
>
> This ground breaking research looks at higher education, museums, housing associations, co-operatives, trades unions, political parties and more. [29]
>
> National Council for Voluntary Action 'giving voice and support to civil society'

There are many different definitions of civil society, or civic society, as it is sometimes called. One of these is provided by the Centre for Civil Society at the London School of Economics, which, it says, captures the multifaceted nature of the concept:

> Civil society refers to the arena of uncoerced collective action around shared interests, purposes and values. In theory, its institutional forms are distinct from those of the state, family and market, though in practice, the boundaries between state, civil society, family and market are often complex, blurred and negotiated. Civil society commonly embraces a diversity of spaces, actors and institutional forms, varying in their degree of formality, autonomy and power. Civil societies are often populated by organisations such as registered charities, development non-governmental organisations, community groups, women's organisations, faith-based organisations, professional associations, trades unions, self-help groups, social movements, business associations, coalitions and advocacy groups. [30]

While the original formulation of the concept of 'civil society' might apparently be traced to the nineteenth century, [31] it came to prominence in the late 1980s and 1990s when it became seen as a way of controlling the state. It was civil society, it has been suggested, that mobilised against the state in Eastern and Central Europe and sparked the Velvet Revolution [32] and it was pressure from civil society that led to the end of apartheid in South Africa. Civil society therefore had to be autonomous of the state and, in the eyes of some, even critical of it.

However, like so many issues in this area, the concept of civil society is not only narrowly defined but also is variously contested. One commentator, for instance, has identified three different uses of the term:

- as a *description* of varieties of association,
- as a *value* advocating the advantages of co-operation,
- as a *democratic ecosystem* – a public sphere in which engagement with the whole future and shape of society takes place (or could take place). [33]

The concept of civil society therefore can be very wide and not easily summarised in just a few paragraphs. Nevertheless, what are, or might be, its links with the third sector? That depends, to some extent, on which use of the term 'civil society' is being considered. If civic society is used to describe varieties of association, then those varieties of association often listed as being in civil society are also listed as being in the third sector. Civil society has been described, for instance, as 'a complex welter of intermediate institutions, including businesses, voluntary associations, educational institutions, clubs, unions, media, charities and churches (which) builds in turn, on the family, the primary instrument by which people are socialised into their culture and given the skills that allow them to live in broader society and through which the values and knowledge of that society are transmitted across the generations'[34]: a list of components very like lists of third sector components.

If, though, the term 'civil society' is used as 'a value advocating the advantages of co-operation', then that might be beyond what is indicated by the third sector, but not possibly beyond the objectives of some advocates of the social economy. As indicated previously, some advocates of the third sector, and particularly of the social economy, look to it to offer a challenge to liberal market forces. So both civil society and the social economy can be associated with advocacy.

If the term 'civil society' is used to indicate a 'democratic ecosystem', then that ecosystem might be said to provide a channel for, and/or a source of, social capital. Social capital has been described as 'the ability of people to work together for common purposes in groups and organisations',[35] and working together for common purposes in groups and organisations is what civil society does. As links are sometimes drawn between social capital and the social economy, as described in Chapter 8, this provides another connection between civil society and the third sector.

Thus, whichever of the suggested uses of the term 'civil society' is considered, links can be found between it and the third sector, and, indeed, the terms are sometimes used interchangeably. However, taken overall, the term 'civil society' might be considered to differ from the third sector, not in the range of organisations it encompasses, but in the wider social and political dimension which for many is the reason for considering it. Therefore, while some people do appear to be looking for a political impact from the third sector, and from the social economy within it, that is not generally highlighted as its main feature. Instead, the concept of the third sector, as the third sector of the economy, focuses on its economic impact. This suggests not that what are labelled 'the civil society' and 'the third sector' are different things, but that those labels emphasise different aspects of what is being considered. The third sector and civic society are clearly linked and might thus be considered to refer to two different facets of the same components of organised human society.

A further dimension to this might be seen in the concept of the Big Society, which is described in Case 3.1. This was introduced as a key idea in the UK Conservative Party's 2010 election manifesto and it could be said to follow the previous Labour government's promotion of a 'third way' between the state and corporate sectors. Thus there has been an emerging policy agenda for decentralisation which would provide new opportunities for the transfer of traditional welfare state functions from the public sector.

Bjerke and Karlsson have explored the entrepreneurial activity in society which is not limited only to private profit. This activity, they suggest, exists 'to a large extent in the business sector but above all in the public sector and to an increasing extent in the third sector, what we refer to as the citizen sector'. They further elaborate that:

> This citizen sector was strong during the nineteenth century, but expansion during twentieth century placed it in the backseat. During the latest 30 years the trend has changed, however, and this has led to a revival of the citizen sector (sometimes denoted as *the social economy*) for three reasons: to a large extent the user has also become his or her own producer; there are increased social imperatives and the advent of the green revolution.[36]

They suggest that there are three kinds of entrepreneurs in a society: entrepreneurs in the public sector, business entrepreneurs, and citizen entrepreneurs; and there are two kinds of citizen entrepreneurs: social entrepreneurs (who aim to spread welfare to people) and social innovators (who devote themselves to building citizenry). However, they do not see social entrepreneurship as being limited only to the citizen sector. Instead, there are also social entrepreneurs in the public sector and some in the private sector, and social entrepreneurship occurs in the area where all three sectors overlap.

Thus, they fully acknowledge that there is a third sector, but, instead of it being identified primarily as consisting of those organisations not in the other two sectors, they see it as having a focus on the increasing efforts of active citizenship (see Illustration 5.5). That suggests that this is a dynamic which could have a significant influence on the future of the sector.

Illustration 5.5 Examples of changing circumstances

Bjerke and Karlsson have identified three key recent trends which are having an impact of the role of the citizenry sector:

- The user has become his/her own producer and the support economy has taken over from the commodity economy. (For instance personalising purchased goods eg by adding apps to mobile phones.)
- There is an increased pressure on the state to provide social services (to which two responses are attempts to introduce private sector production management techniques to increase efficiency or attempts to involve citizens are partners in provision).
- The increasing impact of the green revolution (which is increasingly hard to avoid).

Source: Based on B. Bjerke and M. Karlsson, *Social Entrepreneurship: To Act as If and Make a Difference* (Cheltenham: Edward Elgar, 2013)

Possible influences

So far this chapter has largely considered ideas and perspectives about, or possibly relevant to, the future of the third sector and/or the social economy. However, there are also other factors: things happening in, to, and around the sector, which could influence its future.

Internal factors

The first group of factors to be considered are those that are largely internal to the sector. They include the nature of the sector and the organisations in it, the tensions in the sector, the sometimes contentious issue of funding, and the sector's own efforts to advance itself.

The nature of the sector

Like the private sector, the health of the third sector as a whole does not depend on the health of all of its parts. Third sector organisations can suffer from ill health, fail, and cease to exist, but, unless they all fail at the same time, it does not mean that the overall health of the third sector is failing, just as in an ecology the deaths of some component parts and their replacement by new forms of life is a process which is not only natural, but is even essential for the long-term well-being of the system. Even if many current third sector organisations appear to be in good health, it seems safe to predict that soon some of them will cease to operate. However, if other existing organisations prosper and grow while, at the same time, new organisations are continually being founded as people seek vehicles through which to try to address perceived needs, the future of the sector will thus remain healthy.

It is also clear that the third sector is a very heterogeneous sector (as Pearce's diagram in Figure 2.2 indicates) and therefore it is unlikely that all the organisations in it will respond to the same factors. It is also clear that, at its boundaries, there are no big gulfs and/or sudden changes between it and the other economic sectors. Instead, there is a progression with overlaps and similarities, and, for instance, while some organisations in the third sector are very different from many private sector businesses, there are also enterprises, especially in that part of the third sector often referred to as the social economy, which have a lot in common with many organisations in the private sector. Therefore, trying to consider the future of the third sector in isolation is unlikely to be helpful. The third sector will be affected by many of the same issues as the private sector, and that applies particularly to the social economy which is often the part of the third sector uppermost in people's minds.

Tensions in the sector

There are clearly tensions in the third sector. As well as tensions between it and other sectors, for instance, when some private sector organisations see it as unfair competition and some public sector organisations see it as threat, there are also tensions between different objectives within third sector organisations. On the one hand, third sector organisations are not in the private sector because they do not exist principally to make money, but they do have to acquire money in order to survive. This tension may be most obvious in social enterprises which need to balance the generation of sufficient income to secure financial sustainability with the attainment of the enterprises' social (or other non-financial) goals, and it seems reasonable to suggest that this will continue to be an issue. Social enterprises have often reported tensions when pursuing social and economic goals simultaneously, and some people still appear to see a social enterprise as a potentially unstable mix of an organisation with a social purpose and a business with a social mission, with current trends, such as the emphasis on sustainability, pushing it in the business direction. [37] This social–economic tension can either be resented as a force which has the potential to weaken a social enterprise and to tear it apart or be accepted as a natural part of third sector existence which can serve instead to strengthen an organisation and focus its efforts.

Indeed, both social enterprises and private sector businesses are enterprises, and the 'mushroom' theory presented above suggests that all enterprises have similar origins in that they are formed by their founders to achieve something. Enterprises may differ in their goals but both third and private sector enterprises can have multiple goals, and both have to survive financially if they are to achieve them. In many fundamentals, third sector enterprises, and especially social enterprises, are no different from private (or public) sector enterprises:

> My opinion is that any voluntary sector organisation *must* operate along business lines. The only difference between a social enterprise and normal enterprise is simply that there are no shareholders that receive a dividend, but there are 'shareholders' in terms of the members and the community at large who may benefit from the initiatives that are put together. [38]

Among other characteristics shared with private sector enterprises are the issues involved in employing people, the need to satisfy the requirements of external stakeholders, the requirements of commercial and company law, and the need for leadership. Even size can often be a common characteristic as in both the private and the third sectors many enterprises are small, and, as such, the latter are not very different from other small businesses. Social enterprises may be a newly recognised sector but the difference between them and other small businesses is often no greater than that between other different sectors within the small business ambit.

Funding issues

Funding issues will continue to be a problem for many third sector organisations. Except for those organisations established with a sufficiently large endowment to provide a continuing income, there will always be a necessity to generate sufficient income to cover operating costs. Sometimes it seems that the people behind third sector organisations feel that this is in some way unfair and that, because they are doing useful work, they should be provided with a continuing supply of resources. In particular, some grant schemes have been criticised for only offering relatively short-term funding, thus leaving the recipients of the grants in the lurch when the term of the grant funding comes to an end without a guarantee of any further funding.

One group of organisations which are particularly sensitive to withdrawals of grant funding is made up of those social economy organisations which were created not so much through market forces and the ideas of particular social entrepreneurs, but through government encouragement and the availability of government grants and subsidies. They might call themselves social enterprises but it is said they are probably best labelled 'quasi-public' organisations and have a different logic underpinning them.[39] They may feel that there is a strong case for state funding for their continuation but they may find that they are disappointed.

Indeed, many private sector businesses have an even more hand-to-mouth existence and also have no source of guaranteed income beyond their current orders. They usually realise that they need continually to sell their output in order to renew their sources of income. Therefore, unless government or other external support for the sector includes guaranteed sources of medium- or long-term funding, it is clear that third sector enterprises also may have to accept that selling must be a continuous process at the heart of business, rather than just an occasional one-off separate chore. They may try to 'sell' their benefits to philanthropists, they may try to support their work by trading, they may try joint venturing, or they may try a combination. But if they do not thus help themselves, they may find that no one else will.

The sector's own efforts

The sector's own efforts at advancement, not just as separate organisations but also with a sector-wide voice, could, of course, be influential in its future. If the sector can articulate and communicate some sector-wide (or sub-sector-wide) goals, or if organisations in it can combine to exploit the advantages of scale, that could be influential. Similarly, the sector's own efforts to identify and publicise the benefits it provides could help to bring it more to public attention and gain it more tangible support.

External factors

The above examination of factors internal to the third sector suggests a future of largely more of the same as no significant internal changes are foreseen. If there is to be change, it seems that it will largely be due to external factors such as the expectations people have of the sector; the extent to which they might continue then to promote, fund, guide, and/or otherwise seek to influence it; encroachment on or by the sector; and the wider public perception of the sector.

Expectations of the sector

An important factor relevant to the future of the third sector will be the expectations its various stakeholders have of it, because they will have an impact on the support that might be made available to it. Clearly some of these expectations will be internal, coming from those who are working in the sector, and these can probably be presented in a hierarchy, not unlike Maslow's hierarchy of human needs. There will be people whose immediate requirement is employment which provides them with an income and whose next level of need is probably security of employment. However, there will also be people who, as well as wanting an income, want to feel that they are contributing to society in a useful way. Particularly among the people in the sector who have been responsible for starting or developing third sector organisations, there will be some who are clearly seeking self-actualisation. Those people who just want an income could also seek it in the private or public sector, but for those who are seeking esteem or self-actualisation, the third sector might be the most likely sector in which they think they will find it.

There are stakeholders external to the sector who also have a range of aspirations for the sector. They include people in government responsible for the public sector but who will, in general, support the third sector, or parts of it, because they perceive that it can deliver the sort of benefits which they believe are needed. The benefits they seek may cover a range of issues including the following (see also Chapter 10):

- a way of addressing social exclusion and the tackling of deprivation,
- the creation of more employment,
- assisting with more political aspirations such as
  - providing a vehicle able to deliver more effective or efficient personal and social services than a public sector which is thought to be inefficient and too large;
  - the development of an alternative economic system which avoids the perceived excesses of an unrestrained private sector.

There can be an important tension here between the view of the third sector as a radical alternative to the state or private markets and that of the sector as a more conservative agent of governments in the delivery of a range of services. This is especially so for the social economy, which many think offers an arena which allows the disadvantaged to resist the globalisation of economics and culture by developing their own resources, assets, and skills. This tension has been referred to earlier but how, or whether, it is resolved could influence the sector's future.

In any case it is clear that the sector cannot meet all the different expectations that people sometimes have of it (see Illustration 10.6). Further, the sector is not a single co-ordinated entity, which might therefore easily be steered in a particular direction, but a convenient way of referring to a very heterogeneous set of organisations which have their own disparate aims and objectives and will continue to pursue them.

Promotion of the sector

Unless and until it becomes much clearer that it cannot meet expectations and deliver the benefits sought from it, the third sector, or at least parts of it, can expect to continue to be promoted by the government. There are likely to continue to be a number of government strategies designed to encourage the development of more, bigger, and/or better third sector organisations but it will be important for the sector to recognise that, for governments, such a result will be a means to an end, but not the end itself. Instead, the outcomes sought might include increasing employment as well as countering social exclusion and improving the lot of deprived communities, although that might not always be made clear.

Funding and guidance for the sector

In the public sector, organisations are generally assured of an income stream from public funds for the foreseeable future. In the private sector, they depend upon their own earning efforts. Special sources of funding, together with guidance on how best to access the funding that is available, would obviously be a particular help to the third sector and especially to those organisations which have not learnt how to secure funding on a continuing basis. However, as Chapter 7 indicates, there are already particular sources of funding and advice which have been made available to the third sector in the UK and there is no reason to expect that there will be many more.

It might be argued that helping those third sector organisations which have not learnt how to secure funding with special sources of funding and advice would be unfair on other organisations which have invested in their fund-raising efforts. In any case, it is more logical to tie sources of funding to the outputs and outcomes sought and so to award available funding on the basis of tenders for the efficient supply of those outputs rather than indicating that funding would be available as grants for any suitable organisation that wants it. There is evidence that grants can lead to dependency, and if that leads to fewer grants being available in the future, those organisations which have learnt how to fund-raise in other ways will be better placed to survive.

Encroachment

Another issue for the third sector might be described as encroachment. If it is increasingly appropriated by government (see Chapter 9) to deliver a wide range of programmes and service outcomes, it might lose its edge as a potential radical and radicalising alternative to the power of public sector politics. As indicated in Chapter 6, the public sector can become closely involved in the third sector when it tries to control how the contracts it places are performed or when it is involved in the establishment of third sector organisations to deliver those contracts, and this might lead to third sector organisations adopting public sector cultures and attitudes. At the same time, an increasing emphasis on corporate social responsibility (CSR) in the private sector might seem to be an example of third sector attitudes encroaching on the private sector or it could lead to a bigger private sector influence on some of the social values of the third sector.

Acceptance of the sector

A further area in which the third sector might like help is acceptance. In recent years, it has increasingly been accepted by governments which have tried to promote and support it because of the benefits which they believe it can provide. However, it would also help the sector if it gained wider public recognition and acceptance, both for the value it adds to society generally and for the benefits it can provide for individual participants. It would, for instance, be a considerable help to the sector if it had greater recognition as a source of valid and rewarding careers: careers which might not be among the highest paid in financial terms, but careers which have very considerable potential to make a positive contribution to society. Whether or not the sector develops an appropriate 'brand image' and receives more recognition and acceptance is uncertain at this time.

Will the third sector deliver?

What will be the impact of the third sector? Chapter 10 in particular looks at the benefits that it might deliver and how they might be assessed, but it suggests that there is not much evidence to quantify the extent of the benefits being delivered. An issue for the future of the sector is the extent to which it delivers, or at least appears to deliver, the benefits sought from it. For instance:

- *Employment.* It is clear that it does provide a considerable amount of employment, although how much is often still not clear despite better surveys being conducted of the sector.
- *Addressing exclusion and deprivation.* There does not seem to be clear evidence that third sector organisations have an inherent ability consistently to address issues of exclusion and deprivation.
- *Social capital.* Social capital can be viewed as a cause or an effect in the development of the social economy, but the evidence for the links seems to be more rhetorical than demonstrable. The performance of the sector may be due more to the efforts of individual social entrepreneurs than to the stock of social capital, and organisations in the sector may not, in turn, produce social capital, which, in any case, may not prove to be the antidote to deprivation in the way that has been suggested.
- *Political alternatives.* It is the satisfying of the more quasi-political expectations of the third sector that is probably the hardest to predict. Among the trends that are apparent are that some private sector organisations are becoming more like social enterprises in order to win public sector contracts, which might suggest that the third sector is having a civilising influence on at least part of the private sector. It would also seem that some third sector organisations are becoming, or at least want to appear to be, more like private sector organisations in their efforts to earn money to replace grants as the latter dry up, which might be thought to be a trend in the other direction. In the view, for instance, of the Centre for Employment and Enterprise Development (CEED) based in St Pauls, Bristol, 'CEED does not seek to create an alternative to capitalism – quite the opposite. What CEED seeks to demonstrate is that anyone, regardless of their ethnic background, gender, or postcode can develop successful careers, given the appropriate level of training and support. As such it raises important questions as to how "success" is to be defined and about the factors that underpin success.'[40]
- *The evidence.* A significant problem in analysing these benefits and making predictions from that analysis is often the lack of clear and convincing evidence. That lack of evidence might, itself, be a factor in the sector's future. Thus the sector's own efforts to demonstrate and measure its impact, for instance, through using the new measurement tools which are becoming available, might be important.

Will it still be popular?

The current interest in the third sector has some of the characteristics of a fashion, and fashions often do not last. Government interest in the sector has been triggered by an appreciation of the potential of the sector to deliver particular benefits. That interest is likely to be maintained only if the sector seems to be delivering those benefits more effectively than others and also if government support for the sector seems to increase the amount of benefit thus delivered.

So far there does not appear to be a lot of evidence that either of those requirements is being met, although much of the relevant evaluation work may still be at an early stage.

Many attempts to promote the social economy and social enterprises have come up with very similar support mechanisms to those devised to support small businesses in general, and there is little evidence that those small business promotion strategies have been able to make a clear overall difference. Government support can, however, often be rather like the proverbial oil tanker which takes a long time to turn around once the need for a change in direction is perceived.

If there is evidence that the third sector can deliver what is expected of it, then government interest in it might increase, and government interest also stimulates other areas of interest such as that in business schools and universities. If, on the other hand, third sector organisations prove not to be able to deliver the outcomes sought, or at least if promotional efforts do not produce a proportional increase in those outcomes, then the third sector might find that it eventually ceases to attract government support, and ceases to be promoted in the way that is being done at present. Thus, the current level of interest might increase or wane, but would that make a lot of difference to the sector as a whole, as opposed to just those organisations selected for special assistance?

What might change it?

If the discernible current trends are not likely to lead to significant change in the third sector, what would change it? Historically, it has generally responded to structural changes in society, such as political changes in the nineteenth century and economic developments in the twentieth. But what will be the next such change and what will be its effects? It could be that society will increasingly encourage and welcome voluntary action, and become more dependent on it, and that could have a big effect on the third sector.

However, the third sector is only a part, and an integral part, of the bigger economic picture. What happens in the whole of an economy is likely to affect all its sectors, and what happens in one sector is likely to affect the others. Thus the third sector may not shape its own destiny but will respond to how society organises itself economically and how the private and public sectors develop in response to that. That at least might be the situation in the UK, but the third sector will be influenced by different factors in different countries, because it is in each of those countries. The influence of the society of a country on its third sector and the influences of the sectors of a country's economy on each other are likely to be stronger than the links between the third sectors of different economies.

The context for the future

Part of the context for considering the future is what is happening in, and around, the (other) sectors. The third sector cannot be seen in isolation but also in the context of changes in the other two sectors, and all are being driven by, for example, more powerful and discriminating consumers (see Illustration 5.5). So, what are the typical pressures on organisations in the three sectors?

The public sector. In many countries, the public sector is under pressure to deliver 'value for money' and more 'bang for a buck', to achieve set performance (output) targets, and to achieve efficiency/savings and targets/budget cuts by delivering more for less. This is accompanied, in some quarters, by a (political) distrust of the public sector and its supposed inefficiencies – and therefore a desire/search for alternative provisions. (For instance, the New Public Management (NPM) approach has accountability for performance as a core tenet[41] (an attempt to introduce the pressure of 'market' forces?). Has it changed the sector's relationship with third party organisations which are increasingly seen in the context of options for cheaper delivery? Has this led to a desire to try to control the third sector/social economy?)

The private sector. Many private sector organisations (or at least the larger ones) are generally under pressure to achieve profitability and return on investment. However, the impact of recession has made this harder, and, in some quarters, there has been a reaction against the supposed excesses of the private sector, such as those that led to the banking and other scandals (e.g. Enron) and which have heightened a distrust of the private sector and its supposed ubiquitous greed. Thus, in some quarters, there is desire for an alternative to profit-motivated private business – and is there now a move inside some parts of the sector to show more social responsibility as demonstrated by a stronger emphasis on Corporate Social Responsibility (CSR)?

The third sector. In general, third sector organisations are directed towards satisfying their founders' motivations and achieving their supporters'/backers' objectives. (This applies to some 'private' organisations also.) Are third sector people and organisations thus largely just getting on with their initiatives – trying to keep them going long enough to achieve their objectives – and not worrying/thinking about where the sector as a whole might be going or trying to take over from parts of either the public or private sectors?

Is it time to challenge some assumptions?

This review of new developments and alternative perspectives raises some possibilities which challenge aspects of what is becoming, if not already established as, the conventional wisdom in this area. That wisdom is based on a number of assumptions which it is suggested it might now be appropriate to challenge. Here are some of them, and some of their implications:

- It is assumed that in most economies there are three distinct separate sectors – as indicated in Pearce's diagram (see Figure 2.2). But while the existence and nature of the public and private sectors is generally accepted and understood, there is less clarity about the third sector/social economy and its nature.
- It is assumed that that the traditional demarcations between the three sectors represent real and significant divisions.
  - Because it is assumed that the traditional demarcations are real and significant, it is assumed that the organisations in one sector have more in common with each other than they do with any organisation in another sector.
  - It is also assumed that an organisation will be entirely on one side of a sector boundary and cannot be on one side according to some criteria and on the other according to other criteria.
- It is assumed that the sectors are otherwise similar to each other.
  - Therefore, for instance, it is assumed that if the organisations in one sector have a degree of cohesion and co-operation, then so do, or should, the organisations in other sectors. Thus, because it should be possible to co-ordinate actions between all elements in the public sector in a country or region, some people in the public sector assume that the same can be done in the third sector, or in parts of it such as the social economy.
  - Because the public sector is relatively unified and subject to common controls, and has a clear role, it is assumed that the third sector, or sub-sectors within it such as the social economy or the voluntary and community sector, are also unified and controllable, and have a clear role.

– If, instead of all the sectors being internally similar, it is assumed that there are differences between the public and the private sectors, then it is assumed that the third sector is either like one of them or a mix of them – rather than having its own distinct characteristics.

The reality, it is suggested, is somewhat different:

- *Does an economy consist of three separate sectors?* Most observers agree that there are two clear sectors in an economy and a number of organisations which belong in neither of those sectors. Thus the existence of a third sector has been postulated. Things like the social economy and Bjerke and Karlsson's citizen sector have been identified as possibly being that third sector – or at least as being part of it if there are still organisations which are not in the social economy or the citizen sector or the other sectors.
- *Do the organisations in each sector have at lot in common with each other?* It is suggested that very small (micro) organisations in the private and third sectors (there are no independent organisations that small in the public sector) have more in common with each other than they do with bigger organisations which are supposedly in the same sector as them – and thus at the very small level the sector boundary becomes relatively meaningless. Also, managers in large organisations in all three sectors have a lot in common in that, for instance, they have carefully defined limits to their decision-making powers, they have to keep superiors happy, and, although they may indeed be supportive of the aims of the organisations for which they work, nevertheless they are working there as a career. Pearce's circular, three-sector diagram might thus be redrawn with the main division being between the small and the large, and the three sector divisions being subsidiary to this.
- *Are all organisations entirely on one side of a boundary or on the other?* The assumption that an organisation has to be entirely on one side of a sector boundary, and cannot be on one side according to some criteria and on the other according to other criteria, is being challenged. Instead of being either black or white, in a spectrum of colours it is possible to be both a bit yellow and a bit red – and that might be a better analogy in this situation.
- *Are the relationships within one sector comparable with the relationships within another sector?* The three sectors are very different in their make-up. In the public sector, the makers of the rules (legislative and regulatory bodies) and the controllers of the funds (for instance treasury departments – although generally the funds come ultimately from the taxpayer) have very influential positions. Those influences can do a lot to ensure that all relevant parts of the public sector in any country or region should take a consistent line on any issue and it is thus possible for the public sector to be co-ordinated and as a whole to agree and follow a specific approach to an issue which should be binding on the whole of the sector. In the private sector, the market has an influential role and those businesses big enough, and willing, to join private sector umbrella bodies (such as the CBI in the UK) can help shape agreed approaches – but these are not binding on the whole of the sector. In the third sector, while there are some bodies which aspire to a sort of umbrella role, there is in practice no way to get a co-ordinated agreement or approach for the sector. In other words, the third sector cannot respond as a sector. Inside the third sector there is little feeling of it being a sector (for instance common rules, habits, histories, and customs) – just a variety of individuals and enterprises. Some components may sometimes appear to show a consistent response, but that is usually a common response to market forces such as when grants are offered – like animals showing a common response to the provision of food. Thus public sector concordats

or charters with the third sector (or the social economy or the 'voluntary and community sector'), although desirable from a public sector viewpoint, are not in practice deliverable.

- *Is the third sector like either the public sector or the private sector?* If the third sector has a distinct characteristic, it is that the organisations in it belong in neither of the other two sectors. Beyond that, however, they are a relatively disparate set of organisations. Very few of them co-ordinate things with each other. The public sector may be controllable (like herding animals such as sheep) but the private sector cannot all be controlled like that. The private sector (except the black economy) can be constrained by laws (like fencing animals into a reserve). However, the third sector is neither unified nor controllable (like birds which cannot be fenced in) except insofar as it can be 'bribed' to react in certain ways by things like funding schemes and grants (like using food to motivate animals). Thus, talking about the 'role' of the third sector is inappropriate as it is not driven by such considerations.

So What?

It is beyond the scope of this chapter to make a definitive study of all the questions raised above, not least because it will take a while for some of them to be worked out. However, it may be possible at least to recognise some of the counter-assumptions and/or implications – for instance in 'maps' of an economy. On such attempt is shown in Figure 5.2.

Some features suggested on the map are that:

- There are no clear distinct boundaries between the sectors.
- There are no very small public sector organisations.
- There are few distinctions between very small private or third sector enterprises.
- Large organisations in the three sectors are closer to each other than they are to small organisations supposedly in the same sector.

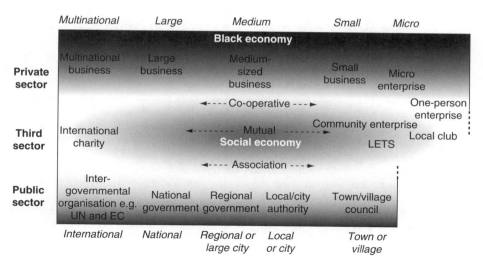

Figure 5.2 The sectors of an economy – An alternative 'map'

Does putting things on a map imply that everything must go somewhere in the picture? No map can be considered to provide a complete picture as it is not possible to represent a dynamic many-dimensioned reality in a static two-dimensional view. Thus, any map only alludes to some aspects of its subject – and Figure 5.2 is no exception. Nevertheless, it is suggested as a way of portraying a more realistic picture than is suggested by views of three separate, distinctly bounded sectors.

Conclusion

The conclusion of this chapter is that, in considering the future of the third sector and/or the social economy, no definitive conclusion is possible. There are many factors and possibilities which might be relevant to that future, some of which are considered here, and the situation is still changing. Not only is no single clear theme or direction thus apparent, but, it has been suggested, even change itself is different and 'we are living in the change of change'.[42]

While the above summaries do not suggest that there is any foreseeable reason to expect major overall changes in the scale, make-up, and direction of the third sector or the social economy, the unexpected often happens. There has been a third sector for as long as the other two sectors of an economy have been distinguishable as separate areas of activity and thus it seems likely that this will continue. Perhaps the future of the third sector will depend more upon the private and public sectors, and on how third sector organisations react to their evolution, than on forces operating directly on it. Therefore, instead of just considering the future of the third sector, it may be more meaningful to explore the future of the combined activity of the three sectors in an interlinked system.

///

Key Points of Chapter 5
- Traditional views tend to support one of three broad choices about the role of the sector – based on an economic/entrepreneurship approach, a social-economic policy approach, and a political/ideological approach.
- New developments which might have an impact on such views include hybridisation, conscious capitalism, and attempts to convert parts of the public sector to social enterprise.
- Other perspectives which might also lead to different views include the aspirations of the people behind third sector ventures, a wider economic perspective, and an increasing recognition of the possible impact of civil society.
- Among the main factors which might influence the future of the third sector are internal factors such as tensions in, and efforts of, the sector itself and external factors such as the expectations that people and governments have of it, the attempts that are thus being made to promote it and the help being given to it, and the extent to which it is gaining wider acceptance.
- There do appear to be grounds for reassessing some of the assumptions behind the conventional wisdom about the sector – which might be recognised in new or different 'maps' of it.
- There is a need to think of the social economy in relational ways and how in particular it is affected by interdependencies among the private, public, and social-economic sectors.

///

Case 5.1 | Green Gold Forestry Ltd

Green Gold Forestry Ltd (GGF) was founded in 2007. It is a sustainable timber company producing premium quality hardwoods, such as flooring and decking, for export to international markets. It operates in the Loreto region of Peru where it is headquartered at Iquitos. It aims to become Peru's leading sustainable timber company.

Sustainability

GGF's management is strongly committed to showing best practice leadership in Peru in social and environmental responsibility. GGF believes both that this is the right thing to do, and that it also reduces business risks through organisational discipline. GGF's forest concessions are managed through very low-impact techniques, extracting an average 2.4 m^3 per hectare per 20 years' rotation. GGF believes that its strong environmental and social credentials will attract high-quality clients and investors. Whilst GGF has not factored higher prices for its Forest Stewardship Council (FSC)-certified timber, GGF believes that certification will widen investor interest in GGF and attract strong sales counterparts. Examples of GGF's sustainability initiatives include:

Vertical integration. Vertical integration gives control over each production stage, which is essential to ensure GGF's high-quality standards. Securing raw materials is the starting point, and GGF's ownership of forest concessions and river transport mitigates supply chain risks.

Renewable energy. Sawmill waste will be used to generate heat (for kilns) and electricity, making GGF more than self-sufficient, and the excess will be supplied to the grid in Iquitos.

Research. GGF sponsors a research programme with the University of Cambridge looking into the ecological sustainability of GGF's low-impact harvesting. The company plans to sponsor a Peruvian PhD student in 2014 to research forest ecology and develop environmental monitoring and reporting programmes.

Chain of custody. GGF is fully certified by FSC for Forest Management and Chain of Custody and is the only timber company in Loreto thus certified by the FSC. GGF has proven chain of custody of its timber from jungle to port. Each tree is measured, recorded, and mapped using GPS, and this legal provenance is essential to comply with US Lacey Act and EU FLEGT legislation.

Community Forestry Programme

From the outset, GGF has worked to develop strong working relationships with government and international NGOs. For instance, GGF signed a cooperation agreement with World Wildlife Fund (WWF) in 2009, and WWF assists it with community liaison and consultation as well as certification. Recently, GGF has been approached by Peru Bosques to partner with USAID and Amazon Alternative to develop community forestry programmes.

Under Peru's Forestry Law, forest communities are entitled to extract timber from allotted community concessions and the Peru Bosques proposal aims to promote community forestry with the ultimate goal of achieving certification of community forests. This venture is attractive to GGF because it reinforces its social commitment, diversifies GGF's supply chain of logs, and builds strong relationships with communities, which can be important when operating in remote jungle areas.

GGF plans to supplement the output from its own concessions by sourcing 30 per cent of its logs from other parties. Its objective is to source these third-party logs from forest communities, which are allocated specific areas of land under Peruvian law. The Loreto region is dotted with hundreds of community settlements, usually sited next to major rivers. These communities typically comprise 'mestizo' groups of 100–200 people who have settled within living history. Most of these groups have legal title to 5,000–10,000 ha of forests and receive some government support including provision of basic teaching and one or two 'public buildings' (concrete huts). Under the Forestry Law, they are allowed to extract timber, so long as they submit formal extraction plans and adhere to the strict criteria regarding methods and legality. However, the reality is that many of these communities fall outside the formal economy and lack expertise and basic business skills, as well as the extraction equipment, required to manage their concessions. This results in many communities either failing to earn revenues, or being exploited by traders who underpay and use illegal extraction methods – thereby contributing to the illegal timber trade and the degradation of forests.

GGF is working with USAID and WWF to develop a credible community forestry model where GGF would provide technical assistance and equipment to help communities manage their concessions, with logs entering GGF's chain of custody. As GGF's chain of custody meets FSC's strict criteria, this guarantees legality as well as adherence to standards for safety, responsible extraction, etc.

In outline, GGF's forest engineers would produce a forest management and extraction plan on behalf of the communities, GGF would part-pay for logs up front through provision of equipment such as chainsaws and hand winches. If required, GGF could also help with extraction using its own heavy machines. GGF would pay a fair and transparent price for the logs and would transport logs to its own mill. GGF would help the communities set up their own bank accounts and tax registration so that they operate within the formal economy. It is GGF's intention to allow the communities to do as much of the work as possible, thus increasing their revenue potential. Because GGF is the only FSC-certified company in Loreto, it is in a unique position to develop this method of community forestry.

The financial and development benefits to communities involved in this programme could be substantial. Over time GGF would expect communities to adopt the skills and expertise so that they could manage their own concessions to FSC standards.

For GGF the benefits of this community programme are very attractive. It would be diversifying its supply of logs, and would not have to purchase the concessions. It believes that by helping to develop community forestry, GGF would further enhance its credentials as one of the leading forestry companies and could attract concessional finance as well as better-quality timber buyers. As demand for FSC-certified and legally sourced timber is on the rise, this could mean that GGF can achieve higher prices in time.

GGF's community programme is still in its early stages, and given the fact that GGF is not yet fully funded, it is not yet in a position to develop this programme fully. However, USAID has said that it is impressed with GGF's social and environmental commitments. It noted that GGF has a strong commitment to employing women: in fact its head forest engineer is one of the very few women to have this role in Peru. GGF also seeks to exceed FSC guidelines on employment standards which include training as well as health and safety, insurance, and benefits.

A profit-distributing business

The above description of the operation of GGF may make it sound like a social enterprise – making money in order to do good. But GGF is a private sector business trying to return a profit to its investors. GGF's motto might be said to be 'Sustainability for profit – not for philanthropy'.

GGF sees social and environmental responsibility as a key component in its profit-making operations – being not only a significant risk-mitigating strategy, but also as a strong supporting driver for growth. It is to this end that GGF is developing innovative projects like the community forestry programme described above, which it believes will deliver significant benefits to some of the poorest groups in the Loreto region of Peru as well as contributing to GGF's own bottom line. At the time of writing, GGF was seeking further expansion capital to enable it to realise its plans to extend its forest concessions to 250,000 ha and invest in additional modern plant and machinery. GGF is confident that it can both make attractive investment returns and help to improve the social conditions of many of the people living at the economic margin in Loreto.

Source: Correspondence with Green Gold Forestry Ltd

Questions, Exercises, Essay, and Discussion Topics

1. Identify five reasons for suggesting that the third sector is not likely to change significantly for the foreseeable future.
2. Identify, with reasons, the five factors most likely to lead to change in the third sector.
3. Is the third sector peripheral to the mainstream economy?
4. Why would a private business be interested in social issues and impacts?
5. To what extent do you think that public acceptance of the third sector will grow?

Suggestions for further reading

A. Amin, A. Cameron and R. Hudson, *Placing the Social Economy* (London: Routledge, 2002).

B. Bjerke and M. Karlsson, *Social Entrepreneurship: To Act as If and Make a Difference* (Cheltenham: Edward Elgar, 2013).

R. Murray, J. Caulier-Grice and G. Mulgan, *The Open Book of Social Innovation* (London: NESTA and the Young Foundation, 2010).

A. Nicholls and A. Murdock (Eds), *Social Innovation: Blurring Boundaries to Reconfigure Markets* (Basingstoke: Palgrave Macmillan, 2012).

F. Powell, *The Politics of Civil Society: Neoliberalism or Social Left?* (Bristol: The Policy Press, 2007).

References

1. C. Borzaga and E. Tortia, 'Social Economy Organisations in the Theory of the Firm', in A. Noya and E. Clarence (Eds) *The Social Economy, Building Exclusive Economies* (OECD, 2007), pp. 38–40.
2. P. Lloyd, 'The Social Economy in the New Political Economic Context', in A. Noya and E. Clarence (Eds), *The Social Economy, Building Exclusive Economies* (OECD, 2007), pp. 67–8.
3. Ibid., p. 77.
4. F. Powell, *The Politics of Civil Society: Neoliberalism Or Social Left?* (Bristol: The Policy Press, 2007), p. 221.

5. K. Alter, '*Social Enterprise Typology*', Virtue Ventures, www.4lenses.org/setypology (accessed 20 April 2013).

6. D. Billis, 'From welfare bureaucracies to welfare hybrids' in D. Billis (Ed) '*Hybrid Organisations and the Third Sector: Challenges for Practice, Theory and Policy* (Basingstoke: Palgrave Macmillan, 2010), p. 3.

7. D. Billis (Ed.) '*Hybrid Organisations and the Third Sector: Challenges for Practice, Theory and Policy* (Basingstoke: Palgrave Macmillan, 2010), back cover.

8. D. Billis, 'Revisiting the key challenges: Hybridity, ownership and change' in D. Billis (Ed) '*Hybrid Organisations and the Third Sector: Challenges for Practice, Theory and Policy* (Basingstoke: Palgrave Macmillan, 2010), p. 254.

9. S. Bridge and K. O'Neill, *Understanding Enterprise, Entrepreneurship and Small Business* (Basingstoke: Palgrave Macmillan, 2013), p. 401.

10. J. Kay, *Obliquity* (London: Profile Books, 2010), p. 8.

11. S. Bridge and K. O'Neill, *Understanding Enterprise, Entrepreneurship and Small Business* (Basingstoke: Palgrave Macmillan, 2013), p. 401.

12. R. Murray, J. Caulier-Grice and G. Mulgan, *The Open Book of Social Innovation* (London: NESTA and the Young Foundation, 2010), p. 3.

13. A. Nicholls and A. Murdock , 'The Nature of Social Innovation', in A. Nicholls and A. Murdock (eds), *Social Innovation: Blurring Boundaries to Reconfigure Markets* (Basingstoke: Palgrave Macmillan, 2012), p. 17.

14. Ibid., p. 2.

15. J. A. Kerlin, 'Considering Context: Social Innovation in Comparative Perspective', in A. Nicholls and A. Murdock (Eds), *Social Innovation: Blurring Boundaries to Reconfigure Markets* (Basingstoke: Palgrave Macmillan, 2012), pp. 68–70.

16. A. Nicholls and A. Murdock, 'The Nature of Social Innovation', in A. Nicholls and A. Murdock (eds), *Social Innovation: Blurring Boundaries to Reconfigure Markets* (Basingstoke: Palgrave Macmillan, 2012), p. 4.

17. Ibid., pp. 4–5.

18. 'Cleveland Fire Brigade Mutual spin-out backed by £95,000 from government', *Third Sector bulletin*, www.thirdsector.co.uk/bulletin (accessed 20 September 2012).

19. 'Government requires health service champions to be social enterprises', *Third Sector bulletin*, www.thirdsector.co.uk/bulletin (accessed 7 January 2013).

20. For more information, see S. Bridge and K. O'Neill, *Understanding Enterprise, Entrepreneurship and Small Business* (Basingstoke: Palgrave Macmillan, 2013), pp. 178–81.

21. A. Amin, R. Hudson and A. Cameron, *Placing the Social Economy* (London: Routledge, 2002), p. 81.

22. F. Fukuyama, *Trust: The Social Virtues and the Creation of Prosperity* (New York: Free Press Paperbacks, 1996), p. 6.

23. Ibid., p. 13.

24. R. Noë, J. A. R. A. M. van Hooff and P. Hammerstein (Eds), *Economics in Nature – Social Dilemmas, Mate Choices and Biological Markets* (Cambridge: Cambridge University Press, 2001).

25. Ibid., p. 18.

26. J. K. Galbraith, 'The Concept of Conventional Wisdom', in *The Affluent Society*, 4th ed. (London: Penguin, [1958] 1991), p. 7.

27. K. Popper, 'Of Clouds and Clocks: an approach to the problem of rationality and the freedom of man', In *Objective Knowledge: An Evolutionary Approach* (Oxford: Clarendon Press, 1972), pp. 206–55.

28. M. Earls, *Herd: How to Change Mass Behaviour by Harnessing Our True Nature* (Chichester, UK: John Wiley & Sons Ltd, 2009).

29. National Council for Voluntary Action (NCVO), *The UK Civil Society Almanac 2008*, executive summary from www.ncvo-vol.org.uk/publications, accessed 31 March 2008.

30. London School of Economics Centre for Civil Society (www.lse.ac.uk/collections/CCS/introduction.htm, accessed 31 March 2008).

31. For instance, G. W. F. Hegel, *Elements of the Philosophy of Right*, 1827 (translated by Dyde, 1897).

32. N. Chandhoke, *The Taming of Civil Society*, www.india-society/com/2005/545 (accessed 28 March 2008).

33. M. Edwards, reported in N. Chandhoke, 'What the Hell is "Civil Society"?' (OpenDemocracy, 2005), www.opendemocracy.net (accessed 29 March 2008).

34. F. Fukuyama, *Trust: The Social Virtues and the Creation of Prosperity* (New York: Free Press Paperbacks, 1996), pp. 4–5.

35. J. Coleman, 'Social Capital in the Creation of Human Capital', *American Journal of Sociology*, Vol. 94 (1988), S95–120, quoted by F. Fukuyama, *Trust: The Social Virtues and the Creation of Prosperity* (New York: Free Press Paperbacks, 1996), p. 10.

36. B. Bjerke and M. Karlsson, *Social Entrepreneurship: To act as if and make a difference* (Cheltenham: Edward Elgar, 2013).

37. For instance, see P. Seanor, M. Bull and R. Ridley-Duff, 'Contradictions in Social Enterprise: Do They Draw in Straight Lines or Circles?', a paper

presented at the 30th ISBE Conference, Glasgow, 2007.

38. A director of a social enterprise (CEED) quoted by A. Amin, A. Cameron and R. Hudson, *Placing the Social Economy* (London: Routledge, 2002), p. 103.

39. P. Lloyd in *Rethinking the Social Economy* (Belfast: Queen's University Belfast CU2: Contested Cities – Urban Universities, 2006), p. 13.

40. A. Amin, A. Cameron and R. Hudson, *Placing the Social Economy* (London: Routledge, 2002), p. 104.

41. Till Bruckner, *Accountability in International Aid: The Case of Georgia* (PhD thesis, University of Bristol, 2011).

42. M. Ferguson, *The Aquarian Conspiracy: Personal and Social Transformation in Our Time* (Los Angeles: Tarcher Ltd, 1980), p. 29.

Part II

The Nature of the Social Economy

Part I of this book looks at the concepts of the social economy and the third sector and maps out the relationships between them, and between the third sector and the rest of an economy. In effect, it tries to describe the 'geography' of the sector by indicating what is considered to be in it and where it is thought to be positioned relative to the rest of an economy.

Part II looks in more detail at what might be described as the 'ecology' of the social economy and the third sector because it concerns how organisations in it behave, how they relate to each other and to other sectors of the economy, and how they might be influenced.

Chapter 6 examines explore key aspects of the nature of social economy organisations including their formation, legal structures, aims, methods, and management.

Chapter 7 considers the sources of finance available to, and used by, social economy organisations. It also examines the diverse financial needs of organisations in the sector, including the need for financial skills.

A key area of potential linkages is then explored in Chapter 8, which looks at the concept of social capital and at the evolution of some of the theories about it and how it might be linked to a wider socio-political concern for the health of civic society.

Governments, and other stakeholders, are often interested in influencing and promoting the development of the social economy and the third sector. Chapter 9 explores the main issues associated with this intervention including both why it is tried and what methods have been used to give effect to policy in the area.

To conclude this part, Chapter 10 reviews the impact the sector is supposed to have and the evidence for that impact.

6

characteristics of social enterprises

contents:

- introduction
- founders
- aims
- legal structures
- ownership
- organisation and management
- employment
- volunteers
- rewards
- measures of success
- conclusion

Key concepts

This chapter covers:

- what social economy organisations are actually like, rather than what theoretical attempts to categorise them might suggest they are like;
- key aspects of social economy organisations;
- some of the issues that these aspects can raise for social economy organisations;
- how, in these aspects, social economy organisations compare and contrast with private sector organisations.

Learning objectives

By the end of this chapter the reader should:

- appreciate the main characteristics shared by most social economy organisations, but not most public or private sector organisations;
- appreciate that social economy organisations do not all share all the characteristics identified;
- be aware that some social economy organisations can share some characteristics with some private or public sector organisations;
- understand that social economy sector organisations do not always behave as theory might suggest they should;
- be aware that there is considerable heterogeneity across social economy organisations;
- be aware that a range of methods are now available to help social economy organisations to account for and report their achievements.

Introduction

Part I of this book explores the position of the social economy in the economy overall and looks at the variety of organisations within it and the various ways in which they can be categorised. There is a wide variety of organisations within the social economy, and the categories of organisations as well as the vocabulary and definitions used for the sector are still evolving and can be confusing. Table 4.1 presents a comparison of definitions which suggests that, even using a narrow definition of the social economy or the third sector, there is little agreement on what characteristics the organisations within it share. Nevertheless, social economy organisations do share a number of characteristics, even if they do not all share all of them. This chapter explores key aspects of social economy organisations in order to indicate the extent to which there might be some shared characteristics.

This chapter, in effect, looks at what social economy organisations, and in particular social enterprises, are actually like, rather than at what theoretical attempts to categorise them might suggest they are like. The issues considered here can help to provide an understanding of the distinctions and similarities across such organisations, and how they compare and contrast with private or public sector organisations. Some aspects of social economy organisations are addressed in more detail elsewhere in this book, however. For instance the type of activity the organisations engage in, or at least the sectors in which they operate, is considered in Chapter 3 and finance for their activities forms the subject matter of Chapter 7, and so these issues are not covered again below.

Founders

An appropriate starting point for considering social economy organisations is their foundation. Yet seeking to characterise the typical founder of such organisations is like trying to define the typical entrepreneur. Both groups of people reveal great heterogeneity coming from all races, social classes, gender, and ages. Indeed, according to many observers, the founders of many social enterprises in particular are just as much entrepreneurs as those who found private sector organisations. There usually has to be someone who cares enough to start it and drive it forward. As with any enterprise, it is clear that, across their founders, there is no stereotypical person or personality. They range, on the international stage, from people such as Mother Teresa, Dr Barnardo, General Booth, and Bob Geldof, to the worker priest, reformed alcoholic, and housewife abuse victim who simply operate within their local communities.

Evidence suggests that very often social enterprises are promoted, established, and/or directed by groups of people, rather than by individuals – indeed it is difficult, if not impossible, to operate as a social enterprise acting alone. As Westall and Chalkley point out, social enterprise is a process rather than a product; it is 'not just about goods and services, but also about political and social co-ordination'.[1] The process will almost always involve groups which may be formed from categories of people such as:

- Those who work or live in areas of long-term disadvantage and seek to address some of its problems, for instance by establishing a training service for long-term unemployed.
- Like-minded groups who organise to meet a community need, solve a problem, take advantage of an opportunity, or fill a gap in provision, for instance by preserving a historic local building from demolition.
- Those within the public sector who seek to encourage the establishment of social enterprises and social partnerships to achieve better local economic or community development, for instance by funding home-based palliative care for cancer sufferers.
- Those in established social economy organisations, such as charities and voluntary organisations, who seek to develop alternative or supplementary ways of meeting their objectives, for instance by developing a trading arm.
- Owners or managers in value-driven businesses seeking to establish social economy businesses to fulfil their social obligations. Examples include the numerous trusts and foundations established by international companies to further support for the arts or educational and social opportunity for disadvantaged groups or young people. This is sometimes referred to as corporate social responsibility (CSR) and is often interpreted as reflecting enlightened self-interest on the part of the founding organisations.

Aims

The aims, or nature of the objectives, of social enterprises or other social economy organisations are often used in studies in this field as the primary, or only, criteria to distinguish such organisations from other ventures. Social aims and objectives are not, though, a unique characteristic of social economy organisations. Many commercial organisations in the private sector will have some sort of social impact on the communities in which they are operating by, for example, providing employment and training or through local purchasing. Typically, though, these social impacts are not explicitly stated by the businesses concerned as being among their objectives. Nor should one confuse strictly commercial organisations which make large donations for worthy causes with social enterprises. The Bill and Melinda Gates Foundation, for example, receives significant donations from the money earned by Bill Gates through his interest in Microsoft. However, the purpose of Microsoft is not to make money for the Foundation – its purpose is to make money for its investors. It is not a social enterprise, however worthy the ultimate philanthropy.

In the social economy, on the other hand, social aims are typically either the primary aims, or are among the primary aims, of organisations in what the language of current times refers to as 'the triple bottom line': alluding to social and environmental objectives as well as, and underpinned by, financial objectives. Sometimes an ethical objective is also added, thus making a 'quadruple bottom line'. The term 'people, planet, and profit' is also entering common parlance as an alternative expression, highlighting the breadth of aims.

The non-economic objectives of social economy organisations can be very varied, ranging from saving souls in the case of churches, to protecting the vulnerable from harm in the case of charities for children, to achieving democracy in the workplace through workers' co-operatives, or to offering opportunities to the disadvantaged through credit unions.

Objectives in the social economy

In the case of many social enterprises, the terms 'non-profit' or 'not-for-profit' (or sometimes more accurately 'not-for-profit-distribution-to-individuals') are commonly used. This indicates that any profits, or surpluses, are not for distribution to the shareholders or other owners for personal gain but are to be reinvested into the enterprise, or otherwise used, to help it to meet better its social, environmental, or ethical objectives. (As noted by Price, with the use of the words 'profit' and 'surplus', there can be an ideological gulf in that there are 'some on the extreme social end of the spectrum who abhor the word profit', just as there are those at the other enterprise end who feel surplus is mealy-mouthed'.)[2] It can also simply mean that the enterprise concerned does not seek to maximise a financial surplus and so arranges to supply its goods or services at prices which are consistent with that aim. Pearce defines non-profit distribution as 'any profit recycled into the enterprise or into the local community rather than distributed to members',[3] recognising the importance of making a profit and focusing attention on how it is used.

However, the way in which a social enterprise re-invests its surplus may not be recognised immediately. Illustration 6.1 highlights what Price refers to as 'more subtle ways' of re-investing.

Illustration 6.1 Some ways to re-invest socially

- *Employ people who are not attractive to other employers*
  - people with disabilities
  - ex-offenders
  - mental health service users
  - those with few educational qualifications
- *Operate in places which are not attractive to other businesses*
  - areas with low educational attainment
  - social housing estates

- post-industrial areas
- sparsely populated rural areas
- *Operate in activities which have lower profit margins than would be acceptable to the private sector*
- *The care sector, particularly looking after people in their own homes*
- *Operate in activities for ideological reasons*
  - renewable energy
  - recycling
  - fair Trade with the developing world

Source: M. Price, *Social Enterprise – What it is and why it matters* (Vale of Glamorgan: Fflan Ltd, 2009), Revised 2nd ed., p. 3

In the USA, a social enterprise may be incorporated as a for-profit or non-profit organisation and the term 'not-for-profit' is common. In essence it can be said that, at least from a UK and USA perspective, the typical social enterprise is a business in a market context that has different and more socially informed values than the typical private sector business, and that uses any profits it does make to pursue objectives other than owner or shareholder value. The popular shorthand phrase is that social enterprises are 'market led but values driven'. [4]

The Social Enterprise Coalition (now Social Enterprise UK) stressed 'that social enterprise is not defined by its legal structure but rather by:

- its nature, its social aims and outcomes;
- the basis on which its social mission is embedded in its structure and governance; and
- the way it uses the profits it generates through its trading activities. In particular, the concept of the multiple "double or triple bottom line" is used to capture the approach and aims of social enterprises to meet financial, social and often environmental goals.' [5]

Objectives for the social economy

When considering the aims for social enterprises or the social economy collectively, or as a sector, differences of purpose and scope can arise.

As elaborated upon in Chapter 4, the European 'political economy' approach to the social economy adopts a wider 'whole society' perspective as opposed to it being viewed as merely 'an alternative business form'. It is about the role of social enterprises as an 'integral component of the social economy' and is essentially people- (citizen-)driven. It is about 'openness, sharing, mutuality, multi-functionality and above all an ethos of independence that gives it a right to promote the cause of the citizenry. It fills gaps, shaves the edges of poverty and exclusion, gives meaning to social life, builds social capital and social discourse.' [6]

Recent developments in Spain, Greece, and Belgium (Wallonia) have seen laws introduced giving definition to the field of the social economy (whether by this name or by that of social enterprises). Spain's Law 5/2011 on Social Economy and Greece's Law 4019/2011 on Social Economy, Social Entrepreneurship aim to establish a common legal framework for the group of entities that make up the sector and applicable promotional measures. In Belgium, the Walloon Parliament's decree of November 2008 on the Social Economy is similar to that of Spain. The Greek law described the social economy as 'the sum of economic, entrepreneurial, productive and social activities, undertaken by juridical entities or associations whose statutory goal is the pursue [*sic*] of collective benefit and the service of wider social interests'.[7]

Overall

The common characteristic of the aims of social enterprises lies not so much in what those aims are, but in what they are not. Those aims are not, or at least not primarily, concerned with enhancing the financial wealth of the organisations' owners, which is a key characteristic of the private sector. Nevertheless, because they do not have recourse to public sector financing sources such as taxation, social economy organisations, like any organisations wishing to sustain their existence, do need to generate enough income to cover their costs.

Legal structures

Social economy organisations have developed differently in different countries, often because of the different regulatory frameworks that exist and the different forms of legal entity that are available. From one country to another the same legal form may not be available to all such organisations and in some countries they might have a choice of legal form available to them. So it is important to recognise that social economy organisations are not typically defined by their legal status.

In the UK there is not a single legal definition of the more limited term 'social enterprise', and many social enterprises regard their legal form or model as merely the vehicle for their activities, not the defining feature. The European Commission description of the term 'social economy' mentions organisations registered as co-operatives, mutuals, associations, and foundations along with social enterprises. The social enterprise sector, in the UK, operates under a complex legal, and regulatory, framework, and the choice of legal form is not narrowly restricted but is often determined by the nature of the activities being undertaken by the social enterprise, the requirements of the key stakeholders, the appropriate governance structure and, crucially, the ability to access the required finance.

A social economy organisation, depending on what sort of organisation it is, may operate as a charity, a trust, an industrial and provident society, a co-operative, a company limited by shares, a company limited by guarantee, a public limited company, an unlimited company, or a partnership. It is sometimes possible to combine forms by, for instance, being both a company limited by guarantee and a registered charity, or by a group structure in which a charity might have a trading company limited by shares as a wholly-owned subsidiary. This is often done to facilitate a variety of activities while taking advantage of tax exemptions and various forms of support (see Table 6.1). In general, in the UK, non-profit organisations may operate 'business' ventures directly through wholly-owned subsidiary companies provided the activities of those subsidiary companies do not conflict with the aims of the parent organisations and remit to the latter any profits made.

Because of the variety of possible legal structures they take, third sector organisations are subject to a variety of regulatory and tax regimes. This means that their registrations and taxation affairs are recorded in a variety of different categories, some of which may also include private sector organisations. This makes it difficult to determine even the number of third sector organisations (See Chapter 10).

GHK in its report[8] argued that it is not necessary to have a multiplicity of legal forms. It noted that in France 'care has been taken in the legislation to provide migration

Table 6.1 Possible forms of legal existence for non–public sector organisations in the UK

This table is a summary, and inevitably a simplification, of what can be quite a complex legal situation. For instance, the separate categories shown are not always mutually exclusive, as, for instance, some trusts are established as companies limited by guarantee.	
Organisations with the following forms will usually be in the social economy	
Company limited by guarantee	A company with members whose liability is limited to the extent of the guarantee they contribute towards its debts, should that be necessary. An upper limit of one pound per member is however often set for this potential contribution. The social or public interest is usually underpinned by a constitutional requirement that profits are not paid out to members
Trust	A trust is a legal means by which control of property is given to a person or institution for the benefit of others (the community), for example, a development trust which is typically community owned and combines community effort with business expertise to foster economic, social, and environmental renewal. It may or may not be registered as a charity
Industrial and provident society (IPS)	Organisations registered under the Industrial and Provident Societies Act become corporate bodies whose members benefit from limited liability. They are regulated by the Financial Services Authority. There are two types of organisations which can thus register: co-operative societies, the activities of which will be primarily for the benefit of the members (see below); and societies formed to benefit the community at large. Both types are known as 'mutuals'
Community interest company (CIC)	A new kind of limited company which exists to benefit the community rather than private shareholders. Thus, while they share features of a limited company (e.g. separate legal existence and limited liability), they also have some key features which make sure they are working to benefit communities. A CIC cannot also be a charity. (See Illustration 6.2.)
Charitable incorporated organisation (CIO)	A new form of legal entity (set out in the 2006 Charities Act) designed for non-profit organisations in the UK. It is an incorporated form of charity which is not a company although it has the features of a company limited by guarantee (including limiting the liability of its members and trustees). While charities can currently be formed as companies, they must be registered with both Companies House and the Charity Commission. The CIO only needs to register with the Charity Commission. This is expected to reduce bureaucracy for the charity and save on costs. (See below.)
NB – Charity: A charity is not typically a distinctive legal form (but see CIO above). An organisation, whether incorporated or not, can apply to be registered as a charity by the Charities Commission (in GB) if its objectives and activities are charitable. Being a charity has tax advantages but also regulatory constraints. The requirements for registration however mean that those organisations which are registered as charities will be in the social economy. (See also section 'Charities' in Chapter 4.)	
Organisations with the following form could be in the social economy or in the private sector	
Co-operative	A co-operative is an association of people united voluntarily to meet their common economic, social, and cultural needs through a jointly-owned and democratically-controlled organisation formed for the primary benefit of its members, not the wider community. Co-operatives are registered under the Industrial and Provident Societies Act but, to be registered as bona fide co-operatives, they have to fulfil a number of conditions, the first four of which reflect the International Co-operative Alliance's statement on the co-operative identity and relate to the community of interest, the conduct of business, the control of the society, and limits on dividend or interest on share and loan capital

Table 6.1 (Continued)

	Many co-operatives are in the social economy but those which limit their membership to their own workers and share the profits among those workers can be considered to be in the private sector
Unincorporated	An unincorporated body may operate as organisation but does not have a legal existence independent of its members. Thus, a club which is unincorporated might have a bank account, buy or sell goods, and even employ people. But it is the members who would be legally liable for any problems
Organisations with the following forms will usually be in the private sector	
Public limited company	A company limited by shares (i.e. shareholders whose liability is limited) a portion of which must be publicly available for purchase
Private company limited by shares	A company limited by shares (i.e. shareholders whose liability is limited) which are not publicly available for purchase
Unlimited company	Differs from the limited company in that the liability of its members is unlimited in return for which it is relieved of some regulatory constraints
Partnership	Formed under the Partnership Acts, the owners (partners) may have limited or unlimited liability. They are commonly used by the professions in a position of trust, for example, architects, lawyers, and accountants

pathways through which existing organisations can easily adapt themselves to new needs'. For the UK, this would mean 'creating bridges' from guarantee companies, charities, IPSs, share companies, and partnerships 'so that any of them could easily become a social enterprise'.

Illustration 6.2 Community Interest Companies

In 2005, the legislation which provides the rules for the creation and operation of community interest companies (CICs) came into force in Great Britain (and in 2007 in Northern Ireland). CICs are created for people who want to conduct a business or other activities for community benefit. In effect, they are bespoke limited liability companies under which social enterprises can trade.

A total of 6391 CICs were registered by March 2012, according to their Regulator,[9] embracing small shops to multi-million turnover operations.

A CIC can be a private company limited by guarantee, or by shares, or a public limited company, but cannot be a charity, an IPS, or an unincorporated organisation. To be a CIC, a company must:

– *Be registered as a CIC*. A CIC must be registered in the same way as a normal company with the same incorporation documents but supplemented by a Community Interest Statement. (Charities cannot be CICs but can form a CIC for trading purposes).
– *Meet the community interest test*. The primary purpose of a CIC is to provide benefits to the community, rather than to individuals. A community for CIC purposes can embrace either the community or population as a whole or a definable sector or group of people either in the UK or elsewhere. It is expected however that the community will be wider than just the members of the CIC. The definition of community interest that applies to CICs is wider than the public interest test for charity.
– *File an annual CIC report*. A CIC must file an annual CIC report with its accounts. The purpose of this CIC report is to show that the CIC is still satisfying the community interest test.
– *Have an 'asset lock'*. 'Asset lock' is a term used to cover the provisions designed to ensure that the assets of the CIC are, subject to meeting its obligations, either retained in the CIC

and used for community purposes, or transferred to another asset-locked body. In the case of a CIC which is a company limited by shares, the payment of dividends to shareholders is permitted but is limited by a dividend cap. Moreover, this precludes any return to shareholders from capital appreciation on an asset. The asset lock is attractive to funders. If the CIC ceases, assets must be distributed to the community. Regular limited liability companies that do not have charitable status find it difficult to ensure that their assets are dedicated to public benefit. There is no simple, clear way of locking assets of such a company to a public benefit purpose other than applying for charitable status. The CIC overcomes this problem.

(*Based on*: 'Community Interest Companies Briefing Pack', prepared by the Regulator of Community Interest Companies, Companies House, Cardiff as distributed in 2007)

Do CICs change the rules?

There has been no legal provision in the UK preventing social economy organisations incorporating as companies limited by shares or preventing private companies limited by shares from acting as though they were social economy organisations. However, such organisations have often found it helpful if they were incorporated, or otherwise registered, in a way which helped to indicate their social economy status. This has often been the case, for instance, when those organisations have sought funding support from public sector grant schemes or private trusts which frequently limit their support to companies limited by guarantee or to charities.

Companies limited by guarantee are precluded from remitting any profit they make to individuals such as their members, and typically their directors have acted in a voluntary capacity as the articles of association have prevented the payment of directors. Funders have liked this because they felt that it served to prevent their funds being passed on to other supporters as dividends or directors' emoluments, but it could also have the counter-effect of lessening the ties between those supporters and/or directors and the companies concerned. If directors are not remunerated, they may feel that their contribution is not valued, or is not as important as their input to other companies which do reward them. Also, if companies are not paying their directors, they can find it hard to demand a proper performance from those directors, such as, for example, regular attendance at meetings.

CICs can be seen as an attempt to bridge this gap by providing funders with an assurance that the companies concerned are acting in the community interest while, at the same time (at least in the case of CICs which are companies limited by shares), allowing some payments to be made to directors and/or investors and thus enabling the companies concerned to demand an adequate performance in return.

Intermixed with these explicit legal structures are a wide range of social enterprise categories such as:

- Charities' trading arms – trading companies owned by the charity, set up to enable them to meet their objectives by generating additional income.
- Community businesses – a business that serves a geographical community or a community of interest (e.g. refugees).
- Credit unions – a financial co-operative, owned and controlled by its members providing access to finance and opportunities to save.
- Development trusts – community based and owned, they permit local communities to bring about social, economic, and environmental renewal.
- Employee-owned businesses – they are often formed to create and preserve jobs in areas where jobs are scarce or under threat.
- Housing associations – the main providers of new social housing, they are run as businesses but do not trade for profit. Any surplus is reinvested and the association guided by a volunteer committee or management board.

- Intermediate labour market (ILM) companies – provide training and work experience for the long-term unemployed.
- Social firms – small businesses created to provide integrated employment and training to people with disabilities and disadvantages.

Ownership

The concept of ownership of many social enterprises is not straightforward. In the case of a company limited by shares, it is clear that the shareholders are the company's owners with the extent of their ownership being determined by the number (and type) of shares they hold. As owners they are entitled to sell their shares in the company and, together, can sell the whole of the company and keep the proceeds of the sale.

In the case of a company limited by guarantee, the ultimate authority in the company is its members and it is they who elect its directors, usually on the basis of one vote per member. Those members, while they may control the company in that way, are precluded from selling off the company and/or its assets and keeping the proceeds. In that sense they are not its owners, but then neither is anyone else. Industrial and provident societies are in a similar position in that the people who control the organisation are not entitled to sell it.

Often the people who control social enterprises are community based. They may be individuals appointed from within the relevant community, elected community representatives, or representatives of other community bodies. In this way there may be an attempt to achieve a genuine sense of local ownership, and to ensure that the organisation values and embraces concepts such as democracy, sharing, empowerment, mutuality, and locality. However, its legal form, and the structure and composition of the controlling team, do not of themselves ensure the incorporation and maintenance of these values in an organisation. The process of leading and managing the organisation plays a vital role in determining the culture and values it embraces (See Illustration 6.3).

Illustration 6.3 A possible drawback of community participation

The Northern Ireland Hospice is a company limited by guarantee. Its members, who normally pay a small annual subscription, elect the Hospice's Council of Management at the Annual General Meeting. The Council is the responsible body for the governance of the Hospice and the employment of its staff. The Hospice was established as a charity in 1981 and began to receive patients in 1983. In 1997 the Council of the Hospice decided to set up a new service for life-limited children and appointed a Project Director for this Children's Hospice. However in 2000 the Council entered into a disciplinary process against the Project Director and in 2001 dismissed him. He appealed and applied to the Industrial Tribunal.

This process led eventually to the then Minister for Health, Social Services and Public Safety in Northern Ireland commissioning a review of the Northern Ireland Hospice in December 2002. The report of this review found that, when the Council was taking its action against the Project Director, large numbers of people began to be enrolled as members of the Hospice and the total number of members grew from under 400 to nearly 2000. Some of these new members were active in support of the Project Director while others supported the Council. However, at the Hospice's 2001 AGM, the members elected a new Council. The new Council reached agreement with the Project Director, which ended the proceedings of the Industrial Tribunal, and referred the matter to an independent panel. The panel concluded that the Project Director had been unfairly dismissed but that he should not be reinstated although he was awarded compensation. The new Council, following its own review, decided to appoint a Chief Executive for the Hospice. The former Project Director applied for this position and was appointed to it. That decision got a mixed reaction and a TV programme about it brought the controversy into the public view. Following that, at the request of the Council, the Minister commissioned his review.

(*Source*: www.dhsspsni.gov.uk/publications/2003/hospice_report.pdf, accessed 19 May 2007)

Comment

The case of the Northern Ireland Hospice illustrates the potential problems of community participation in the control of social economy organisations. The increase in the Hospice's membership at the time of action against the Project Director was thought by some to be the result of a reaction by his supporters, who set out to recruit new members who would support his case. As a result, by signing up many like-minded people, his supporters were able to secure the appointment of a new Council and thus to some extent dictate the policy of the organisation. Depending on the point of view taken, this outcome could be considered either to be representative of the community's reaction and wishes, or to be a form of coup perpetrated on the community by a particular faction. To reduce the possibility of such a coup in their affairs, there has been a tendency by some other third sector organisations to specify, in their constitutions, that there should be a limit to the number of their members and/or that new members must be acceptable to the controlling body. In that way, the organisations concerned hope to be able to remain true to their founders' intentions, but such approaches might be viewed as limiting community involvement and therefore to be undemocratic.

There is also a range of organisations in which the owners are not only the members but are also the beneficiaries. In other words, the extent of mutuality varies. Many social enterprises, charities for example, are run for the benefit of non-members, but credit unions and some community businesses, co-operatives, and community enterprises are run primarily for the benefit of the members themselves. Moreover, the degree of democratic participation by members also varies enormously.

As noted in the previous section, French Société Coopérative, Intérêt and Collective (SCICs) (unlike CICs in the UK) embody the concept of democratic ownership, one of the criteria proposed by EMES, the European research network, in its definition of social enterprise. It sees a participatory approach as important, whereby not only the users of the social enterprise's services but also its employees, owners, public authorities, volunteers, and other representatives contribute to decision-making. Some see democratic ownership as a key factor in sustainability as it may help to maintain closer links with stakeholders and their needs as well as keeping the organisation grounded in its community. On the other hand, given the proposed increasing role of social enterprise in public procurement, consideration needs to be given to potential conflicts of interest if stakeholder relationships become too close and varied.

Undoubtedly, a strong view exists that the ethos of the social enterprise requires ownership to be shared across stakeholder groups, particularly users (consumers) and deliverers (employees) – despite the obvious tensions that may be exacerbated as the drive for greater commerciality is pursued by some.

Organisation and management

The best approach to leading and managing people, and to structuring an organisation and its processes, will be influenced by many factors, not least the external environment and the organisational purpose. While no two organisations are alike, it is possible to discern some general organisation and management challenges as well as the characteristics often associated with the social enterprise sector.

Borzaga and Solari[10] have identified the following management challenges facing social enterprises across Europe:

- reshaping a supportive legislative and regulatory environment
- ensuring the quality of products and services
- upgrading skills and jobs
- securing management expertise and support
- developing finance sources for start-up and growth
- developing networks and co-operation
- establishing adequate governance structures

Bull and Crompton highlight, from their project on social enterprises, a number of characteristics common to the sector as a whole. Those relating to organisation and management are summarised in Illustration 6.4 as typical of the responses received mainly from their interviewees.[11]

Illustration 6.4 Some common social enterprise organisation and management issues

Business, Planning, and Plans

- One of the difficulties observed is that many people running social enterprises do not see themselves as 'being in business' or their organisations as 'businesses'.
- Because of the insecurity and short-term nature of much funding, many social enterprises felt they were not in control of their own destiny – or of where their businesses were heading. Business plans were commonly deemed irrelevant.
- Business courses tend to be aimed at market exploitation, maximising human and capital resources, and are judged not to cater for more philanthropic aims.
- Business planning was something that many felt was either informal or out of date, yet visioning led by mission strategies was more appropriate.
- Social enterprises create a range of social and environmental impacts beyond their financial return. They experience tension and conflicts between these priorities that mainstream businesses do not face.

Management Structures and Systems
- Social enterprise organisations tend to have less hierarchal organisational structures, more informal communications systems, but a participatory culture with a strong sense of social mission and community.

Role of the Board
- In many cases the Board of Directors was a key feature in propagating values, decision-making, giving direction, and passing on expertise within social enterprises. Whilst many reported that their board's involvement was critical to the success of the organisation, there were a few exceptions:

   The Board met once every two months, they came in here when everyone's gone home, they never see the business operating. They get sent information the week before – but they don't read it – so how can they make decisions? . . . their suggestions are not very good either.[12]

Other Management and Organisational Issues

- Another weakness is to have a board which can be bullied or cajoled into doing exactly what senior management want – forgoing the necessary checks and balances. As reported by Price:

  > One senior person in a charity said to me, when I queried the legality of some of their business practices: 'We do good for people with learning disabilities. We can do what we like.'[13]

- Issues were raised about aligning bases with organisational structures (management functions and roles and responsibilities).
- Social enterprises were constantly wrestling with insufficient resources and meeting immediate impact needs and service delivery levels.
- Short-term funding adversely affects sustained employment in social enterprises where contracts are tied to short-term funding periods.
- Inclusive decision-making was highly regarded.
- Organisational structure was a key issue for the management.
- Informality and flexibility were key attributes of social enterprises.
- Boards of Directors were key attributes in organisational knowledge, bringing in higher-level management skills – some, but not all, totally appropriate to the small social enterprise.
- Informal communication processes were stifling growth past micro-stage or organic growth phases.
- Social enterprises were slow to update structures, systems, and procedures.

Source: Based on M. Bull and H. Crompton, *Business Practice in Social Enterprise* (Manchester: Manchester Metropolitan University Business School, June 2005)

Balancing social and financial issues

As can be deduced from some of the comments in Illustration 6.4, a significant issue for those involved in decision-making in social enterprises is dealing with the multiple bottom line, and reconciling social and environmental objectives with financial objectives poses real problems for many of them. In a private business, the objective is reasonably straightforward to express – to maximise profit over the medium to long term – although not all owners choose to maximise, but instead 'to satisfice' (i.e. to balance the earning of a satisfactory and sustainable return with the expenditure of reasonable amount of effort).

When one is seeking to meet the needs of poorer households with services such as housework, shopping, childcare, elderly care, help with schoolwork, and gardening, for example, it is difficult to know what emphasis to put on maximising profit, even if it is retained in the business to subsidise services in the future. How management prioritises and balances these sometimes conflicting goals is a major challenge. Should it be about purely social aims or purely commercial aims or is there a defensible and rational middle ground, especially in the absence of readily available measures of social impact? (See Illustrations 6.5 and 6.6 and see Case 6.1.)

Central to many of the problems which arise in this area is the issue of pricing. There is a chronic tendency for social enterprises to under-price their goods and services (as there often is with small private businesses). This can arise for a number of reasons, including undervaluing the worth of what is offered, wishing to minimise the expense to the client, treating receipt of grants as a reason for subsidising prices, or simply misunderstanding the true costs. (See Illustration 6.7.)

Illustration 6.5 Choosing among alternatives: The multiple bottom line

Organisations which are trying to survive financially while also achieving their primary purpose are often faced with awkward choices such as the following:

- To raise prices or to cut services?
- To employ disabled people or to put productivity first?
- To purchase 'green' products at higher prices or to select cheaper but less 'ethical' products?
- To recruit the most suitable person for a job or to recruit someone who can most benefit from it for their future employment?
- To rely on external funding and donations to support the work of meeting the needs of the disadvantaged, or to seek financial autonomy at the expense of range of services and quality?

Illustration 6.6 Ethics or profits – An example of conflicting values

One of the authors asked a colleague if he would like to facilitate a strategy formulation session for a newly formed social enterprise. The colleague however found it to be a very frustrating experience and his subsequent report was brief but informative:

I no longer wish to be with people who devote more time to arguing whether it is unethical to price products at £9.99 instead of £10 than to considering how and where they could generate additional sales income.

Illustration 6.7 Full-cost or marginal cost?

Typical of an area of decision-making which can cause considerable disagreement, if not confusion, is that of pricing. It is a common criticism of (grant-aided) social enterprises by public procurers, as well as private sector competitors, that they too often price their goods or services at marginal cost, or at least below what full-cost recovery would dictate. The following is an extract from a NCVO case study on Ealing Community Transport:

It is also important, surrounded as we are in the sector by animated discussion about core costs to ensure that we always charge on the basis of average, not marginal, costs. Demand the full amount of what it costs you to deliver the service, not just the project costs, but all the costs that go into making that project happen – lighting, heating, rent, the Chief Executive's salary – in other words, demand 'full cost recovery'.

Source: 'Real-life tales of earning – Ealing Community Transport', http://www.ncvo-vol.org.uk/advice-support/funding-finance/sustainable-funding/ealing-community-transport (accessed 14 January 2013)

There is no doubt that maintaining stakeholder satisfaction is a constant trade-off between financial constraints and service needs for many enterprises. It can be argued that democratic participation and inclusive decision-making processes can make the resolution of the challenge simpler. But, equally, it can produce more complex and slower decisions based on 'the least unacceptable' option.

Corporate governance

A further area of difficulty for many social enterprises which cuts across a number of the issues identified above is the matter of 'corporate' governance. Corporate governance involves the roles and relationships existing across an organisation's management, its board, its stakeholders, and the mission and goals for which the organisation is governed – all in the context of market and regulatory constraints.

In recent years there has been considerable interest among policy-makers in reforming corporate governance arrangements across the private, public, and third sectors. Much of the initial impetus for these changes came from the private sector, and many of the reforms that were initiated there have had an influence in the other sectors.

Indeed, the diversity of the third sector and the differing regulatory requirements have led to various sub-sectors often developing their own codes of practice. In addition, there has been an increasing number of initiatives aimed at increasing awareness of the responsibilities of board members and providing them with appropriate advice, support, and training, as reported by Spear et al. They note that

> In the voluntary and community sector one of the most significant recent develop-
> ments was the establishment of the Governance Hub in 2004, one of several hubs
> set up with government money to build the capacity of the third sector. The hub
> played an important role in developing and disseminating the code of practice for vol-
> untary and community organisations, developing a wide range of governance advice
> and training, and developing national occupational standards for trustees and board
> members.[14]

The key problems affecting governance, highlighted by Spear et al., are as follows:

- *Recruiting board members with the right skills and experience* – becoming more difficult in a sector where most board members are volunteers.
- *The absence of a dominant external stakeholder and the need to balance a range of interests* – between, for example, funders, users, and beneficiaries.
- *Managing membership* – which can come to be dominated over time by an elite of board members and/or full-time staff.
- *The power of boards to control management* – as professional managers may run organi-sations to further their own interests rather than the interests of their stakeholders, the board becoming merely a 'rubber stamp'.
- *Managing the interdependencies between boards and management* – a contrasting complaint about boards is that they often stray into management's territory, meddling in their affairs.
- *Balancing of social and financial goals* – boards may be faced with quite difficult trade-offs among different types of goals.[15]

A move towards private sector practices?

The issue of the organisation and management of third sector organisations is closely linked to their 'ownership', and, within the social enterprise segment in particular, it has been the subject of much debate in recent times. This has been generated in part by the greater emphasis in some quarters on the sustainability of these organisations, not least in times of tightened public funding.

Increasingly in the UK, for example, public services which are not delivered directly by the public sector are being subjected to market forces by being put out to competitive tendering. As a consequence, third sector organisations, which had formerly relied on grant income from government or philanthropic organisations to support the delivery of their services, are now having to change to a business-based 'contract culture' in which, in order to survive, they must compete with other social or private enterprises to secure contracts (and perhaps forming socially responsible partnerships with the business sector in order to do this). (See Illustration 6.8.)

Illustration 6.8 A disadvantage of separation from the market?

The disadvantage of creating temporary work schemes which are prohibited from trading in the market is that their employees are prevented from building links with the mainstream economy and hence prevented from integrating. A more promising approach is to award a wage subsidy to individuals who suffer some disadvantage in the labour market, and then allow the enterprise that employs him or her to trade freely.

Source: GHK, *Social Enterprise: An International Literature Review*, Report to SBS/SEnU (March 2006), para. 143, p. 35

Bull and Crompton[16] state that 'competition, scarce resources and the push towards sustainability through non-profit commercialisation has led to an emphasis on competitive strategies' and 'models or tools imported or copied from the business world'. In addition, there are demands for even greater accountability to funders and for transparency and public accountability.

The UK's (former) Department of Trade and Industry asserted that 'the ability to show that a social enterprise is meeting both its financial and its social bottom lines – reconciling its mission and its money – will be increasingly important...' and '... to help achieve this, it may be helpful to develop...minimum standards of behaviour or an accreditation system...'.[17] It further stated that it wanted to 'make social enterprises better businesses'.[18]

Thus it is evident that in many instances the dividing line between commercial and social enterprise is blurring, at least in the US/UK model of the latter. This convergence has not met with universal approval. Because the non-profit organisation has multiple bottom lines, Anheier sees it as a conglomerate of multiple organisations. He states:

> the notion of non-profit organisations as multiple organisations and as complex, internal federations or coalitions requires a multi-faceted, flexible approach, and not the use of ready-made management models carried over from the business world or public management. This is the true challenge non-profit management theory and practice face: how to manage organisations that are multiples and therefore intrinsically complex.[19] (See Illustration 6.9.)

Illustration 6.9 Tensions between 'social' and 'enterprise'

There were three key findings. Firstly, in the minds of practitioners tensions exist between the social and economic domains and goals. Many will only entertain dominant economic thinking where it supports social goals, overcomes barriers to funding, or enables survival. There are multiple attitudes ranging from: enthusiasm and acceptance of business-like behaviour; acceptance of an ebb and flow between social and economic; a radical view of enterprise as the 'dark side' to be raided on a smash and grab basis, or avoided all together. Not all practitioners perceive a need to pursue a business model (even to obtain necessary funding) as numerous income streams (grant aid, contracts and partnerships) remain.

Source: P. Seanor, M. Bull and R. Ridley-Duff, 'Contradictions in social enterprise: do they draw in straight lines or circles?', Paper presented at Institute for Small Business and Entrepreneurship Conference, Glasgow (November 2007), p. 15

One commentator has sought to draw comparisons between the managerial and organisational characteristics of market-led or private sector organisations and those in the social economy which are value led with social objectives, as shown in Table 6.2.

With the emphasis on performance measurement, the adoption of tools developed in the business world remains controversial. Bull and Crompton[20] quote the Social Enterprise Partnership as reporting that 'many social enterprises see impact measurement as a burden, rather than ... a useful management tool' and 'little work has been done at a sector wide level to see how existing tools work for social enterprises'.

Or a move towards public sector practices?

At the same time as some people are detecting a move towards private sector practices in some parts of the third sector, others are highlighting the danger of importing aspects

Table 6.2 Comparison of market sector and social economy characteristics

Issue	Market sector characteristic	Social economy characteristic
Responds to	Demand (which generates profit)	Need (which generates sympathy and appreciation)
Objectives	Profit	Financial and social return
Strategy	Product/market led	Need/competence/value driven
Organisation structure	Hierarchical	Flat
Pricing	What the market will bear	What client can afford
Decision-making	Quick, one boss, single bottom line	Slow, participative, based on trade-offs, multiple bottom lines
Culture	Stand-alone, viability	Dependency, grant driven
Ethos	Autocratic, effective	Democratic, caring, laid-back
Approach to risk	Managed	Mainly averse
Managerial attitude	(Get out of) my way	All together, communal, shared approach, shared vision
Business model	Production (emphasising efficiency and results)	Administrative/strategic (emphasising process and people)

Source: Based on a presentation by P. Quinn to a joint INCORE and Cresco Trust seminar the Magee Campus of the University of Ulster on 5 May 2006

of public sector culture. This, they suggest, can arise when the public sector is closely involved in controlling how contracts it places are performed or, even more, when it is involved in the establishment of third sector organisations to deliver those contracts (see Illustration 5.3 and Chapter 9).

Borzaga and Solari, in turn, stated their concern about the social enterprise–public sector interface as follows:

> Social enterprise managers must continue to provide the public sector with innovative projects and a broader view of the evolution of social needs. Autonomy and an ability to devise new markets and new strategies are crucial for the legitimisation of social enterprises with respect to public-sector organisations. Social enterprises are at risk of a reaction by the public sector, which may seek to gain direct control over them. The consequences would be the hampering of innovation and the confinement of social enterprises to the organisation of a secondary labour market. [21]

Overall

The competing pulls of the public and private sectors on at least the social economy part of the third sector arise because, according to some definitions, the social economy exists at that part of the private returns/social returns continuum in which activities undertaken to create social value can also create financial returns. While third sector organisations can in turn reapply financial returns for social purpose, those managing them, with other stakeholders, need increasingly to be clear about the ways in which their enterprises contribute to the creation of social value and articulate it in a balanced way alongside the financial return they create.

The drive towards contracts and market commercialisation is likely to continue and will lead to increasing pressure on social enterprises having to develop 'business-like' strategies and a greater requirement for accountability and transparency and the measurement of social performance indicators – output measures. According to Bull:

> This challenge has been met with … tools [which] help social enterprises develop strategies for social accountability. But these merely seek to package the output and delivery performances of the services – the 'what comes out of what they do'. They do not challenge the business-like practices within the organisations, the 'how they do what they do' which is vitally important to the development of the sector. [22] (See section 'Measures of success' later in this chapter.)

Employment

The issue of employment can often provide particular challenges, as well as benefits, in the third sector. To date in the UK there has not been an adequate empirical base upon which to form solid conclusions on employment characteristics. Nevertheless, there is an area which continues to be topical and is worthy of consideration, and that is the quality of jobs in the sector.

Job quality

The social economy is often faced with the assertion that the jobs it generates are 'low quality'. The meaning of 'low quality' in this context often seems to lack precision but it appears generally to reflect a perception that many jobs in the sector have low remuneration and are relatively unskilled, temporary, and/or part-time. There is, however, a lack of reliable or recent data upon which to substantiate or refute such assertions.

The factors which contribute to a prevalence of low remuneration and temporary and/or part-time employment, if that is the case, are seen to be not only a consequence of the market factors of supply and demand (see Illustration 6.10) but also in many ways intrinsic to the sector.

Illustration 6.10 Should an issue of supply and demand lead to low wages?

'Don't let charities bid for services' – Amicus

In November 2006 trade union Amicus urged the Treasury to bar voluntary and private sector organisations from bidding for public sector contracts.

The union met Stephen Timms, the chief secretary to the Treasury, to try to persuade him to abandon procurement processes that allow charities to bid. It claims the competition leads to a deterioration in services for users and in conditions for staff.

'The most cost-effective bid wins the contract', Rachael Maskell, national officer at Amicus, told Third Sector. 'Organisations cut back on terms and conditions to shave off margins.'

She said some of its voluntary sector members had complained about a decline in their working conditions because charities were cutting corners to produce competitive bids. The union wanted a more collaborative approach.

'If all stakeholders met to decide what the service is, what the cost is and how they are going to deliver it, that gives greater consideration to the actual service rather than placing the emphasis on the procurement process', Maskell said.

Stephen Bubb, Chief executive of Acevo, said: 'Amicus is living in cloud-cuckoo-land. We should focus on what public services are there for – providing a service to communities.'

He refuted Maskell's claim that staff working for charities delivering public services saw any decline in their working conditions.

Source: http://www.thirdsector.co.uk/Channels/Fundraising/Article/621812   (accessed 14 August 2007)

If the remuneration is low, some of the causes may be:

- The task content of many social economy jobs is often quite basic requiring limited skills and consequently earning low levels of remuneration.
- Social enterprises may often themselves be operating at the margins of sustainability and therefore only be able to afford to pay low wages, and/or they may recruit, as a matter of policy, those who find it difficult to get into the labour market and who do not expect a higher wage.
- The social economy is not yet perceived as a valid career or employment option by many people and so it attracts less well qualified and less able people for whom higher levels of remuneration would not be justified.
- As the social objectives of social enterprises may have primacy, it may be assumed that in some ways employees are attracted by the mission and values and are less concerned about the financial rewards of their employment.
- As social non-profit organisations, or charities, dependent often upon donations and grants, it might be assumed that there should be a strict, if not parsimonious, attitude to remuneration levels.

- That, as the recipients of the sector's services are often the disadvantaged, marginalised, and excluded, this should be reflected in restraint, or even sacrifice, by the providers of those services in order to deliver as much service as possible from limited budgets. Thus, it might be perceived that high levels of remuneration would be inappropriate or even unethical.
- A blurring of the distinction between employees and volunteers can occur, inducing an attitude that employees are 'paid volunteers'.

Similarly the temporary nature of jobs may be attributed to:

- The unpredictability of the funding base of organisations, which means that their ability to offer 'permanent' or continuous employment is limited.
- The lack of a clear distinction, at times, between the role of volunteers (including board members) and that of professional staff in meeting the needs of the community.
- An almost unconscious mindset which perceives that this is 'how the sector does things'.
- In the absence of a strong business culture amongst the directors and senior staff, a dilettante approach to the commercial necessities of organisational life can develop.

It can also be relevant to ask what a 'quality' job is in this context. Many people might feel that a quality job would be one which required high skills/qualifications, was well remunerated, had status and stability, was full-time and permanent, and included regular training and opportunity for professional advancement. However, an indication of a high-quality job might also be a low employee turnover rate. A low turnover rate might indicate that the people concerned liked their jobs, or at least preferred them to alternatives available, and that preference might not depend only on the set of criteria just listed.

Quality can also be interpreted as meaning 'fitness for purpose', instead of just 'degree of excellence', and in the context of employment, there can be more than one purpose for a job. If, for instance, a job is seen as contributing to economic development, then it might be hoped that it would be high value-adding, export-producing, new technology and/or knowledge-based, full-time, and long-lasting. From the point of view of a job-seeker, on the other hand, the purpose of a job might be to support a lifestyle, and, in that case, issues such as convenience of working hours and accessibility of location, prospects for career progression and learning opportunities, an acceptable working environment, flexibility allowing for other tasks such as child-rearing, and making a 'useful' contribution to society might all be very relevant.[23] On that basis many social economy jobs, even if not very well remunerated, may offer other compensating features and provide some people with what are, for them, better-quality jobs than the alternatives. In short, quality jobs may be interpreted as those which support, or at least are compatible with, the sort of life people want to live. Many would argue that many social economy employment opportunities are of this sort.

Indeed, Borzaga and Defourny[24] note that a telling feature of Italian social co-operatives is the measure of job satisfaction reported by workers. In comparison to their counterparts in the public sector, workers in social co-operatives are more satisfied with job quality and the overall employment environment, including their perception of their work as a key source of self-fulfilment. This sense of job satisfaction is directly related to the perception that they work in an environment of shared values, and their status as decision-makers in the design and delivery of the co-operative's services.

Martin and Thompson, in similar vein, argue that as social enterprises may not be paying the full market rates to employees, building motivation and commitment to the mission of the organisation is important, and that 'motivation is even more important in a social enterprise than it is in a for-profit SME'. [25]

Volunteers

Illustration 6.11 Volunteering perspectives

The Welfare Society is that which delivers welfare beyond the State. At the heart of the Welfare Society is the army of people who, for love of neighbour and community, shoulder the massive burden of care. I think of the daughter caring for a sick mother, the volunteer in a children's hospice, the ex-addict helping others escape drugs. Within Britain's welfare society nearly all forms of need are being overcome by somebody, somewhere. The Welfare Society remains the largest deliverer of care in Britain today, dwarfing the State; without it the State would be overwhelmed.

Source: Conservative Party Social Justice Policy Group, 'Breakthrough Britain: Third sector', www.volunteering.org.uk, 25 October 2007

Despite a plethora of initiatives, rates of volunteering remain low, especially among charities tackling poverty and communities suffering from social exclusion. Independent research suggests that perhaps only 19% of the adult population is volunteering at present.

Source: Conservative Party Social Justice Policy Group, 'Breakthrough Britain – Briefing Paper 6: Third sector', p. 1, www.centreforsocialjustice.org.uk/UserStorage/pdf20%Exec%20summariesBBExecThirdSector.pdf (accessed 11 January 2013)

One characteristic of many social enterprises is that they rely, at least in part, on volunteer labour. Indeed, as Chapter 3 notes, the sector, or part of it, is sometimes referred to as the voluntary sector. It could be said that the nature of the sector makes the use of volunteers both necessary and possible. It is necessary because many social enterprises do not have enough resources to pay for all the labour needed to run them and it is possible because some of the labour is only required part-time, so those providing it can earn a living from other full-time jobs, and because those providing the labour want to contribute in that way to the organisations' activities. Indeed, sometimes people establish organisations of this kind to provide a vehicle for their volunteer contributions.

Volunteers can help social enterprises at all levels. At the strategic level the directors or trustees of companies limited by guarantee, trusts, and similar organisations are often not paid for their input, and the constitutions of many of those organisations actually preclude such remuneration. At the operational level many organisations rely on volunteers to carry out much, if not all, of their service delivery work. In between, some social enterprises have management or specialist staff who are paid, because they need them full-time or because they could not otherwise obtain their services on a reliable and consistent basis. Often a lack of volunteers can result in a greater dependence on external funding sources, a weakened human resource potential, as well as reduced monitoring and quality control in organisations.

Yet volunteering can be seen as the extreme of low pay. Indeed, it very often involves the supply of services that neither the public sector nor private individuals are willing to pay for. However, just because it is not paid, volunteering is not without value. It can be beneficial both to the volunteer and to the recipient organisation, which is why it continues. The benefit to the recipient organisation is that it is provided with the labour it needs. The benefits to the volunteer can include not just a sense of making a contribution to the organisation and its work but also help with their personal development. Some volunteer work is even promoted for this benefit because it can help unemployed people to re-enter the labour market by means such as:

- Giving them training and work-related skills.
- Giving them the experience of regular work.
- Helping them to acquire, and to show that they have acquired, work disciplines such as regular time-keeping.
- Enabling them to apply for jobs from a position of regular employment.

The existence of volunteers can nevertheless make the management of an organisation more difficult. Traditional management approaches to rewards and punishment are often related to financial remuneration, which does not apply to volunteers. They have to be motivated by a different set of incentives. Indeed, given that the ability to recruit and train volunteers is essential to the business model of many organisations in the sector, it is a relatively neglected area.

That volunteering underpins so much of the work of the third sector and its social enterprises is recognised in various ways (see Illustration 6.11) and, in the UK and elsewhere, has led to the formation of voluntary associations promoting the concept. The UK government estimated the contribution that volunteers make 'to service provision and support' is 'equivalent to over 1 million full-time workers'.[26] It further stated that over 20 million people in England volunteered formally or informally, equating to half the adult population, and that almost one quarter of employees work for an employer with a scheme for volunteering.[27]

The *Civil Society Almanac* reports that 39 per cent of adults in England, during 2010–2011, said that they had volunteered formally at least once in the previous 12 months, with 25 per cent volunteering formally at least once a month. (Formal volunteering is interpreted as giving unpaid help through groups, clubs, or organisations to benefit other people or the environment.) This 'equates to 16.6 million people in England volunteering formally at least once a year and 10.6 million people in England volunteering formally once a month. If the survey results were equally valid for the UK adult population as a whole, these estimates would increase to 19.8 million (once a year) and 12.7 million (once a month).'[28]

Rewards

Employees in the sector, including volunteer employees, seek some reward for their efforts. Except for the volunteers, the rewards sought and expected by employees include money, and that is common across all three sectors of an economy. There is little doubt, however, that in terms of financial remuneration, the rewards at least for senior staff in the third sector fall, on average, significantly below that of their counterparts in the private and even public sectors (but see Illustration 6.12).

Illustration 6.12 City pay culture has spread to charities?

The leaders of Britain's charities face accusations that their six-figure pay packets are excessive and part of a culture of greed polluting the voluntary sector. Research seen by *The Independent* shows that more than 50 charity chief executives received between £100,000 and £210,000 last year. In one case, a charity paid its chief executive nearly £400,000. Unite, the union which represents 60,000 charity workers, said too many charity bosses were paying themselves more than the Prime Minister's salary of £197,000. But Unite's attack... drew a fierce response from the organisation representing charity chief executives:

> Unite seems to think the charity sector is stuck in the Victorian age, where our organisations are run by volunteers who rely on jumble sales and raffles – we have moved on from those days.

Source: www.independent.co.uk/news/uk/home-news/city-pay-culture-has-spread-to-charities-union-says-1817725.html, 10 November 2009 (accessed 11 January 2013)

That private sector rewards can be relatively very large is very apparent. The media regularly expresses its concern, if not outrage, at the latest announcement of salary/bonus awards for directors and CEOs of large corporations. Indeed, even owners of small- and medium-sized businesses can earn substantial sums if their businesses are successful. Many such people, when questioned, will contend that money is not pursued for money's sake (nor even for what it can buy), but that it is their way of measuring their success. It is a form of scorecard that reflects the result of their efforts and many strive consistently to improve that score. Satisfaction derives from such improvement and provides the motivation to continue to strive.

While senior public sector employees do not typically reap the same level of financial rewards at the top end of the scale as their private sector counterparts, they can receive other forms of reward which provide a motivation for them. Recognition through the award of honours, for example, is common for senior civil servants and presumably compensates in some way for the shortfall in earnings compared to the private sector. Honours are clearly not the preserve of those employed in the public sector but they receive disproportionately more of them than those in the private sector, who in turn rely on senior public sector support for their endorsements. Similarly it can be argued that security of employment is greater in the public sector to which can be attached a monetary equivalent. Senior staff in the third sector, however, receive on average less than their counterparts in either of the other two sectors.

Some of the reasons why this situation prevails have been highlighted already (see section 'Job quality' above). That it has existed for so long and shows little signs of changing in the foreseeable future suggests that senior staff are motivated by something more than the level of the financial remuneration. It is reasonable to deduce that such motivation derives from fulfilling the mission and sharing the values of the organisation employing them. Such emotional, even spiritual rewards, are likely to count substantially to the sense of well-being of leaders of value-driven organisations. Whenever someone is acting to reduce the number of road deaths, heart attacks, cancer patients, or animals ill treated, he/she is often totally committed to the central *raison d'être* of their organisation. As in Maslow's hierarchy of needs/wants, once one's basic material needs are met, individuals strive for emotional fulfilment and ultimately 'self-actualisation'.

Market economics would suggest that rewards, whatever form they take, should equate across sectors, assuming that the competences sought in senior staff are similar and transferable. That financial rewards vary significantly is due, inter alia, to the non-monetary 'rewards' inherent in certain occupations. Undoubtedly, the job satisfaction deriving from the desire to generate social, ethical, environmental, cultural, or sporting benefit constitutes a significant non-monetary reward for many in the third sector.

Measures of success

It is generally perceived that 'business' is about profit and making money for the business owner(s). This view is reinforced, at least in countries such as the UK, by legal requirements that most companies should prepare and submit annual financial accounts and by the traditional format of company annual reports, which always include the financial accounts showing, on the 'bottom line', the financial profit or loss made by the business during the year. Most 'business' is private sector business and is generally thought to have a single objective and so have a single bottom line, or measure of success, which is the level of its financial profit.

As already noted, social enterprises can have more than one objective. Their objectives can be social, but they also need to maintain their financial viability if they are to survive. Without that, nothing else is possible, and the more financial profit they make, the more they have available to put back into their operations. Financial profitability is of interest therefore to third sector organisations, but as a means to an end, rather than as the end itself or as a measure of business success. Thus, the success of a social enterprise is measured not only, or even mainly, by its financial profit (or surplus) but also by its social, environmental, cultural, and/or ethical impact, and this has given rise to the concept of the double, triple, or even quadruple bottom line, depending on how many kinds of key objective the organisation has.

The existence of a double (or multiple) bottom line suggests forms of measure expressed in terms wider than just financial profitability. It may be in terms of one or more of a wide range of social, environmental, or other impacts, such as the number of people helped into employment, the number of hungry people fed, the number of lives saved, the number of persons reached by an artistic venture, the scale of CO_2 emissions eliminated, or other impacts. As it has been put in relation to the social enterprise, the financial figures tell you about the 'enterprise' part, but they do not tell you about the 'social' part.

Thus, in the late 1990s, the concepts of 'social accounting' and 'social auditing' emerged in their latest manifestation, along with various related measurement tools, to help the social enterprise to develop the monitoring, documentation, and reporting systems for recording its impacts across all its objectives. Through a social accounting and audit process, the social enterprise, it is argued, can both understand and account for its social, environmental, and economic impacts on its beneficiaries in the surrounding community. It may also be hoped that, in so doing, the enterprise will be more accountable and will engage more with its key stakeholders because it can measure and demonstrate its value in both quantitative and qualitative ways, and also possibly see where its performance might be improved. Ultimately, the communities served should be better able to evaluate its contribution and investors to assess whether their investment in the enterprise has achieved the added value intended.

While the term social auditing has been used to cover the process of both recording and checking social achievement, there is now a tendency to differentiate the activities. Social accounting refers to the process of gathering and using data to report to stakeholder groups in the accounts. Social auditing seeks to verify (vouch and check) the performance claims made in those accounts. While the terms are also observed to be used interchangeably, strictly the distinction is like that between financial accounting and financial auditing.

There is no single method of social accounting for use by third sector organisations (and others)[29] – not least because there is no one single social objective shared by all third sector organisations nor indeed by their funders. Advocates of social accounting would also stress that, in this sense, it is not like an external evaluation. Rather, it is for the 'social and community enterprises themselves to identify their values and their social, environmental and economic objectives and take responsibility for fully reporting on them, including consulting with the stakeholders'.[30] The stakeholders can include customers, employees, local communities, the public at large, business partners, and government at the national, regional, or local level.

Overall, it has been said that what the social auditing process, or really the whole social accounting, auditing, reporting, and feedback process, 'boils down to' is:

- Do you know what is important to you and to your stakeholders?
- Do you know what your impact is and what your stakeholders think of it?
- Are you responding to this?[31]

'At its broadest', according to Price, 'it is used to capture the whole set of values, issues and processes that must be addressed in order to minimize any harm resulting from any activities and to create economic, social and environmental value.'[32]

Undoubtedly, there is in the UK an increasing pressure, especially for those servicing government-funded contracts, to demonstrate in measurable form their impacts as a basis for continued funding. The emphasis on assessing social enterprises in a holistic way is likely to grow and represents an additional challenge to managers in this sector. To date, there is little evidence to suggest that many social enterprises are measuring their social and environmental impacts. While recognising the pressure to become more proactive in recording and marketing their social values, most social enterprises limit themselves to mission statements incorporating values and aspirations or to responding merely to the requirements of funders for measures. There are, however, now a number of bodies which will advise on social accounting and/or perform an independent social audit of the results of a social accounting process.

Accounting and audit tools

There is a range of accounting and audit tools from which to choose, and these are complemented by strategy and performance/quality improvement systems. By no means all of these concepts or tools are new or innovative. Many are adapted from the traditional business world. Tables 6.3 and 6.4 offer a sample of the approaches and tools which are currently available to help the enterprise to focus, measure, control, and ultimately publicise its impacts. The 'proliferation of organisations that produce social accounts and the diversity of social accounting techniques'[33] available have led to increased efforts to establish international standards for the practice of social and ethical accounting, auditing, and reporting.

Measuring outputs and outcomes

There is a further aspect of performance measurement that is particularly relevant to those organisations, whether in the third sector or sometimes in the private sector, which receive grants for aspects of their activity. It is the need sometimes to distinguish outputs from outcomes and to ensure that both are measured. In this terminology, outputs are the things that an organisation undertakes to provide, such as a car manufacturing business undertaking to produce cars. The outcomes are then the benefits which it is hoped that having the outputs will lead to, such as the social status which having a particular type of car might be thought to indicate. Understanding this distinction can be important because

Table 6.3 Examples of social accounting management tools

Focus	Tools
(For fuller explanations see 'Sources of social accounting guidance and tools' in 'Suggestions for further reading' at the end of this chapter)	
Holistic accounting and reporting	Social Accounting and Audit
	AA 1000 Assurance Standard
Measuring impact and performance	Social Return on Investment
	Eco-mapping
	GRI (Global Reporting Initiative)
	KSCPIs (Key Social and Co-operative Performance Indicators)
	LM 3 (Local Multiplier 3)
Quality/performance improvement systems	Prove It!
	DTA (Development Trust Association) Healthcheck
	EFQM (European Foundation for Quality Management)
	PQASSO (Practical Quality Assurance System for Small Organisations)
Strategic management	IIP (Investors in People)
	Social Enterprise Balanced Scorecard
	Social Firms Performance Dashboard

Source: Adaptation of PowerPoint slides of Martin Cooper, new economics foundation, presented at University of Cambridge, April 2006

Table 6.4 Prominent approaches to quality and methods and tool for assessing social impact

Social Return on Investment (SROI)
Theory of Change
Social Accounting and Audit (SAA)
Logic Models
Social IMPact measurement for Local Economies
Third Sector Performance Dashboard
Social Enterprise Balanced Score Card
Volunteering Impact Assessment Toolkit
Local Multiplier 3 (LM3)
Quality Evaluation
Measuring Environmental Impact
Consultant Facilitated Impact Assessment
Outcomes Star
The Rickter Scale

Source: www.socialimpactscotland.org.uk/understanding-social-impact-/methods-and-tools-.aspx (accessed 14 January 2013)

it is the outputs which are contractual whereas it is the anticipated outcomes which are usually the reason for the grants being given.

For instance, a third sector organisation might undertake to provide training courses for unemployed people in the expectation that the recipients of the training would more readily find employment. The delivery of the training courses would be the output and the subsequent employment would be the anticipated outcome. Sometimes outcomes are separated into shorter-term results and longer-term impacts, and in the training case, the qualifications obtained would be a result and the employment obtained through the possession of those qualifications an impact. (See Figure 6.1.) This distinction between outputs and outcomes, between what is contracted and what is desired, is relevant to the measurement process and can be helpful in determining why things work well, or in identifying where the problem lies when they go badly (as Illustration 6.12 describes).

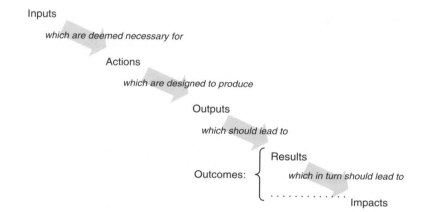

Figure 6.1 The sequence from inputs to impacts?
Source: S. Bridge and K. O'Neill, *Understanding Enterprise, Entrepreneurship and Small Business* (London: Palgrave Macmillan, 2013), p. 300

Illustration 6.13 An example of outputs and outcomes

This analysis of a project from a remote farming community illustrates the difference between outputs and outcomes.

In this community, farm incomes were low and, as a result, young people were leaving the area. To encourage them to stay and to keep the community alive, the local community enterprise devised a scheme to improve farm incomes by improving the quality of the cattle the farms produced.

The planned *output* of the scheme therefore was that the farms would produce better quality cattle, and the *outcomes* hoped for from this were that farm incomes would increase and that more young people would stay in the area to take over the farms. In this case the increase in farm incomes was the anticipated *result* and the retention of young people was the *impact* which it was hoped this would have.

The community enterprise was successful in obtaining a rural development grant to help it to implement the scheme which involved introducing better AI to provide better genetic stock and better silage-making and better byres to provide better over-wintering feed and care for the cattle. What actually happened as a result of the scheme was that the farms involved did produce better quality cattle which was demonstrated by veterinary inspections and the fact that they sold in better quality markets. So the scheme delivered what it was contracted to deliver. However farm incomes did not increase as a result because, in the meantime, the BSE problem had arisen and depressed the price for all cattle. The scheme could not be blamed for this but it did mean that the hoped-for result was not achieved. In this case however there was some evidence that more young people were staying on the farms, possibly because they saw that some attention was now being given to the area. Thus the desired impact, to some extent, was happening. Without that distinction between outputs and outcomes and, within outcomes, between results and impacts, and without some measurement of each aspect separately, it would not have been possible to analyse properly the effectiveness of the project.

Source: Based on S. Bridge and K. O'Neill, *Understanding Enterprise, Entrepreneurship and Small Business* (London: Palgrave Macmillan, 2013), p. 300

Problems/Dangers

There are reasons put forward for the slow uptake of these relatively new forms of measurement and some dangers highlighted also, which are as follows:

- A lack of resources, typically time and money, or perhaps expertise, to prepare for and carry out the measurement.
- Lack of knowledge on how to get commitment (or 'buy-in') within the organisation and to effectively embed the processes.
- Being too ambitious in scope when implementing the accounting/audit process for the first time. It is deemed useful to prioritise objectives and take each in turn to allow the processes to evolve in manageable 'chunks'.
- The process can become dysfunctional if there is too strong a desire to produce results to meet unreasonable expectations from key stakeholders. In such a situation the learning and improving dimension of the accounting process may be lost. Moreover, the 'quality of social performance verification has been severely criticised'.[34]

Benefits

While there are problems and dangers as noted above, three distinct sets of benefits from measuring social achievements are frequently articulated. They are as follows:

- supporting business credibility, increasing productivity, and enhancing corporate reputation
- improved relations with stakeholders
- marketing performance improved from listening to customer demands[35]

Conclusion

Third sector organisations are not completely different from private or public sector organisations, as noted in Chapter 5. They all involve groups of people supposedly trying to achieve a common purpose. Third sector businesses, such as social enterprises, are, in many respects, like private sector business, especially in their need to earn sufficient income to maintain their existence. There is a significant difference, however. For a profit-seeking private sector business, having raised income and/or reduced costs enough to be 'in the black', making the profit sought then involves doing more of the same. For a third sector business, while being 'in the black' is essential for survival, achieving the organisation's purpose then involves not only delivering more financial surplus, but also delivering social, environmental, cultural, and/or ethical outcomes on top of that.

This might suggest that, size for size, managing a third sector organisation can be more challenging, than managing a private business.

Such might not be the public perception, and sometimes private sector managers might seem to be under greater pressure to get results than third sector managers. That perception might, however, reflect a lack of understanding of the third sector. In their aims, legal structures, ownership, organisation, and measures of success, third sector organisations face many similarities with organisations in the other sectors, but also some significant differences. This chapter has tried to describe some of them.

Key Points of Chapter 6

- Third sector organisations, and social enterprises in particular, share some characteristics with organisations in other sectors but have other characteristics which are unique to this sector.
- Consideration of the particular characteristics of social enterprises throws light on aspects of their uniqueness. They include:
  - the founders and their motivations
  - the variety of aims of the sector's organisations
  - the possible legal structures and their suitability and flexibility
  - the concept of ownership and its complications
  - their organisation and how they are affected by, for example, culture, values, style, staffing, and multiple bottom lines
  - employment profiles and perceptions of job quality
  - the role and management of volunteers
- With a wide range of aims, social enterprises often have a complex task in reporting to stakeholders on their effectiveness and on the success, or otherwise, of their efforts. There is now a proliferation of accounting and audit tools with the potential to help with this.
- It is useful to distinguish, in performance terms, between outputs and outcomes, and between results and impacts.

Case 6.1 | Developing income streams while balancing social and commercial objectives

Being innovative is seen as a characteristic of successful social enterprises, not least in developing income streams to maintain sustainability. At the same time, the social enterprise often has to manage the tensions between its social mission and its commercial imperatives. The case below illustrates how one such enterprise has approached these issues.

Based in Canning Town Public Hall, East London Community Links is a network of community initiatives working, since 1977, with children, young people, and adults learning and developing new ways of tackling the familiar problems of disadvantaged communities. Community Links' trading activity takes several forms and is based on two types of assets as follows:

Visible assets

Community Links negotiated with the local authority to transfer Canning town hall on an annual peppercorn lease on condition that Community Links restore the decaying building within two years: if they failed and the restoration was not achieved, the property would revert to council control. They succeeded.

Although the freehold on the building is not owned by Community Links – meaning that it cannot be shown on the balance sheet and used as equity for attracting loan finance – the acquisition saved significant sums in rent and enabled Community Links to expand significantly the range of services that it provides in the local community.

Visible assets also extend to equipment. A corporate sponsor asked Community Links if it could hire its nursery's bouncy castle for an employee family day. Now the community centre has developed an occasional trading enterprise whereby it sells a complete package to corporate family days: it hires out the bouncy castle and other toys and sends along a couple of young people who have completed a short course as children's entertainers.

Invisible assets

Beyond the tangible, Community Links has generated considerable revenue from selling a training package developed from its own volunteer training programme to Thames Water. It relies on voluntary action and, in building such a wealth of social capital, it has accumulated a great deal of know-how on training and motivation. A private company values that know-how highly.

'We get results – motivation and team building – from people who aren't paid, which is what interested our sponsor Thames Water', says Community Links' Director. 'They asked us to run a training programme for them, on the clear understanding that we'd be paid at commercial rates.'

That's an example of mission-related trading designed purely to make money for other aspects of the organisation's work. However, the other trading activity developed from Community Links' core activity, makes money, and advances its mission simultaneously.

The *Ideas Annual* has been published for 12 years now. The first edition simply aimed to collate the good ideas that different community groups were putting into practice, and stop them duplicating each other's work. Like many successful publications, it ended up being repeated every year, with focuses on different themes and geographical regions. Priced on a scale of £5–25, the *Ideas Annual* makes enough money to cover its own costs, freeing up other income.

The 'First Steps' training course, which draws on the expertise built up over 21 years of working with community groups, has a similar sliding pricing structure that allows it to pay in part for itself and, by sharing expertise, develop the core aim of tackling the familiar problems of disadvantaged communities.

Some trading activities are designed to make money to help finance other, unrelated initiatives taking place within the organisation; others are developed as part of a self-financing project furthering core aims.

The Director is, however, clear on the balance between making money and sticking to mission, on the extent to which services can be developed as self-financing ventures.

'You have to agree your limits, but sometimes it's OK to say there's a social purpose and you'll also make some money.' But other potential spin-offs were thought not to be an option.

A café, for example, located in the building's spacious front hallway might have been conceived as a means of making money. Instead, it has been cast as an extension of core services, and Community Links has accepted that its earning potential is restricted.

'We want a café where you can sit over a cup of tea for an hour: we could make a lot more out of a different sort of place, but we don't want that,' explains the Director.

At some places there is money-making potential, and at others there is not. In the case of this cafe, mission and money were hard to combine.

In all instances, income generation is an additional source of income, not a replacement for all grant income.

'I'd say we cover about 70 per cent of our costs now, without distorting our original purpose. There'll always be a mix.'

Conclusion

This is an example of what turns up when you look really closely at an organisation's assets – visible and invisible – and at ways of developing a sustainable funding mix across a broad base of diversified income streams. It is also an illustration of being very clear as to when an activity can and cannot generate its own income and how social and commercial objectives can conflict.

Source: Adapted from http://www.ncvo-vol.org.uk/advice-support/funding-finance/sustainable-funding/community-links (accessed 6 February 2013)

Questions, Exercises, Essay, and Discussion Topics

1. Of the issues considered in this chapter, what are the characteristics revealed which are shared by many third sector organisations, but not by most public or private sector organisations?
2. Of the organisations listed in Table 3.1, which ones share those characteristics?
3. Is it possible, in a moral rather than a legal sense, to be an investor in a CIC (see Illustration 6.2) taking a dividend from the investment while also being a benefactor of the community by virtue of the same investment?
4. In Illustration 6.3, who were the 'owners' of the Northern Ireland Hospice who should have had the final say in directing its affairs: the founders of the Hospice, the original membership which grew in number to just under 400, the new membership of nearly 2000, or the Council of the Hospice?
5. In what ways does the management of a social enterprise tend to differ from that of a private sector organisation?
6. When is it likely to be worth the investment of time and money to prepare social accounts?

Suggestions for further reading

G. Dees, J. Emerson, and P. Economy, *Strategic Tools for Social Entrepreneurs* (New York: Wiley, 2002).

O. Foka, 'The FSM: A holistic approach to measuring social and ethical performance', *Business Ethics: A European Review*, Vol. 12, No. 4, pp. 314–24.

J. Pearce, *Social Audit and Accounting: Manual, Workbook and CD-Rom* (West Calder: Community Business Scotland Network and Liverpool, Social Enterprise Network, 2001).

SEPGB Quality and Impact Project – Social Accounting Manual and Quality Impact ToolKit, www.proveandimprove.org, accessed 16 June 2013.

Social Audit Network, www.socialauditnetwork.org.uk, accessed 16 June 2013.

Institute of Social and Ethical Accountability (ISEA) – AA100, accessed 16 June 2013.

Sources of social accounting guidance and tools

Social Accounting and Audit: www.socialauditnetwork.org.uk

AA 1000 Assurance Standard – reporting standards propagated by AccountAbility, an international not-for-profit organisation: www.accountability21.net/default.aspx?id=54

Social Return in Investment (SROI) – a calculation methodology that monetises impacts to demonstrate to social investors the value creation for society of projects and programmes: www.neweconomics.org/gen/newways_socialreturn.aspx (and www.sroi.london.eu)

Eco-mapping – a tool to analyse and manage a small enterprise's environmental behaviour: www.proveandimprove.org/new/tools/ecomapping.php

GRI (Global Reporting Initiative) – another form of reporting framework (called G3): www.globalreporting.org/ReportingFramework/ReportingFrameworkoverview

KSCPIs (Key Social and Co-operative Performance Indicators) – an alternative way to assess impact: www.co-operatives-UK.coop/live/dynamic/login2.asp?component

LM 3 (Local Multiplier 3) – a tool to assess how a business or initiative impacts on the local economy. Based on the Keynesian multiplier, it measures three rounds of spending: www.neweconomics.org/gen/tools_lm3.aspx

Prove It! – a method for measuring the effect of community regeneration projects on the quality of life of local people: www.proveandimprove.org/new/tools/proveit.php

DTA (Development Trust Association) Healthcheck – a diagnostic tool for reviewing performance and facilitating best practice: www.dta.org.uk/activities/services/healthcheck/

EFQM (European Foundation for Quality Management) – a framework for self-assessment, benchmarking, and improvement: www.efqm.org/default.aspx?tabid+35

PQASSO (Practical Quality Assurance System for Small Organisations) – a quality system designed for voluntary sector organisations facilitating setting of priorities and improved performance: www.ces-vol.org.uk/index.cfm?pg=42

IIP (Investors in People) – a framework to help improve performance through the effective management and development of an organisation's people: www.investorsinpeople.co.uk/Pages/NewCustomersHomePage.aspx

Social Enterprise Balanced Scorecard – a mechanism to track quantitative and qualitative data simultaneously allowing an organisation to measure and communicate its social impacts: www.sel.org.uk/balanced_scorecard.html

Social Firms Performance Dashboard – a tool developed for emerging and established social forms which seeks to offer a simplified version of the Social Enterprise Balanced Scorecard (see above): www.proveandimprove.org/new/tools/socialfirm.php

References

1. A. Westall and D. Chalkley (Eds), *Social Enterprise Futures* (London: The Smith Institute, 2007), p. 27, http://www.smith-institute.org.uk/file/Social EnterpriseFutures.pdf (accessed 31 December 2012).

2. M. Price, *Social Enterprise – What it is and why it matters* (Vale of Glamorgan: Fflan Ltd, 2009), Revised 2nd ed., p. 2.

3. J. Pearce, *Epose Regional Report – UK, Community Business Scotland Networks* (1999), p. 2, www.cbsnetwork.org.uk/EPOSErep.html (accessed 5 June 2007).

4. *Rethinking the Social Economy.* An unpublished paper based on a forum sponsored by the Belfast Local Strategy Partnership and The Queen's University of Belfast, January 2006.

5. GHK, *Review of the Social Enterprise Strategy, a final report submitted by GHK* (London: GHK, 2005), p. 1.

6. *Rethinking the Social Economy.* An unpublished paper based on a forum sponsored by the Belfast Local Strategy Partnership and The Queen's University of Belfast, January 2006.

7. I. Nasioulas, 'CIRIEC Working Paper 2010/11', paper presented at the 3rd International CIRIEC Research

Conference on the Social Economy (Valladolid, Spain: 6–8 April 2011), pp. 5–6.

8. GHK, *Social Enterprise: An International Literature Review*, a report submitted to SBS/SEnU (London: GHK, 2006), p. 26.

9. Office of the Regulator of Community Interest Companies, *Annual Report 2011/2012 – Regulator of Community Interest Companies*, 2012, p. 22.

10. C. Borzaga and L. Solari, 'Management Challenges for Social Enterprises', in C. Borzaga and J. Defourny (Eds), *The Emergence of Social Enterprise* (London: Routledge, 2001), pp. 335–7.

11. M. Bull and H. Crompton, *Business Practice in Social Enterprise* (Manchester: Manchester Metropolitan University Business School, June 2005), pp. 21–38.

12. Ibid., p. 33.

13. M. Price *Social Enterprise – What it is and Why it Matters* (Vale of Glamorgan: Fflan Ltd, 2009), Revised 2nd ed., p. 44.

14. R. Spear, C. Cornforth and M. Aiken, 'The governance challenges of social enterprises: evidence from a UK empirical study', *Annals of Public and Cooperative Economics,* Vol. 80, No. 2 (2009), p. 255.

15. Based on R. Spear, C. Cornforth and M. Aiken, 'The governance challenges of social enterprises: evidence from a UK empirical study', *Annals of Public and Cooperative Economics,* Vol. 80, No. 2 (2009) p. 255.

16. M. Bull and H. Crompton, *Business Practice in Social Enterprise* (Manchester: Manchester Metropolitan University Business School, June 2005), p. 12.

17. DTI, *Social Enterprise: a strategy for success* (London: HM Treasury, July 2002), p. 9.

18. Ibid., p. 77.

19. H. K. Anheier, 'Managing non-profit organisations: Towards a new approach', Civil Service Working Paper 1 (2000), www.ise.ac.uk/collections/CCS/publications/CSWP/cswp1-abstract.html (accessed 6 June 2008).

20. M. Bull and H. Crompton, *Business Practice in Social Enterprise* (Manchester: Manchester Metropolitan University Business School, June 2005), p. 14.

21. C. Borzaga and L. Solari, 'Management Challenges for Social Enterprises', in C. Borzaga and J. Defourny

(Eds), *The Emergence of Social Enterprise* (London: Routledge, 2001), pp. 335–7.

22. M. Bull, *Balance: Unlocking Performance in Social Enterprises* (Manchester: Centre for Enterprise, Manchester Metropolitan University Business School, December 2006), p. 15.

23. Based on S. Bridge, *Quality Jobs,* report to Department of Agriculture and Rural Development for Northern Ireland (2001).

24. Based on C. Borzaga and J. Defourny (Eds), *The Emergence of Social Enterprise* (London: Routledge, 2001).

25. F. Martin and M. Thompson, *Social Enterprise: Developing Sustainable Businesses* (Basingstoke: Palgrave Macmillan, 2010), p. 50.

26. Cabinet Office, *The Future Role of the Third Sector in Social Regeneration: Final Reports,* CM 7189 (London: HM Treasury, July 2007), p. 35.

27. Ibid., p. 45.

28. *UK Civil Society Almanac 2012,* (NCVO, 2012), p. 8, http://www.ncvo-vol.org.uk/sites/default/files/uk_civil_society_almanac_2012_section.pdf (accessed 2 January 2013).

29. Some primarily private sector businesses have used social auditing to help them to demonstrate non-financial impacts, which are increasingly of interest to their shareholders and the wider public.

30. Social Audit Network, *CD2 Social Accounting and Audit: a framework for social, environmental and economic (SEE) reporting* (Undated), p. 1.

31. Said by Simon Zadek at *Improve it: social auditing to win business,* a seminar organised by The Cat's Pyjamas and *Social Enterprise Magazine* and held in London on 29 April 2003.

32. M. Price, *Social Enterprise – What it is and Why it matters* (Vale of Glamorgan: Fflan Ltd, 2009), Revised 2nd ed., p. 51.

33. M. O'Carroll, 'Social Enterprise Performance Verification: an analysis of three social audit tools', Paper presented at Annual Conference of the Institute for Small Business and Entrepreneurship (Cardiff: October/November 2006), p. 2.

34. Ibid., p. 3.

35. Ibid., p. 8.

7

financing the social economy

contents:

- introduction
- finance for the social economy
- social economy finance schemes
- financial instruments
- financial skills for the social economy
- conclusion

Key concepts

This chapter covers:

- the distinctive financial environment of the social economy and how it differs from private and public markets;
- the type and range of financial supports available to the sector;
- how the financial market operates within the social economy in both the demand and supply of resources;
- the distinctive financial obstacles to capitalising the social economy;
- the variety of social finance products including more recent innovations in community shares and Social Impact Bonds;
- how to make the financial supports for the sector work more effectively in growing and developing the social economy.

Learning objectives

By the end of this chapter the reader should:

- understand the importance of financial resources for the development of the social economy;
- appreciate the range of financial supports and products and how they are used to support social enterprises with different development needs;
- be able to identify the strategic and operational obstacles to financing the sector and capitalising social enterprises;
- evaluate the importance of community development finance for investment in the social economy;
- appreciate the importance of business support and skills development for strengthening financial management in the social economy.

Introduction

Animals cannot survive without food, and businesses and other organisations cannot survive without money. And just as an animal needs food to provide both the energy it needs to survive and the building materials it needs to grow, so too an organisation needs money both to cover the costs of its operations and to provide the resources needed for growth.

There are many sources of food available to animals but not all sources will be appropriate to all animals. So too there are many different sources of finance for organisations but they are not all appropriate for every organisation. Financial sustainability is crucial to the creation of a viable social economy and knowing what type of finance is required is a key skill in the management of social enterprises. Nicholls[1] (2008) sets out the key features of market failure in the social finance market and the challenges facing social enterprises. Some of these relate to access to capital, skills shortages, and the lack of distinctive support for social finance:

- Conventional notions of the role of finance and financial markets are increasingly inappropriate for a discussion of social investment.
- Few metrics exist to account for social and environmental externalities (whether positive or negative).
- Concepts of social investment are blurring the boundaries between private, public, and third sector investment.
- Social investment players operate in a fragmented landscape with little exchange of information or incentives for co-operation.
- There are considerable information asymmetries and co-ordination problems across the landscape.

- There is a lack of financial literacy in social purpose organisations that supports a risk-averse approach to new resource strategies.
- Regulation and legislation are lagging behind trends in social and environmental investment.

There are complex and interlinked challenges in financing the social economy, and this chapter thus considers the sources of finance used by third sector organisations and in particular those products which are used mainly, or exclusively, by social enterprises or have been developed especially for them. Interest has also grown in the whole idea of community banking as a real alternative to private financial institutions, which is creating new pressures on the sector:

> The third sector, as it grows in importance, will need access to finance to expand its activities and to adapt to meet the ever changing demands of communities it serves. At the same time, the people managing these organisations will have to accept that borrowing and a certain degree of financial risk will enable them to achieve far more than if they take a more restricted view of their capacities.[2]

As indicated above, an organisation generally needs finance for two things: to pay for the 'capital' costs associated with the start-up, expansion, or redevelopment of the organisations and to pay for all the organisation's day-to-day operating expenses. A sustainable organisation is one which attracts enough income to cover its operating costs, but all organisations, at least at the start-up stage, need some external capital finance, although some of them can, and do, fund later expansion from retained operating surpluses.

A Bank of England[3] review of finance for social economy organisations highlighted the range of ways in which they raise money and the often complex financial mix required to maintain their financial sustainability. One of the most important and traditional areas of support for the social economy has been grant aid. Grants are still important for many social enterprises, especially during their start-up phase, as they may otherwise lack the finance needed to create a viable business. The Bank of England review highlighted the difficulties of grant funding, including the problems associated with creating surpluses, the restrictions on what agencies can do with the aid, and the potential of 'mission drift', whereby organisations adapt their plans to meet funders' priorities. Therefore, there has been an emphasis on diversifying the funding streams for social enterprises, especially in encouraging innovation and reducing dependency from non-tradable activities. Non-grant sources have a number of benefits including their longer-term nature, which can facilitate more effective planning, strengthening organisational efficiencies, and enabling greater flexibility in the activities in which the organisation can engage so as to support service delivery.

Brown and Swersky[4] estimated that the demand for social investment could rise from £165 million of deals done in 2011 to £286 million in 2012, £750 million in 2015, and to as much as £1 billion by 2016. The growth will be caused by increased outsourcing of public services to private and social providers; a new statutory requirement for commissioners to consider social value when awarding contracts; and a shift towards higher-risk models of payment, such as payment by results, which will encourage social organisations to favour social investment over the commercial sources.

The Bank of England report also shows that lack of access to finance is one of the major obstacles to growth, and so this chapter reviews the issues in funding for the social economy and social enterprises in particular. It looks first at the range of financial sources open to social enterprises before describing specific schemes, especially in a UK context. The chapter then examines the diverse needs of organisations in the sector and the mix of supply dealing with enterprises of different size, scale, and stage of development. The final part of the analysis highlights the implications for skills development in finance and fiscal initiatives tailored to the sector.

Finance for the social economy

Social economy organisations have access to many of the same commercial sources of funding as private sector businesses, limited only by their ability to offer sufficient return on investment. They also have access to private sources of funding and, like private sector businesses, they can earn income through their operations. In addition, they have access to a number of other sources which, in either kind or degree, are not normally available to the private sector.[5]

Kickul and Lyons[6] draw on the work of the F. B. Heron Foundation which has developed a mission-related investment continuum to make the most of asset allocation and build a diverse portfolio from grant funding at one end to equity investment at the other. The degree of risk increases as market or near-market returns are expected from debt as opposed to grant finance. For Kickul and Lyons, effective social entrepreneurs understand the relationship between risk, return, and impact – and aligning the values of the enterprise with those of the investor is a crucial skill, especially in scaling the businesses and moving to more market-rate investors. Within this broad categorisation, the main sources of funding for social enterprises that are considered below can be divided into four types:

- commercial sources of funding.
- private sources of funding.
- earned income.
- special sources of funding.

Commercial sources of funding

Commercial sources of funding include the banks offering, for example, overdrafts and loans, venture capital, the stock market, and various forms of equity finance. However, most social enterprises are limited in their ability to avail of such sources. Often, because they have a constitution which prevents them from distributing profits to investors, they are unable to attract commercial investments from sources which are specifically seeking a significant financial return. Also, because their focus is on their social purpose as well as on sustainability, they may not generate enough income to cover the interest on, and eventual repayment of, significant loans, although they may avail of an occasional overdraft facility.

Private sources of funding

Private sources of funding are often summarised as the three F's: family, friends, and foolish strangers. However, these categories of funders also often hope for some return from their investment, or at least expect eventually to get their money back. So it can be harder for social enterprises to attract their support, unless it is in the form of a donation to support the purposes of the organisation, and in that case it might be considered to come into the special sources category.

One UK initiative to allow social enterprises to return some of their earnings to shareholders, and thus to facilitate some private investment finance, albeit with a social purpose, was the legislation which provides for the creation and operation of community interest companies (CICs). In effect, a CIC is a bespoke company limited by shares, which allows some payments to be made to directors and/or investors (see Chapter 6).

Earned income

Social enterprises, trading by selling goods or services, do earn income through their operations. Because they do this in order to cover operating costs and seek to reapply any surplus to support their social purpose, they may be less able than comparable private sector businesses to fund the development of the business from retained earnings.

Special sources of funding

While social enterprises do use commercial methods of funding, such as overdrafts, as noted above, they are generally less able to avail of those sources which are the main financers of private sector businesses. Many organisations in the sector engage in their own fund-raising, often soliciting charitable donations in various forms. This form of funding can be sustainable provided the organisation can continue successfully to solicit donations. Some churches, for instance, have sustained themselves for many hundreds of years on this basis. Endowments, it might be argued, are just a form of donation but, if big enough, can contribute to sustainability because the recipient organisation can cover at least part of its operating costs from the interest the endowment can earn. Donations, often in the form of grants, might be sought from those trusts and foundations which give money to social enterprises. Grants might also be sought from a number of public sector sources which have budgets to use for supporting specific activities and some of these are set out in Illustration 7.1.

No one, it has been suggested, has ever parted with money without expecting to get something in return. The traditional highwayman was supposed to have offered the victim his or her life in exchange for the victim's money, and charity flag sellers offer a clearer conscience to those who donate something. Therefore, it is suggested, that what donations, endowments, and grants have in common is that they are two-way transactions, because, even if it is not obvious, the source of the money nevertheless wants something in return for that money. In this sense, those sources are customers and the potential 'suppliers' are more likely to secure a deal if they can identify what those 'customers' are looking for and showing how their service will offer it. Appreciating that the donor will want to know 'what's in it for me?', even if the question is not framed in that way, can indicate how to phrase a request for funding.

Illustration 7.1 Grant programmes

In the UK there is a wide variety of grant programmes and they do not all apply just to social enterprises. Nevertheless, although some private sector businesses can and do use the programmes to which they can apply, grants are, on the whole, more important to the third sector, and especially to social enterprises. While some grants are given out by third sector organisations, such as foundations, they are normally considered in the context of public sector grants, whether awarded directly by government departments and their agencies, or by other public sector bodies such as the lottery funding bodies.

When they are available, grants are normally requested using a dedicated application form, and then, after a decision process which may or may not include further negotiations with the applicant, they are awarded by the issue of a letter of offer. The letter of offer usually states the amount of grant offered together with some indication of how it is to be used (although this may only be a reference to the original application and a set of conditions).

Grants are used by social enterprises, if and when they can get them, both to provide the funding needed for capital investments and to cover operating costs. For a number of social enterprises grant finance has been crucial both for their start-up or expansion and for their day-to-day operation.

Grant schemes have sometimes been criticised when they are made available to cover operating costs because there is generally no guarantee, and often little possibility, of further grant support for the same activity, which means that the activity may not be sustainable. Public sector grant-givers, however, while wanting to support certain activities, do not want to commit their budgets for long periods into the future. This encourages organisations to engage in certain activities with a once-off grant, often of up to 100 per cent of the funding required, but with no guarantee that they can or will be repeated. Grants have therefore been said to encourage dependency while not being able to deliver continuing support.

An alternative view of grant schemes

Although grant letters of offer, once accepted, become legally binding contracts, grant schemes are not often seen by either the grant-givers or the grant recipients as two-way transactions. Instead they are often viewed, at least by the grant recipients, as some form of entitlement, rather like unemployment or other statutory benefits. Thus grant recipients may often resent the monitoring requirement which the grant-givers then seek to impose. That however is not a helpful attitude. Morrissey and Bridge,[7] for instance, have argued that the grant system is essentially a customer-supplier relationship and that the grant-giver is, in essence, trying to buy something with its money, the delivery of which it should seek to monitor. (Social impact investment, such as Social Impact Bonds, would suggest a move in this direction.) But both the lack of a clear indication that the system is a two-way process, and the absence from many grant letters of offer of a clear statement of what is to be delivered in exchange for the grant, contribute to a lack of clear communication.

The sort of issues that cause confusion about the real nature of grants can include the following:

- Social enterprises often fail to view grant-givers as potential one-off customers and to decide whether or not to engage with them on that basis. Many private sector businesses would be pleased to sell to one-off customers – although they might prefer to get customers who might come back – and do not have customers lined up for years ahead.
- What the grant-giver may actually want is the potential benefits (or 'outcomes') of the process, not the process itself and its direct deliverables (which are sometimes referred to as the 'outputs'). For instance, training courses for unemployed people might be funded in the expectation that unemployed people would then find employment because they had enhanced skills, but it is only the delivery of the training, not the subsequent employment, which should be made contractual, as the delivery of the training is within the supplier's control, whereas the subsequent employment of the people trained is subject to other external factors such as the availability of suitable jobs.
- Grant applicants might consider the desirability of investing in making a good sales pitch if they want to have a reasonable chance of securing an order. However, the availability of grants may have led some third sector organisations to become better at writing successful grant applications than at the subsequent delivery of their projects. It is suggested that sometimes organisations which could rely on debt or mixed forms of finance have instead become effective in making grant applications but, in doing so, are squeezing out other organisations which do indeed need the grants.

Social economy finance schemes

The need for special social economy finance schemes

The demand for social finance varies from small grants and loans to more sophisticated financial products including equity capital. The new economics foundation (nef) argued that the rising number, size, and complexity of social enterprises has created demand for social equity capital in which issuing shares in the company through an equity listing is a route to raise significant capital. This builds the number of stakeholders, offers an exit for early stage investors, and provides a basis for future investment.[8] Its study calls for the development of a social equity capital prototype, stronger links with ethical investors, developing market intermediaries to build awareness, and supporting businesses to attract social equity investment.

According to Iona et al.,[9] the key priorities for social enterprise finance are:

- to stimulate demand for finance by building awareness, marketing products, and developing a preliminary understanding of the grant–loan relationship;
- developing the capacity of investees to help them become investment-ready, to improve their financial literacy and ability to scale up or replicate successful business models;
- processing demand and supply by supporting intermediaries to generate bankable deals. It is important to ensure that the market is not over-stimulated creating a shortage of processing capacity among intermediaries; and
- developing financial products that appeal to investors as well as investees.

There has been considerable change in social finance in the UK with the coalition government aiming to develop products for social ventures and the creation of a new asset class to enable social ventures to access mainstream capital.[10] The Big Society Bank has been established by the government, not directly to fund businesses, but to invest in social finance intermediaries which lend on to social enterprises. As with other sectors, the social economy is increasingly supported by financial infrastructures developing in the traditional centres of capital and finance. Thus, Lloyd[11] argued that 'the London hub has become a recognised preserve for a supporting group of successful entrepreneurs, financiers and fund managers who have migrated into social investment looking for potentially lucrative solutions to social and environmental problems'.

While most small business owners probably feel that they have faced difficulties in finding the finance needed to start or develop their businesses, commentators have pointed out that many social enterprises face additional barriers specific to that sector. For instance, according to the DTI:

> At present many social enterprises are under-capitalised and struggle to access external finance, particularly when starting up, growing or moving away from grant dependency. Whilst this is often to do with a lack of financial skills, in many social enterprises it is also a result of an understandable reluctance to take on debt. In addition, it is sometimes that investors do not understand the social enterprises' market and this situation is exacerbated for those social enterprises located in disadvantaged areas where the transaction costs associated with such investments can be extremely high.[12]

According to Mayo et al. in an extensive review of community investment in the United Kingdom, the demand and supply barriers which limit access to capital for community businesses are:

1. Lack of viable proposals:
   - Voluntary organisations are resistant to using private capital.
   - There is a lack of skills for putting a business case together.
   - There is a lack of credit history to satisfy banks.
2. Return:
   - The risk means that interest rates are set too high.
3. Information asymmetries:
   - Lenders are unable to assess the risk of repayment from voluntary agencies.
   - There is a lack of understanding of the sector among bankers.

4. Transaction Costs:

   • The financial costs of administering small loans to micro enterprises are high.

5. Risk:

   • Bank underwriting criteria are inappropriate for certain voluntary/community markets.
   • Bankers may reject viable projects. [13]

The 2000 report of the Social Investment Task Force (SITF) and the research papers that underpinned its conclusion have provided an important and comprehensive series of recommendations on the development of the social economy in the UK. [14] A core concern of the Task Force was the barriers that stood in the way of enterprise and wealth creation in under-invested communities which it identified as: a systematic failure among government, banks, and sources of capital; public sector grants and charitable funding which create over-dependence and stifle enterprise; and weak incentives for private investment in communities.

As a result of this investigation, the core recommendations of the Task Force were that there should be:

• A Community Investment Tax Credit to encourage private investment in under-invested communities, via Community Development Finance Institutions (CDFIs).
• A Community Development Venture Fund – a matched funding partnership between government on the one hand and the venture capital industry, entrepreneurs, institutional investors, and banks on the other.
• Disclosure by banks of their commitments to business finance in deprived areas.
• Greater latitude for charitable trusts and foundations to invest in community development initiatives.
• Technical support for CDFIs.

Figure 7.1 summarises the Task Force's recommendations, and this is useful because it highlights the need for a mixed community development finance sector comprising community development banks, a community loan fund, and micro-loan funds standing

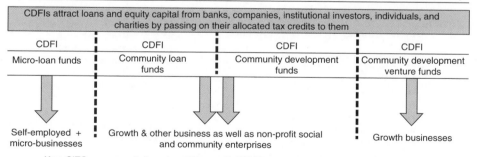

Government agency accredits

1. CDFIs for CITC allocation to be passed on to lenders and equity investors in CDFIs

2. CDVFs for matching govt funding

CDFIs attract loans and equity capital from banks, companies, institutional investors, individuals, and charities by passing on their allocated tax credits to them			
CDFI	CDFI	CDFI	CDFI
Micro-loan funds	Community loan funds	Community development funds	Community development venture funds
Self-employed + micro-businesses	Growth & other business as well as non-profit social and community enterprises		Growth businesses

Key: CITC = community investment tax credit; CDVF = community development venture fund; CDFI = community development finance institution"

Figure 7.1 The Social Investment Task Force vision of a community investment finance sector

Source: Based on Social Investment Task Force, *The Report of the Social Investment Task Force* (2000), p. 9

between government, banks, and other investors on the one side and businesses and social community enterprises on the other. The proposed Community Investment Tax Credit is designed to help to increase the scale and capacity of CDFIs by increasing private investment flows. But other actions were also suggested to bolster this process:

- Organisations that wish to become national (or regional) intermediaries should equip themselves with the business expertise and skills in this arena.
- CDFIs should work closely with Regional Development Agencies (now replaced by Local Enterprise Partnerships) and Local Strategy Partnerships.
- Government should help by supporting CDFI development through the Phoenix Fund (now discontinued), and banks and large corporate organisations and entrepreneurs should also be encouraged to help.

The range of social economy capital finance schemes

Table 7.1 sets out the types of social finance available, and Sattar and Fisher[15] highlighted the different scale of finance from Triodos, which operates as a social bank in Britain, the Netherlands, and Belgium, to the Aston Reinvestment Trust, which is a community loan fund in inner-city Birmingham. Similarly, the Prince's Trust offers a good example of a micro-loan fund aimed at business start-up in the UK.

Mayo et al.[16] described the functions of community finance as providing the catalytic capital resources or means of risk reduction to secure the interest of mainstream finance in enterprise development and to provide the means for widening economic opportunities for marginalised individuals, business, and communities. Table 7.2 describes

Table 7.1 Types of social economy finance schemes

- ethical share issues using the plc rules
- withdrawable share capital
- community finance loans
- mutual guarantee mechanisms by a federation of mutuals
- non-profit licensing of new technology
- mezzanine finance
- social business angels

Source: Finance for Social Enterprises, www.renewal.net (accessed 2004)

Table 7.2 Different initiatives and arrangements for communities

Circumstances	Action	Reason
If a community: Needs fewer financial services and in smaller amounts (including cheque and savings accounts to consumers) Needs an institution that is less expensive to form or adapt than a commercial development bank Wants to focus on low-income consumers Has little or no other access to savings and credit facilities	Community credit union	Sustainable at a much smaller scale of activities than other initiatives, community credit unions have volunteer support and lower overheads. They can service more small accounts, are competitive on loan interest rates, and are well suited to encourage members to increase savings *But* many community credit unions have lower asset sizes than is ideal for sustainability

Table 7.2 (Continued)

Circumstances	Action	Reason
If a community or sector: Needs flexible, high-risk business financing or potentially equity capital Needs specialist or locally responsive and knowledgeable regeneration finance for housing, charities, social enterprise, or small business	Community loan fund	Such loan funds can operate at a smaller scale than commercial banks and can be formed by a skilled group of committed people. They have significantly more leeway in the kinds, sizes, and terms of loans they make. They have the potential to develop relationships with mainstream banks as a local partner or agent *But* this is an evolving model, which to date has required significant development time and still faces the dilemma of how to provide high-risk loans with capital from social investors that may be intended as low risk
If a community: Needs credit for micro-enterprises, including disadvantaged borrowers; Needs other micro-level financial services	Micro-finance fund	These are attractive for the innovations they make, such as peer and group lending, for managing risk, and for reducing operating costs through outsourcing costs to group borrowers *But,* while highly effective in poor countries, schemes in industrialised countries rarely achieve the same scale of operation and financial sustainability
If small businesses: Need access to development finance or better terms from banks Have capital they are willing to pool as a guarantee fund	Mutual guarantee society	This is a creative, self-help way of responding to finance needs among small businesses, encouraging better terms from banks and developing mutual support *But* these are relatively new in the UK and it will not always make sense for entrepreneurs to tie up liquidity in guarantee funds. Credit unions that offer finance for micro-entrepreneur members may be more suitable for small loans
If a community or sector: Can support a dedicated finance institution with assets of £5 million or more Needs a variety of services Can attract the necessary organisers, banking experience, and capital	For-profit social bank or sub-sidiary/initiative of a commercial bank	A for-profit bank is viewed as a credible and solid institution. They provide a range of services including deposits. If profitable, they can produce income sufficient to attract mainstream equity investors But large organising costs, substantial initial capitalisation, and regulatory demands are major hurdles. Some argue that EU banking directives make it too difficult for new social banks to emerge. Some community loan funds aspire to become banks in due course

Source: Based on E. Mayo, T. Fisher, P. Conaty, J. Doling and A. Mullineux, *Small Is Bankable: Community Reinvestment in the UK* (York: Joseph Rowntree Foundation, 1988), p. 40

different community development finance initiatives and how they can be used in different circumstances.

As Illustration 7.2 shows, there is increasing sophistication in the mix of community finance suppliers and products in the UK. These range from community loan funds and micro-finance to venture capital and social banks.

Illustration 7.2 Community Development Finance Institutions in the UK

A 2002 report by the UK Social Investment Forum[17] divided the CDFI sector into six different types of organisation:

- *Community loan funds* – the majority of the CDFI sector: organisations that provide loans to for-profit and/or social enterprises, often with an overarching social mission and sometimes focused on a particular geographic area;
- *Micro-finance funds* – a sub-sector of the above: organisations that specialise in providing very small loans to micro enterprises;
- *Community development venture capital* – operates like mainstream venture capital but with a community development mission;
- *Social banks* – operate as mainstream banks but with strict ethical policies and social and/or environmental goals;
- *Community development credit unions* – credit unions (i.e. co-operatives owned and controlled by members with a 'common bond') with a particular community development mission; and
- *Mutual guarantee societies* – formal associations of SMEs that pool their savings in banks in order to provide collective guarantees.

The Community Development Finance Association (CDFA) currently lists 74 CDFI members or associate members, a figure which has seen consolidation since 2006 following rapid growth from 2003, and is confident that its membership constitutes the substantial majority of the CDFI sector in the UK. The value of lending capital held by the CDFI sector increased by 22 per cent, from £201m in 2006–2007 to £246m in 2008–2009; average CDFI fund size increased by 25 per cent, from £3.5m to £4.3m in 2008–2009; the growth of a handful of large national social enterprise lenders (such as Charity Bank) is also evident (indeed it has been necessary to remove Triodos Bank from the analysis since it is as large as the rest of the CDFI sector combined).

Source: GHK, *The National Evaluation of Community Development Finance Institutions (CDFIs): An Action-Orientated Summary for the Sector* (London: BIS and The Cabinet Office, 2010)

Community Development Finance Institutions (CDFIs)

Community Development Finance Institutions (CDFIs) are specialist organisations whose primary mission is to promote social welfare and not to make a private profit. They support communities by providing affordable finance that would otherwise not be available to businesses, social enterprises, and individuals who find difficulty in getting finance from high-street banks and loan companies. Most are based within the UK's most disadvantaged communities. Many CDFIs are run with funding from the government and charitable trusts, alongside other funding sources, and do not take savings or deposits like banks do.

Notwithstanding the organisational heterogeneity evident in the sector (see Illustration 7.2), CDFI numbers are estimated to have stabilised at 'somewhere between 70 and 80 during the last few years after a period of substantial numerical growth in the last decade. The sector's financial size continues to grow with total capital available nearing the £600m mark and the value of current outstanding loans by the sector stood at over £330m.'[18]

nef showed CDFIs that they have been effective in getting funding into under-invested areas but that most are small and growing slowly and that there is over-optimism about their economic impact (see Chapter 10). nef argues that the government needs to have a longer-term and better-resourced vision for the sector in which funding is more secure to allow CDFIs to sustain their portfolios in the longer term.

Overall, we found that CDFIs are at a critical juncture. Without renewed support the sector will become increasingly fragmented and weak. CDFIs could wither and many may disappear, providing another set-back to disadvantaged communities. With the right support from government, regional agencies, funders and banks, however, CDFIs could play a major role in addressing issues of access to finance in the UK. [19]

nef outlined a particular approach to Community Banking Partnerships, which brings together both credit union(s) and a Community Reinvestment Trust whose members jointly form a charitable trust. A Community Reinvestment Trust is a non-profit organisation providing loans and other financial services to small businesses, community enterprises, and individuals in under-served communities. The approach aims to open credit to non-bankable residents and to attract clients from local, high-cost moneylenders in particular. The Partnership combines access to credit with money and debt advice, bill payment services, and energy advice, especially given high levels of fuel poverty in disadvantaged areas. Some examples of venture social capital include the following international schemes:

- The first specific law in Europe for social enterprises helped to establish the Banca Popolare Etica in Italy in 1998. The bank provides innovative financing for social and ecological ventures in particular.
- In France, Club Cigales is encouraged by a national tax credit to target micro-social business (fewer than 10 employees). It operates a business angel approach to provide risk capital along with management and marketing expertise.
- The Clann Credo fund in Ireland, capitalised initially by several religious orders, has been deploying social venture capital for growth projects in the social economy.

The Bank of England review

In 2003 the Bank of England produced one of the most comprehensive and authoritative accounts of the financing of social financing in the UK. [20] The key findings of this research were:

- Demand for debt finance among social enterprises is limited both by the availability of other, cheaper forms of funding such as grants, and by a cultural aversion to the risks associated with borrowing.
- Larger, more established organisations use a range of financial instruments to address cash flow difficulties or to purchase or develop assets.
- Social enterprises are more likely to be rejected for finance than SMEs with possible explanations being lack of available security and personal financial stake, use of organisational structures and grant funding streams with which lenders may be unfamiliar, some element of credit and behaviour scoring, reputational risk to the lender, and low levels of investment readiness among some social enterprises.
- There is little evidence of demand for, or supply of, conventional venture capital or business angel finance to the social enterprise sector.

One area where the Bank of England research showed evidence of demand was for some form of patient capital:

> The term is variously defined to range from 'investment' grants to products that are structured as debt or equity, where investors are willing to accept lower, and in some cases uncertain, financial returns in exchange for social outputs. [21]

According to the Bank, a key issue in tapping into the social investment market is the ability of the social enterprise to describe and account for social costs and benefits, and in this context the methodology of social auditing is encouraged for social enterprises (see Chapter 6).

In order to stimulate demand, the Bank of England recommended:

- Advertising and transferring best practice models of lending across the social economy.
- The devolved administrations could ensure that mainstream business support arrangements recognise the particular needs of social enterprises.
- Public sector agencies should expand their funding on researching on the feasibility of a business idea.
- Building on existing financial awareness programmes could increase the level of investment readiness of social enterprises.
- A greater emphasis on providing more information and guidance on access to social finance sources.

On the supply side, the Bank of England recommended:

- Increasing the amount of money available to CDFIs specialising in the social enterprise from regional authorities and the private sector and through take-up of the Community Investment Tax Relief (CITR).
- Developing joint lending (e.g. between banks and CDFIs) and encouraging co-financing where possible.
- Encouraging CDFIs that lend to social enterprises to become approved lenders under the Small Firms Loan Guarantee Scheme.
- As important, the development of clearer means of distinguishing social enterprises from other borrowers especially by identifying financial indicators specific to the sector.
- The development of a brokerage service at a local level by an expert in the range of finance services available to the sector.
- The reviewing by banks of their procedures for ensuring that broad policy intentions at head office level related to lending to social enterprises are implemented effectively at branch level.
- The British Bankers' Association could usefully act as a source of information for banks on social enterprises via their website and other communication channels.
- Grant providers, including government, could review the administration of grants so as not to impede the ability of social enterprises to leverage in other forms of finance.

Micro-finance initiatives

In the UK, micro-finance initiatives aim:

> to widen the access of disadvantaged people and neighbourhoods to capital and other financial services. Such services include micro-financial services provided for example by credit unions; neighbourhood regeneration initiatives, such as community loan funds; and loan funds and social banks targeted at relevant sectors, such as small businesses, community and social enterprises, or charities. [22]

Moseley and Steel highlighted their value in disadvantaged areas of the UK by offering loans, advice, and business support to self-employed people and micro-enterprises that were viewed as un-bankable by the mainstream commercial sector. [23] However, Dyson et al. [24] point out that micro-finance providers continue to struggle to provide market returns and meet their social objectives, and that it is difficult to do both and achieve long-term fund sustainability.

A number of writers and commentators have been concerned about the lack of a co-ordinated approach to the support of these interventions over time and across countries. Parker and Lyons, for instance, were critical of government and policy support for the development of CDFIs in Australia but suggest that, as well as a clearer policy framework and investment, the sector also needs to support itself via effective networking and cross-learning among the active organisations.[25] They also highlighted the need for greater spatial integration of services and access to money, and nef has pointed out that both domestic and business finance were needed in under-invested communities.[26]

Street UK is a Midlands-based organisation set up in 2000 to offer loans, advice, and business support to self-employed people and micro-enterprises that were considered as un-bankable by the mainstream commercial sector. As well as financial services, Street UK offers software and back office support and mortgages and home loans. The scheme has supported more than 200 clients with bespoke business support and credit finance, especially in assisting businesses in the transition from undeclared to declared economy. Williams[27] evaluated the initiative and highlighted the multiple business, economic, and social benefits and improvements from small amounts of credit released via not-for-profit finance. These included:

- moving from part-time to full-time work;
- moving from home to business premises;
- keeping basic level records;
- keeping higher level accounts;
- purchasing public liability and employers' liability insurance;
- hiring employees on a Pay As You Earn (PAYE) basis;
- using a bank account for their business transactions;
- obtaining the required licences and permits to operate the business such as health and safety inspection certificates;
- graduating off all non-work state benefits;
- graduating from majority cash revenues to majority invoiced revenues;
- incurring a formal business tax liability; and
- becoming VAT registered.[28]

Experience in the United States

Much of the development of the social economy in the United States originated from the implicit and explicit exclusion of some ethnic neighbourhoods where banks, building societies, and insurance companies would not invest. The Community Reinvestment Act (1997) states that financial institutions have an affirmative obligation to meet the credit needs of communities where they are based. The 1993 Community Development Finance Institutions Fund Act provides public support through a development fund for community finance initiatives and for bank subsidiaries promoting community reinvestment. There are around 1000 certified CDFIs with a collective $25 billion in assets.[29] Lowry also showed that every state in the US has a CDFI but the heaviest concentrations are in New York and California and emerging markets include dedicated Native American and healthy food funds.[30] Mayo et al. pointed out that there are typically five models of community finance in the US:

- community development banks (more than 10);
- community development credit unions (130+);
- community development loan funds (46);
- micro-finance funds (50+); and
- neighbourhood equity funds.

Some initiatives have emphasised their 'community capitalisation' by helping to stabilise or prevent the collapse of the local economy. They often seek to work with other specialist non-profit parties, multi-purpose development agencies, or coalitions providing advice or technical support. CANDO was formed in Chicago in 1979 in response to the Community Reinvestment Act. It is the largest local urban partnership coalition in the US with 100 non-profit neighbourhood development organisations as members and more than 130 private affiliate members. CANDO's programmes include lobbying, developing publicly owned land especially for local housing projects, organising local business groups to revive brownfield land, and helping to revive local retailing.

Bernholz[31] describes the expansion of the social economy in the US, especially through the development of bespoke social impact investment products and philanthro-capital giving. Impact investing is emerging as a separate social class that involves actively financing companies that produce social and financial returns, and Bernholz shows that 42 social impact investing funds managing $1.9 billion are currently registered. In 2010, philanthropic giving in the US reached $290 billion with the bulk ($211 billion) coming from individuals. There are more than 650 social businesses registered with a collective income of $4 billion and there are almost one million public charities with annual revenues of more than $1.4 trillion.

Financial instruments

Demand for, and supply of, finance for the social economy

As with any financial market, maintaining a satisfactory relationship between the demand for, and the supply of, capital is essential for sustained growth and business development. A key issue for the social economy within the wider macro economy is the asymmetry between the supply of and demand for investment. In an extensive review of 'patient capital' (see Illustration 7.3) in Scotland, CEiS (Supporting Enterprise in Communities)[32] showed that there was a strong undercurrent of investor interest based on the desire of the public sector to shift from grants to more commercial arrangements and to the more straightforward profit motive of the private sector. It makes the point that traditionally the private sector has invested in social enterprises for philanthropic or promotional reasons but that they are being increasingly attracted by returns available in growth areas of the sector. Picking up on this pattern, the Bank of England report on social enterprise finance[33] showed that this emerging investment lay in commercial businesses concerned with ethical issues (recycling or ethical trading) rather than in social economy businesses per se.

The CEiS review argued that there was no technical bar to linking supply and demand but identified a number of dimensions to market failure including:

- *Information and knowledge* is the primary obstacle to efficient market operation both in terms of those seeking resources and among those attempting to make investments.
- *A sustainable deal flow* has two dimensions in that the size of investment and availability of a commercial return will dissuade private investors especially on a comparative basis with other sectors.
- *Exit strategies* are not clear for investors in social enterprises. It might be clear how they put money into the organisation but it is less clear how they get it out easily and efficiently.
- *Transaction* costs on equity deals tend to be high given the technical competencies and systems required to maintain the investment.

- *Culture and skills gaps* especially in moving the community and voluntary sector from a grant- to loan-based funding arrangement is a significant short-term obstacle. The CEiS highlighted the contradictory value base of the public sector and its concern for accountability and the private sector with its acceptance of risk and flexibility in investment decisions.

The CEiS report[34] also highlighted the need to harness the skills of the private investment community in mainstreaming social economy equity investment. In particular, it stressed:

- the need to educate the marketplace on both demand and supply sides;
- action is needed to create and retain surpluses in social economy organisations;
- the need to unblock constraints to developing an effective lending market which includes:
  - the absence of exit mechanisms for investors;
  - the limited size of the market and its effects on transaction costs;
  - the relatively high cost of development support;
  - the lack of appropriate investment skills in the social economy; and
  - the need to foster demand that is latent, via education, marketing, and demonstration projects.

In their report *Revaluing the Social Economy in Scotland,* McGregor et al.[35] pointed out that 54 per cent of all organisations surveyed identified difficulty in obtaining appropriate or sufficient funding as the main obstacles to sustaining or developing their organisation. The research showed that:

> the lending as opposed to granting agenda will be difficult to deliver, on the assumption we are talking about loans that must be repaid notwithstanding the patience of the lender in terms of when this happens. However, one of the key constraints is revenue out of which to pay off debt, and the evidence of the survey is that revenues from charges have grown only modestly with even the largest social economy organisations still looking to grant funding in the first instance.[36]

McGregor et al. also point to the contradiction in funding regimes whereby organisations that make surpluses are penalised by a progressive withdrawal of mainstream grant income. They are simultaneously being told to 'be entrepreneurial but don't make surpluses'.[37] However, the report also showed that the bigger organisations attract more mainstream funding, and that the larger they become, the less likely they are to locate in or employ people from areas of high disadvantage. Dayson also made the point that:

> there has been a systematic failure with a 'grant culture' that has led to over-dependence and there were no incentives for private sector investment. Additionally a risk adverse culture was limiting business start-ups and entrepreneurship.[38]

Illustration 7.3 Patient capital

The main characteristics of patient finance are:

- It is long term in nature, enabling it to be used for both start-up and subsequent development funding.
- If structured as debt, it could have capital and interest payment holidays, perhaps to the extent of deferring all capital repayments until the end of the loan. Alternatively, it could be structured as a zero-interest loan, analogous to a recoverable grant.

- If structured as equity or quasi-equity, it would involve little ceding of control and would not require an explicit exit strategy.
- However structured, the financial returns would be sub-market, in return for social gains.

In suggesting an extension of patient capital, the Bank of England recommended that:

- Government may need to extend the availability of support, such as subordinated, matched funding or tax relief.
- The Social Enterprise Coalition could investigate the possibility of establishing a 'social angels' network to match social investors with social enterprises needing investment.
- The results of pilots such as the Adventure Capital Fund and Futurebuilders would provide more information on how innovative approaches might be applied across government.
- Patient finance could be stimulated by sharing best practice and by encouraging larger social enterprises to invest in start-up projects.
- In view of the regulatory and cost burden on social enterprises wishing to make a public share offering, the government and the Financial Services Authority could review current regulatory exemptions relating to share issues, in the light of the particular characteristics of social enterprises.
- Social auditing techniques should ensure that they meet the needs of investors and provide a means of benchmarking performance.

Source: Bank of England, *The Financing of Social Enterprises: A Special Report by the Bank of England* (London: Bank of England, 2003)

Supply of finance

Metcalf et al.[39] referred to the current supply of community finance as a 'jumble' while Collin et al.[40] argued that even soft loans raise problems about their sustainability, community involvement, and accountability. Here, Copisarow[41] argues that micro-finance needs to be targeted to ethnic minorities and women, specifically to improve self-confidence, business survival rates, and access to finance. Dayson usefully identified the reasons for the patchy development of community development finance initiatives in a UK context as:

- problematic definition of a charity;
- failure to provide the right mix of grant and loan funding;
- a cultural inability to understand that 'not for profit' is not charity or 'for loss';
- a difficulty for banks to support CDFIs undertaking the same activity as themselves in areas they rejected and by using different methodologies;
- a lack of integrated welfare to work incentives;
- a lack of appropriate legislation and regulation;
- credit unions having difficulties with bespoke lending, while the requirement to save before borrowing can exclude or delay clients;
- soft-loan schemes being too focused on the most deprived and often providing no opportunity for second loans.[42]

In a separate report that helps to address these structural and cultural obstacles, Westall et al. identified the key characteristics of European-wide community development finance activity, and these are shown in Table 7.3.

Collin et al. state that soft loans are short term, supported by a government agency or a programme, which cover part of the operating costs and are usually life limited.[43] Soft loans were, in particular, regarded as a method to help shift organisations from grant to lending. Collin et al. were highly critical of soft loans because a high proportion were

Table 7.3 Good practice in community development finance lending in Europe

* lending to groups or individuals often based on peer lending where collateral is based on mutuality and social ties;
* providing pure credit with business support;
* financing of start-ups or existing businesses;
* funding is targeted at specific groups such as women or ethnic minorities;
* unlike Credit Unions, most CDFIs only offer loans due to local banking regulations; and
* they provide 'free loans' or charge a commercial rate which imposes financial discipline on the borrower and helps the CDFI become sustainable.

Source: A. Westall, P. Ramsden and J. Foley, *Micro-entrepreneurs: Creating Enterprising Communities* (London: IPPR and nef, 2000)

un-lent, because default rates are also comparatively high, and because of their poor dis-closure practices.[44] Copisarow argues that most CDFIs have started small which has made them reliant on public subsidy for longer and at a higher cost. For Dayson,[45] the agenda for development consists of a number of interconnected stages:

* A cultural shift in both the operation of schemes including realistic interest rates and debt collection.
* Improvements in structures and the quality of governance, management, and manage-ment information systems needed to transfer soft funds into sustainable CDFIs.
* A crucial need to achieve cost minimisation by streamlining services through a techno-logically driven back office service with revenue maximisation (i.e. issuing many loans), which overcomes the danger of limited growth enhancement in lost minimisation approaches.

Community shares and bonds

Iona et al.[46] point out that bond issues or loan stock issues are offers to several people to lend money to an organisation on similar terms for several years and as such are a form of long-term debt capital. Share issues are a way of obtaining long-term risk capital, and the majority of share issues made by community enterprises have been by Industrial and Provident Societies (IPSs), some of which were charitable. An IPS can ask any individual or limited company to invest up to £20,000 each in the share capital of the IPS to pursue its objectives. However many shares they purchase, investors will still only have one vote in the society.

Investors have to become members of the IPS; the conditions surrounding their invest-ment will normally be presented in a simple invitation to invest. This will include an outline of the business case, the dividend the investor can expect to receive, the risk in the investment, and the terms on which they can withdraw their money. The would-be investor then simply pays the IPS and receives a share certificate. Brown[47] points out that liquidity is an issue that would need to be taken into account in designing a community share offer. Companies normally issue transferable share capital, which means that they can be exchanged between third parties, and withdrawable shares also provide an agreed exit route for the investor through the ability to sell shares back to the IPS.

The advantage of shares over other forms of finance is that if the shares carry limited rights to withdrawal or are transferable, there is no obligation to repay them. In general, dividends are paid out of the profits of the organisation linked to its business performance in the normal way. The main difference between a share and a bond issue is that, in the latter case, there is a commitment to repay the amount invested after a number of years. While this makes it easier to raise the money in the first place, the business case has to show the ability to repay the loans (or raise another loan to repay the initial investors) within the stated time.

Social Impact Bonds (SIBs)

According to Loder,[48] 'A Social Impact Bond is a financial instrument that raises capital, and links financial returns to the achievement of a particular socially desirable outcome. Outcomes are chosen so that improvements to the outcome produce savings as well as social good, and so fund the financial returns (see Illustration 7.4).' The SIB involves three parties:

- a funder, who puts up the initial capital to fund the intervention;
- an operator, who performs the intervention; and
- a payer, usually the central government, which makes payments to the investor based on the impact achieved.

Loder argues that the central purpose of SIBs is more effectively to realise social goals: creating more *good for less* money and achieve this by creating incentives, promoting innovation, and accessing new capabilities. In particular, they shift the emphasis to outcomes rather than inputs or activities in programme delivery, and by incentivising performance they aim to align the interest of the payer, operator, and funder.[49]

Illustration 7.4 Social Impact Bonds

Social Impact Bonds are a form of outcomes-based contract in which public sector commissioners commit to pay for significant improvement in social outcomes (such as a reduction in offending rates, or in the number of people being admitted to hospital) for a defined population. Social Impact Bonds are an innovative way of attracting new investment around such outcomes-based contracts that benefit individuals and communities. Through a Social Impact Bond, private investment is used to pay for interventions, which are delivered by service providers with a proven track record. Financial returns to investors are made by the public sector on the basis of improved social outcomes. If outcomes do not improve, then investors do not recover their investment. Social Impact Bonds provide up front funding for prevention and early intervention services, and remove the risk that interventions do not deliver outcomes from the public sector. The public sector pays if (and only if) the intervention is successful. In this way, Social Impact Bonds enable a re-allocation of risk between the two sectors.

Source: http://www.socialfinance.org.uk/work/sibs (accessed January 2013)

The economic environment

Despite the more attractive taxation environment for social finance funding, the Scottish Council for Voluntary Organisations (SCVO) has identified important limitations to the impact of fiscal instruments in the community and voluntary sector. It showed[50] that 70 per cent of the UK population give to charity in a typical year but fewer than 10 per cent use the tax breaks available. Lack of awareness and assumptions that it would be technically difficult to operate seem to lie behind the low tax relief take-up rates. The Gift Aid scheme rewarded donations to charity through tax relief at the basic rate of income tax (currently 20 per cent), and the scheme has been progressively widened and simplified over time. SCVO highlights the opportunity to pursue payroll giving, deeds of covenant, and gifts of quoted shares and securities as ways of responding to the uncertain financial climate faced by charities and voluntary sector groups. Illustration 7.5 provides an outline of the CITR scheme in the UK.

Illustration 7.5 Community Investment Tax Relief (CITR)

Community Investment Tax Relief (CITR) is available to individuals and corporate bodies investing in accredited Community Development Finance Institutions (CDFIs), which in turn provide finance to qualifying profit-distributing enterprises, social enterprises or community projects. CITR will enable an accredited CDFI to offer tax relief as an incentive to investors willing to provide it with patient capital for at least five years. These funds can then be on-lent by the CDFI to borrowers within its target market. The design of CITR draws a distinction between loans made by CDFIs to profit-distributing small and medium-sized enterprises (SMEs) and those to 'community projects'. The latter category includes both non-commercial activity as well as commercial activity that is small-scale and purely local in nature. Many social enterprises will therefore be included within the scope of that description and thus benefit from the greater flexibility permitted in CDFI transactions with community projects. In particular, when using funds raised under CITR, an accredited CDFI:

* may make a loan of up £250,000 to a community project, compared with a limit of £100,000 for loans to profit-distributing SMEs;
* is not required to apply the European Commission Hurdle Rate as a minimum interest rate when making loans to community projects, which it must do when lending to profit-distributing SMEs;
* may make an equity investment of up to £250,000 in a community project, but may not make equity investments in profit-distributing SMEs.

Source: Bank of England, *The Financing of Social Enterprises: A Special Report by the Bank of England* (London: Bank of England, 2003)

Financial 'wholesaling' for the social economy

Ainger et al.[51] researched the possibility of a wholesale intermediary for community finance and found that a fully commercial wholesaler, even partly capitalised by government, would not be viable in the short term. However, they found that some form of interim or transitional central funding organisation could provide a valuable catalyst towards a more commercially sustainable future for the community development finance initiative sector. A recent example of the restructuring of wholesale social finance in the UK is the Big Society Bank established by the Conservative government under their wider Big Society initiative (see Illustration 7.6).

Illustration 7.6 Big Society Capital in the UK

To support the implementation of the Big Society in the UK [see Case 3.1] the UK government established Big Society Capital Ltd as a company limited by shares, with a mission to act as a social investment wholesaler and to promote and develop social investment and the social investment market in the UK. BSC's purpose is to achieve its social mission rather than to maximise profits for shareholders. BSC shares are owned 60 per cent by the Big Society Trust and 40 per cent by the four 'Merlin' Banks (Barclays, HSBC, Lloyds and RBS). The BST will always hold at least 80 per cent of the voting rights in BSC and the Merlin Banks no more than 20 per cent.

Big Society Capital (BSC) has an overall budget that will reach £600m. It will invest in social investment finance intermediaries (SIFIs) – organisations that provide finance and support to social sector organisations. It will invest £400m from dormant bank accounts and £200m from the high street banks.

Source: http://www.bigsocietycapital.com/our-organisation (accessed January 2013)

According to Ainger, the long-term aim of the wholesaler would be to raise private and public sector financing to on-lend to CDFIs to support their development and growth and increase their scale and impact. They set out seven functions for intermediaries.

1. An intermediary with specialist experience in raising private finance could bring a measure of coherence to the scramble for funds amongst CDFIs and give greater coherence to potential investors.
2. An intermediary could also contribute to quality control among CDFIs.
3. The wholesaler might jointly finance larger loans to community groups, where such loans are too large to be taken into the CDFIs' books for reasons of prudence.
4. The wholesaler could play an important role in the syndication of tax incentives for investment in CDFIs under the Community Investment Tax Relief (CITR) scheme.
5. The wholesaler could reduce the costs of fundraising for both funders and recipients.
6. An intermediary might help to keep resources to the sector flowing.
7. An intermediary could provide a more secure source of funds than grants or subsidised funds, which are neither secure nor likely to be sustained over the long term. [52]

Thake and Lingayah[53] show that the Adventure Capital Fund (ACF) had, in total, been allocated £14.4 million to enable investment in independent, medium-sized, community-based organisations in order that they could develop successful social enterprise initiatives (see Illustration 7.7). Their final evaluation showed not only that there was sufficient demand for loan finance but that lending improved the financial and organisational sustainability of participating businesses. The programme enabled enterprises to diversify activity, grow faster, and strengthen their skills base, and the wider fund enabled a degree of innovation in understanding the multiple social effects of lending programmes.

Illustration 7.7 Adventure Capital Fund

The Adventure Capital Fund was established in 2002 in order to pilot a range of approaches to investing directly in independent community based organisations working in disadvantaged areas.
    The Fund included:

- A £360,000 Bursary Fund to invest in approximately 20 revenue bursaries to staff, each up to £15,000. The bursaries are intended to strengthen and assist in the development of its investment readiness.
- A £2 million Patient Capital Fund to invest in 10 capital investments with a ceiling of £400,000. The Patient Capital Investments are designed to establish/strengthen the asset base and increase the scale of operations of the selected community enterprise.

The Adventure Capital Fund is delivered by a community sector partnership comprising the Local Investment Fund, the Development Trust Association, the Scarman Trust and the new economics foundation, with the active participation of the Active Community Unit of the Home Office. The designers of the Adventure Capital Fund programme have incorporated a number of process elements designed to strengthen the delivery process. The introduction of the Supporters Programme, the use of balanced score cards, the exploration of measures of social impact, the development of strong interlocking partnership arrangements and an innovative approach to the evaluation process strengthen the social impact of the Fund.

Source: Based on S. Thake, *Sustainable Futures: Investing in Community-Based Organizations* (London: nef, 2004)

A summary

Table 7.4 indicates the range of instruments which, according to the (former) Department of Trade and Investment (DTI, now the Department of Business Innovation and Skills BIS), are now available to grow the social economy in general and social enterprises in particular.

Financial skills for the social economy

The East of England Development Agency (EEDA) [54] has highlighted the importance of preparatory assessment work before selecting from the range of financial products that

Table 7.4 The supply-side funding regime

Source	Details
Cooperative Action	New foundation established to support the development of new forms of co-operative and mutual enterprise by giving grants and making loans of between £5,000 and £200,000 in developing or supporting new or existing co-operative enterprises, organisational structures, and research
Community Investment Tax Relief	Encourage up to £1b investment in start-up businesses and social enterprises in deprived areas
Community Development Finance Institutions (CDFIs)	Independent financial institutions providing capital and other financial support to enterprises in disadvantaged areas
Industrial Common Ownership Finance (ICOF)	ICOF was set up in 1973 and is a loan fund for employee-owned cooperatives and social enterprises. It is supported by pubic shares and is fully self-sustaining
Local Investment Fund	The fund was established with support from government, Business in the Community, and the private sector, and by Natwest. Since it was established, it has offered 25 loans totalling £29m and has leveraged £15m into community regeneration
Bridges Community Development Venture Fund (CDVF)	CDVF, a 50/50 partnership between government and the venture capital industry aimed at supplying venture capital, was launched in 2002 by the Chancellor of the Exchequer. Capital finance is for firms operating in some of the most disadvantaged areas in England. More details of the fund can be found at wwww.bridgesventures.com
Charity Bank	The bank has attracted £10m in exempt deposits and gifts to provide finance and related support to help charities and other organisations develop sustainable charitable ideas
Business angels	Business angels can provide total finance at a key stage and often business advice. Social enterprises are potentially a prime recipient of attention from business angels who want to put something back into society
Community asset transfer	The Active Community Unit has been exploring the potential to transfer physical assets such as community centres, parks, and redundant building to social enterprise management

Source: Based on Department of Trade and Industry, *Access to Finance for Social Enterprise* (London: DTI, 2003)

are on offer. In particular, it suggests that there needs to be a stronger assessment of what social enterprises need, of the skills and staff they need to access and manage non-grant finance income, and of how to set prices and understand markets in developing sustainable services and products. It is not, therefore, enough just to create additional sources of finance for third sector organisations. If that finance is to be applied success-fully, those sources need to be made readily available and third sector organisations need to know how to access and use that finance.

It has been suggested that there is, in particular, a shortage of professional finance staff working in social enterprise organisations. Many social enterprises need funders to provide the financial skills they lack and often lack information about the range of types and sources of finance available, meaning that it is difficult to assemble the mixed finance packages that are often required. This is because finance organisations operate in isolation and there is a lack of intermediaries able to broker deals on behalf of social enter-prises.[55] Aston Reinvestment Trust (Case 7.1) highlights the need to combine finance with technical support to make businesses viable.

Conclusion

Micro-finance initiatives have proved critical in communities where the absence or with-drawal of the banking sector has left many poor communities at the mercy of predatory lenders. Grants and endowments are still important, especially in supporting incuba-tion or fledging organisations, and the tension between tradable and charitable aims of a community sector organisation is a distinctive pressure facing new entrants to the social economy. There are also structural barriers to finance including the technical proficiency of enterprises as well as awareness and understanding of financial suppliers. New 'prod-ucts' have emerged to support the sector, especially to sustain itself on a commercial basis, and initiatives such as the Adventure Capital Fund have proved important in diversifying the supply of finance to the sector.

Key Points of Chapter 7

- Social enterprises, like other enterprises, need access to finance to start, develop, and grow.
- There are various ways in which social enterprises can access financial support including grants, endowments, and commercial loans.
- More recently, there has been a growth in the sophistication of financial supports for the sector, reflecting its diverse needs. This includes the availability of patient capital and soft loans, social equity finance, and impact investment.
- Fiscal measures, in the form of Community Investment Tax Relief, are attempting to incentivise investment into the community and voluntary sector, whilst growing interest for ethnical investment is also attracting commercial resources to the social economy.
- There are important obstacles to more effective assembly and use of funding cocktails including the capacities and preparedness of organisations to manage investment and the lack of awareness of risk-sensitive commercial lenders.
- There is growing importance attached to making the financial market work better for the social economy, with intermediates attempting to connect supply and demand more efficiently across businesses.

Case 7.1 | Aston Reinvestment Trust

Aston Reinvestment Trust (ART) is one of the best-known Community Development Finance Institutions (CDFIs). It operates in Birmingham as a mutual society providing loans to the voluntary organisations and SMEs which have viable projects that cannot obtain funding from mainstream banks.

Supporting groups with technical support and advice is an important part of the organisation's approach. ART's overall aim is to create local jobs for local people, and its main features, as an industrial and provident society, are:

- one member, one vote;
- maximum shareholding of £20,000 (individual or corporate), withdrawal of shares with 3 months notice; no prospectus or opening and closing dates required to issue shares;
- regulations of IPS similar to that of credit unions.

ART raises money from private companies, personal investors, housing associations, charitable foundations, and the public sector. Regional Growth Funding is provided to ART through its trade association, the Community Development Finance Association (CDFA), and is matched by funding from the Unity Trust and co-operative banks. This means ART has £1.6m to lend under the scheme in 2012 with the potential of £4.8m in total over the following three years, subject to funding availability and providing it meets its targets for lending to small businesses to enable them to create or safeguard jobs in Birmingham or Solihull.

Source: www.reinvest.co.uk (accessed November 2012)

Questions, Exercises, Essay, and Discussion Topics

1. What do you understand by the term patient capital?
2. Why are there different types of financial support for the social economy?
3. Are the financial support needs of the social economy different to those of the private economy?
4. What sort of organisation might need social venture capital?
5. What are the obstacles to the effective financing of social enterprises?
6. What knowledge set and skills do social enterprises need among their staff to manage their finances effectively and efficiently?
7. Describe the different forms of finance available to social economy enterprises.
8. When might a social enterprise need social equity finance and how might this be used?
9. How might fiscal initiatives such as Community Investment Tax Relief aid the development of social enterprises?

Suggestions for further reading

J. Iona, L. de Las Casas and B. Rickey, *Understanding the Demand for and Supply of Social Finance* (London: NESTA, 2011).

A. Nicholls, *The Landscape of Social Investment: A Holistic Topology of Opportunities* (Oxford: Said Business School, 2008).

T. Thorlby, *Finance and Business Models for Supporting Community Asset Ownership and Control* (York: JRF, 2011).

References

1. A. Nicholls, *The Landscape of Social Investment: A Holistic Topology of Opportunities* (Oxford: Said Business School, 2008).
2. A. Cadbury, *A Vision of Community Finance, in Up-scaling Social Investment: Fifty Case Studies* (Paris: INAISE, 2000), pp. 8–9.
3. Bank of England, *The Financing of Social Enterprises: A Special Report by the Bank of England* (London: Bank of England, 2003).
4. A. Brown and S. Swersky, *The First Billion: A Forecast of Social Investment* (Boston: Boston Consulting Group, 2012), p. 1.
5. F. Capber, *A Greater Space for Social Banking: Up-scaling Social Investment: Fifty Case Studies* (Paris: INAISE, 2000).
6. J. Kickul and T. Lyons, *Understanding Social Entrepreneurship: The Relentless Pursuit of Mission in an Ever Changing World* (London: Routledge, 2012).
7. M. Morrissey and S. Bridge, *Lessons of Peace II: A Review for Proteus* (Belfast: Proteus, 2006), pp. 30–2.
8. New economics foundation (nef), *Developing a Social Equity Capital Market* (London: nef, 2006), p. 11.
9. J. Iona, L. de Las Casas and B. Rickey, *Understanding the Demand for and Supply of Social Finance* (London: NESTA, 2011).
10. T. Thorlby, *Finance and Business Models for Supporting Community Asset Ownership and Control* (York: JRF, 2011).
11. P. Lloyd, *The Social Economy? What Future* (Belfast: Building Change Trust, 2011), p. 8.
12. Department of Trade and Industry (DTI), *Social Enterprise: a strategy for success* (London: DTI, 2003), p. 64.
13. E. Mayo, T. Fisher, P. Conaty, J. Doling and A. Mullineux, *Small Is Bankable: Community Reinvestment in the UK* (York: Joseph Rowntree Foundation, 1988).
14. Task Force, *The Report of the Social Investment Task Force (SITF)* (London: SITF, 2000).
15. D. Sattar and T. Fisher, *The Scope and Opportunity for Social Investment in the UK, Social Investment Taskforce Papers* (London: New Economics Foundation, 2002).
16. E. Mayo, T. Fisher, P. Conaty, J. Doling and A. Mullineux, *Small Is Bankable: Community Reinvestment in the UK* (York: Joseph Rowntree Foundation, 1988).
17. UKSIF, *Community Development Finance Institutions: A New Financial Instrument for Social, Economic and Physical Renewal* (London: UKSIF, 2002).
18. GHK, *The National Evaluation of Community Development Finance Institutions (CDFIs): An Action-Orientated Summary for the Sector* (London: BIS and The Cabinet Office, 2010), p. i.
19. New economics foundation (nef), *Reconsidering UK Community Development Finance* (London: nef, 2007).
20. Bank of England, *The Financing of Social Enterprises: A Special Report by the Bank of England* (London: Bank of England, 2003).
21. Ibid., p. 1.
22. B. Rogaly, T. Fisher and E. Mayo, *Poverty, Social Exclusion and Microfinance in Britain* (Oxford: Oxfam, in association with the New Economics Foundation, 1999), p. 3.
23. P. Moseley and L. Steel, 'Microfinance, the Labour Market and Social Inclusion: A Tale of Three Cities', *Social Policy and Administration*, Vol. 38, No. 7 (2006), pp. 721–43.
24. K. Dyson, P. Mosely, P. Lenton and P. Vik, *The Social Impact of UK Microfinance* (Salford: University of Salford, 2010).
25. K. Parker and M. Lyons, *Community Development Finance Institutions, Evidence from Oversees and Australia* (Sydney: Accord University of Technology, 2004).
26. New economics foundation (nef), *Community Banking Partnership: A Joined up Solution for Financial inclusion* (London: nef, 2004).
27. C. Williams, 'Harnessing the hidden enterprise culture; the Street UK Community Development Finance Initiative', *Local Economy*, Vol. 21, No. 1, pp. 13–24.
28. Ibid., p. 19.
29. S. Bernanke, 'Community Development Financial Institutions: Challenges and opportunities', in *Community Development Investment Center, The Economic Crisis and Community Development Finance: An Industry Assessment* (San Francisco: CDFC, 2009, pp. 2–5), p. 3.
30. S. Lowry, *Community Development Financial Institutions (CDFI) Fund: Programs and Policy Issues* (Washington, DC: Congressional Research Service, 2012).
31. L. Bernholz, *Philanthropy and the Social Economy: Blueprint 2013* (New York: Grant Craft, 2012).
32. CEIS, *Sharing in Success Patient Capital for the Social Economy in Scotland* (Glasgow: CEIS, 2002).
33. Bank of England, *The Financing of Social Enterprises: A Special Report by the Bank of England* (London: Bank of England, 2003).

34. CEIS, *Sharing in Success Patient Capital for the Social Economy in Scotland* (Glasgow: CEIS, 2002), p. 4.

35. A. McGregor, A. Glass and S. Clark, *Revaluing the Social Economy* (Glasgow: University of Glasgow, 2003).

36. Ibid., p. 34.

37. Ibid., p. 35.

38. L. Dayson, *Community Finance Solutions* (Bristol: Bristol City Council, 2003), p. 9.

39. H. Metcalf, H. Crowley, T. Anderson and C. Bainton, *From Unemployment to Self-employment: The Role of Micro Finance* (London: ILO, 2000).

40. S. Collin, T. Fisher, E, Mayo, A. Mullineux and D. Sattar, *The State of Community Development Finance* (London: nef, 2001).

41. R. Copisarow, 'The application of micro credit technology to the UK: key commercial policy issues', *Journal of Micro Finance*, Vol. 2, No. 1 (2000), pp. 13–42.

42. L. Dayson, *Community Finance Solutions* (Bristol: Bristol City Council, 2003), p. 13.

43. S. Collin, T. Fisher, E, Mayo, A. Mullineux and D. Sattar, *The State of Community Development Finance* (London: nef, 2001).

44. Ibid.

45. L. Dayson, *Community Finance Solutions* (Bristol: Bristol City Council, 2003).

46. J. Iona, L. de Las Casas and B. Rickey, *Understanding the Demand for and Supply of Social Finance* (London: NESTA, 2011).

47. J. Brown, *Community Shares: One Year On* (London: Cooperatives UK, 2010).

48. J. Loder, *Social Impact Bonds in Health* (London: The Young Foundation, 2012), p. 1.

49. Social Finance, *Social Impact Bonds, Rethinking Social Finance* (London: Social Finance, 2009).

50. Scottish Council for Voluntary Organisations (SCVO), *Tax Effective Giving to Charity* (Edinburgh: SCVO, 2002).

51. A. Ainger, R. Brocklehurst and S. Forster, *Feasibility Study into a Wholesale Intermediary for Community Development Finance* (London: Housing Finance Corporation, 2002).

52. Ibid., pp. 8–9.

53. S. Thake and S. Lingayah, *Investing in Thriving Communities: The Final Evaluation of the Adventure Capital Fund* (London: London Metropolitan University, 2009).

54. East of England Development Agency (EEDA), *Finance Think Tank: Issues for Social Enterprise Finance* (Norwich: EEDA, 2005).

55. Bank of England, *The Financing of Social Enterprises: A Special Report by the Bank of England* (London: Bank of England, 2003), p. 7.

8

social capital: a vital enterprise ingredient

contents:

- introduction
- the concept of social capital
- definitions and different forms of social capital
- the advantages of social capital
- social capital and economic performance
- the types of social capital: a 'vitamin' view
- social capital, networks, and entrepreneurship
- social capital and social enterprise
- social capital and regeneration
- the dark side of social capital
- measuring social capital
- does the social economy create social capital?

Key concepts

This chapter covers:

- the origins of social capital across a range of different intellectual and policy traditions;
- the relationship between social capital and other forms of capital relevant to development;
- the role of social capital in economic, enterprise, and community resilience;
- the negative effects of social capital, especially linked to the delivery of broad-based economic development practice;
- some of the issues in measuring social capital.

Learning objectives

By the end of this chapter the reader should:

- understand origins of social capital as a conceptual and applied policy concept;
- appreciate the connection between social capital and other forms of capital resources essential for local development;
- understand the connection between the concept of social capital and the performance of the economy and the social economy in particular;
- recognise the connection between the social economy and regeneration and community resilience;
- identify the limits of social capital, especially as it is applied to the social economy;
- understand the problems in measuring social capital across time and place.

Introduction

This chapter looks at social capital, at its relationship to the social economy and the third sector, and at its role in addressing deprivation. Some academics and policy-makers consider social capital to be a necessary prerequisite for effective economic growth,[1] whilst for others it is a by-product of community-inspired responses to economic disinvestment.[2] However, critics suggest that social capital and notions of community cohesion are weak alternatives to the provision of hard economic resources such as jobs, cash, skills, and opportunity.[3] Concepts such as empowerment and capacity-building ring hollow in places and communities which economic capital has abandoned or ignored.[4]

Nevertheless, the connection between social capital and the necessary means for community advancement is a potentially attractive one for programme managers and policy-makers concerned with the improvement of disadvantaged neighbourhoods across the developed world.[5] A viable stock of social capital in the form of organisations, networks, trust, and norms can, it is suggested, be an important foundation for local economic mobilisation and for the creation of a virtuous circle of economic and social growth in both urban and rural communities.[6]

Baron et al.[7] argue that the current interest in social capital reflects a growing recognition of the excesses of individualism and a concern that, in the market-orientation politics of the 1980s, valuable social assets and morals were eroded, which in turn had deteriorating effects on communitarianism and the quality of life. Francis Fukuyama[8] also argued that the success of the strongest and most advanced capitalist societies has been based on a relatively high level of trust in business and politics. In countries such as Japan and Germany, social capital is the defining factor that explains the strength of their political economy as well as their cultural vitality. Capitalism has proved to be a more successful and enduring system than the failed communist order, and within capitalism, trust facilitates friction-free economic development and political maturity.

Not surprisingly, the potential capacity of social capital to enrich or even rescue civic society has a powerful appeal to politicians, not least in the UK where notions of a stake-holding society and Big Society politics (see Case 3.1) focus attention on the erosion of civility and social cohesion.[9] The decline of civic society is 'real and visible . . . it is seen in the weakening sense of solidarity in some communities and urban neighbourhoods, high levels of crime and the break-up of marriages and families'.[10] For Giddens, the repair process involves government and civil society working in partnership, community renewal through harnessing local initiative, and involvement of the third sector in service delivery. He is especially attracted to the notion of social investment whereby the state works with multiple actors, especially in the community and voluntary sectors, in the production of a broader and more shared sense of a welfare society, not a welfare state:

> Since the revival of civic culture is a basic ambition of third way politics, the active involvement of government in the social economy makes sense. Indeed some have presented the choice before us in stark terms, given the problematic status of full employment: either greater participation in the social economy or facing the growth of 'outlaw cultures'.[11]

This has been extended in ideas around Big Society politics and the responsibilities and rights of civic society to control the assets that matter in people's lives.[12] Social enterprises have been repositioned as a way of delivering failing public services and neighbourhood facilities and strengthening consumer control over health and social care. This chapter presents the concept of social capital, therefore, in relation to other forms of capital, and aims to show the relationship between civic society, social capital, and the social economy in practical ways. It begins with a brief review of the concept of social capital before look-ing in more detail at its application to the economy, enterprise, and entrepreneurship. The analysis also considers whether social capital has specific contributions to make to, or a specific dependence upon, the social economy, which are distinct from its relationship to business performance in private markets and the added value it may contribute to economic development generally.

The concept of social capital

The concept of social capital is not new. Its intellectual roots in the social sciences rest with a concern for communitarianism, pluralist associated life, and both representative and participative forms of democracy.[13] Pierre Bourdieu re-energised the study of social capital by connecting it to both cultural and material economic assets. The capital that individuals are able to accumulate defines their position in the social class order but there are important distinctions in the way in which these forms of capital work in practice. For Bourdieu, social capital is not reducible to economic or cultural capital but it is not independent of them either, and economic capital is the most efficient form of capital in shaping class and society in advanced countries. The reproduction of economic capital, on its own, creates wealth and power disparities, but, in Bourdieu's model, the individual has 'the capacity to exercise control over one's own future and that of others'.[14] Social capital is thus the aggregate of real and potential resources which are linked to durable relational networks between individuals and institutions.[15] This suggests that it has two dimensions:

- First, it is a resource that is connected to group membership and social networks and the volume of social capital possessed by an individual depends on the size of the network created; and

- Second, it is about the quality of these relationships and especially the capacity of the groups to mobilise resources in their own interests. [16]

Bourdieu used the term narrowly, being primarily interested in explaining how some people gained access to power and resources via their social connections. Coleman's analysis shared some of these ideas but he viewed social capital as a functional concept that could also be employed neutrally or in non-political ways. Coleman saw social capital consisting of two components that reflect some aspects of social structure and facilitate the actions of actors within that structure. This structure is passive and can be used in positive or negative ways, which, in each case, is determined by the motivation and objectives of actors within any given network. Thus, it simultaneously reproduces greater connection between the actors and imposes obligations and sanction on the membership. [17]

Portes in particular criticised Coleman's version of social capital, especially for its definitional vagueness. [18] Here, he stressed the distinction between the membership of social structures and the resources gained via such membership. Coleman's work drew heavily on 'dense networks' such as kinship and neighbourhood links, which understates the importance of weak or informal ties in securing economic advantage. Like Putnam, Portes criticised Coleman's understanding of social capital as functionalist and organic which places particular value on the family. This has left the approach open to criticism from feminists and by those who identified the exploitative labour practices sometimes associated with familial business commitments.

Few writers have done more to boost the status of social capital, in the West at least, than Robert Putnam. His early definition referred to social capital as 'the networks, norms and trust that enable participants to act together to effectively pursue shared objectives'. [19] In his later work he shifted the emphasis from trust to reciprocity and an acknowledgement that social capital has a dark side, especially in multi-ethnic societies. [20,21] His approach is examined in greater detail later in the chapter but it has attracted particular criticism from those who argue that it is a neoliberal concept urging conformity with, not resistance to, the pervasive power of public and private markets. Law and Mooney [22] in particular argued that Putnam's work represents a constructivist, simplistic, and descriptive account of social capital that fails to theorise power relations and the dominant role of economic capital in creating social exclusion.

Definitions and different forms of social capital

Social capital, like the social economy, has a multitude of definitions. These reflect different emphases such as the strength of networks, the quality of structures and institutions, or the intended outcomes or beneficiaries from its activation in particular settings. For example, Kay's interpretation of social capital is especially interesting as he makes the connection between resources generated by its presence and a vibrant social economy. For Kay, social capital is:

> that tangible 'something' that exists among individuals and organisations within a community; the connections and trusting contacts that people make while going about their daily business. These contacts can be used on a mutual and reciprocal basis both to further their own ends and/or for the development of the community. [23]

Others have highlighted different aspects, and Table 8.1, based on a UK Cabinet Office discussion paper, [24] lists a few of the definitions and the different emphases they place on social capital and its economic, political, and social purposes.

Table 8.1 Definitions of social capital

- '... features of social life – networks, norms, and trust – that enable participants to act together more effectively to pursue shared objectives ... Social capital, in short, refers to social connections and the attendant norms and trust' [25]
- 'Social capital is seen as the foundation on which social stability and a community's ability to help itself are built; and its absence is thought to be a key factor in neighbourhood decline.' [26]
- '... the institutions, relationships and norms that shape the quality and quantity of a society's social interactions' [27]
- 'networks together with shared norms, values and understandings that facilitate co-operation within or among groups' [28]
- 'The term "social capital" is increasingly used by policymakers as another way of describing "community," but it is important to recognise that a traditional community is just one of many forms of social capital. Work-based networks, diffused friendships and shared or mutually acknowledged social values can all be seen as forms of social capital.' [29]
- 'Social capital ... should be interpreted as interpersonal networks where members develop and maintain trust in one another to keep their promises by the device of "mutual enforcement" of agreements' [30]

Sustainable livelihoods

The UK Department for International Development (DFID) developed an approach to understanding vulnerability and its management in different situations. This 'sustainable livelihoods' approach suggests that there is a range of factors, each of which needs to be addressed to achieve sustainable routes out of exclusion and deprivation:

> The livelihoods approach is concerned first and foremost with people. It seeks to gain an accurate and realistic understanding of people's strengths (assets or capital endowments) and how they endeavour to convert these into positive livelihood outcomes. The approach is founded on a belief that people require a range of assets to achieve positive livelihood outcomes; no single category of assets on its own is sufficient to yield all the many and varied livelihood outcomes that people seek. [31]

The 'sustainable livelihoods' model (see Figure 8.1) is highlighted here because it includes social capital as one of five types of 'capital' asset which are considered to be important in building a strong community but which have limited substitution potential. The five-capitals pentagon lies at the core of the livelihoods framework as it highlights the important interrelationships between the various assets affecting people's quality of life.

DFID pays particular attention to the relationship between social capital and other assets that even the poorest communities can secure to improve their chances. Government policy can provide some assets, such as the provision of essential infrastructure, and determine access to assets and influence their ownership and control through, for instance, the operation of the taxation system. Transforming structures and processes within the livelihoods framework are the institutions, organisations, policies, and legislation that shape livelihoods. They operate at all levels, from the household to the international arena and across both public and private markets in order to determine:

- access (to various types of capital and to decision-making bodies and sources of influence);

- the terms of exchange between different types of capital; and
- returns (economic and otherwise) to any given livelihood strategy.

The DFID model may therefore be looking at a different level than that of many social enterprises or other forms of business but it is introduced here to show the potential

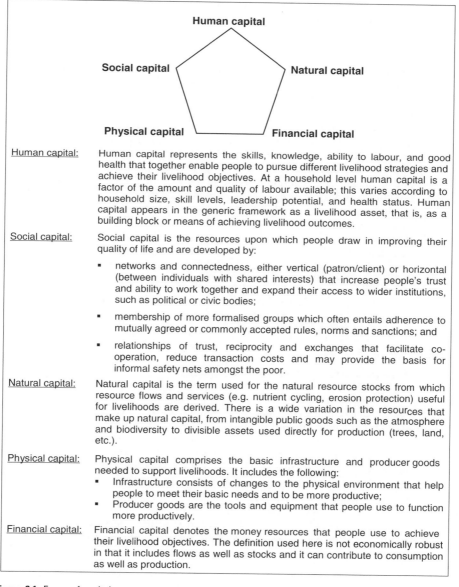

Human capital:	Human capital represents the skills, knowledge, ability to labour, and good health that together enable people to pursue different livelihood strategies and achieve their livelihood objectives. At a household level human capital is a factor of the amount and quality of labour available; this varies according to household size, skill levels, leadership potential, and health status. Human capital appears in the generic framework as a livelihood asset, that is, as a building block or means of achieving livelihood outcomes.
Social capital:	Social capital is the resources upon which people draw in improving their quality of life and are developed by: ▪ networks and connectedness, either vertical (patron/client) or horizontal (between individuals with shared interests) that increase people's trust and ability to work together and expand their access to wider institutions, such as political or civic bodies; ▪ membership of more formalised groups which often entails adherence to mutually agreed or commonly accepted rules, norms and sanctions; and ▪ relationships of trust, reciprocity and exchanges that facilitate co-operation, reduce transaction costs and may provide the basis for informal safety nets amongst the poor.
Natural capital:	Natural capital is the term used for the natural resource stocks from which resource flows and services (e.g. nutrient cycling, erosion protection) useful for livelihoods are derived. There is a wide variation in the resources that make up natural capital, from intangible public goods such as the atmosphere and biodiversity to divisible assets used directly for production (trees, land, etc.).
Physical capital:	Physical capital comprises the basic infrastructure and producer goods needed to support livelihoods. It includes the following: ▪ Infrastructure consists of changes to the physical environment that help people to meet their basic needs and to be more productive; ▪ Producer goods are the tools and equipment that people use to function more productively.
Financial capital:	Financial capital denotes the money resources that people use to achieve their livelihood objectives. The definition used here is not economically robust in that it includes flows as well as stocks and it can contribute to consumption as well as production.

Figure 8.1 Forms of capital

Source: Department for International Development (DFID), *Sustainable Development Guidance Sheets* (London: DFID, 1999), p. 5

width of the application of social capital in human activity, including enterprise – not least because humans are a social species:

> The notion that we are rational individuals who respond to information by making decisions consciously, consistently and independently is, at best, a very partial account of who we are. A wide body of scientific knowledge is now telling us what many have long intuitively sensed – humans are a fundamentally social species, formed through and for social interaction.[32]

Other views on social capital

The DFID model has also been described here to provide a framework within which other views can be compared and contrasted. Hirschman, for instance, helpfully unpacks the concept of social energy into interpersonal or human friendship, ideals or a shared sense of values, and ideas which underscore the value of intellectual capital in the formation of valuable communal structures and networks.[33] Putnam points out that 'whereas physical capital refers to physical objects and human capital refers to properties of individuals, social capital refers to connections among individuals – social networks and the norms of reciprocity and trustworthiness that arise from them'.[34] This distinction is important and highlights the reinforcing value of social capital with other assets that places and communities possess or need to acquire in order to secure long-term development.

The contributions of other authors have also added to the confusion about the nature of social capital, but, in view of its relative newness as a concept, it may not be surprising that no single clear, widely accepted description seems to have been established. Schuller et al. have commented, for instance, that 'the relative immaturity of social capital as a concept... [and its] rapid proliferation has allowed a diversity of approach', and, in summary, they suggest that:

> Social capital has several adolescent characteristics: it is neither tidy nor mature; it can be abused, analytically and politically; its future is unpredictable; but it offers much promise.[35]

The advantages of social capital

Increasing attention has been paid to community resilience in the face of major global risks such as climate change, ageing, and terrorism.[36] Pelling and Dill[37] argue that understanding vulnerability and the multiple stresses that disadvantaged communities face is important but that it has tended ideologically to dominate and/or encourage dependent approaches rather than one which sees assets and capital as a basis for 'adaptation'. Adaptation and risk reduction is primarily about resilient development and transformative change. Reactive resilience that simply allows a community to return to its original state or bounce back after a shock event is insufficient, but proactive resilience means developing a portfolio of capital or assets to engineer systemic change.[38]

Table 8.2 describes some of the advantages attributed to social capital in the exercise of public participation, in engaging the private sector, and in service provision. These include specifically that:

- By improving the efficiency of economic relations, social capital can help increase people's incomes and rates of saving (financial capital). (Isolated studies have shown that communities with 'higher levels' of social capital are wealthier – but questions remain about measuring social capital.)

- Social capital can help to reduce the 'free rider' problems associated with public goods. This means that it can be effective in improving the management of common resources (natural capital) and the maintenance of shared infrastructure (physical capital).
- Social networks facilitate innovation, the development of knowledge, and the sharing of that knowledge. There is, therefore, a close relationship between social and human capital.
- Social capital, like other types of capital, can also be valued as a good in itself. It can make a particularly important contribution to people's sense of well-being (through identity, honour, and belonging).

Governments and policy-makers are naturally attracted to the wider economic benefits of social capital.[39] The Performance and Innovation Unit (PIU) in the UK Cabinet Office in 2002 concluded that:

> Social capital may contribute to a range of beneficial economic and social outcomes including: high levels of and growth in GDP; more efficiently functioning labour markets; higher educational attainment; lower levels of crime; better health; and more effective institutions of government.[40]

The Unit also highlighted the factors that lead to a healthy stock of social capital, including history and culture, whether social structures are flat or hierarchical, the family, education, the built environment, residential mobility, economic inequalities and social class, the strength and characteristics of civil society, and patterns of individual consumption and personal values. The accumulation of social capital, it argues, should be prioritised as an outcome of government policy, which intellectually draws on Putnam's wider interpretation of the relationship between capital and changing familial and social structures.

According to PIU,[41] social capital has multiple social, political, and economic effects. It can enhance economic performance by strengthening the levels of trust in business-to-business relationships. Fukuyama suggests that global enterprise requires a high degree of trust in order to grow, trade across cultural and fiscal boundaries, and secure markets and strategic partnerships; where it is not present, business models remain muted and vulnerable.[42] Social capital can create information symmetries between businesses and between producers and consumers and helps, in part, to explain the localised strength of business clusters, especially in high-growth sectors of the economy evidenced by the dynamism of Silicon Valley in California. Social capital can help labour markets to work more effectively: it can increase knowledge and awareness of job opportunities and identify

Table 8.2 The strengths of relational webs

Strength	Description
Transaction	Networks of civic engagement increase the potential costs to a defector in any individual transaction: in other words, he/she will lose in other and future transactions by not being involved
Norms	Networks of civic engagement foster robust forms of reciprocity, understanding of the rules and expectations governing relationships, and reinforcing of reputation and trust between actors
Communications	Networks build civic engagement, facilitate communication, and improve the information flow about the trustworthiness of individuals
Collaboration	Networks build on past successes of collaboration and build informal routines and continuity between actors

Source: Based on R. Putnam, *Making Democracy Work: Civic Traditions in Modern Italy* (Princeton: Princeton University Press, 1993), pp. 173–4

supplies of the skills required by growing industrial sectors. Education can benefit by tapping into physical and intellectual resources and crime is reduced as a stronger sense of local identity strengthens community values as well as offering sanctions against deviant behaviour. Finally, the PIU argue that social capital improves health by bolstering community support systems and strengthens government institutions by developing citizens as more sophisticated political consumers.

Social capital and economic performance

One of the main criticisms of local development approaches is that they are based on extensive descriptions of social need that strengthen dependency and reliance on outsiders to provide solutions. [43] For proponents of social capital, the emphasis should be placed on the *assets* that are locally available and which are interdependent in creating sustainable communities. [44] Kay thus argues that the best way to see the value of social capital is to look at communities where it is absent or where there are few social networks, a lack of trust, or limited shared commitment to place, cohesiveness, and development.

Social enterprises generate social capital in their area, mostly by using social capital. Explicit, shared values create solidarity between like-minded social enterprises. Trust and reciprocity build up into co-operation and collaboration. Informal and formal social networks are actively built upon – bonding the social enterprises together and also bridging to other social enterprise organisations outside the immediate group. [45]

Crucially, he draws on the DFID analysis to suggest that social capital alone cannot build the social economy and that financial, human, and physical resources need to be present in sufficient quantities, and linked together to create sustainable development. In a local community, the market, public sector, and community activity exist together and effective social capital helps to reduce transaction costs, provide services, and facilitate synergy across the three sectors in any given place. Social capital provides a framework for integrating the third sector, putting it to work, providing strategic guidance, and helping to clarify how the social economy needs to work in concert with both private and public markets.

The idea of social capital as a theoretical concept, relevant to policy and politics, was given particular impetus by the work of Robert Putnam. In his study of Italy, he argued that co-operation for mutual benefit is at the heart of the differential economic performance between the north and south of the country:

> Success in overcoming dilemmas of collective action and self-defeating opportunism that they spawn depends on the broader social context within which any particular game is played. Voluntary cooperation is easier in a community that has inherited a substantial stock of social capital in the forms of norms, reciprocity and networks of civic engagement. [46]

Here, therefore, social capital refers to features of social organisations including trust, norms, and networks that can improve the efficiency of society by facilitating coordinated actions. Putnam's analysis of the regions of Italy suggests that social trust has been a key ingredient sustaining economic dynamism and government performance in the north in contrast with Naples and the wider south. Similarly, Fukuyama[47] argued that relationships form a virtuous circle of growth in which trust encourages co-operation and co-operation breeds trust in the steady accumulation of social capital. Social trust in modern societies arises from norms of reciprocity and networks of civic engagement. Norms of reciprocity evolve because they lower transaction costs between people, groups, or interests and because they facilitate mutual co-operation. In turn, reciprocity can be of two types:

- Balanced reciprocity refers to a simultaneous exchange of items of equivalent value.
- Generalised reciprocity refers to a continuing relationship of exchange that involves mutual expectations that benefit granted should be repaid in the future.

Generalised reciprocity is likely to be associated with a dense or *thick* network of social exchange. Formal or informal communication and exchange can be either horizontal, which brings together interests with equivalent status and power, or vertical, which connects with unequal agents in a hierarchical relationship.

For Putnam it is the quality and durability of personal and business networks that are critical in explaining the difference between competing and declining economies. Table 8.2 shows that rational benefits result from belonging to, and maintaining, relational webs that might have a vertical or horizontal character. Putnam argues that vertical networks cannot sustain social trust and co-operation as those lower down the hierarchy may have less influence and control in these types of relationships. Yet for others, who refer to this relationship as linking social capital, it is connections that provide those outside public or private markets with access to decision-making arenas, although dependent relationships based on patron–client exchanges are more likely to be characterised by opportunism than by mutuality.[48]

Horizontal relationships, he contends, have a more robust quality, but Putnam makes an important distinction between internal and external relationships in group dynamics:

> Dense but segregated horizontal networks sustain cooperation *within* each group, but networks of civic engagement that cut across social cleavages nourish wider cooperation. This is another reason why networks of civic engagement are such an important part of the community's stock of social capital.[49]

Putnam's most recent work also acknowledges the multiple forms and purposes of social capital (see Table 8.3) and the crucial distinction between bonding (exclusive) and bridging (inclusive) social capital. Bonding social capital is good for mobilising solidarity and cohesion and can provide important socio-psychological networks for mutual support among groups that share a common set of interests as varied as ethnic minorities or entrepreneurs. Bridging networks, on the other hand, are better for linking to external assets and resources and for both spreading and exchanging knowledge and ideas. Bonding social capital forms what Putnam refers to as, 'sociological superglue',[50] which might have negative side effects in the exclusion, for example, of the out-group and negative consequences of '*otherisation*'.

Table 8.3 Types of social capital

- Bonding social capital – characterised by strong bonds (or 'social glue'), e.g. among family members or among members of an ethnic group.
- Bridging social capital – characterised by weaker, less dense but more cross-cutting ties ('social oil'), e.g. with business associates, acquaintances, friends from different ethnic groups, friends of friends, etc.
- Linking social capital – characterised by connections between those with differing levels of power or social status, e.g. links between the political elite and the general public or between individuals from different social classes.

Source: Based on Performance and Innovation Unit, 'Social capital: A discussion paper' (London: Cabinet Office, 2002), pp. 11–2

The types of social capital: a 'vitamin' view

Reference is made above to different types of social capital, and Table 8.3 suggests three types that are not substitutable one for another. Although, in *Bowling Alone*, Putnam uses a one-dimensional measure of the amount of social capital in a society, nevertheless in the same book he suggests that there are different forms of social capital which are not necessarily complementary – and cannot therefore usefully be summed to a one-dimensional total. Instead, if the different 'capitals' in models like the DFID model (see Figure 8.1) are likened to the different components of food, then, following the example of Halpern,[51] Bridge suggests that social capital should be likened to vitamins rather than to other components such as protein.[52] For instance, if a diet is short of protein, then different forms of protein, such as those from animal and vegetable sources, can both contribute to making good that deficiency. If, however, a diet is short of one or more vitamins, then the specific vitamins missing need to be supplied.

Bridge also suggests that this lack of interchangeability is a feature of the different forms of social capital and means that, in at least some respects, vitamins offer a better analogy for the different aspects of social capital than do proteins. Other similarities are that it took some time for the role of vitamins in diet to be recognised, not least because they are normally present in fresh food and a lack was not noticed until preserved food was used for a significant period – for instance in long ocean voyages. Also, once the existence of vitamins was recognised, it still took very many years to identify all of the vitamins relevant to human life.

Thus, it is not necessarily surprising that, if the vitamin analogy is correct and there are different non-substitutable forms of social capital, that no definitive list is available of all those different forms. The six headings listed in Illustration 8.2 indicate some distinctions and Table 8.3 presents three possible forms: bonding, bridging, and linking. From Case 8.1 the following possibilities might be extracted, some of which may, or may not, overlap with the Table 8.3 distinctions:

• support from within the local community.
• guidance from outside the local community.
• obtaining relevant information.
• trust and vouching.
• encouragement of specific behaviours.

However, this suggestion that there may be more different forms of social capital than are described in Table 8.3 is not yet widely agreed. Also, if it is correct, it is likely that some forms have not yet been clearly identified and/or described. Nevertheless, it might be helpful to be aware of the possibility of a number of different forms and to question which form is being considered and/or relevant in any particular context.

Social capital, networks, and entrepreneurship

In 2007 the *International Small Business Journal* dedicated an entire edition (Vol.25 No.3) to the connection between social capital and entrepreneurship. In particular, the contributions to the Journal valued the quality of networks and relationships as a resource and asset which could help explain the performance of entrepreneurs:

> Relationships clearly matter to entrepreneurs, but understanding how they function requires an appreciation of social capital. The presence or absence of social capital is

likely to influence the very nature of the entrepreneurial venture. Social capital involves social interaction and would appear to reside in and between connections to others. It could even be regarded as representing 'networking capital' since in essence it is really a relational phenomenon and a term that actually refers to the social connections entrepreneurs use to obtain resources they would otherwise acquire through expending the human or financial capital.[53]

Anderson et al. saw social capital as 'a relational artefact, produced in interactions but that resides within a network. Individuals may have a high or low propensity to develop social capital, but they can only do so within social interactions.'[54] Thus it is not a capital asset in any conventional sense but is a condition that adheres to, and is determined by, the number, range, and quality of social interactions. As a result, the literature on the economic and entrepreneurial value of social capital places a particular emphasis on business networks and interpersonal trust in the development and maintenance of efficient production chains.[55]

Casson and Della-Giusta argue that different types of networks are needed to support entrepreneurship at different stages of development. The network literature suggests that social capital can be defined as the creation of high-trust social networks, and to Casson and Della-Giusta these are evident at the local, regional, national, or global level. Given the emphasis on interpersonal contact, much research has concentrated on the local level, but in regional and national interests shaped around sectors such as tourism or mining, more mobile and adaptive networks can be identified. Place, in short, does not restrict the scope or quality of networks.

Casson and Della-Giusta also further stratify the definition to look at local business networks, social networks, and physical networks (such as a common transport spine or rail hub), which are all important to entrepreneurial performance. These networks can vary therefore in their shape and in the way communications and trust flow between actors. A web-based network is more informal and based on shared mutual pursuits whilst a hub-based network is centred on a point where large number of concentrations converge or where a dominant agent drives the relationships. Both rely on ease of communications and trust. Ease of communications is clearly facilitated by a shared language, customs, cultures, and efficient technologies. Trust is based on the obligations between parties and the rational interest they have in reciprocal exchange of these obligations in business transactions.

Casson and Della-Giusta also distinguish between vertical networks in the chain of production and horizontal connections between people engaged in the same stage of production such as suppliers or manufactures or retailers. The latter improve economic performance and competitiveness or simply yield scale economies that would be missed by individuals working on their own. Interestingly, Casson and Della-Giusta are critical of network approaches with exclusively social concerns where the dispossessed are brought together in relationships that often accentuate their victim mentality and marginalisation. This social exclusion rationale has limits, and bridging to those with entrepreneurial expertise and values may stimulate new thinking and financial resources to tackle exclusion.

In their review of leadership in the social economy Chambers and Edwards-Stuart[56] identify the common features of successful social entrepreneurs, which include:

- integrative, speculative thinkers;
- high drive and persistence;
- strong value base;

- strong focus;
- developed sense of self;
- good reading of others;
- strong networking;
- sense of responsibility for others and for outcomes; and
- creating a sense of excitement, vibrancy, and progress.

They argue that entrepreneurs need support throughout the cycle of business development including incubation, start-up, building a sustainable organisation, and growth or replication of the organisation. They further argued that there are common success traits in successful social entrepreneurs who have been pivotal in the establishment of their businesses: they have had strong relationships with their supporters based on a common value or belief system, they were active and inquisitive learners, and they tended to be self-sufficient and less reliant on procedures and system to manage their organisations.

Social capital and social enterprise

Evans and Syrett drew an important link between the presence of social capital and the stimulation of social enterprises' development. 'The importance of social capital in the local economic development process resides in its ability to lever in and maximize the use and development of other sources of capital within local arenas'. [57] Similarly, a number of writers have critically examined the relationship between social capital, the social economy, and social enterprise. Chell [58] highlighted the value of research into enterprise that drew upon social constructionism in which attention is paid to the social embeddedness of entrepreneurial practices. She has indicated the social as well as the material value of entrepreneurs as agents of change. Entrepreneurs garner a range of resources and use various forms of human, financial, and social capital in order to create wealth and add social value.

Johnstone and Lionais [59] also highlight a central contradiction in community business initiatives which expected that part of the market to fix what capitalism has used up or abandoned in de-industrialised or depleted communities. It might be expected that a different type of entrepreneur would emerge but it raises important issues about the deployment of locally based social capital networks as a resource for redevelopment. Thus, Birch and Whittam [60] highlight an important contradiction in the social capital functioning of entrepreneurs which questions the logic of regional and local development policy. They draw upon Dees [61] to define the characteristics of the *public entrepreneur*:

- adopting a mission;
- pursuing new opportunities to achieve that mission;
- continually innovating, adapting, and learning;
- avoiding limitations of current resources; and
- being concerned with accountability to their clients and that community.

Fulfilling these functions creates a central paradox in that the social entrepreneur needs to collaborate with many disparate groups, maintain that network, and develop and use it in the pursuit of the social objective. These weak ties outside the strong bonding ties with the local community are critical for success and the two may not be reconcilable:

> Social entrepreneurship can therefore be positioned as a response to the exclusivity and closed structure within community networks. It operates as a linking capacity

between groups, bringing together agendas and resources in the pursuit of particular projects; such 'gate-keepers' draw on a range of different capacities within the community. It is therefore a version of weak networks that connect disparate groups and enables social cohesion through stopping fragmentation. Because social entrepreneurs pursue projects, it is a temporary process that provides links dependent upon the individual capabilities of the entrepreneur or entrepreneurial organisation involved. The social capital inherent within social entrepreneurship can be characterised in contrast to that inherent within communities, which implies that the proposition of the former will be detrimental to the retention of the latter. [62]

Linked to this, there is a range of criticisms about the policy rationale for promoting social entrepreneurship:

- The development of a strong trading ethos within a social enterprise inevitably reduces the rationale of a community link in order to sustain development or provide a cost service.
- The emphasis on market-reoriented activities reduces attention paid to the value base of the organisation.
- There are inevitable displacement effects with well-developed communities receiving the benefits of social capital whereas others are left with either none or the remnants of entrepreneurial activity.

Howarth [63] also questioned the market-led values and assumptions underpinning the enterprise shift within community development policy and programme delivery. He traced the adoption of social entrepreneurship in Western policy discourse to the established tradition of community economic development, to a concern for civic emancipation and neighbourhood self-reliance, and to a response to top-down market economics of the 1980s and early 1990s. However, uncritically interlocking social capital and entrepreneurship has not been without theoretical, practical, and operational difficulties. Howarth showed that many social entrepreneurs had a strong sense of communal and kinship values directing the value base of their work. Whilst they exhibit characteristics associated with private sector entrepreneurs, including being proactive, opportunity seeking, and risk taking, these characteristics were part of a wider process of community change rather than the preserve of individual 'leaders'.

Social capital and regeneration

Illustration 8.1 Social capital and disadvantage: Two views

We still don't have a good word to describe what is missing in Cameroon, indeed in poor countries across the world. But we are starting to understand what it is. Some people call it 'social capital', or maybe 'trust'. Others call it 'the rule of law', or 'institutions'. But these are just labels. The problem is that Cameroon, like other poor countries, is a topsy-turvy world in which it's in most people's interest to take action that directly or indirectly damages everyone else.

Source: T. Harford, *The Undercover Economist* (London: Little Brown, 2006), p. 201

In terms of social capital, deprived neighbourhoods with relatively stable populations may have levels of intra-community 'bonding' social capital that are equal to, or above, that of more affluent districts. The downside of heavily bonded communities is an insular and exclusionary local culture which limits connections to external networks. There is often an absence of extra-community 'bridging' social capital, which connects different groups and individuals to a wider range of social networks that extend beyond their community.

Source: D. North and S. Syrett, *The Dynamics of Local Economies* (London: Department for Communities and Local Government, 2006), p. 9

Illustration 8.1 shows that some commentators have identified a connection between deficiencies in social capital and the spirals of decline experienced by communities and even countries. Among others, Miles and Tully made the connection between social capital and urban and regional degeneration:

> In a national economy an absence of social capital is often seen as a feature of market failure, in which co-operation, collective action, risk sharing, innovation and entrepreneurship are lacking or severely constrained. This form of market failure can also characterize regional economies and disadvantaged local communities.[64]

They suggested that there are a number of reasons why social capital might assist in area-based regeneration including improving the ability of an area to recover from a shock such as a factory closure, to rebuild itself by enabling access to decision-makers and politicians, and to open access to the labour market via formal and informal networks. However, their review, based on the North-East of England, again emphasised the need for local social capital to connect more formally with tangible economic assets capable of providing work, income, and investment to a neighbourhood:

> A combination of traditional support programmes (e.g. area-based integrated labour markets (ILMs), education and training, enterprise development) with social capital building (e.g. promoting community/business co-operatives, support networks, labour and cultural exchanges etc.) is perhaps required.[65]

Forrest and Kearns[66] and Callois and Aubert[67] also highlighted the fundamental point that internal social capital aimed at social cohesiveness has limits, especially when the economic sustainability of a place is increasingly dependent on globalisation and regional economic performance. Looking at the problems of peripheral rural areas in France, Callois and Aubert noted that sociological factors are vital in helping communities organise themselves but that business, personal, and political networks that bridge outside the region are becoming more important in determining the pace of economic and agricultural restructuring in such areas.

Thus, Moulaert and Nussbaumer[68] made the point that the study of social capital at the neighbourhood level needs to acknowledge that:

- social capital is not held by individuals and groups but is part of the social relationship between agents;
- there is a link between social and other forms of capital and whilst these are variously intertwined, economic capital or its absence can negatively affect the effectiveness of social capital;
- development trajectories of areas are important so that long-lasting economic decline can deplete and even paralyse social capital; and
- the interaction between various types of capital (human, ecological, business, social, or institutional) can have both destructive and creative effects.

Kleinhans et al.[69] noted that policy-makers and practitioners have acknowledged the diverse and interconnected quality of various forms of localised capital, especially in the presence and depth of relationship-building around area-based and housing redevelopment programmes. Forrest and Kearns set out the domains of social capital exhibited at a neighbourhood level and how and where policy-makers should support them (see Table 8.4). Their work moves beyond abstraction, unpacking social capital in a spatial context and describing an area-based agenda that connects social capital and community cohesion.

A criticism of highly localised approaches is that they concentrate on micro-variables such as the performance of housing management systems, street parties, or localised actors such as wardens, but that, at least in part, they fail to address the deeper structural problems facing disadvantaged neighbourhoods.[70] Woolcock argues that micro and

Table 8.4 Domains of social capital and supporting policies

Domain	Description	Local policies
Empowerment	The people feel they have a voice which is listened to; are involved in processes that affect them; can themselves take action to initiate changes	Providing support to community groups; giving local people 'voice'; helping to provide solutions to problems; giving local people a role in policy processes
Participation	That people take part in social and community activities; local events occur and are well attended	Establishing and/or supporting local activities and local organisations; publicising local events
Associational activity and common purpose	That people co-operate with one another through the formation of formal and informal groups to further their interests. Developing and supporting networks between organisations in the area	Developing and supporting networks between organisations in the area
Supporting networks and reciprocity	The individuals and organisations co-operate to support one another for either mutual or one-sided gain; an expectation that help would be given to or received from others when needed	Creating, developing, and/or supporting an ethos of co-operation between individuals and organisations which develop ideas of community support; good neighbour award schemes
Collective norms and values	That people share common values and norms of behaviour	Developing and promulgating an ethos which residents recognise and accept; securing harmonious social relations; promoting community interests
Trust	The people feel they can trust their co-residents and local organisations responsible for governing or servicing their area	Encouraging trust in residents in their relationships with each other; and delivering on policy promises
Safety	That people feel safe in their neighbourhood and are not restricted in their use of public space by fear	Encouraging a sense of safety in residents; involvement in local crime prevention; providing visible evidence of security measures
Belonging	That people feel connected to their co-residents, their home area, have a sense of belonging to the place and its people	Creating, developing and/or supporting a sense of belonging in residents; boosting the identity of a place via design, street furnishings, naming

Source: R. Forrest and A. Kearns, 'Social cohesion, social capital and the neighbourhood', *Urban Studies*, Vol. 38, No. 12(2001, pp. 2125–43), p. 2140

macro forms of social capital are essential, especially if local communities are to influence or work with governments, corporate institutions, and wider civic society.[71] Thus, Amin et al. suggest that we have over-emphasised the importance of place and that the most successful examples of social enterprises are those which connect to external circuits of capital, knowledge, supply, and demand in the formation of a sustainable business model. They made the point that:

> the spatial context matters in how the social economy is locally instantiated rather than as a social context reduced to particular types of place (e.g. low- or high-trust environments, spaces of face-to-face familiarity, powers of community, circuits of local need). Places, in our study, have mattered as social formations with varying geographies of connectivity, not as spatial formations.[72]

Table 8.5 is drawn from their work, which identifies the factors that can create a sustainable social economy premised on strong internal and external networks of social capital.

Amin et al. argue that it is the capacity of the social economy to be different from private or public markets that gives it its reformist potential. The social economy can:

> never become a growth machine or an engine of job generation, or a substitute for the welfare state, but it can stand as a small symbol of another kind of economy, one based on meeting social needs and enhancing social citizenship. For this, the characterisation of the social economy as a 'localised' solution to the problem of social exclusion must be broken.[73]

This requires the sector to be seen as a way of organising alternative economic models and ideas, fostering social solidarity, and developing human capabilities, not as a local substitute for welfare or work. In sum, they identify the influences on effective performance of the social economy in the UK, which include:

- the quality and inspiration of visionary leaders of social entrepreneurs and intermediaries;
- clarity of purpose and an ability to retain focus on a clearly expressed and agreed set of aims and goals;
- systematic and careful market research that explores the sustainability of businesses, products, and services beyond local areas and needs;
- risk intermediation and patient support for emerging enterprises which acknowledges market obstacles and realties as essential qualities often unrecognised in short-term, audit-led, and risk-averse government programmes;

Table 8.5 Elements of a successful local social economy

1. The presence of voiced minority cultures expressing non-mainstreamed needs and values.
2. The presence of a market for welfare intermediaries in between the state and the private sector, such as contracted-out services.
3. An open, willing, and supportive local state such as a local authority.
4. A strong political culture of protest and values.
5. Connectivity with other communities, the local authority, and other areas and linkages to the wider economy and labour markets.
6. The extent of local socio-economic disadvantage as those areas with large-scale structural unemployment, depleted social capital, and limited demographic heterogeneity have restricted resources on which to base a thriving social economy.

Source: Based on A. Amin, A. Cameron and R. Hudson, *Placing the Social Economy* (London: Routledge, 2002)

- the strength of the wider economy and its capacity to generate employment needs, surplus capital, and intellectual or technical resources.

The dark side of social capital

> Those excluded from power, consequently, often do not see their goal as *solidifying* the existing status quo, but *challenging* the very foundations upon which the 'community', including its boundaries, membership and norms, is constituted.[74]

Even the most enthusiastic supporters of social capital as an instrument of social and economic reform acknowledge that it has a dark side.[75] Putnam highlights the intellectual and empirical connection between social capital and the historic debate, in the US at least, with community and communitarianism. Without doubt the existence of community groups which have failed to legitimise their activities among community residents can dilute the rationale and potential for capacity-building. Instead of acting as the 'glue that holds a community together'[76] or as a 'moral resource'[77], such groups can be viewed by residents as self-serving, irrelevant, remote, and hierarchical. In addition, there is no universal law that communities must be guided by natural and shared values or by communal tastes for collective action. In addition, many communities are composed of diverse groups that compete among themselves for both resources and influence. As his own exploration of social capital developed, Putnam revealed a concern for the role that race, religion, and organised ethnic groups played in reproducing segregation in American society, arguing that 'in the short to medium run, immigration and ethnic diversity challenge social solidarity and inhibit social capital'.[78] Constructing durable, bridging social capital networks is, he argues, the great challenge in redrawing the lines of social identity around a respect for diversity.

The social turn in local development policy produced a broad debate on the nature of discursive flows within area-based strategies, the inclusive capacity of new governance forms, and the knowledge infrastructure and competencies of local activists.[79] However, much of this literature treats 'community' uncritically and as a distinctive and, for the most part, unitary concept.[80] Edwards argued that 'more rhetorical fluff attaches to "community" than most other words in the social science lexicon (with the possible exception of "empowerment"). We still seem to have a romantic conception of community; all unitary values and communitarianism'.[81] Capacity-building and the formation of social capital have attracted both theoretical and policy interest, as developing 'the features of social organisation, such as trust, norms and networks that can improve the efficiency of society by facilitating co-ordinated actions'[82] was vital to the efficient and effective delivery of a whole range of programmes. However, for Levitas, this debate has more dangerous overtones:

> My first worry about 'capacity building', as about 'community development', is that it often seems to be a way of expecting groups of people who are poorly resourced to pull themselves up by their collective boot straps. So-called social capital is expected to take the place of economic capital. The imputed absence of social capital is potentially stigmatising and laid at the door of (mainly) poor people themselves. 'Capacity building' may be an alternative to economic regeneration. A large part of the effective resourcing therefore takes the form of unpaid work.[83]

Law and Mooney[84] argued that social capital is about political and social conformism and that New Labour had emphasised the neoliberal attributes of the concept at the expense of social inclusion and alternative economics. In order to avoid this sort of conservatism, they suggest a more politically active 'recalcitrant voluntarism'. This involves resisting capital accumulation projects which dictate and direct social relations, and not seeing social capital in isolation from the political economy (in the way in which they argue that Putnam does). Leonard[85] also made the point that bonding social capital in Belfast enabled the communities to counter discrimination, provide economic and welfare services, and mobilise in the context of violence and conflict. The conditions for bridging social capital, she argues, require excluding some, especially the more vulnerable, from networks designed to build new economic and political relationships outside the neighbourhood. There are also displacement effects with efficient and well-resourced middle-class communities successfully organising to resist unwanted building developments (not in my backyard) that disorganised working class communities would find difficult to counter.[86]

However, Bridgen argues that this merely illustrates the multiple interpretations of social capital and of what it is and how it is said to work. He makes a distinction between Putnam's concern with social capital as a public good and Bourdieu's conceptualisation of social capital as a weapon: a resource to be used by those who possess it to wield power and influence. Bourdieu defines social capital as:

> The aggregate of the actual or potential resources which are linked to the possession of a durable network of more or less institutionalized relationships of mutual acquaintance and recognition – or in other words to membership in a group – which provides each of its members with the backing of the collectively owned capital.[87]

Taylor[88] advocated a more radical agenda to develop social capital and community empowerment less reliant on state resources and patronage. She argued that despite the rhetoric of governance beyond the state, new governance spaces are still inscribed with a state agenda, However, her research shows that there is potential for communities to become 'active subjects' and manipulate prevailing discourses to their own advantage, and to identify the opportunities that new governance spaces have opened up. This necessitates a clearer understanding of the skills and techniques involved in acting politically, which in turn requires a level of community sophistication simply not present in the most disadvantaged neighbourhoods. Additionally, successful community governance requires the building of a movement, on all scales, that will be both political and social. It requires:

- the building of a political alliance, dedicated to the principles and practice of participatory democracy; members of this alliance can work within a number of different political parties but with common objectives with regard to the transformation of UK political institutions and beyond;
- programmes for making UK institutions, both public and private, more democratically controlled and accountable to the people, for example through processes of mutualisation.[89]

Measuring social capital

It is difficult to talk about social capital as a real and meaningful concept, and as something that policies might be designed to create, without considering how it can be measured. However, as Pearce admits, 'the measurement of social capital is not easy. This is because the definition remains rather woolly and because each of the elements is qualitative and open to subjective interpretation.'[90] Nevertheless, attempts have been made to measure levels of social capital using proxy indicators. Pearce cites one occasion, the Conscise

Project, in which this was attempted, and, although it 'was inconclusive due to the small size of the sample and other biases, it did demonstrate that the measurement of social capital may not be impossible'.[91] Illustration 8.2 provides a summary of the Conscise Project and its proxy indicators.

Illustration 8.2 The Conscise Project

The Contribution of Social Capital in the Social Economy to Local Economic Development in Western Europe (Conscise) project's first report looked, among other things, at definitions, measures and indicators of social capital. For this it encapsulated the key parts of definitions of social capital under the six headings of:

Trust.
Reciprocity and mutuality.
Shared norms and behaviour.
Shared commitment and belonging.
Both formal and informal social networks.
Effective information channels.

To try to measure social capital in a local area, the project then used proxy indicators in the form of statements about which local people were asked to indicate the extent of their agreement. For example:
Two statements on trust:

- When everything is taken into account, this locality is a safe place to live.
- If I were looking after a child and in an emergency I needed to go out for a while, I would trust my neighbours to look after the child.

Two statements on reciprocity and mutuality:

- By helping other people you help yourself in the long-run.
- If I see litter in the neighbourhood, I normally pick it up even if I have not dropped it there.

Source: J. Pearce, *Social Enterprise in Anytown* (London: Calouste Gulbenkian Foundation, 2003), p. 76

Putnam's suggested approach to measurement concentrated on measuring community activism, volunteering, and sociability.[92] The measure of trust and engagement in public issues is also identified via a range of attitudinal and numeric counts of a range of activities (see Illustration 8.3).

Illustration 8.3 Measuring engagement and trust

1. Measures of community organisational life:
   - percentage served on committee of some local organisations in last year;
   - percentage served as officer of some club or organisation in last year;
   - civic and social organisations per 1000 population;
   - number of club meetings attended in last year; and
   - mean number of group membership
2. Measures of engagement in public affairs:
   - turnout in presidential elections, 1998 and 1992; and
   - percentage attended public meeting on town or school affairs in last year

3. Measures of community volunteerism:
    *   number of non-profit organisations per 1000 population;
    *   mean number of times worked on community project last year; and
    *   mean number of times did volunteer work last year.
4. Measures of informal sociability:
    *   agree that 'I spend a lot of time visiting friends'; and
    *   mean number of times entertained at home last year.
5. Measures of social trust:
    *   agree that 'Most people can be trusted'; and
    *   agree that 'Most people are honest'.

Source: R. Putnam, *Bowling Alone: The Collapse and Revival of American Community* (New York: Simon & Schuster, 2000), ch. 16

In the UK in 2000–2001, the Office of National Statistics introduced a social capital set of questions into the General Household Survey (GHS) (see Illustration 8.4). This takes the key dimensions of social capital, especially as offered by Putnam, and operationalises them as a series of attitudinal and behavioural questions.

Illustration 8.4 GHS measurement of social capital

Theme	Description
View of local area	This topic looks at the physical environment in which people live, the facilities in their area, and whether they feel safe in the area. People's feelings about their physical environment can relate to each of the other aspects of social capital
Civic engagement	This looks at people's role in their community, and whether they feel they can influence events within the community. Indicators of civic engagement and trust of civil institutions and processes are central to Putnam's understanding of social capital. It is measuring the amount of self-empowerment and control that people think they have and their involvement with the community
Reciprocity and local trust	This section looks at how many local people respondents know and trust, and whether people would do favours for them, or vice versa. Trust of the stranger is a central dimension of Putnam's concept of social capital
Social networks	This section looks at how often respondents see or speak to relatives, friends or neighbours, and how many close friends or relatives live nearby. Social networks are seen as an important aspect of social capital, as the number and types of exchanges amongst people within the network, and shared identities that develop, can influence the amount of support an individual has, as well as giving access to other sources of help
Social support	This section looks at how many people the respondent could turn to if they needed help ranging from practical to financial to emotional support. This section also asks to whom they would turn for help. The degree of individual support a person has can influence health outcomes and health behaviour

Source: Office of National Statistics, *Assessing People's Perceptions of Their Neighbourhood and Community Involvement* (London: ONS, 2002)

Bullen and Onyx used survey-based techniques to audit and plot social capital in localised communities and showed how these can be aggregated across time and different spatial scales.[93] Also working in Australia, Stone[94] offered a different perspective on measurement by concentrating on the range and strength of networks rather than on attitude and behaviour. These include:

- network size and capacity;
- local and global networks;
- open and closed networks;
- dense and sparse networks;
- homogeneous and heterogeneous networks; and
- vertical and horizontal network relations.

Measurement is clearly a problematic area, especially in the way in which social capital is quantified with a battery of statistics and quantitative techniques that give the illusion that it can be determined with precise point measures. This methodological reductionism is especially shaky when it comes to large-scale comparative and international studies, where different social, cultural, and developmental conditions determine the type and depth of social capital.[95] There are also temporal issues, as social capital changes across both space and time slowly and in response to different pressures and opportunities. Disaggregating the deadweight influences on the reproduction of social capital over time becomes particularly challenging in complex economic systems. Linked to this is a scalar argument which assumes that social capital can be aggregated, in measurement terms, from the individual, community, regional, national, and even global levels.

Baron et al. also raised the issue of circularity in that it can be difficult to distinguish between social capital as a characteristic of a flourishing society and the social capital that achieves or helps to achieve growth in the first place. Often, indicator approaches fail to distinguish between the cause and effect dimensions of social capital and, crucially, how it accumulates (or depletes) in measurement terms. Finally, there is the issue of what Baron et al. call normative control, by which they mean the application of norms that produce negative as well as positive forms of social capital. An emphasis on measuring what social capital is *for* needs to acknowledge that it has multiple effects and relationships that have both advantageous and disadvantageous effects.

Also, with regard to the vitamin view of social capital outlined above, it might be relevant to consider whether attempts to measure social capital have actually been measuring the amount of social capital, and if so which forms – or whether they have instead been measuring the media through which it is passed or acquired.

Does the social economy create social capital?

As a final comment on social capital, it is noted that there have been suggestions that the social economy has a particular potential to help disadvantaged communities through the mechanism of social capital. Such claims are, for instance, summarised by Birch and Whittam, who report that:

> The lack of social networks, usually referred to as social capital, has been highlighted within both policy and academia as the main method to empower communities. The social economy is supposed to be a means to encourage the development of social capital by encouraging mutualism amongst communities through grassroots empowerment based on 'active participation' and a 'stakeholder society'. In a

somewhat circular conceptualisation, social entrepreneurship is supposed to provide the means to achieve this mutualism through the social economy. [96]

This claim, in effect, reduces to the two assumptions that for disadvantaged communities the key lack is often social capital and that the social economy creates social capital. From these two assumptions the conclusion is drawn that the social economy will therefore help disadvantaged communities.

However, as the earlier part of this chapter shows, the relationship between social capital and disadvantaged communities depends on just what is meant by social capital, because it is a very diverse concept. There are nevertheless grounds for saying that there is something which is often referred to as social capital which is frequently lacking in disadvantaged communities and which is probably an essential component for improvement. Whether it alone can effect improvement is much less certain, and whether the social economy creates social capital is also debatable. Again, depending on which meaning of social capital is used, it might be argued that all enterprises can create social capital, just as all businesses can create financial capital, but they can also lose it and generally they only create it when the conditions are particularly favourable. Examined in this way, therefore, the 'social economy helps disadvantage' claim does not seem to be particularly strong. Indeed a counter argument is that, just as financial capital is needed to start businesses, so too is social capital needed to start enterprises, including social enterprises, and, as disadvantaged communities often lack social capital, they are not good places in which to start social enterprises. As Amin et al. conclude:

> We find, against the dominant communitarian and Third Way thought (that local community mobilisation for local provision can help resolve local social exclusion), that rarely is the social economy genuinely rooted in the resources of local communities. Indeed, areas of marked social exclusion are precisely those that lack the composite skills and resources necessary to sustain a vibrant social economy, resulting in either highly precarious and short-lived ventures that fail to meet local needs, or ventures reliant on public sector leadership, peripatetic professionals and social entrepreneurs, dedicated organisations such as religious or minority ethnic bodies, or market links that stretch well beyond the modest offerings available locally. [97]

Key Points of Chapter 8

- Social capital is not a new concept, but is a contested one.
- Some writers argue that the current interest in social capital is about governments getting communities to conform and even deliver policy implementation as they withdraw from welfare delivery.
- For others it acts as a resource for communities and interests to resist governments and markets and support their resilience and capacity to adapt to vulnerability.
- Social capital can best be understood as offering the vitamins needed to achieve strong social enterprises, and different components of social capital are thus required to ensure resilient organisations.
- Trust, reciprocity, and norms of civic engagement have been placed at the centre of studies of social capital and claims about its capacity to restore communities, economies, and even society at large.
- The stock of social capital is seen as both cause and effect, especially in developing area regeneration, social enterprise, and entrepreneurship.

- The concept is a difficult one to measure and evaluate and international audits have difficulty comparing the stock of social capital across very different cultural, political, and economic contexts.

///

Case 8.1 | Holywood Old School Preservation Trust

Holywood is a small town close to Belfast and the Old School was built there in about 1845. After being used as a school, it then became the parish offices and was used by the Scouts. However, by the beginning of the twenty-first century, the condition of the building had deteriorated to the extent that it was it was no longer used by anyone and it seemed to be under threat of demolition.

The Holywood Old School Preservation Trust was formed to try to restore it. A feasibility study indicated that the building could be restored and that a sustainable use might then be found for it. It then took the Trust about two years to raise the money needed, but then the building was successfully restored and now operates as a sustainable social enterprise providing premises for community activities.

To achieve this, the Trust researched its potential market and developed a plan; selected, interviewed, and appointed competent conservation architects as its professional advisers; and identified potential sources of grants and made successful applications to several of them. It also generated a lot of local support including financial contributions. What had helped it to do this?

Amongst the trustees was a business consultant who had worked with small businesses and administered funding schemes. He was used to handling funding applications and understood what funders were looking for and how the applications were likely to be assessed. He had also been able to use a connection with the local council to get help with the selection of the Trust's professional advisers.

Another trustee had originally trained as a solicitor. She had also become interested in conservation and served on the committee of the local architectural heritage society. Through this she had met others engaged in conservation including members of other building preservation trusts, conservation architects, and representatives of conservation funding bodies. She was therefore able to get advice about forming a trust and about different aspects of a building's restoration. She also knew whom to ask to produce a suitable list of conservation architects to tender to be the trust's professional advisers.

The other trustees included a retired insolvency lawyer, an insurance manager, a carpet supplier, and someone who had for many years been organising fund-raising events, each of whom brought their own experience and/or contacts to the task. Between them the trustees had:

- Some experience of directing and advising social enterprises.
- An insight into how to write funding applications.
- An understanding of the need for careful financial control.
- Introductions to the good conservation architects in the area.
- A good contact with another nearby building preservation trust which was happy to talk about what was involved and to explain what had worked, or not worked.
- Contacts with like-minded people and bodies who could and did offer advice and encouragement.

- A network which included several people on the boards or committees of funding organisations or were their advisers. These people were often happy to explain the funders' requirements to the Trust and/or were in a position to vouch for it.
- Experience of what was involved in running fund-raising events and credibility in asking others to support them.

A study of the process of forming and operating the Trust suggested that it included many examples of the application of social network resources, including the following:

- *Contact within the local community*. Within the local community there was a regard for the building and a clear appreciation of the need to do something to preserve it. This was also manifest in contacts with like-minded people willing to be involved by becoming trustees, support from local schools and a local printer, and a good response to local fund-raising efforts.
- *Contact outside the local community*. Relevant contacts outside the local community included a neighbouring building preservation trust which provided the trustees with an understanding of what such a venture might involve, contacts in the grant funding system, and people who could suggest which conservation architects might be invited to bid to be the Trust's professional advisers and advise on how to manage that tendering process.
- *Obtaining relevant information*. Contacts who provided the trustees with key relevant information including how much grant they might realistically ask for from a key funder, how to recruit a caretaker, and how to recruit professional advisers for the first stage of the process without precluding them from obtaining grants for their professional advice in the second stage.
- *Trust and vouching*. The Trust was able to obtain an overdraft facility from a local bank branch without the need for personal guarantees. It is understood that the reputation of several of the trustees, established through personal banking at that branch, helped the branch to vouch for their bona fides and credibility as trustees.
- *Encouragement of specific behaviours*. Local approval was expressed in a number of ways for the formation of the Building Preservation Trust and for its attempts to save the building. This helped to reinforce the commitment of the trustees to their task.

Those examples of interactions were all beneficial to the venture and did seem to be examples of social capital. However, at least four of them appeared to represent specific applications of social capital which were not transferable or substitutable for each other. For instance:

- Contacts within and contacts outside the local community were both valuable, but a shortage of one could not have been addressed by more of the other.
- Contacts who were able to provide specific information were very helpful, and this could not have been found from general contacts whether within or outside the community.
- The credibility established by the trustees with the bank was dependent on their specific dealings with the bank. If they had not built up this reputation, it could not have been provided in other ways.

Thus, the case study suggests that the Holywood Old School Preservation Trust benefitted from a number of specific, non-substitutable aspects of social capital and that, if any of these had been missing, a general provision of more social capital of another sort may not necessarily have helped.

Source: Based in part on S. Bridge and K. O'Neill, *Understanding Enterprise, Entrepreneurship and Small Business* (Basingstoke: Palgrave Macmillan, 2013), pp. 278–9

Questions, Exercises, Essay, and Discussion Topics

1. In Case 8.1, try to produce an inventory of the social capital of the Trust. How does this inventory compare with the various definitions of social capital given above?
2. Trace the origins and development of social capital.
3. Why has social capital become an important political and policy concern across the globe?
4. What are the different interpretations of social capital and its role in local development?
5. Describe some of the methods used for measuring social capital, and state what are their limits in auditing the stock of social capital across time and place?
6. What is the link between social capital and the development of the social economy?

Suggestions for further reading

J. Field, *Social Capital: Key Ideas* (London: Routledge, 2008).
D. Halpern, *Social Capital* (Cambridge: Polity Press, 2005).
R. Putnam, *Bowling Alone: The Collapse and Revival of American Community* (New York: Simon & Schuster, 2000).

References

1. S. Szreter, 'Social capital, the Economy and Education in historical perspective', in S. Baron, J. Field and T. Schuller (Eds), *Social Capital: Critical Perspectives* (Oxford: Oxford University Press, 2000), pp. 56–77.
2. M. Cattel, 'Having a Laugh and Mucking in together; using social capital to explore dynamics between structure and agency in the context of declining and regenerated neighbourhoods', *Sociology,* Vol. 38, No. 5 (2004), pp. 945–63.
3. A. Portes, 'Social capital: Its origins and applications in modern sociology', *Annual Review of Sociology,* Vol. 124 (1998), pp. 1–24.
4. J. Field, *Social Capital: Key Ideas* (London: Routledge, 2008).
5. R. Forrest and A. Kearns, 'Social cohesion, social capital and the neighbourhood', *Urban Studies,* Vol. 38, No. 12 (2001), pp. 2125–43.
6. S. L. Hofferth and J. Iceland, 'Social Capital in Rural and Urban Communities', *Rural Sociology,* Vol.63 No.4, 1998, p. 574–598.
7. S. Baron, J. Field and T. Schuller (Eds), *Social Capital: Critical Perspectives* (Oxford: Oxford University Press, 2000).
8. F. Fukuyama, *The End of History and the Last Man* (New York: Free Press, 1992).
9. W. Hutton, *The Stakeholding Society* (Cambridge: Polity Press, 1999).
10. A. Giddens, *The Third Way: the Renewal of Social Democracy* (Cambridge: Polity Press, 1998), p. 78.
11. Ibid., p. 127.
12. New economics foundation (nef), *Cutting It: The Big Society and the New Austerity* (London: nef, 2010).
13. D. Halpern, *Social Capital* (Cambridge: Polity Press, 2005).

14. C. Calhoun, E. LiPuma and I. Postone, *Bourdieu: Critical Perspectives* (Cambridge: Polity Press, 1993), p. 4.

15. P. Bourdieu and L. Wacquant, *An Invitation to Reflexive Sociology* (Cambridge: Polity Press, 1996), p. 119.

16. F. Sabitini, *Social Capital, Public Spending and the Quality of Economic Development: The Case of Italy* (Milan: Fondazione Eni Enrico Mattei, 2006).

17. J. C. Coleman, *Foundations of Social Theory* (Cambridge, MA: Harvard University Press, 1994).

18. A. Portes, 'Social capital: Its origins and applications in modern sociology', *Annual Review of Sociology*, Vol. 124 (1998), pp. 1–24.

19. R. Putnam, 'E Pluribus Unum: diversity and community in the twenty-first century', The 2006 Johan Skytte Prize Lecture, *Scandinavian Political Studies*, Vol. 30, No. 2 (2007), pp. 137–74.

20. R. Putnam, 'Who killed civic America?', *Prospect*, March (1996, pp. 66–72), p. 66.

21. M. Leonard, 'Bonding and bridging social capital: Reflections from Belfast', *Sociology*, Vol. 38, No. 5 (2004), pp. 927–44.

22. A. Law and G. Mooney, 'The maladies of social capital I: The missing "capital" in theories of social capital', *Critique*, Vol. 34, No. 2 (2006), pp. 127–43.

23. A. Kay, 'Social capital in building the social economy', in J. Pearce, *Social Enterprises in Anytown* (London: Calouste Gulbenkian Foundation, 2003), p. 75.

24. Performance and Innovation Unit, *Social Capital A Discussion Paper* (London: Cabinet Office, 2002).

25. R. Putnam, 'Turning in, turning out: the strange disappearance of social capital in America', *Political Science and Politics*, Vol. 28 (1995), pp. 1–20.

26. A. Middleton, A. Murie and R. Groves, 'Social capital and neighbourhoods that work', *Urban Studies*, Vol. 42, No. 10 (2005), pp. 1711–38.

27. World Bank, http://www.worldbank.org/poverty/scapita, accessed May 2013; Department for International Development (DFID), *Sustainable Development Guidance Sheets* (London: DFID, 1999).

28. OECD, *The Well-Being of Nations: The Role of Human and Social Capital* (Paris: OECD, 2001).

29. Based on Performance and Innovation Unit, *Social Capital A Discussion Paper* (London: Cabinet Office, 2002), p. 10.

30. A. Dasgupta, 'A matter of trust: Social Capital and economic development', in J. Yifu Lin and B. Pleskovic (Eds), *Social Capital* (Washington, DC: World Bank, 2011), pp. 119–56.

31. Department for International Development (DFID), *Sustainable Development Guidance Sheets* (London: DFID, 1999), p. 1.

32. J. Rowson and I. McGilchrist, *Divided Brain, Divided World* (London: RSA, 2013), p. 3.

33. Ibid.

34. R. Putnam, *Bowling Alone: The Collapse and Revival of American Community* (New York: Simon & Schuster, 2000), p. 19.

35. T. Schuller, S. Baron and J. Field, 'Social Capital: A Review and Critique', in S. Baron, J. Field and T. Schuller (Eds), *Social Capital: Critical Perspectives* (Oxford: Oxford University Press, 2000), pp. 24, 35.

36. J. Coaffee, M. Ward and P. Rogers, *The Everyday Resilience of the City: How Cities Respond to Terrorism and Disaster* (Basingstoke: Palgrave Macmillan, 2009).

37. M. Pelling and K. Dill, 'Disaster politics: tipping points for change in the adaptation of socio-political regimes', *Progress in Human Geography*, Vol. 34, No. 1 (2010), pp. 21–37.

38. C. Folke, 'Resilience: The emergence of a perspective for social-ecological systems analyses', *Global Environmental Change*, Vol. 16, No. 3 (2006), pp. 253–67.

39. M. Evans and B. Syrett, *Informal Economic Activities and Deprived Neighbourhoods* (London: Department for Communities and Local Government, 2006).

40. Performance and Innovation Unit, *Social Capital: A Discussion Paper* (London: Cabinet Office, 2002), p. 5.

41. Ibid., p. 5.

42. F. Fukuyama, *The End of History and the Last Man* (New York: Free Press, 1992).

43. M. Aiken, B. Cairns, M. Taylor and R. Moran, *Community Organisations Controlling Assets: A Better Understanding* (York: Joseph Rowntree Foundation, 2011).

44. New Economics Foundation (nef), *Plugging the Leaks: Making the Most of Every Pound That Enters Your Local Economy* (London: nef, 2002).

45. A. Kay, 'Social capital in building the social economy', in J. Pearce, *Social Enterprises in Anytown* (London: Calouste Gulbenkian Foundation, 2003), p. 78.

46. R. Putnam, *Making Democracy Work: Civic Traditions in Modern Italy* (Princeton: Princeton University Press, 1993), p. 167.

47. F. Fukuyama, *Trust: The Social Virtues and the Creation of Prosperity* (London: Hamish Hamilton, 1995).

48. Community Evaluation Northern Ireland (CENI), *Toolkit to Measure the Value Added of Voluntary and Community Based Activity* (Belfast: CENI, 2005).

49. R. Putnam, *Making Democracy Work: Civic Traditions in Modern Italy* (Princeton: Princeton University Press, 1993), p. 175.

50. R. Putnam, *Bowling Alone: The Collapse and Revival of American Community* (New York: Simon & Schuster, 2000), p. 23.

51. D. Halpern, *Social Capital* (Cambridge: Polity Press, 2005), p. 35.

52. S. Bridge, *Rethinking Enterprise Policy* (Basingstoke: Palgrave Macmillan, 2010), p. 187.

53. J. Cope, S. Jack and M. Rose, 'Social capital and entrepreneurship: An introduction', *International Small Business Journal,* Vol. 25, No. 3 (2007), pp. 213–9.

54. A. Anderson, J. Park and S. Jack, 'Entrepreneurial social capital', *International Small Business Journal,* Vol. 25, No. 3 (2007), pp. 245–72.

55. See for instance H-H. Hohmann and F. Welter (Eds), *Trust and Entrepreneurship: A West–East Perspective* (Cheltenham: Edward Elgar, 2005).

56. C. Chambers and F. Edwards-Stuart, *Leadership in the Social Economy* (London: School for Social Entrepreneurs, 2007).

57. M. Evans and S. Syrett, 'Generating social capital? The social economy and local economy development', *European Urban and Regional Studies,* Vol. 14, No. 1 (2007), p. 71.

58. H. Chell, 'Social Enterprise and entrepreneurship: Towards a convergent theory of the entrepreneurial process', *International Small Business Journal,* Vol. 25, No. 1 (2007), pp. 5–26.

59. H. Johnstone and D. Lionais, 'Depleted communities and community business entrepreneurship: revaluing space through place', *Entrepreneurship and Regional Development* (2004), pp. 217–233.

60. K. Birch and G. Whittam, 'Social entrepreneurship: The way to sustainable regional development', Paper read at the Institute for Small Business and Entrepreneurship, 31 October–2 November (Cardiff: ISBE, 2006).

61. J. Dees, 'The meaning of social entrepreneurship' (2001), CASE, Duke University, Durham, NC, , http://www.fugua.duke.edu/centers/case/doicuments/dees_SE.pdf, accessed May 2013, quoted in Birch and Whittam (2006), p. 4.

62. Birch and Whittam (2006), p. 7.

63. C. Howarth, 'Resisting the Identity of Social Entrepreneur', Paper read at the Institute for Small Business and Entrepreneurship, 31 October–2 November (Cardiff: ISBE, 2006).

64. N. Miles and J. Tully, 'Regional development agency policy to tackle economic exclusion? The role of social capital in distressed communities', *Regional Studies,* Vol. 41, No. 6 (2007, pp. 855–66), p. 857.

65. Ibid., p. 863.

66. R. Forrest and A. Kearns, 'Social cohesion, social capital and the neighbourhood', *Urban Studies,* Vol. 38, No. 12 (2001), pp. 2125–43.

67. J-M. Callois and F. Aubert, 'Towards indicators of social capital for regional development issues: The case of French rural areas', *Regional Studies,* Vol. 41, No. 6 (2007), pp. 809–21.

68. F. Moulaert and J. Nussbaumer, 'Defining the social economy and its governance at the neighbourhood level: A methodological reflection', *Urban Studies,* Vol. 42, No. 11 (2005), pp. 2071–88.

69. R. Kleinhans, H. Priemus and G. Engbersen, 'Understanding Social Capital in Recently Restructured Urban Neighbourhoods: Two Case Studies in Rotterdam', *Urban Studies,* Vol. 44, Nos 5/6 (2007), pp. 1069–91.

70. A. Crawford, ' "Fixing Broken Promises?": Neighbourhood Wardens and Social Capital', *Urban Studies,* Vol. 43, Nos 5/6 (2006), pp. 957–76.

71. M. Woolcock, 'Social capital and economic development: Toward a theoretical synthesis and policy framework', *Theory and Society,* Vol. 27, No. 2 (1998), pp. 151–208.

72. A. Amin, A. Cameron and R. Hudson, *Placing the Social Economy* (London: Routledge, 2002), p. 120.

73. Ibid., p. 125.

74. W. Potapchuk, J. Crocker and W. Schechtler, 'Building community with social capital', *National Civic Review,* Vol. 86, No. 2 (1997), pp. 129–139.

75. R. Putnam, *Bowling Alone: The Collapse and Revival of American Community* (New York: Simon & Schuster, 2000), p. 350.

76. W. Potapchuk, J. Crocker and W. Schechtler, 'Building community with social capital', *National Civic Review,* Vol. 86, No. 2 (1997), pp. 129–39.

77. R. Putnam, *Making Democracy Work: Civic Traditions in Modern Italy* (Princeton: Princeton University Press, 1993), p. 130.

78. R. Putnam, 'E Pluribus Unum: Diversity and Community in the Twenty-first Century', The 2006 Johan Skytte Prize Lecture, *Scandinavian Political Studies,* Vol. 30, No. 2 (2007, pp. 137–74), p. 138; R. Putnam, *Making Democracy Work: Civic Traditions in Modern Italy* (Princeton: Princeton University Press, 1993), p. 167.

79. N. Ginsburg, 'Putting the social into urban regeneration policy', *Local Economy,* Vol. 13, No. 5 (1999), pp. 55–71.

80. P. Burton, 'Power to the People: How to judge public participation', *Local Economy,* Vol. 19, No. 3 (2004), pp. 193–198.

81. J. Edwards, 'Urban policy: the victory of form over substance', *Urban Studies,* Vol. 34, Nos 5–6 (1997, pp. 825–43), p. 831.

82. R. Putnam, *Making Democracy Work: Civic Traditions in Modern Italy* (Princeton: Princeton University Press, 1993), p. 167.

83. R. Levitas, 'Community, utopia and New Labour', *Local Economy,* Vol. 15, No. 3 (2000, pp. 188–97), p. 196.

84. A. Law and G. Mooney, 'The maladies of social capital II: resisting neo-liberal conformism', *Critique,* Vol. 34, No. 3 (2006), pp. 253–68.

85. M. Leonard, 'Bonding and bridging social capital: Reflections from Belfast', *Sociology,* Vol. 38, No. 5 (2004), pp. 927–44.

86. M. Mayer, 'The onward sweep of social capital: causes and consequences for understanding cities, communities and urban movements', *International Journal of Urban and Regional Research,* Vol. 27, No. 1 (2003), pp. 110–32.

87. P. Bourdieu, 'Forms of capital', in J. Richardson (Ed.), *Handbook of Theory and Research for the Sociology of Education* (New York: Macmillan, 1986), pp. 248–9.

88. M. Taylor, 'Community Participation in the real world: opportunities and pitfalls in new governance spaces', *Urban Studies,* Vol. 44, No. 2 (2007), pp. 297–317.

89. P. Sommerville, 'Community governance and democracy', *Policy and Politics,* Vol. 33, No. 1 (2006, pp. 117–44), pp. 136–7.

90. J. Pearce, *Social Enterprise in Anytown* (London: Calouste Gulbenkian Foundation, 2003), p. 75.

91. Ibid., p. 76.

92. R. Putnam, *Bowling Alone: The Collapse and Revival of American Community* (New York: Simon & Schuster, 2000), Ch. 16.

93. J. Onyx and P. Bullen, *Measuring Social Capital in Five Communities in New South Wales: An Analysis,* Working Paper No. 41 (Sydney: Centre for Australian Community Organisations and Management, University of Technology, Sydney, 1997).

94. W. Stone, *Measuring Social Capital* (Melbourne: Australian Institute of Family Studies, 2001).

95. S. Baron, J. Field and T. Schuller (Eds), *Social Capital: Critical Perspectives* (Oxford: Oxford University Press, 2000), p. 27.

96. K. Birch and G. Whittam, 'Social Entrepreneurship: the Way to Sustainable Regional Development?', *ISBE Conference,* November 2006, p. 5.

97. A. Amin, A. Cameron and R. Hudson, *Placing the Social Economy* (London: Routledge, 2002), pp. vii, ix.

9

advancing the social economy

contents:

- introduction
- why the social economy is promoted
- who is promoting the social economy
- how the social economy is promoted – the components of policy
- where the social economy is promoted – comparing the delivery of policy
- conclusion

Key concepts

This chapter covers:

- the reasons why the social economy is promoted;
- the various parties promoting the social economy, including governments;
- the range of strategies followed by governments to promote the sector, and the various components of those strategies.

Learning objectives

By the end of this chapter the reader should:

- appreciate why the social economy is being promoted;
- understand who is promoting it;
- appreciate the range of promotional strategies and the different components in their evolution.

Introduction

Governments and other stakeholders are often interested in the third sector, because they think that it has the potential to help them to achieve some of their objectives. Therefore, they are prepared to intervene to promote the sector and to encourage and support its establishment and development. This chapter explores the main issues associated with this promotion. In particular, it looks at why the sector is promoted, who is promoting it, how and where it is being promoted, and what the results of this promotion appear to be.

The declared focus of promotional efforts may be the third sector or the social economy or some of the social enterprises of which it is composed. As indicated in Chapter 4, definitions of these terms vary. In the absence of a single common terminology, that of the country whose policy is being considered is used.

Why the social economy is promoted

It is suggested in Chapter 1 that among the reasons why interest in the social economy has grown is the apparent potential of this sector of the economy to address some of the problems in, or of, society. Chapter 3, for instance, among other things, indicates why the social economy and social enterprises are sometimes seen as having a key role to play in regeneration and social cohesion strategies. The sector is seen therefore as having the ability to provide a variety of benefits in a number of areas including the following (see also an expanded list in Chapter 10):

- the provision of goods, services, and social benefits which the public sector does not adequately provide and a means for addressing some problems of the welfare state;
- the provision of jobs for people who might not otherwise be employed;
- the fostering of enterprise and economic competitiveness;
- the promotion of environmental sustainability, or ethical operations;
- the creation of social capital and social cohesion. This is sometimes seen as giving it the ability to reach parts that other initiatives cannot reach, in particular when trying to tackle disadvantage through urban and rural regeneration projects (see also the comments on social capital in Chapter 8).

Government interest

Many of these areas are of interest to governments. As a result, many governments have shown an interest in promoting the sector. As the section 'Paradigm differences' in Chapter 3 indicates, a country's perception of what particular benefits it would like to get from the sector often influences which bits of the sector it wishes to support and how it attempts to define them. A review, commissioned by the UK's Social Enterprise Unit (SEnU), reported in March 2006 on the social economy policy objectives of a number of European countries and the US.[1] It not only confirmed similarities but also noted some differences, not least in respect of the UK policy. The review recognised that, while in Europe social enterprises and the wider social economy have multiple objectives, it is possible to identify a tradition and a prevailing interest in the use of social enterprise as a means of

- integrating disadvantaged members of the community into employment (e.g. the long-term unemployed and the disabled);
- augmenting the delivery of public services, especially in the areas of health and social care.[2]

The contribution of social enterprise to social inclusion and cohesion (at the level of individual and local areas) is shared as a common policy interest across a number of countries including the US (and arguably more in other countries than in the UK), the report asserts. Also, the role of social enterprises in delivering public services is also well established in the countries reviewed and 'has attained a renewed vigour and purpose under UK policy'.[3]

The UK differs in at least one significant way from other countries in the emphasis it often puts on the potential of social enterprises to contribute to economic competitiveness and development, both regionally or nationally. This is re-enforced by an expectation that they should be financially self-sustainable, generally through some form of trading activity. This aspect seems to be less of a concern in other countries, where the sector's contribution is often seen as a response to market failure, and, with that, there is a greater willingness to recognise the additional costs associated with addressing such market failures. Therefore, it appears that financial sustainability is not, for them, a main aim. Moreover, other countries often retain a broader perspective on the social economy in terms of focus and approach, placing emphasis on a wider range of characteristics of the sector such as democratic control, citizen initiative, and user participation.

The development of government policy for the sector

While many governments want to encourage the social economy, support for it is still a developing policy field. Thus, according to Graefe, 'it is difficult to foresee what directions policy will end up taking, what its results will be, and who will stand to benefit most'. This, he suggests, will 'depend crucially on the relative ability of the interested actors to embed their vision for the social economy in state policy', and, in this, there are two conflicting visions:

> On the one hand, there is the project borne by the social economy's champions, seeking to re-embed footloose capital, to spark local economic and social regeneration, and to counter social exclusion. On the other hand, there are those backing stage accumulation strategies of a more neoliberal bent who seek to employ the sector as a cut rate welfare state and a basin of low wage jobs.[4]

Because of these conflicting visions, interpretations of the focus of, and approaches to, policy and its consequences can differ. It is also apparent that there is no single good or bad, or right or wrong, policy framework; the different organisational models and their varying dominance in the sector, which are apparent in different countries, offer routes for the achievement of different policy goals.

It is also worth noting at this stage that any meaningful policy framework, whether on a supra-national, national, or local level, requires clarity in terms of objectives and targets. This is true in the field of public policy in general and in policies to assist social enterprises in particular. Thus, policy-makers should, as far as possible, be explicit about the contribution which they seek from their social enterprises. They should clearly articulate in what ways (and to what extent) they think that social enterprise can contribute and to which policy goals.

However, therein lies a problem: often the objectives are either not explicit or not quantified, which makes it difficult not only to implement but also to understand and evaluate strategies (see Chapter 10). Moreover, within the social economy itself, measurement of its impact is at a very early stage of development. In the UK, the (then) DTI, for instance, has contended that while it was building 'intellectual capital about the sector, . . . rhetoric rather than a robust evidence base continues to inform most arguments for growth and support'.[5] Nevertheless, this chapter and the next seek to provide an overview of what is generally known about these issues.

Other interests

Other organisations, as well as governments, are also interested in promoting part or all of the social economy. Some of these are organisations formed specifically to assist the sector and to promote its interests, and examples of them are given in Table 9.1. Some are

Table 9.1 Examples of the different types of national or regional social enterprise support agencies in the UK

Type	Example
Social enterprises	Social Enterprise UK
	Social Enterprise Scotland
	Social Enterprise NI
	Welsh Social Enterprise Coalition
	Community Action Network
	The Community Development Finance Association
Community businesses	Community Business Scotland Network/CBSN
	Co-operative Futures
Business/worker co-operatives	Co-operatives UK
Housing co-operatives	Confederation of Cooperative Housing UK
Employee-owned enterprises	Employee Ownership Association
	Employee Share Ownership Centre
Development trusts	Locality (which is a merger of the British Association of Settlements and Social Action Centres and the Development Trusts Association)
Social firms	Social Firms UK
Credit unions	Association of British Credit Unions

Source: Based on D. Smallbone et al., *Researching Social Enterprise*, SBS Research Report RR004/01 (July 2001), p. 23

organisations whose interest in promoting the sector appears to lie in its potential to provide a counter to the supposed power and influence of either the private or the public sectors. Such politically linked agenda are related, for instance, to the different paradigms of the social economy already noted above, and a range of their interests is discussed below.

Who is promoting the social economy

The social economy and its sub-sectors are being promoted by various people and organisations. Indeed, social enterprise has become a truly global phenomenon in recent years. It has ceased to be on the margins of debate about economic and social development policies. Over the past 15 years, it has moved now to occupy an increasingly important position in discussions on such policies and on state reform. This is a trend which can be observed in 'the northern and southern hemispheres and from East to West.[6]

Governments

The social economy is promoted by government bodies at international, national, regional, and local levels. For instance,

- At an international level, the European Commission has stated that it wishes to 'promote social enterprises across Europe',[7] and the most recent example of its actions is its Social Business Initiative which 'provides a short-term action plan to stimulate the creation, development and growth of social businesses'.[8] The Commission further states that its

  > objective is to create an ecosystem conducive to developing social businesses and to facilitating their access to funding. The initiative also builds on the *Communication on the Innovation Union*, the *Platform against Poverty and Social Exclusion* and on the recent Commission proposal for establishing a *Programme on Social Change and Innovation*.[9]

- At a national level, the UK government's Coalition Agreement sought to 'support the creation and expansion of mutuals, co-operatives, charities and social enterprises',[10] while the predecessor government asserted that 'Departments across government are developing and deepening their relationships with and understanding of social enterprise'.[11]
- In Scotland, the *Enterprising Third Sector Action Plan 2008–2011*[12] explains how the Scottish government intends to create the right environment in which an enterprising third sector can fulfil its role in the development, design, and delivery of policy and services in Scotland.
- In Wales, its *Social Enterprise Action Plan*, launched in early 2009, sets out 'how we will provide an environment in which social enterprises can continue to grow and assist in delivering *One Wales* commitments'.[13]
- At a regional level, in Northern Ireland, the Department of Enterprise, Trade and Investment established a social economy branch and led the preparation and publication in 2004 of a cross-departmental strategy – *Developing a Successful Social Economy* – and followed up with a *Social Economy Enterprise Strategy 2010–2011*, which was 'in recognition of the potential of the social economy to make a significant contribution to both social and economic regeneration'[14] and 'to ensure that social economy enterprise is valued, encouraged and supported'.[15]

- At a local level, in the late 1970s, the Community Business scheme began in Paisley. It then extended to other parts of Glasgow and became, in the 1980s, the largest social enterprise development programme in the UK.[16]

Umbrella bodies

There are many organisations and groups which champion the sector and lobby for it, seeking to give it visibility and voice. Research undertaken for the Home Office revealed that there were at least 256 umbrella bodies in the UK representing the sector at a national level,[17] and in April 2007 the UK Cabinet Office set aside £2.4 million for 3 years 'as additional support to the social enterprise sector to raise its own profile and influence public debate'.[18] Some of the different types of these bodies are illustrated in Table 9.1 and include the following:

- Social Enterprise UK – formerly the Social Enterprise Coalition (SEC), – was formed with UK government support in 2002 'to address the lack of a coherent, representative voice for social enterprises', bringing together 'the range of existing umbrella bodies operating in the sector'.[19] The SEC, describing itself as 'the UK's national body for social enterprise', purported to lead 'a combined membership of over 10,000 organizations'.[20] And now, as SE (UK), it reports as having 'a network of almost 9,000 organisations'.[21]
- Social Enterprise NI (the recently-created successor to the Social Economy Network) in Northern Ireland is a membership-based, government-funded organisation comprised of social economy enterprises and networks. It has a mission to build an active social economy which aims for excellence in meeting community needs. Its responsibilities include being a voice for its members on relevant issues, a signposter to best practice, and a source of help and advice as well as to stimulate government action in support of the sector, influencing its policies and programmes.
- The Community Development Finance Association (CDFA) is the umbrella body or trade association for Community Development Finance Institutions (CDFIs). These are specialist financing bodies for social enterprises (and SMEs). (See Chapter 7.)
- The National Council for Voluntary Organisations (NCVO), which has recently merged with Volunteering England, the Association of Chief Executives of Voluntary Organisations (ACEVO), the Association of Chief Officers of Scottish Voluntary Organisations (ACOSVO), the Institute of Fundraising, and the Charity Finance Group are also sector representative bodies that lobby, share best practices, and measure performance on behalf of their members. They cover bodies across the social economy spectrum.
- The National Association for Voluntary and Community Action (NAVCA) is the umbrella body for Councils for Voluntary Action throughout England, which are themselves umbrella bodies for more than 160,000 local community and voluntary groups. NAVCA was originally a project of the NCVO (National Council for Voluntary Organisations) but became independent in 1991. Until 2006, NAVCA was called NACVS (the National Association of Councils for Voluntary Service). It describes itself as a bridge between local groups and the national government. The organisation provides its members with information, advice, support, and development services and in turn seeks to influence government policy.

Other organisations

There are a range of other organisations which for a variety of reasons promote the third sector or its components, often because they are social economy organisations themselves operating within the sector and/or generating income from it. Examples include the following:

- The new economics foundation (nef), founded in 1986, is an example of an independent 'think and do tank'[22] organisation that describes itself as wishing to 'promote innovative solutions that challenge mainstream thinking on economic environment and social issues'.[23] Thus, it promotes the third sector, inter alia, as a means of finding innovative solutions.
- The Charity Bank ('Banking for the Common Good'), launched in October 2002, is the first-ever charity to be granted a banking licence and the world's first not-for-profit bank. It aims to increase the capacity of the charitable/non-profit sector by remedying the gap in their financial services not filled by the traditional banking sector. Its goal is to move the sector away from grant dependency to self-sustainability with a pool of capital which could be ever recycled into the sector and to make a cultural shift within the sector.
- Social Firms UK aims 'to create employment opportunities for disadvantaged people through the development and support of Social Firms. Social firms are market-led businesses that are set up specifically to create good quality jobs for people severely disadvantaged in the labour market.'[24] Social Firms UK recognises that many organisations lack the resources to identify viable business opportunities or to turn an idea into a business. 'Flagship Firms' is the name of its programme of franchising, licensing, and replication which offers business opportunities, perceived as having the potential for successful ventures by social firms, to those seeking new businesses.
- UnLtd, the Foundation for Social Entrepreneurs, is a charitable organisation set up in 2000 to promote social entrepreneurship. In 2002, it was granted a £100 million legacy by the Millennium Commission, which it has invested to fund its Millennium Awards scheme in perpetuity. UnLtd gives awards to young people to set up community projects and offers practical as well as financial support.
- The School for Social Entrepreneurs (SSE) was established to develop the competences of aspiring social entrepreneurs utilising the principles of 'action learning'. It offers a training and mentoring service with the aim of accelerating the numbers, growth, and quality of social enterprises.

The sector itself

In addition to the advocacy generated by the sort of organisations listed above can be added the exhortations of others in the sector itself. Indeed, some have argued that, due to the voluntary sector's 'babble of tongues',[25] there are 'too many overlapping voices struggling to be heard'[26] and 'charities' regional voice is fragmented',[27] so that, overall, there has been the absence of a consistent message and of effective leadership.

How the social economy is promoted – the components of policy

The reasons why governments consider intervention to support the social economy and/or social enterprises to be appropriate have been discussed. This section looks at some ways in which this intervention is conducted, and the following section looks at how policies are applied in different countries.

Anyone trying to understand the different components of policy and its application might be confused by the different steps in the process and the variety of items or components that are presented for each step. Figure 9.1, with examples from UK policy,

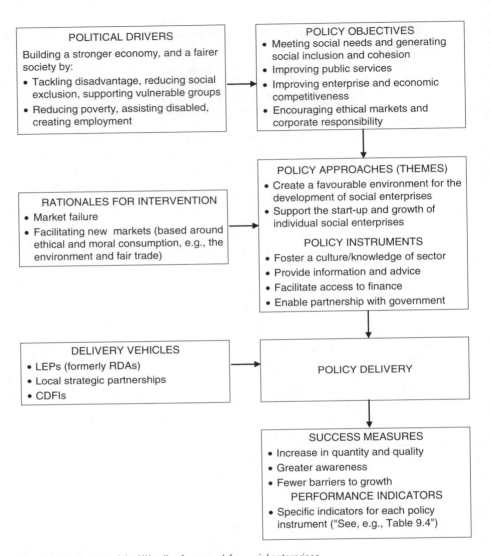

Figure 9.1 A diagram of the UK policy framework for social enterprises

has therefore been prepared as a model of an overall framework for this process. Brief explanations of the components then follow.

Political drivers

The political drivers can be interpreted as the core political reason for having a particular policy, albeit sometimes this is rarely highlighted. In the case of the UK government's published social enterprise policy, the following statements can be found:

- 'The Government's vision is of dynamic and sustainable social enterprise sustaining an inclusive and growing economy.'[28]

- The vision is 'dynamic and sustainable social enterprises, contributing to a stronger economy and a fairer society'. [29]
- 'The Government recognises that social enterprises contribute to its vision "of a fairer, more just society..."'. [30]
- 'The Government believes that the innovation and enthusiasm of civil society is essential in tackling the social, economic and political challenges that the UK faces today.' [31]

Policy objectives

The policy objectives are the overall aim of the policy in question and they can be stated qualitatively, quantitatively, or in both ways. Sometimes, however, the overall aim is described as a vision or mission statement while the term objectives is confined to quantified targets that enable one to determine when the mission has been accomplished. In the case of UK policy, the following are presented:

- *Social cohesion.* Social enterprise is perceived as adding to the contribution of the community and voluntary sector in the regeneration of disadvantaged communities: 'empowering individuals and communities, encouraging the development of work habits and increasing employment diversity'. [32]
- *Public service delivery.* Social enterprise activity is seen as being a means to improve the quality and efficiency of public service delivery.
- *Economic competitiveness.* A role is seen for social enterprise in its efforts to support enterprise (including the number of people going into business), especially in disadvantaged areas, and sustainable improvements in the economic performance of UK regions.
- *Ethics and responsibilities.* Social enterprise is seen as setting an example in encouraging an ethical approach to business and to corporate responsibility.

Rationales for policy intervention

Although a government may identify certain objectives, government intervention to achieve them may be counterproductive unless there is a good justification for it. The justification frequently used (whether adequately assessed or otherwise) is that of 'market failure'. The implication is that a gap needs to be filled because of the lack of private provision and inadequate public service delivery (and that, *inter alia*, the benefits of intervention exceed the costs of so doing).

There appear to be two factors that provide the rationale for intervention in support of social enterprises in the UK:

- *Market failure.* The social economy is seen as capable of making available products and services that would not otherwise be available in particular places or for particular people. 'Social enterprises create new goods and services and develop opportunities for markets where mainstream business cannot, or will not, go.' [33]
- *New markets.* With shifts in public attitudes towards greater social and environmental responsibility, social enterprises are perceived as being in the vanguard in meeting ethical consumers' needs, the private and public sectors being slower to respond.

Policy approaches and instruments

To achieve the objectives of intervention, two broad approaches are generally available. One concentrates on the creation of an environment favourable to the establishment and growth of social enterprise and the other supports the actual start-up and growth of individual enterprises. Within each approach, a number of specific instruments can then be used. The two approaches are not mutually exclusive and both can be seen in the policy instruments in the UK, which include the following (see also Table 9.2):

* *Fostering a culture of social enterprise*, for instance, through publications, award competitions, and support for networks such as the Social Enterprise UK.
* *Providing access to finance*, for instance, through organisations such as CDFIs, tax relief schemes such as the Community Investment Tax Relief (CITR), and guidance on best practice in funding.
* *Providing information and advice*, for instance, through publications, business advisers, and key business support agencies.
* *Enabling partnership with government*, for instance, by providing advice on creating better working relationships between government and the sector, not least in the area of procurement.

Table 9.2 A taxonomy of policy instruments

Among the range of policy instruments potentially available to achieve government objectives for the social economy are the following, all of which have been, at one time or another, deployed by the UK government:
Raising the profile and providing information • research/evidence-based publications • award schemes and best practice dissemination campaigns • information and advice (e.g. procurement toolkit, working with private sector)
Advocacy and lobbying • informing and involving government departments, such as the Cabinet Office and the Office for Civil Society, the Department for Business, Innovation and Skills • liaison with representative organisations (e.g. Social Enterprise UK)
Deregulation and simplification • legal form (e.g. Community Interest Company) • legislative exemptions • procurement procedures
Sectoral and problem-specific policies • rural enterprises • inner-city enterprises • ethnic enterprises • procurement (e.g. Procurement Pledge/Public Services – and the Social Value Act)
Financial assistance • community Development Finance Institutions • big Society Capital • local Enterprise Growth Initiative (LEGI) • grants • loan funds • venture capital and other funds (e.g. Adventure Capital Fund and UnLtd) • tax relief (CITR)
Indirect assistance • influencing mainstream business support • training for advisers, staff, volunteers, and public sector purchasers • mentoring • network development

Delivery vehicles

In order to undertake the work of implementing its policy, a government needs delivery vehicles. In the case of the UK government's social enterprise policy, the principal delivery agent, at least in England, had been the Regional Development Agencies (RDAs) through their Business Links – until they were both abolished in 2012 and replaced by Local Enterprise Partnerships – and other partners. However, other organisations, such as the CDFIs and Social Enterprise UK, have also had a part to play.

Policy delivery

Having put all that together, policy delivery should then take place. The effectiveness of that delivery can then be assessed through success measures and/or performance indicators.

Success measures and performance indicators

In its *Social enterprise action plan: Scaling new heights*, the UK government identified a trend indicator, which was 'an upward trend in the number of businesses that fit the Government's definition of social enterprise',[34] as well as performance indicators for each of the four ways (policy instruments) in which it planned to encourage growth in social enterprises (see Table 9.3)

Where the social economy is promoted – comparing the delivery of policy

The social enterprise sectors of different countries have distinctive characteristics, reflecting the needs, and uniqueness, of each country's political economy. Nevertheless, there is considerable similarity in the experience and development of the sector and associated policies across many countries, with each tending to face the same broad strategic issues.

Table 9.3 An example of performance indicators

Strategy: Encourage growth in social enterprise in four ways			
Fostering a culture of social enterprise	Ensuring that the right information and advice are available	Enabling access to appropriate finance	Enabling social enterprises to work with government
Performance indicator	Performance indicator	Performance indicator	Performance indicator
Levels of involvement in social enterprise through employment and awareness Source: DTI Household Survey	Measurement of penetration and satisfaction rates for social enterprises using Business Link Source: RDAs	Comparison of social enterprises' access to finance with matched samples of commercial businesses Source: Additions to the DTI's survey on small business finance	Assessment of social enterprises/third sector organisations' experience of government procurement Source: Office of the Third Sector (which will consult on the most appropriate measure)

Source: Cabinet Office/Office of the Third Sector, *Social enterprise action plan: Scaling new heights* (London: HM Treasury, November 2006), p. 62

This section considers the promotion of the social economy in a number of European countries and in the US.

Policy in the UK

The UK policy framework is considered in some depth as England has been described as having 'a more advanced state of social economic policy initiatives than many other countries'.[35] After the Labour government came into office in 1997, a number of initiatives were launched to facilitate the growth and transformation of the social economy, financially, legislatively, and rhetorically. Then the succeeding coalition government in 2010 stated in its Coalition Agreement the intention, inter alia, to 'support the creation and expansion of mutuals, co-operatives, charities and social enterprises, and enable these groups to have much greater involvement in the running of public services'.[36] (The UK government has used the terms 'social economy' and 'social enterprise' in a range of policy initiatives designed to stimulate, support, and develop the 'third sector'.)

Three broad policy themes have emerged in the areas of:

- Philanthropy: involving initiatives to stimulate the giving of time and/or money.
- Voluntary and community sector: involving initiatives to facilitate the sector to build its organisational infrastructure and relationships with government.
- Social enterprise: involving initiatives to stimulate a broader range of social enterprises (such as social businesses, co-operatives, and friendly societies) and to support social entrepreneurs.

Because the UK government has focused on different parts of the third sector in different ways, with reforms remaining largely independent of each other, it can be said to have resulted in 'a loss of momentum to construct a single social economy framework'.[37]

Some key stages in the evolution of the UK policy

Late 1990s – Policy action teams
While social enterprise has existed in various forms for many years, as noted in Part I, and was the subject of policy initiatives at the European level in the 1990s, a significant step change took place in the UK in the late 1990s. This occurred as a result of the work of a number of Policy Action Teams (PATs), which, in 1999, produced reports to contribute to the National Strategy for Neighbourhood Renewal.[38]

Three of the reports drew attention to social enterprises in the context of disadvantaged communities. One report in particular, *PAT 3*, emphasised the role of social enterprise as a way of facilitating enterprise development and community self-help. This message was re-enforced by other reports, and led to three general focus areas for social enterprise policy:

- One focus was that of economic competitiveness and enterprise.
- A second focus, which emanated from the PAT reports, articulated a link between economic regeneration and the engagement of local communities – suggesting, in effect, that social enterprises could generate greater social cohesion and social capital.
- The third focus which developed was the delivery of public services for which social enterprises offered an alternative to private and public sector providers – a third way.

2001 – Social Enterprise Unit
A growing interest in strengthening the sector led to the establishment, in October 2001, of the Social Enterprise Unit (SEnU) as the policy-making body for social enterprise in

Table 9.4 Major barriers to growth of the social enterprise sector in the UK

- poor understanding of the particular abilities and value of social enterprise;
- little hard evidence to demonstrate the impact and added value of social enterprise;
- fragmented availability of accessible, appropriate advice and support;
- difficulty accessing and making use of what is perceived to be limited appropriate finance and funding available;
- limited account taken of the particular characteristics and needs of social enterprise within an enabling environment;
- complexity and lack of coherence within the sector, combined with widely varying skills and knowledge bases.

Source: DTI, *Social Enterprise: a strategy for success* (2002), p. 9

the UK. It was formed within the (then) DTI's Small Business Service section and was tasked with being the focal point 'for strategic decision-making across Government'. [39]

The SEnU set up eight Working Groups, which identified 'the major barriers to growth of the social enterprise sector' [40] (see Table 9.4), and, in tackling the barriers, three key outcomes were to be sought:

- create an enabling environment;
- make social enterprises better businesses; and
- establish the value of social enterprise. [41]

In May 2006, the SEnU was absorbed into the newly created Office of the Third Sector (within the Cabinet Office), which was established 'in recognition of the increasingly important role the third sector plays in both society and the economy', [42] and its remit was described as:

- acting as a focal point for policy making affecting social enterprise;
- promoting and championing social enterprise;
- taking action needed to address barriers to growth of social enterprises; and
- identifying and spreading good practice. [43]

2002 – Social enterprise strategy

The Working Groups' reports were completed in February 2002 and this was followed, in July 2002, by the publication of a social enterprise strategy from the (then) DTI. This document was entitled *Social Enterprise: A Strategy for Success* (SES 2002) and it stated that 'the Government's vision is of dynamic and sustainable social enterprises strengthening an inclusive and growing economy', adding that 'successful social enterprises can play an important role in helping deliver on many of the Government's key policy objectives'. [44] This cross-departmental strategy set out a 3-year programme designed to promote and sustain social enterprise activity and served as the policy framework for the UK (together with the strategies which have been developed by the devolved administrations of Scotland, Wales and Northern Ireland).

The government reviewed progress on the implementation of the strategy and its action plan in October 2003 recorded three areas of activity:

- Improving the evidence: for example mapping the sector and using social accounting tools.
- Structures and networking: for example joint working and partnerships, facilitating networking, awareness raising and integrated business support; and

- Technical assistance: for example capacity-building asset transfer, support for CDFIs, other specialist finance and the provision of incubation space.[45]

These areas bear a general similarity to the types of initiatives taken over the last 15–20 years to support the SME sector. They centre around evidence gathering and awareness raising, improving the flows of advice, information and finance, and assisting structures and networks.

A fuller review of the government's progress in delivering its strategy was published in 2006 drawing upon an independent review by consultants GHK.[46] The latter noted that continued support for enterprise and economic competitiveness was apparent in a variety of ways and concluded that, since 2002,

> developments in the broader policy environment concerning economic competitiveness, social cohesion and public service delivery have all acted to re-enforce the potential role of the social enterprise sector in the delivery of government objectives for the UK economy and society.[47]

2006 – Social enterprise action plan

This review was followed in 2006 by the government's 3-year strategy document for the way forward, entitled *Social enterprise action plan: Scaling new heights.*[48] This document included a review of progress made since the launch of SES 2002 and laid out the government's plans for continuing support for social enterprises. It restated government support for the sector as contributing to its vision of a fairer, more just society and identified the contribution of social enterprise as meeting social needs, encouraging ethical markets, improving public services, and increasing enterprise.[49]

It recognised that government does not create social enterprises, but stated that 'government, working with social enterprises and the organisations that represent them, can create the conditions that enable social enterprises to thrive, and government can tackle the market failures that would otherwise frustrate them'.[50] Specifically, it said the government will

- foster a culture of social enterprise;
- ensure that the right information and advice are available to those running social enterprises;
- enable social enterprises to access appropriate finance;
- enable social enterprises to work with government.[51]

2007 – Final Report

In July 2007, the UK government published the 'final report' of the joint Cabinet Office – Treasury review of the future role of the third sector in social and economic regeneration.[52] (Note the change in vocabulary from 'social enterprise' in the 2006 action plan to 'third sector' in the 2007 report, which further reflected the Cabinet Office's move away from the 'better business'-focused approach apparent in the language of the (then) DTI.) This 'final report' was described as setting out 'a new agenda on social action' and as presenting a 'vision of a partnership in which government empowers and enables individuals and organisations working for positive social change'.[53] It effectively re-emphasised the thrust of its earlier strategy documents.

The review identified four major areas of common interest between the sector and the government: an enabling voice and campaigning, strengthening communities, transforming public services, and encouraging social enterprise. To these was added supporting a thriving, healthy third sector to produce five main themes for which an agenda was set out – see Illustration 9.1 (which could be criticised as a mix of ends and means: 'drivers', 'objectives', and 'approaches' – see Figure 9.1).

Illustration 9.1 The five themes of the 2007 *Final Report*

Enabling voice and campaigning
- A new focus on enabling the third sector's role in campaigning and providing voice for many vulnerable groups.

Strengthening communities
- A new £50 million local endowment match fund.
- At least £10 million of new investment in community anchor organisations and asset and enterprise development.
- £117 million of new resources for youth volunteering.

Transforming public services
- Building capacity of third sector organisations to improve public services through the Futurebuilders fund, training for public sector commissioners, and evidence on opportunities.

Encouraging social enterprise
- Additional investment to raise awareness of the social enterprise business model, and support for government departments to investigate areas for social enterprise delivery.

Supporting a thriving, healthy third sector
- Better mechanisms to drive best practice in funding the third sector.
- Building the third sector evidence base, including a new national research centre.
- A new third sector skills strategy.
- Over £80 million of new investment for third sector infrastructure development.
- Continued focus on the National Compact (launched in 1998) as a means to build the relationship between the third sector and all levels of government.

Source: Taken from www.cabinetoffice.gov.uk, Press release (accessed 10 August 2007), and HM Treasury/Cabinet Office, *The Future Role of the Third Sector in Social and Economic Regeneration: Final Report* (London: HM Treasury, July 2007)

2010 – Big Society and Social Value Act

The election of the new government in 2010 has led to a reinforcement of the previous government's policy direction and the generation of a number of further initiatives. The Office of the Third Sector was renamed the Office for Civil Society (OCS) and takes responsibility for charities, social enterprises, and voluntary organisations in the Cabinet Office. It is interesting to note that the ministerial role has been designated at the level of parliamentary secretary, more junior than that enjoyed by the final minister for the third sector, who was a minister of state.

The Office will 'take the lead in implementing the Big Society agenda' (see Case 3.1 for more on the Big Society) and 'translating the Big Society vision into practical policies to deliver a radical change in the relationship between citizen and state' and more specifically to:

- make it easier to run a charity, social enterprise or voluntary organisation;
- get more resources into the sector and strengthen its independence and resilience; and
- make it easier for sector organisations to work with the state.[54]

Early initiatives under the new government have focused on volunteering, access to finance, and procurement. Increasing volunteering is being facilitated through support for organisations such as the National Citizen Service, Community Organisers, and Community First so as to encourage people to get involved in their communities. Examples of financial initiatives include Big Society Capital (see Illustration 7.6), the Social Incubator Fund, and the Investment and Contract Readiness Fund. On procurement, the government has given a Procurement Pledge, which established a set of principles about how government will procure services with a range of providers. In addition, a Public Services (Social Value) Act 2012 has been introduced in England and Wales. This 'Social Value Act' requires public authorities to take into account social and environmental value when they choose suppliers, rather than focusing solely on cost. Thus, if a third sector organisation can demonstrate that it will not only deliver efficiency, but also add value, the latter should influence the winning of the contract.

> In theory . . . this will rebalance a public services provider market that currently favours big organisations with financial muscle and expert bid-writing capabilities. It will require authorities to put a value on the knowledge, expertise and local connections of smaller, community-based social enterprises. The hope is that, as a result, charities and small businesses will get a bigger share of the public services cake. [55]

Prior to the Social Value Act, the government introduced a 'Right to Request' Programme to the National Health Service (NHS). It enabled front-line clinical staff employed by primary care trusts (PCTs) to request that they deliver their services to NHS patients through a social enterprise. Contracts could be awarded for the provision of services for an initial period of up to 5 years, and once proposals were approved and the new social enterprise set up, staff would transfer with their existing terms and conditions of employment legally protected at the point of transfer[56] (see Illustration 5.3). However, suggestions have been made that this programme does not promote smaller, community-based social enterprises in the same way that the Social Value Act does.

Overall, it is too soon to judge the impact of these measures individually or of the Big Society vision and agenda generally.

Social economy policy in the EU

The European Commission currently states that its

> policy towards 'social economy' enterprises is to guarantee to them a level playing field in which they can compete effectively in their markets and on equal terms with other forms of enterprise, without any regulatory discrimination and respecting their particular principles, modus operandi, needs, particular goals, ethos and working style. [57]

In recognising that many of the enterprises are small or medium sized, it treats them, by and large, as it would other SMEs. The policy context is complicated by the absence of clear definitions as to what is included in the social economy.

The development of EU Policy

1989 – Social Economy Unit
The first significant EU official recognition of the social economy could be said to have occurred in 1989 when the European Commission established a dedicated unit to handle the social economy portfolio. Called the 'Social Economy Unit', it was created within DG XXIII, which was responsible for 'Enterprise Policy, Distributive Trades, Tourism and the Social Economy'. For this, the European definition of the social economy

included co-operatives, mutuals, associations, and foundations (CMAFs), as well as social enterprises.

From 1994 – Multi-annual Programme

Two strands have been identified[58] in the subsequent development of policy for the social economy in the EU, and they are similar to those in the UK. The first strand emerged in February 1994 within the areas of enterprise policy when the Commission agreed a Multi-annual Programme (MAP) of work for the period 1994–1996. It sought to lay down the infrastructure seen as necessary for the development of the sector and to stimulate innovation within it. The MAP resulted in three European CMAF statutes, strengthening the role of the social economy as a vehicle for EU policies, a representative body to act as a dialogue partner (a consultative committee), and improved statistics. It also led to pilot projects to assist financing the sector and communication.[59]

The Enterprise and Industry DG (see below) has developed subsequently MAPs for enterprise and entrepreneurship, and support of social enterprises is a part of those programmes (albeit a small part). Mirroring the subsequent emphasis in the UK's Social Enterprise Strategy, the MAP 2001–2005, for example, sought, for social enterprises, to

* raise the degree of understanding and visibility;
* review the regulatory framework;
* better assess their economic impact.

From the mid-1990s – Employment policies

The second strand of policy development came from within the area of employment policy, reflecting mid-1990s' concerns about 'jobless growth'. The social economy was thought to have the potential to create jobs in areas such as personal services, culture, and the environment, and local economic development initiatives were also seen as having a significant role for social enterprise.[60] A pilot action called 'Third System and Employment' (TSE) was introduced (1997–2001), and the evaluation of this action identified a range of barriers to the development of the sector (see Table 9.5), similar to those articulated in the UK (see Table 9.2).

Out of the employment considerations emerged the EU initiatives named Adapt and Employment followed by EQUAL. This latter initiative, funded through the European

Table 9.5 Barriers to the development of the social enterprise sector in the EU

External barriers
• political preferences for market or state solutions
• inadequate social and fiscal policies
• inappropriate contracting procedures
• inappropriate legal frameworks for third sector activity
Internal barriers
• a lack of managerial and professional skills
• a lack of quality control systems for social services provided by private organisations
• a lack of co-ordination, leading to price competition among service deliverers
• difficulty in accessing finance
• an inadequately developed system of second-level support organisations

Source: Adapted from GHK, *Social Enterprise: An International Literature Review*, a report submitted to SBS/SEnU (March 2006), p. 6, quoting M. Campbell, *The Third System, Employment and Local Development – Volume 1 – Synthesis Report* (Leeds: Leeds Metropolitan University, August 1999)

Social Fund, tested and promoted new means of combating discrimination and inequalities in labour markets, frequently through transnational co-operation. While it did not take the lead in policy for the social economy, it was, nevertheless, the EU's most significant source of financial support for it (€300 million from 2002 to 2008 – a figure matched by national contributions).

Some of the recommendations which emerged from EQUAL 'development partnerships' (DPs)[61] were again very similar to those already being implemented or considered in the UK, such as:

- ensuring that public procurement tender includes social criteria to enable social enterprises to have access to public markets;
- developing measures of social added value;
- improving legal frameworks;
- developing a braided support structure combining specialist with mainstream business support;
- having a department in government which has a clear responsibility for liaising with the social enterprise sector.

The job creation potential of the social economy (including meeting new needs) has been regularly commented upon by the EU in this period. Nevertheless, it has been suggested that, as the employment strategy developed, 'the social economy has been progressively sidelined'.[62] For instance, in the Integrated Guidelines for Growth and Jobs (2005–2008),[63] explicit reference is made only once to 'the social economy' in contrast to the increasing emphasis placed by the UK government on both the social economy in general and social enterprises in particular. There is more recent evidence of a reversal of this trend.

2000 – Directorate General for Enterprise and Industry
While the two strands identified above continued to guide support into the twenty-first century, the Social Economy Unit itself was downgraded. In 2000, a Directorate General for Enterprise and Industry was created through a merger of DG III (Industry), the Innovation Unit of DG XIII (Information Technology), and DG XXIII (Enterprise Policy, Distributive Trades, Tourism and the Social Economy). The Social Economy Unit was subsumed into this new DG, where it became one of the responsibilities of the Unit for Small Enterprises, Crafts, Co-operatives and Mutuals (Unit ENTR/E3).

However, the focus on the sector seemed to gain momentum at the end of the decade. According to a CIRIEC report, there are a number of reasons why this happened. They included the depth of the economic crisis and consequent questioning of the European institutions, leading the Commission to seek alternative solutions and a new wave of social and institutional demands. Examples including the position paper on European civil society and the social economy and those of Social Economy Europe and Cooperatives Europe, the European academic world's 'From words to action: Supporting cooperative and social enterprises to achieve a more inclusive, sustainable and prosperous Europe' open letter of October 2010, the European Parliament's 2009 'Resolution on the social economy' (the Toia report), or the European Economic and Social Committee Opinion on the 'Diverse forms of enterprise'[64] required the Commission to put a greater focus on the social economy in its policies encouraged by the parliament and to recognise the social economy as a social partner and as a key actor in achieving the Lisbon Strategy objectives.

Moreover, the application of the Small Business Act passed in 2008 (which explicitly cited the social economy) was in need of review, leading to interest in social businesses; 'finally, but no less importantly, there were circumstantial factors such as certain European policy makers' noticing the exceedingly high profile of social enterprises'.[65] The Small Business Act and the Single Market Act were seen as central in this respect.

Thus, in 2009, the European Parliament passed a resolution stating 'that the European Union and the Member States should recognise the social economy and its stakeholders – cooperatives, mutual societies, associations and foundations – in their legislation and policies'[66] as well as calling for other forms of institutional recognition.

2010 – Social Business Initiative

Following on from the EU Parliament's resolution and within the framework of the European Platform against Poverty and Social Exclusion, the commission took a significant initiative. It undertook to

> support the development of the social economy as a tool for active inclusion by proposing measures to improve the quality of the legal structures relating to foundations, mutual societies and cooperatives operating in a European context, proposing a "Social Business Initiative" in 2011, as well as facilitating access to relevant EU financial programmes.[67]

Following the above communication, the Single Market Act of 2011 contained a section entitled 'Social business' setting out the commission's intentions. While focusing almost exclusively on the provision of finance, it proposed a Social Business Initiative.

Thus, in 2011, the European Commission undertook the introduction of two initiatives on social enterprises: the *Social Business Initiative (SBI)* and the *Proposal for a Regulation on European Social Entrepreneurship Funds* – the latter Proposal aiming to enable investors more easily to identify funds that focus on investing in European social businesses. It is part of the SBI, itself being part of the Single Market Act. The SBI is the joint responsibility of three DGs: DG Internal Market and Services, DG Employment Social Affairs and Inclusion, and DG Enterprise and Industry, with the former in the lead. It incorporates 11 actions under the following main themes:

- improve access to funding
- improve visibility
- improve the legal environment

Sector representative bodies

There are a significant number of bodies representing the social economy sector at EU level, more so than in the UK. Some of the best known are listed in Table 9.6. The associations that represent social economy companies and organisations have mainly been formed with a sector ('family') perspective. Most of these European-level representation organisations are in turn members of Social Economy Europe's European Standing Conference of Cooperatives, Mutual Societies, Associations and Foundations (set up in November 2000 under the name of CEP-CMAF), which is currently the highest-level European social economy interlocutor.

Groupings are not all of the family or sectoral type. Groups represent 'the social economy, government bodies (such as town councils) and/or companies and other social organisations that are actively encouraging the social economy'.[68] Examples include REVES, the European Networks of Cities & Regions for the Social Economy, ENSIE, the European Network for Social Integration Enterprises, and FEDES, the European Federation of Social Employers.

Table 9.6 Social enterprise sector representation at EU level

1. Cooperative family:
– EUROCOOP: European Community of Consumer Cooperatives
– CECODHAS: European Liaison Committee for Social Housing – cooperative section
– CECOP: European Confederation of Workers' Cooperatives, Social Cooperatives and Participative Enterprises
– COGECA: General Confederation of Agricultural Cooperatives
– GEBC: European Cooperative Banking Group
– UEPS: European Union of Social Pharmacies
– Cooperatives Europe is the umbrella organisation of all these representative bodies of the European cooperatives.
2. Mutual society family:
– AIM: International Association of Mutual Societies
– AMICE – Association of Mutual Insurers and Insurance Cooperatives in Europe
3. Association and social action organisation family:
– CEDAG: European Council of Associations of General Interest
– EFC: European Foundation Centre
– European Platform of Social NGOs
4. Platforms for Social Enterprises:
– CEFEC: Social Firms Europe, the Confederation of European Social Firms, Employment Initiatives and Social Cooperatives

Source: J. Monzón and R. Chaves, *The Social Economy in the European Union* (Brussels: CIRIEC study commissioned by the European Economic and Social Committee, 2012) pp.43–4

Some comments on EU policy

As described in Chapter 4, the EU has indicated that it considers social enterprises to be one of the categories of organisation included in the social economy. However, beyond that, it has no agreed definition of a social enterprise. Whether or not the EU has had a coherent policy (or, as some might contest, any policy) towards social enterprises is somewhat unclear. Jeremy Kendall has observed that in relation to EU policy and the third sector, there is 'sustained policy salience but contested policy substance' and that 'the topic will stay alive, as a contested and fraught domain characterised by competing interests and ideas'.[69] He also added that:

- Definitions of the third sector are politically constructed, as they determine who benefits from subsequent regulatory and funding decisions.
- Most policy refers to the 'vertical' policy field (referring to social issues such as poverty or employment), though certain 'horizontal' issues (cross-cutting issues that cover all organisations under consideration) have emerged, such as legal status, citizenship, consultation, funding and volunteering.
- The most important level of interaction between the third sector and government is at the local level, as this is where the policy is delivered, not at national or European [level].[70]

However, it has also been said that a 'policy towards social enterprise is slowly emerging' and that 'there is evidence of a more joined-up view', illustrated in the past by 'the treaties of Maastricht and Amsterdam, the Commission communication on voluntary organisa-tions . . . , the management of the Structural Funds and the governance debate'[71] and more recently by the development of the Social Business Initiative (see above).

Policy towards social enterprise has been easier to identify and articulate in the UK than at an EU level. UK policy also has a coherence, which derives in part from the consensus which largely exists as to what constitutes the concept of 'social enterprise'. In Europe, there is no such consensus, and the differing national conceptions have tended to produce a fragmentary approach towards policy with considerable fluctuations in the resources made available over time.

While the Social Business Initiative suggests a more coherent and a less ad hoc and reactive approach to policy in the sector, with its distinct parallels to the UK strategy for the sector, it is too soon to say what will eventually be achieved. There is no doubt that the current financial crisis, with its restraints on the public social budget and pressure for efficiency savings in the public sector, has helped to push the possible benefits from the sector further up the agenda of the EU Commission.

Social economy policy in other European countries

The following is a summary of some of the features of social enterprise policy in selected European countries. It is based substantially on the findings of two reviews,[72, 73] submitted respectively to the UK's Social Enterprise Unit and to DG Enterprise and Industry of the European Commission.

Belgium

- The social economy falls under the jurisdiction of the regions, each of which applies a different definition to it. Moreover, the German-speaking community authorities support the social economies in different ways. Therefore, a social enterprise can take different legal forms.
- As in a number of European countries, social enterprise has a dual meaning in Belgium. The first meaning generally refers to service organisations that are developing commercial activities. The second refers to those cooperatives or associations with initiatives targeted at integrating disadvantaged people, excluded from the labour market, into work.
- The development of social enterprises aiming to create jobs for low-qualified workers dates back essentially to the 1960s, when the first 'sheltered workshops' were created to provide work for handicapped people. From the end of the 1970s and onwards, especially during the 1980s, various other initiatives targeting disadvantaged groups were created.
- Progressively, public authorities have created a legal framework for various types of work-integration social enterprises and implemented subsidies to support them.
- As in the UK, the Belgian authorities place an emphasis on the self-sufficiency of social enterprises.

France

- The idea of the 'social economy' first grew in France in the nineteenth century but was subsequently eclipsed by the co-operative and public sectors. The French model has, however, been influential on broader European thinking.
- French policy now tends to use the term 'social and solidarity economy' rather than 'social enterprise'. There is no official definition of social enterprises.
- The concept of social economy developed in the 1970s based on the recognition of the shared values of the three 'families' (co-operatives, mutual companies, and associations, which permeate almost every field of activity and walk of life).

- Cohesion within the sector has been encouraged and facilitated through simple legal frameworks.
- There are positive examples of the integration of provider and user voices within enterprises. For instance, strong stakeholder relationships including democratic ownership and the involvement of both customers and employees can enhance the sustainability of enterprises.
- The social benefits delivered by the social and solidarity economy have been recognised through economic instruments for the sector, for example, '*cheques domiciles*': vouchers for services provided by social enterprises.
- In France the cohesion in the sector was felt to have suffered in 2002 by 'the integration of different social economy sectors into different ministries – cooperatives were integrated into the Ministry of Solidarity and Employment while associations were in the Ministry of Sport and Youth'.[74] However, the new French government, which took office in 2012, appointed a Minister Delegate for the social economy within the Ministry of the Economy, the Treasury and Foreign Trade.

Germany

- Policy in Germany has followed a relatively strict division between co-operatives (pursuing self-help) and welfare organisations (performing a public duty). The family of co-operative organisations is strong but has a weak attachment to the idea of social enterprise.
- Within government, the main policy drivers of support for the sector are to reduce unemployment, to integrate disabled people into the workforce, and to combat poverty, social exclusion, and racial discord. However, there is no co-ordinated government dialogue with social enterprises, and development has been hindered by the absence of a long-term vision for the sector.
- Innovation in the sector is hindered by regulations and procedures which constrain the ability of social enterprises to trade in the open market and in areas of the economy that are 'additional' to the activities of existing businesses.
- As long as social enterprise is seen primarily as a means for short-term job creation, instead of as a contributor to local economic development, community development and social capital, innovation, and self-sufficiency in the sector may be hampered.

Ireland

- There is no legal or official definition of a social enterprise in the Republic of Ireland. The term 'social enterprises' is taken to mean enterprises that have been established to support the development of local communities.
- Traditionally, Irish social enterprises have played a central role in tackling problems associated with disadvantage and exclusion. More recently, social enterprises have been associated with two aims: providing unmet community needs and addressing the problems of long-term unemployment and labour market marginalisation.
- The Community Services Programme evolved from the Social Economy Programme and is managed for the Department of Social Protection by Pobal, a not-for-profit company that manages programmes on behalf of the Irish government and the EU.
- The Community Services Programme supports community businesses to provide local services and employment opportunities for disadvantaged people. The programme also enables the benefit of other public investment to be realised (as in the case of investment in community centres and resources).

Italy

- The third sector in Italy is seen as one of the strongest in Europe. The role of the co-operative movement is anchored in Italy's constitution and it is large and well organised. In contrast, associations in Italy are relatively badly structured. The country has been responsible for some innovative partnership ideas but it is the co-operative family that has been the engine for innovation. There are many examples of multi-stakeholder structures (involving employees, users, volunteers and supporters) within the sector.
- Although the terminology varies, the social economy is normally thought of as including all co-operatives, along with mutuals, associations and foundations. However, for some, there are divergent concepts of its scope. There is a business concept that sees it as consisting mainly of co-operatives which coexists with a non-market concept that sees it as largely comprising associations, social co-operatives and other non-profit organisations.
- The third sector, or third system, is the part of this that works for the public benefit and does not distribute profit. The legal structure adopted by social enterprises has to be one of those as provided by the Italian Civil Code (*libro V*).
- Italian government policy towards the third sector has historically been unsystematic and pragmatic. Since the 1990s, however, a more stable government framework has grown within which the third sector has been able to work more coherently.
- Tax relief is used to reflect the social benefits delivered by the sector, and the social co-operative sector is working to transform the business advice system and to establish the legitimacy of social enterprise among business advisers. The sector thus benefits from an advisory support system which takes social enterprise seriously.

Poland

- In Poland, the term 'social economy' is chiefly associated with the country's associations and foundations although there is no official definition of a social enterprise. The social economy in Poland had rich traditions between the wars but became a tool of centralised planning under communism. Nowadays, as in other former Soviet Bloc countries, they often give their projects names other than terms like 'co-operative' because they had been used by the communist regimes.
- The main motivation of the Polish government to support the development of social enterprises has been as a source of jobs to counter high unemployment. However, the government does recognise the useful role of the social economy in tackling a wide range of issues including entrepreneurship, employment, youth unemployment, drug abuse, social inclusion, and promoting democracy.
- The term 'social enterprise' is not much used in Poland, where the term 'third sector' is more common.
- European networks are being used to develop the sector, and public finance is available for sector development. Regional initiatives and local actions have stimulated the growth of the sector carried out within the framework of a coherent regional policy.

Points from a comparison

Various conclusions have been drawn from comparisons of the policies of European countries, including the UK, as well as further afield. The following are some of the observations made, including those in the two reviews noted above or, where indicated, from other sources:

- The economic and political dynamics of a given country tend to dictate the scope, nature, treatment, and even recognition of the 'social economy'. The socio-economic and regulatory institutions shape the opportunities for social enterprises. The distinction with the public sector is not clear in some cases.

- In the newer member states of the EU, the concept of social organisations as hybrid organisations which combine entrepreneurial principles and a social aim is new. In most cases, it has been driven by the European Social Fund (ESF).
- The role of the organisations in the social economy of countries within Europe is increasing. However, due to differences in the definitions used, comparable data for the various activities in which they are involved are not available. Consequently, the relative importance of the sector within various countries is not clear.
- There is no 'right or wrong' policy framework. There is considerable diversity of organisational models in the social enterprise sector, and certain models can best fit certain policy goals.
- There are common aims for social enterprises and the social economy in the fields of social cohesion and public service delivery. Unlike in the UK, there is less of a concern about its role in promoting economic competitiveness.
- In most countries, the *de facto* policy ministries are those which regulate and fund the sector. In countries where policy is highly decentralised (e.g. Germany and Spain), regional and local authorities play an important role in policy creation and in the nature of relationships with the sector. 'Only the UK, France and Italy have appointed a specific authority in charge of co-ordinating, at least in part, the national policy for the sector.'[75]
- There is strong belief that the social economy needs and builds human and social capital and that it is an instrument to address social and economic exclusion.
- Throughout Europe, social enterprises that (re-)integrate disadvantaged persons into the labour market or provide workplaces for people with special needs (disabled, learning disability, etc.) seem to receive most attention from policy-makers.
- Some governments encourage social enterprises to become more self-sufficient (UK, France, Belgium).
- There is a perceived need for micro-finance as a necessary mechanism to support social economy enterprises.
- Social enterprises seem to be of rather small size and most often act at a local level. Thus the role of regional structures is important in developing the sector, linking national strategy with local activity. In the UK, this suggests a valuable role for the devolved administrations and perhaps Local Enterprise Partnerships (which have replaced RDAs).
- There is also variation among those groups to whom these measures are targeted (disabled, unemployed, ex-prisoners, poor, disadvantaged persons, etc.). Thus, the promotion and development of social enterprises impacts upon social policy, employment policy, and industrial policy.
- There is less interest in evaluating the social benefits of the sector in other European countries than in the UK and the DIES[76] in France.
- The main national policy instruments used in support of the sector are[77]
  - special legal forms and regulations,
  - favourable tax system,
  - grants and subsidies,
  - incentives for fund-raising, and
  - support for voluntary work and job generation (e.g. paid days off work, tax exemptions on expenses).

A general review of literature in this field as well as analysis of EU and European national systems of support for the social enterprise sector would suggest, for those wishing to advance the sector, seven principles of good practice:

1. Political commitment

There needs to be genuine belief that the sector has a strategic and long-term role to play in the social and economic systems of the country, such belief exhibiting itself in appropriate support policies.

2. A clear focus for the sector

There should be a recognition that the sector has a distinctive contribution to make and agreement on what that contribution is and its clear articulation.

3. Vertical and horizontal integration

There should be a strategic approach appropriate to the needs of the social economy at the local level, recognising and integrating horizontal issues common to the sector and vertical issues common to its various areas of involvement (e.g. employment, health care). In addition, co-operation and integration of social enterprises themselves should be facilitated to further their common objectives and meet their common needs.

4. Independent financial resources

Access to financial resources (other than grants) should be facilitated, for instance, borrowing against assets to enhance the prospects of sustainability.

5. Skills, education, and training

There should be a support and advisory system that can deliver critical mass whilst recognising the distinctiveness of the sector applied to the various stakeholders including staff, board members, volunteers, and supporters. Education *about* the social economy should rest alongside education *for* the social economy.

6. Social entrepreneurship

There should be recognition and support for the phenomenon of the social entrepreneur as a catalyst in developing innovative ways of addressing social problems.

7. A shared vision

Processes which lead to a shared vision should be in place comprising appropriate structures in the public sector and in the social economy, maintaining shared objectives, resources, and dialogues addressing common issues.

Policy in the USA

The third sector is claimed to be the fastest-growing part of the US economy, and the US has one of the highest levels of voluntary sector activity anywhere in the world (at almost 10 per cent of the economically active working for a civil society organisation). [78] The third sector in the US is said to comprise a mix of 'non-profit' or 'not-for-profit' organisations and co-operatives. [79]

The terms 'social economy' and 'social enterprise' have not been much used, and neither is the term 'social entrepreneurship', although there is now a rapidly growing social entrepreneurship movement developing around universities, foundations, and not-for-profit organisations.

Kerlin contrasts the definitions of the academic (and consulting) worlds where social enterprise is understood to include 'those organizations that fall along a continuum from profit-oriented businesses engaged in socially beneficial activities (corporate philanthropies or corporate social responsibility) to dual-purpose businesses that mediate profit goals with social objectives (hybrids) to nonprofit organizations engaged in mission-supporting commercial activity (social purpose organizations)'. Outside academia, 'much of the practice of social enterprise in the United States, termed as social enterprise, remains focused on revenue generation by nonprofit organizations (specifically those registered as 501[c][3] tax-exempt organizations with the United States Internal Revenue Service)'.[80]

The US's Social Enterprise Alliance definition is as follows:

> Social enterprises are businesses whose primary purpose is the common good. They use the methods and disciplines of business and the power of the marketplace to advance their social, environmental and human justice agendas.[81]

The alliance will encompass, however, for-profits 'whose driving purpose is social'.[82] In other cases, an organisation may not qualify as a social enterprise unless it directly addresses social needs through its products or services or the numbers of disadvantaged people it employs.

In the US, as in other countries, the role of government in supporting the sector needs to be interpreted within the particular political, economic, and social characteristics of the country. Indeed, some would draw a sharp contrast between the UK/US social enterprise approach to the sector and the European social economy approach. In the former, the social or not-for-profit enterprise has its rationale as a business in the market context (albeit with more socially informed values and for which it uses its surpluses). It is suggested that on

> the basis of US experience it can even claim to be becoming 'fashionable' – merging in with new corporate management methods (to privilege trust and worker empowerment), the drive for good corporate citizenship . . . as a vehicle to add a second (social) and third (environmental) bottom line to good corporate practice . . . an alternative business vehicle.[83]

The European approach differs in that the social economy has its roots in political economy as opposed to economic sociology or business management. In this context, the social enterprise is more than 'just another kind of business'. In summary, the US emphasises the 'enterprise' element, whereas in Europe the 'social' element is more prominent in driving policy.

In the US, organisations in the sector generally have higher levels of commerciality than their counterparts in Europe. Moreover, there is a much higher level of corporate philanthropy than in European countries, with philanthropic foundations serving as important investment vehicles for third sector activity (for instance, the Schwab, Ashoka, and Skoll foundations). These foundations were often established to focus on supporting an organisation's social mission. However, when the downturn in the economy came in the late 1970s, it led to welfare retrenchment and to significant cutbacks in federal funding. Nonprofits then began to expand their commercial activities to fill the gap in their budgets through the sale of goods or services not directly related to their mission.

Private foundation support for the development of social enterprise was begun in the 1980s and 1990s by a number of organisations. Some

focused on basic information collection on social enterprise and the creation of networks (Kellogg Foundation, Kauffman Foundation, Surdna Foundation, Rockefeller Foundation). Others turned their support towards social enterprise start-ups (Roberts Enterprise Development Fund), social enterprise business competitions (Goldman Sachs Foundation, Pew Charitable Trusts), and increasingly towards individual social entrepreneurs through intensive education programs and/or grants some of which are international in nature (Draper Richards Foundation, Skoll Foundation, Echoing Green, Ashoka, Schwab Foundation).[84]

This trend was strengthened 'by the blooming of institutions, initiatives and consulting practices to support this new "industry" along the 1990s. Moreover, the National Gathering of Social Entrepreneurs, promoted by a few thought leaders in 1998, greatly helped this emerging community of practitioners and consultants to reach a critical mass.'[85]

The situation contrasts with many European countries, where the institutional environment for strategic support of social enterprise is much more tied to government and European Union support. Government support for social enterprises in the US is mainly in the form of grants and tax incentives – a recent example of the former being the creation of a Social Innovation Fund, in 2010. It will 'direct funding through innovative, hands-on grant makers (or intermediaries) across the country. These grant makers will identify fund and support over a period of years promising nonprofit organizations working in low-income communities.'[86] Government is also important as a contractor of services, not least in health care. In addition, tax concessions support worker buy-outs and succession buy-outs.

The conclusions[87] to be drawn about support for the third/social economy sector in the US include the following:

- Corporate philanthropy, which is supported by tax breaks, has a significant influence on sector development.
- The sector benefits from high levels of commerciality and is also driven by increasing social entrepreneurship.
- There are some government grants for the sector (about 8 per cent of the revenue of reporting charities), and government contracting for services plays a dominant role in the health-care sector.
- A significant support role is played by an extensive array of diverse structures at state level and trade associations.
- Government support for employee ownership also assists the expansion of the sector.

Kerlin's summary of the key distinctions between the US and Europe is presented in Table 9.7.

Conclusion

This chapter is about promoting the social economy through interventions which are designed to encourage, support, focus, and/or grow it. It started by considering why there is an interest in promoting the sector and then looked at who is promoting it. Much of that promotion is instigated by governments, and therefore a considerable section of the

Table 9.7 Comparative overview of social enterprise in the United States and Europe

Emphasis	*United States* **Revenue Generation**	*Europe* **Social Benefit**
Common Organizational Type	Nonprofit (501(c)(3))	Association/Cooperative
Focus	All Nonprofit Activities	Human Services
Types of Social Enterprise	Many	Few
Recipient Involvement	Limited	Common
Strategic Development	Foundations	Government/EU
University Research	Business and Social Science	Social Science
Context	Market Economy	Social Economy
Legal Framework	Lacking	Underdeveloped but Improving

Source: J. A. Kerlin, 'Social Enterprise in the United States and Europe: Understanding and Learning from the Differences', *Voluntas*, Vol. 17, No. 3 (2006), p. 259

chapter is devoted to government strategies for the sector and particularly for the social economy within it. Governments in different countries approach the sector in different ways and with different perspectives, sometimes placing a different focus on its potential and attempting to help it by somewhat different means.

Nevertheless, it is clear that there has been, is, and will continue to be, considerable interest in the sector from international governmental organisations such as the EU, from national governments, and also from regional and local government bodies. This chapter therefore suggests a model of how, in these government strategies, political drivers and objectives, rationales, approaches and themes, instruments and delivery vehicles, and success measures and performance indicators can be linked, although not all strategies will formally acknowledge all these components.

As the first part of this chapter explains, these interventions are generally undertaken because of the apparent potential of the social economy to address some of the problems in, or of, society. Governments and others therefore believe that the social economy has the potential to help them to achieve some of their social, and economic, objectives, and thus they promote it in order to make it stronger and able to deliver more. But do these promotions work? Is the social economy, or at least some of its components, stronger as a consequence, and are they as a result delivering more? That question is considered in the next chapter.

Key Points of Chapter 9

- The social economy, or at least parts of it, is perceived to provide benefits such as augmenting welfare state provision and generating jobs, enterprise, social cohesion, environmental sustainability, and ethical operations.
- Governments and others have an interest in some, if not all, of these benefits, and so they promote and encourage the social economy. Government support can be at the international, national, regional and local levels.
- To understand government strategy, it can be useful to have a model linking policy drivers and objectives, rationales, approaches and themes, instruments, delivery vehicles, and success measures and performance indicators (or their equivalents).

- The UK is viewed as being one of the countries with advanced social economy policies and has published a series of strategies/action plans over recent years describing its goals, plans, and performance.
- Policy development in the UK has centred around fostering a culture of social enterprise, easing access to finance, providing information and advice, as well as enabling partnership with government.
- At the EU level, social economy policy developments have tended, until recently, to be embraced within enterprise and employment policy but with a diminishing emphasis and in a somewhat fragmentary way. Since 2010, new initiatives are underway under the Single Market Act (Social Business Initiative).
- Different European countries have different regulatory frameworks and organisation structures within which policy is applied. These result mainly from their unique political, economic, and social histories.
- The institutional environments in the United States and Europe tend to reflect a private/business focus and a government/social service focus, respectively. The US supportive institutional context largely consists of private organisations that provide financial support, education, training, research, and consulting services for social enterprises.
- Some lessons can be drawn about the social economy sector by reviewing its development and promotion across a number of countries, as can some tentative principles of good practice.

Case 9.1 | Key points on business support for social enterprises

As noted in this chapter, the social economy sector is seen as having the ability to provide a variety of benefits. Thus efforts are made by government bodies at the international, national, regional, and local levels to develop policies to promote and support social enterprises (SEs). It is also noted that there is no single good or bad, or right or wrong, policy framework. It depends on circumstances. One recent UK study sought, inter alia, to highlight points which were believed to be key to enabling appropriate business support to be delivered to the sector.

The study was funded by the Office for Civil Society and managed by the Department for Business, Innovation and Skills. It was carried out and reported on by Durham University in 2011. Its overall intention was to provide a fuller understanding of the opportunities and challenges SEs face and to examine the availability and quality of business support to overcome those challenges. Its key points for effective business support are summarised as follows:

- Broadly, the business support needs of SEs are similar to other SMEs*, in the general areas of support sought and generic support courses (e.g. basic book-keeping). However, they are distinguished by a commitment to a social mission and decision-making processes and operational models which are non-mainstream, leading to complications in applying mainstream support products, mainly geared towards an ultimate end of increasing the income of the owner or business.
- The diversity of SEs – in terms of operating models, constraints and social/environmental missions – means that there can be no one-size-fits-all SE support model.

- There may be a lack of understanding of differences on the supply side and resistance on the demand side. Support needs to take account of differences in emphasis and terminology, recognising that standard metrics such as turnover or profitability should be complemented by harder to measure social impact outcomes.
- In some areas – finance, governance/legal structure and managing volunteers in particular – there are specific support needs which are distinct from those of other SMEs. SEs tend to take longer to develop and to reach a position of marketisation than private sector SMEs. In this early phase, they may require a greater degree of 'hand-holding'.
- While SEs are as likely or even more likely than SMEs to seek support, there is wariness about mainstream and generalist providers. This is driven in part by the variability in service provided, varying levels of the understanding of social objectives and can be dependent upon the individual advisor.
- There can be a lack of self awareness in the SE sector along with some general resistances to marketing and self promotion. When it comes to marketing the sector's USP – its social objectives and ways of operating – this may be better communicated via generalised promotional activity.
- Support delivered through specialist providers or peer learning methods, such as role models and networking and brokered specialised support through a trusted intermediary organisation, is more likely to be received positively.

*SMEs are small and medium-sized enterprises (authors' note).

Source: G. Allinson, P. Braidford, M. Houston, F. Robinson and I. Stone, *Business Support for Social Enterprises: Findings from a Longitudinal Study* (Durham: University of Durham, Policy Research Group, 2011), pp. 37–8

Questions, Exercises, Essay, and Discussion Topics

1. Does the social economy need to be promoted any more than other areas of the economy? Discuss.
2. What categories of organisation promote the sector? Are there too few or too many voices for the sector?
3. Identify the main components of a cohesive strategy for policy support for the sector.
4. Describe the main policy instruments used by the UK government to promote social enterprises.
5. Are the commonalities of policy across countries greater than the differences?
6. Describe some best practice principles to guide policy support for social enterprises.

Suggestions for further reading

Some key publications relevant to the development of the social enterprise sector in the UK (listed chronologically by date of publication):

DTI, *Social Enterprise: a strategy for success* (London: Department of Trade and Industry, 2002).

ECOTEC Research and Consulting Ltd, *Guidance on Mapping Social Enterprise* (London: ECOTEC Research and Consulting Ltd, 2003).

GHK, *Review of the Social Enterprise Strategy*, a final report submitted by GHK (London: GHK, 2005).

GHK, *Social Enterprise: International Literature Review*, a report submitted to SBS/SEnU (London: GHK, 2006).

Office of the Third Sector, Cabinet Office, *Social Enterprise Action Plan: Scaling New Heights* (London: Cabinet Office, 2006).

Office of the Third Sector, Cabinet Office, *Social Enterprise Action Plan: One Year On* (London: HM Treasury, 2007).

Office of the Third Sector, Cabinet Office, *Social Enterprise Action Plan: Two Years On* (London: HM Treasury, 2008).

In addition, the following offer a perspective on Europe, the US, and globally:

J. Defourny and M. Nyssens, 'Conceptions of social enterprise and social entrepreneurship in Europe and the United States: Convergences and divergences', *Journal of Social Entrepreneurship*, Vol. 1, No. 1 (March 2010), pp. 32–53.

J. A. Kerlin (Ed.), *Social Enterprise: A Global Comparison* (Lebanon, NH: University Press of New England/Tufts University Press, 2011).

Study on Practices and Policies in the Social Enterprise Sector in Europe: Final Report, conducted on behalf of the European Commission, DG Enterprise & Industry (Vienna: Austrian Institute for SME Research and TSE Entre, Turku School of Economics, Finland, June 2007).

References

1. GHK, *Social Enterprise: An International Literature Review*, a report submitted to SBS/SEnU (London: GHK, 2006).

2. Ibid., p. iv.

3. Ibid., p. 68.

4. P. Graefe, 'The social economy and the state: Linking ambitions with institutions in Quebec, Canada', *Policy and Politics*, Vol. 30, No. 2 (2002), p. 248.

5. DTI, *A Progress Report on Social Enterprise: a strategy for success* (London: HM Treasury, October 2003), p. 49.

6. F. Lyon and L. Sepulveda, 'Social Enterprise Support Policies: Distinctions and Challenges', in R. Blackburn and M. Schaper (Eds), *Government, SMEs and Entrepreneurship Development: Policy, Practice and Challenges* (Farnham: Gower, 2012), p. 215.

7. http://cc.europa.eu/enterprise/coop/social-cinafagenda/social-enterp (accessed 29 August 2007).

8. http://www.eubusiness.com/topics/social/social-business (accessed 5 November 2012).

9. Ibid.

10. Cabinet Office, *The Coalition: Our Programme for Government* (London: HM Treasury, May 2010), p. 29.

11. Cabinet Office/Office of the Third Sector, *Social enterprise action plan: Two years on* (London: HM Treasury, November 2008), p. 3.

12. R. R. Donnelley, *Enterprising Third Sector: Action Plan 2008–2011* (Edinburgh: Scottish Government, 2008).

13. Welsh Assembly Government, *The Social Enterprise Action Plan for Wales 2009* (Cardiff: The Publications Centre, 2009), p. 5.

14. Social Economy Branch, Department of Enterprise, Trade and Investment, *Social Economy Enterprise Strategy 2010–2011* (Belfast: Social Economy Branch, DETI, March 2010), p. 8.

15. Ibid., p. 7.

16. A. Amin, R. Hudson and A. Cameron, *Placing the Social Economy* (London: Routledge, 2002), p. 61.

17. http://www.thirdsector.co.uk/News/DailyBulletin/613394/Umbrella-groups-need-this (accessed 21 August 2007), p. 1.

18. Cabinet Office, *Social Enterprise: Scaling New Heights*, Action Plan Draft (London: HM Treasury, 2006), p. 45.

19. Office of the Third Sector/Cabinet Office, *Social Enterprise Action Plan: Scaling New Heights* (London: Cabinet Office, 2006), p. 60.

20. http://www.socialenterprise.org.uk/page.aspx?SP=1346 (accessed 19 August 2007).

21. Social Enterprise UK, *Social Enterprise UK Annual Review* (January 2012), p. 2, http://www.socialenterprise.org.uk/uploads/files/2012/02/seuk_annual_review_2011.pdf (accessed 18 December 2012).

22. http://www.neweconomics.org/gen/
m1i1aboutushome.aspx (accessed 19 August 2007).
23. Ibid.
24. http://www.socialfirms.co.uk (accessed 19 August
2007).
25. http://www.thirdsector.co.uk/News/DailyBulletin/
613394/Umbrella-groups-need-this (accessed
21 August 2007), p. 1.
26. Ibid.
27. http://www.thirdsector.co.uk/news/Article/921196/
Charities-regional-voice-fragmented-says-IPPR/
(accessed 5 November 2012).
28. DTI, *Social Enterprise: a strategy for success*
(London: HM Treasury, July 2002), p. 7.
29. Office of the Third Sector/Cabinet Office, *Social
Enterprise Action Plan: Scaling New Heights*
(London: Cabinet Office, 2006), p. 3.
30. Cabinet Office, *Social Enterprise: Scaling New
Heights*, Action Plan Draft 0.8 Version for
DA Committee (London: HM Treasury, 2006), p. 9.
31. Cabinet Office, *The Coalition: Our Programme for
Government* (London: HM Treasury, May 2010),
p. 29.
32. DTI, *Social Enterprise: a strategy for success*
(London: HM Treasury, July 2002), p. 20.
33. Ibid.
34. Office of the Third Sector/Cabinet Office, *Social
Enterprise Action Plan: Scaling New Heights*
(London: Cabinet Office, 2006), p. 62.
35. Canadian Government draft of 'Europe – Social
Economy; Synthesis and Analysis of Environmental
Scans' (Unpublished, circa 2005).
36. Cabinet Office, *The Coalition: Our Programme
for Government* (London: HM Treasury, May
2010), p. 29.
37. Canadian Government, Europe – Social
Economy, p. 45.
38. Neighbourhood Renewal Unit, PAT reports, www.
neighbourhood.gov.uk, accessed 16 June 2013.
39. DTI, *Social Enterprise: a strategy for success* (2002),
p. 8.
40. Ibid.
41. Ibid.
42. http://www.sbs.gov.uk/sbsgov/action/layer
(accessed 15 April 2007).
43. Based on GHK, *Review of the Social Enterprise
Strategy*, a final report submitted to SBS/SEnU
(London: GHK, 2005), p. 5.
44. DTI, *Social Enterprise: a strategy for success*
(London: Department of Trade and Industry,
2002), p. 8.
45. DTI, *A Progress Report on Social Enterprise: a
strategy for success* (London: HM Treasury, October
2003), p. 7.
46. Based on GHK, *Review of the Social Enterprise
Strategy*, a final report submitted to SBS/SEnU
(London: GHK, 2005).
47. Ibid., p. 12.
48. Office of the Third Sector/Cabinet Office, *Social
Enterprise Action Plan: Scaling New Heights*
(London: Cabinet Office, 2006).
49. Ibid., p. 13.
50. Ibid., p. 3.
51. Ibid., pp. 3–5.
52. HM Treasury/Cabinet Office, *The Future Role of the
Third Sector in Social and Economic Regeneration:
Final Report*, Cm 7189 (London: HM Treasury, July
2007).
53. www.cabinetoffice.gov.uk – press release (accessed
10 August 2007).
54. http://www.cabinetoffice.gov.uk/resource-library/
office-civil-society-structure-finalised (accessed
5 November 2012).
55. www.guardian.co.uk/society/2013/feb/05/
social-value-act-public-services (accessed
25 March 2013).
56. http://www.thirdsector.co.uk/news/Article/1041388/
Final-wave-Right-Request-will-create-32-social-
enterprises-says-Andrew-Lansley/ (accessed
25 March 2013).
57. http://ec.europa.eu/enterprise/policies/sme/
promoting-entrepreneurship/social-economy/
(accessed 12 November 2012).
58. GHK, *Social Enterprise: An International Literature
Review*, a report submitted to SBS/SEnU (March
2006), p. 5.
59. Commission of the European Communities, COM
(1997) 241 final, *Promoting the Role of Voluntary
Organisations and Foundations in Europe*
(Luxembourg: Office for Official Publications of the
European Communities, 1997).
60. Commission of the European Communities, *Local
Development and Employment Initiatives:
An Investigation in the European Union* (Luxembourg:
Office for Official Publications of the European
Communities, 1995).
61. DPs are strategic partnerships bringing together
geographical and sectoral representatives who
agree on a common work programme to meet
EQUAL's objectives.
62. GHK, *Social Enterprise: An International Literature
Review*, a report submitted to SBS/SEnU (March
2006), p. 9.
63. COM (2005) 141 final of 12 April 2005. Quoted in GHK
(ibid.), p. 9.
64. J. Monzón and R. Chaves, *The Social Economy in the
European Union* (Brussels: CIRIEC, 2012), pp. 99–100.
65. Ibid., p. 100.

66. European Parliament resolution of 19 February 2009 on Social Economy (2008/2250(INI)), *Official Journal of the European Union* (25 March 2010), 2010/C 76 E/04. Or see http://eur-lex.europa.eu/LexUriServ/ LexUriServ.do?uri=OJ:C:2010:076E:0016:0023:EN:PDF, Accessed 15 June 2013.

67. Commission of the European Communities COM (2010) 758 final, *The European Platform against Poverty and Social Exclusion: A European framework for social and territorial cohesion* (Brussels: European Commission, 2010), p. 18.

68. J. Monzón and R. Chaves, *The Social Economy in the European Union* (Brussels: CIRIEC, 2012), p. 44.

69. J. Kendall, Third Sector European Policy: organisations between market and state, the policy process and the EU. TSEP Working Paper 1 (London: The Centre for Civil Society, London School of Economics and Political Science, 2005).

70. As reported in GHK, *Social Enterprise: An International Literature Review*, a report submitted to SBS/SEnU (March 2006), p. 7.

71. Ibid.

72. Ibid.

73. *Study on Practices and Policies in the Social Enterprise Sector in Europe: Final Report* (Vienna: Austrian Institute for SME Research and TSE Entre, Turku School of Economics, Finland, June 2007), pp. 20–22. This study was conducted on behalf of the European Commission, DG Enterprise & Industry.

74. M. Alaitru and E. Drábková, *Social economy in France*, p. 27, from www.thelearningnetwork.net/ Downloads/.../SocialEconomyinFrance (accessed 12 November 2012).

75. KPMG Consulting and EIM Small Business Research and Consultancy, *The European Observatory for SMEs, Sixth Report Executive Summary* (Zoetermeer, the Netherlands: EIM, 1999), p. 14.

76. The DIES is the French Interdepartmental Delegation for Social Innovation and the Social Economy. Established in 1981, it serves to create a favourable policy environment for the associative sector.

77. KPMG Consulting and EIM Small Business Research and Consultancy, *The European Observatory for SMEs, Sixth Report Executive Summary* (Zoetermeer, the Netherlands: EIM, 1999), p. 14.

78. GHK, *Social Enterprise: An International Literature Review*, a report submitted to SBS/SEnU (London: GHK, 2006), p. 62.

79. C. Gunn, *Third Sector Development: Making up for the Market* (New York: Cornell University, 2004), pp. viii, 2.

80. J. A. Kerlin, 'Social Enterprise in the United States and Europe: Understanding and Learning from the Differences', *Voluntas*, Vol. 7, No. 3 (2006), p. 248.

81. https://www.se-alliance.org/ why#whatsasocialenterprise (accessed 17 November 2012).

82. Ibid.

83. P. Lloyd, 'Rethinking the Social Economy'. A paper based on a Forum sponsored by the Belfast Local Strategy Partnership and The Queen's University of Belfast (January 2006), pp. 7, 8.

84. J. A. Kerlin, 'Social Enterprise in the United States and Europe: Understanding and Learning from the Differences', *Voluntas*, Vol. 17, No. 3 (2006), pp. 254–5.

85. J. Defourny and M. Nyssens, 'Conceptions of Social Enterprise and Social Entrepreneurship in Europe and the United States: Convergences and Divergences', *Journal of Social Entrepreneurship*, Vol. 1, No. 1 (March 2010, pp. 32–53), p. 38.

86. http://www.whitehouse.gov/blog/2010/02/17/ introducing-social-innovation-fund (accessed 6 December 2012).

87. Based on GHK, *Review of the Social Enterprise Strategy*, a final report submitted to SBS/SEnU (London: GHK, 2005).

10

the impact of the social economy

contents:

Key concepts

This chapter covers:

- the range of benefits the social economy might deliver;
- how those benefits might be measured;
- some indications of the scale of the social economy;
- some of the issues associated with evaluations of government promotion of the social economy, and some of their findings.

Learning objectives

By the end of this chapter the reader should:

- understand the variety of impacts attributed to the social economy;
- be aware of some methods suggested for auditing the impact of social economy organisations;
- appreciate the indicated scale of the social economy;
- understand some of the issues involved in evaluations of government efforts to promote the social economy, and some possible limitations of their findings.

Introduction

As Chapter 1 indicates, some economic textbooks, even modern ones, still give the impression that there are only two significant sectors in a mixed economy: the private sector and the public sector. Yet, as Chapter 2 shows, for as long as there have been distinct private and public sectors, there has also been a third sector, which, as noted in Chapter 1, is sometimes seen as synonymous with the social economy and sometimes has a wider meaning.

Attempts have been made, under the so-called communist systems, to produce a society in which all activity was public sector activity, done through or by the state, but these have not lasted. 'Market' economies with private sectors, in some form or other, have proved to be more efficient at co-ordinating many aspects of human endeavour than single-sector 'command' economies. Indeed, communist societies still had private sector activity, although it might have been illegal, or at least unofficial, and they still had some third sector activity carried out neither by the state nor purely for personal gain. At the other extreme, even the most capitalistic of societies have had third sector activity in their economies.

Third sector or social economy activity, however defined, is clearly old and it clearly endures, but why? Why do we seem to need it and why do people engage in it? What impact does it have and what benefits does it deliver? Does it deliver the benefits that are claimed of it and does it justify the variety of support provided for it? To try to answer such questions, this chapter considers some of the things that social economy organisations are at least reported to do and considers how they might be 'audited' to assess their contribution. It also considers what is sometimes expected of the sector from its governmental supporters, how such support programmes might be evaluated, and what is known about their impact.

Benefits

What does the third sector deliver?

Asking what the third sector delivers is a bit like asking what the public sector delivers: it depends on both where the question is being put and who is being asked to respond. That is because the relative strengths of different parts of the sector differ from country to country and, within countries, can differ from region to region. It is also because different people have different views on what the sector and its components can, or should, do. Nevertheless, the list below attempts to indicate the wide range of things that have, at one time, or in one place, or another, been attributed to the this sector or to one of its components.

The list is not exhaustive and some of the things listed address more than one of the impact areas under which they are categorised. For instance, the creation of jobs has both an economic and a social benefit but, to avoid a very long list, is only listed under one of them. Also, if the whole is considered to be more than the sum of its parts, such a list might be considered to be an unwarranted disaggregation of the sector. The format of the list, however, is not intended to suggest that the sector can be split into separate impacts but that the totality of its impact can be considered to have aspects of all the things listed (see Illustration 10.1).

Illustration 10.1 The contribution of social enterprise

A View from the Social Enterprise Coalition (now Social Enterprise UK)

Social enterprises are dynamic businesses with a social purpose, working all around the UK and internationally to deliver lasting social and environmental change. They operate across an incredibly wide range of industries and sectors, from childcare and social housing to fair trade and farmers' markets.

The social enterprise sector is extremely diverse, encompassing co-operatives, development trusts, community enterprises, housing associations, football supporters' trusts, social firms, and leisure trusts, among others.

As innovators, social enterprises are often at the leading edge, pioneering groundbreaking ways of doing business and meeting new challenges. Their added value comes from the engagement of stakeholders and the way in which profit is used to maximise social and environmental benefits.

Social enterprise offers the government a range of solutions to meet its goals – whether on sustainable economic development or on public service reform.

A business model

Social enterprise is a distinct way of doing business that seeks to meet social and environmental needs rather than maximising shareholder value. It has a role in creating wealth and employment and in enhancing choice and diversity in a more plural, resilient, and sustainable economy.

Thriving communities

Social enterprises are able to harness the power of local communities – catalysing regeneration and promoting active citizenship. Development trusts have pioneered sustainable approaches to development, and an increasing number of housing associations are taking an enterprising approach. Housing co-operatives have a proven track record in community empowerment and cost-effective property management, and in rural areas community-owned shops and pubs are vital to locking in long-term prosperity.

An essential element of many of these approaches is community ownership of buildings and land. It can transform even the most struggling community – energising local people and providing the long-term foundation for enterprise and renewal. By locking in land value, community ownership can support the development of mixed-income housing, vital local services, and public space, enabling community involvement in local planning decisions and preventing people and businesses being priced out of an area.

Public services

There is an ongoing debate around increasing choice through diversity of provision and how to make services more centred on the needs of the individual and local communities. So far the discussion has mostly been split between improving direct provision by the state through additional resources and targets, and the introduction of private companies who can bring market-based efficiencies. What has been largely missing from this debate is the role that social enterprise can play in providing quality services that are truly value for money.

By combining the entrepreneurial drive of a business approach with a public service ethos, social enterprise brings together the best of the public and private sectors. The debate around choice needs to focus on social enterprise as a practical new way to deliver public services.

Within a number of key areas – for example childcare, social care, and health – there is the potential for social enterprises to play a bigger and more strategic role delivering public services. They are certainly not the only solutions social enterprise has to offer, but they represent areas where a fresh look at service delivery could reap real rewards.

Education and entrepreneurship

Entrepreneurship is a set of life skills such as self-confidence, self-reliance, and the ability to bring resources together to innovate and create change. Enterprise teaching in schools must be about developing these skills rather than a narrow focus on 'teaching business', and should incorporate social entrepreneurship and social enterprise into the mainstream enterprise curriculum.

Incentives to work

Many social enterprises, for example social firms (businesses set up specifically to create employment for disabled people), help disadvantaged groups into meaningful work.

Other social enterprises, particularly those in disadvantaged areas, are set up by people on benefits as a way of creating community benefit and employment. However, in many instances, 'traps' within the benefits system, particularly for those receiving incapacity benefits, actively discourage people from entering employment or from donating their time voluntarily in order to set up a social enterprise.

Research shows that people with a financial cushion are more likely to apply for a job in contrast to those living from week to week. Therefore, a benefit system that works in favour of those who choose to move towards employment is a vital component of any attempt to increase levels of employment among disadvantaged and marginalised groups.

Source: Based on Social Enterprise Coalition, 'There's more to business: A manifesto for social enterprise', www.socialenterprise.org.uk (accessed 15 October 2007)

Within the third sector, there are organisations which have:

- An *economic impact*, through
  - producing goods and services;
  - fostering enterprise and competitiveness;
  - creating employment, often focusing particularly on the socially excluded;
  - training people and assisting them into employment;
  - facilitating economic/social development by providing grants (e.g. from foundations) and low-cost loans (e.g. from credit unions).
- A *social impact*, through
  - supplementing the public sector social services and addressing welfare state problems by, for instance, providing affordable childcare, domiciliary care, and day care;

- fostering innovations in services and often playing a pathfinder role in the introduction of new or improved services later taken up by the public sector;
  - providing an alternative social service business model;
  - aiding regeneration by reaching areas and people other initiatives cannot or do not reach;
  - fostering social inclusion and social cohesion and the building of social capital;
  - enhancing civic involvement through the use of volunteers.

- A *local impact*, through

  - contributing to enterprise in areas with low levels of private entrepreneurship;
  - creating and managing workspace;
  - facilitating community ownership of land, buildings, and other resources, putting them to community use;
  - providing local facilities, such as shops and pubs for remote communities;
  - reusing old buildings and thus preserving parts of local history which might otherwise be redeveloped;
  - providing local public amenity space.

- An *environmental, cultural, artistic, or sporting impact*, through

  - promoting and practising environmental sustainability;
  - operating recycling schemes when there is not enough financial return for the private sector;
  - facilitating artistic activity;
  - facilitating sports activity.

- An *educational impact*, through

  - providing mainstream education in third sector schools and colleges;
  - complementing traditional approaches and subjects (e.g. Young Enterprise).

- A *political impact*, through

  - advocating, or helping to deliver, a fairer society, democratic participation, and involved citizenship;
  - facilitating greater stakeholder engagement and pluralism (see Illustration 10.2);
  - providing an alternative economic approach and showing that business does not have to be solely concerned with profit maximisation and personal enrichment;
  - providing a counterculture (or a way of reintroducing socialism?);
  - providing an alternative paradigm. (Do some people seek the support of the third sector in their aspirations to reduce the power of either the private or the public sector?)

- A *moral and ethical impact*, through

  - promoting religion and spirituality, a more caring society, and/or the development of a set of moral and/or ethical values;
  - enhancing the philosophy of giving in society as opposed to receiving.

- A *personal impact*, through

  - helping their founders and operators to achieve personal goals and to 'self-actualise'.

Illustration 10.2 Community bodies 'are more engaging'

An evaluation of the Northern Rock Foundation's Money and Jobs grant programme said that disadvantaged people involved in the programme are getting richer 'both financially and in terms of personal wellbeing'. It also said that community-based organisations are 'in general, better at this engagement than statutory agencies and therefore make a distinct and valuable contribution to social and economic provision, including current government labour market policies'.

Source: Based on a report at www.thirdsector.co.uk (accessed 21 August 2007)

Audits of the social economy

Tools for measuring the impact of third sector enterprises are at an early stage of development and tend to be applicable mainly to social enterprises. Some tools are being developed and assessed – but they are not being used by many organisations. Also, there are many different aspects of impact to be measured which cannot easily be reduced to a single common dimension in the way that private sector returns may all be summarised in terms of money.

In many cases there is no legal requirement to produce and declare social accounts. An exception in the UK is the case of Community Interest Companies (CICs) (see Illustration 6.2), which must file an annual CIC report with their accounts to show that they are still satisfying the Community Interest Test. Otherwise, all that is available are the relatively few voluntarily published social reports and/or accounts, and even these have not been consistently reviewed and summarised. Furthermore, many of them are not produced by social enterprises but by private sector businesses to fulfil a commitment to demonstrate corporate social responsibility.

Other researchers have also found little quantitative data and have relied instead on anecdotal evidence. For instance, under the heading 'evidence for impact', Smallbone et al., in their 2001 report on researching social enterprise, referred to case studies, not statistics:

> Part of the case for encouraging and supporting social enterprises is based on their wider social contribution which can include helping to reduce social exclusion, encouraging environmentally friendly practices, contributing to community regeneration and offering work and educational experiences to young people. This can be illustrated with *selected examples* drawn from our enterprise case studies. [1] (emphasis added)

Despite this lack of information, there are a number of brochures and other documents produced for or about the social economy by bodies wishing to advance its interests. These, however, are often designed to promote the sector, rather than to evaluate it, and as a result sometimes appear to be subjective in their assessment.

Benefit audits

Chapter 6, in the section entitled 'Measures of success', looked at some of the methods by which individual social enterprises, and other social economy organisations, can try to measure their success. Some of those methods have been referred to as social auditing but, unlike financial auditing, they often cover the initial accounting for success, rather than the subsequent verification of that accounting, which is the role of the financial auditing function.

Those measures of success are often like the financial accounts of a business in that they assess what the organisation has delivered rather than its value as an investment. There are, though, some techniques which do look at this additional dimension of what an organisation's backers might have got in return for the resources which they invested. An example is Social Return on Investment (SROI), which was pioneered in the 1990s by the Roberts Enterprise Development Fund, a San Francisco-based venture philanthropy fund, as a means to illustrate the value generated through an investment in its programmes.[2] It has been taken up by the new economics foundation (nef), based in London, which describes SROI as an innovative approach which 'places stakeholders – the people that matter – at the heart of the measurement process' and:

> shows how social and environmental outcomes translate into tangible monetary value, helping organisations and investors of all kinds to see a fuller picture of the benefits that flow from their investment of time, money and other resources. This investment can then be seen in terms of the 'return' or the value created for individual, communities, society or the environment.[3]

The approach of nef involves assessing the net present value of the benefits produced, allowing for the 'deadweight' of what would have happened anyway, and looking at the ratio between that net present value and the net present value of the investment used to create it. As nef's guide says, 'those who invest in an organisation can learn more about how their input directly contributes to social value creation'.[4] This is, however, a relatively recent development, and, while the nef guide includes a case study of SROI application, it does not yet appear to have been widely used and there is no compilation of audits using it upon which a wider assessment of the overall value created by the sector might be based.

The scale of the social economy

One overall aspect of the social economy relevant to the amount of benefit it delivers, and for which some assessment attempts have been made, is its composition and size. However, current national accounting rules in the EU 'do not acknowledge the SE as a differentiated institutional sector, making it difficult to draw up regular, accurate and reliable economic statistics on the agents of which it is composed. Internationally, the heterogeneous criteria employed in drawing up statistics prevent comparative analyses.'[5]

Earlier chapters have on occasion given some indications of its scale in particular countries, or of the scale of some of its components. What follows is a wider collection of statistics, almost all about the social economy, from different parts of the world. Indeed, the UK example serves to illustrate how difficult it is to get reliable figures as it shows significant differences between the figures reported by different government sources for the same year, and over different years. Moreover, while Lyon et al. argue that the UK is 'relatively unique in terms of the amount of investment by the government in measuring and mapping social enterprise', they assert that 'this investment has been in diverse and uncoordinated approaches which have led to an element of confusion rather than clarity'.[6] A brief review of Lyon et al.'s analysis is given below.

UK

Attempts to assess and compare the scale of the social economy are generally based on efforts to identify and measure its component social enterprises. However, a problem in assessing the population of social enterprises, as noted, arises from the variety of different research approaches used to measure and map them. According to Lyon et al., each study 'has taken a different approach, using different definitions and different sampling frames in order to examine slightly different elements'.[7]

Kendall, in his book on the voluntary sector, included an assessment that in 1995 there were nearly 1.5 million full-time equivalent employees in the UK's 'Broad Nonprofit Sector', and an additional 1.6 million full-time equivalent volunteers.[8] More recently, and on a narrower basis, the Small Business Service (SBS) in 2005 published *A Survey of Social Enterprises across the UK.*[9] This survey followed an earlier Department for Trade and Industry (DTI) exercise to assess the feasibility of mapping social enterprises, which concluded that while social enterprises may take a range of legal forms, companies limited by guarantee and industrial and provident societies were the most popular. Therefore the survey, instead of claiming to describe the total population of social enterprises, focused only on these two legal forms but excluded some on the basis that their Standard Industrial Classification meant that they were unlikely to include much social enterprise activity.

Despite its shortcomings, this survey was groundbreaking in its attempt to survey social enterprises across the UK and appeared to be the most complete survey at that time. Among its findings were the following:

- There were around 15,000 social enterprises in the UK registered as companies limited by guarantee or as industrial and provident societies.
- In terms of the overall business population that meant that social enterprises accounted for 1.2 per cent of all enterprises with employees in the UK.
- The annual turnover of these social enterprises was just under £18 billion approximately, which was just under 1 per cent of the turnover of all UK businesses.
- These social enterprises employed 475,000 people, of whom two-thirds were employed full-time. A further 300,000 people worked for the social enterprises on a volunteer basis.
- The typical social enterprise employed 10 people. Almost half (49 per cent) employed fewer than 10, 38 per cent employed between 10 and 49, 11 per cent between 50 and 249, and 2 per cent employed 250 or more.

Nevertheless, in 2006, the UK government's social enterprise action plan stated that there were an estimated 55,000 social enterprises across the country and that they had an annual turnover of more than £27 billion and contributed more than £8 billion a year to GDP.[10] These figures were repeated in the UK government's 2007[11] report setting out its vision for the third sector, which added that the estimate that there were 55,000 social enterprises was for the year 2005 and that they had accounted for around 5 per cent of all businesses with employees at that time. It added that there were also hundreds of thousands of small community groups.

These figures are based upon the Annual Small Business Survey (ASBS) 2005–2007, which used of a sample of SME businesses with and without employees and found that 5 per cent of them defined themselves as social enterprises. Lyon et al. claim that it is the most quoted source of information on social enterprise in the UK, 'being found in political documents and speeches of politicians of all parties as well as a range of lobbying organisations, and academic publications'.[12] Based on a 3-year rolling average, the number rose in 2009 to '62,000 social enterprises . . . contributing £24 billion to UK output'.[13] However, in a 2009 assessment, the National Survey of Third Sector Organisations (NSTSO) used a narrower definition of social enterprises as organisations that derive more than 50 per cent of the income from trading and self-define as social enterprise – excluding organisations with a private sector legal structure. This assessment suggested that there were 16,000 social enterprises in the UK. Using the definition of social enterprise employed in that study, it is estimated that in those enterprises there were 'at least 227,000 employees and a turnover of at least £8.5 billion'.[14]

Other studies have produced yet different figures based on varying definitions and databases.[15] Figure 10.1 is Lyon et al.'s interpretation of how particular surveys can be combined to provide different figures corresponding to the definitions of social enterprise selected. Table 10.1 is a summary of the results of some of the major UK surveys undertaken, revealing widely different estimates.

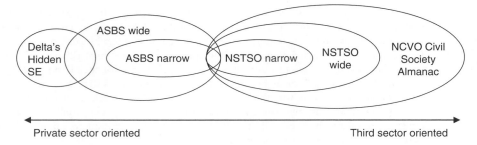

Figure 10.1 The overlapping data sources on social enterprise
Source: F. Lyon, S. Teasdale and R. Baldock, 'Approaches to measuring the scale of the social enterprise sector in the UK', Third Sector Research Centre, Working Paper 43 (Birmingham: University of Birmingham, 2010), p. 17

Table 10.1 Data sources presenting information on the scale of social enterprise

Data source	Description	Sample details	No. of orgs (000s)	T/O (£bns)	Employees (000s)	Comments
IFF 2005	>25% income from trading and self defining	Only companies limited by guarantee (CLG) and industial and provident societies (IPS)	15	18	475	
ASBS narrow	SE with employees	Dominated by private, under representing TS	70	15.5	248	Only 8,000 in a third sector legal form
ASBS wide	All enterprises meeting SE tests	As above	234	23.6	410	Only 10,000 in TS legal form
NSTSO narrow	>50% income from trading and self defining	Third sector only	16	8.5	227	
NSTSO wide	>50% income from trading but not self defining	As above	21	10.7	272	
NCVO	SE activity	All civil society		77		
Delta	Businesses wanting to make a difference	Private, less than 2 years old with >£200K income	232	97		Not self defining

Source: F. Lyon, S. Teasdale and R. Baldock, 'Approaches to measuring the scale of the social enterprise sector in the UK', Third Sector Research Centre, Working Paper 43 (Birmingham: University of Birmingham, 2010), p. 18

However, previous estimates are questioned by Ridley-Duff and Bull, who draw attention to work by the EU Commission to define and study the European social economy.[16] The figures in Table 10.2 use the EU definition of social economy and indicate that the annual contribution of social enterprises to the UK economy is about 5 times greater, at £112

Table 10.2 The 'mutual'* sector in 2011

Sector	Number	Members	Jobs	Revenue
Building Societies	52	25,000,000	42,000	£3,700.000.000
Co-operatives	3339	10,290,000	159,000	£24,230,000,000
Co-operative Trust Schools	159	–	–	0
Craft Unions	424	808,700	980	£39,000,000
Clubs and Societies	11,600	7,000,000	20,000	£463,000,000
Employee Owned Businesses	250	–	130,000	£30,000,000,000
Football/Rugby Supporter Trusts	170	270,000	214	£11,000,000
GP Co-ops and Mutuals	34	–	7,500	£120,000,000
Housing Associations	1694	6,727,000	170,410	£14,039,000,000
Leisure Trusts	101	–	21,400	£739,000,000
Mutual Insurers and Friendly Societies	56	8,500,000	17,200	£7,800,000,000
NHS Foundation Trusts	136	1,900,000	481,060	£30,700,000,000
TOTAL	**18,015**	**60,495,700**	**1,048,764**	**£111,841,000,000**

*In the sense used in the *Mutuals Yearbook*

Source: Kellogg College, Oxford University, *Mutuals Yearbook 2011* (Borehamwood: Mutuo c/o Westminster Bridge Partnership Ltd, 2011), p. 6

billion in 2011, than some earlier estimates and those enterprises employ in excess of 1 million people. (This estimate includes the contribution of all co-operatives, mutuals, and associations that produce goods or services to improve human well-being – all of which are labelled 'mutuals' by this source.)

Other statistics available[17] suggest that:

- The vast majority (89 per cent) of social enterprises are located in urban areas. A fifth alone are in London.
- Most UK social enterprises operate in the health and social care sector (around 33 per cent). This is mostly related to day care, childcare, welfare and guidance, as well as accommodation services.
- Social enterprises also commonly derive their main income from 'community or social services' (21 per cent) and property (20 per cent). A much smaller percentage of social enterprises trade in the educational sector (15 per cent) or wholesale and retail (3 per cent).
- However, a big growth area for trading social enterprises has been the rising popularity of Fairtrade products – the biggest example of which is the coffee company Cafédirect.
- There are now more than 3400 Fairtrade retail and catering products available and the industry as a whole grew by 81 per cent between 2006 and 2007. UK sales now equate to an annual half a billion pounds.

It is also reported[18] that, in England and Wales, at the end of 2006 there were 168,000 registered charities (and an estimated 110,000 unregistered charities) and 567 registered credit unions, while at the end of 2005 there were over 8100 registered industrial and provident societies.

Recent figures from National Council for Voluntary Organisations (NCVO) indicate that on its definition of 'civil society', there are an estimated 2 million people who are paid staff and 'this is equivalent to 7% of the total UK workforce and is larger than the NHS workforce (1.4 million people, the UK's single largest employer [*sic*]. When compared to an industry sector, it is clear that civil society organisations are major employers – employing as many people as the construction sector (2.0 million). Voluntary organisations employ 765,000 people and account for more than one-third (37%) of the civil society workforce – thus making them the largest category employer within civil society'[19] (see Table 10.4). A breakdown of paid staff is shown in Table 10.3 (which includes all those in mutuals (see Table 10.2), the voluntary sector, and other civil society organisations).

Some additional statistics presented by the same body, NCVO, are shown in Table 10.4.

Table 10.3 Paid staff by type of civil society organisation, UK, 2009–2010

General Charities	765,000
Universities	387,400
Housing Associations	170,400
Cooperatives	159,000
Sports Clubs	143,500
Employee-owned businesses	130,000
Other	285,700
Total	**2,041,000**

Source: http://data.ncvo-vol.org.uk/almanac/about-the-almanac/fast-facts/ (accessed 1 January 2013)

Table 10.4 NCVO's civil society statistics

	2009/10
Civil society	
Number of organisations	900,000
Total income	£170 billion
Civil society paid workforce (headcount)	2.0 million
Voluntary organisations	**2009/10**
Number of voluntary organisations	163,763
Total income	£36.7 billion
Voluntary income	£14.1 billion
Earned income	£20.1 billion
Investment income	£2.4 billion
Income from individuals	£14.3 billion
Income from statutory sources	£13.9 billion
Income from National Lottery distributors	£0.5 billion
Income from other sources	£8.0 billion
Total current expenditure	£36.3 billion
Expenditure on charitable activities (excluding grants)	£26.5 billion
Expenditure on grants	£4.6 billion
Expenditure on generating funds	£4.1 billion
Expenditure on governance	£1.0 billion
Net assets	£90.2 billion

Giving		2010/11
Mean amount donated per person in last four weeks		£31
Proportion giving to charity	Men	56%
	Women	61%
Workforce		**2010**
UK voluntary sector paid workforce (headcount)		765,000
Employment status	Full-time	477,000 (62%)
	Part-time	288,000 (38%)
Gender	Female	522,000 (68%)
	Male	244,000 (32%)
Volunteering		**2010/11**
Proportion of people formally volunteering	at least once a month	25%
	at least once a year	39%

Source: http://data.ncvo-vol.org.uk/almanac/about-the-almanac/fast-facts/ (accessed 12 January 2013)

Europe

Illustration 10.3 CMAFs in Europe

According to Social Economy Europe (formerly the European Standing Conference of Cooperatives, Mutual Societies, Associations and Foundations: CEP-CMAF), the social economy represents 10 per cent of all European businesses, which means 2 million businesses employing more than 20 million workers.

For example:

- the mutual health funds provide social coverage to more than 150 million people in Europe;
- the cooperatives represented in Cooperatives Europe comprise 250,000 cooperative enterprises, 163 million members and 5.4 million jobs;
- associations form a network of over 50,000 associations and 9 million members;
- foundations from over 30 countries in Europe have assets totalling some 111 billion Euro.

Source: www.socialeconomy.eu.org (accessed 20 April 2013)

The European Commission estimated in 2010 that

> social economy enterprises represent 2 million enterprises (i.e. 10 per cent of all European businesses) and employ over 11 million paid employees (the equivalent of 6 per cent of the working population of the EU). Out of these, 70 per cent are employed in non-profit associations, 26 per cent in cooperatives and 3 per cent in mutuals. Social economy enterprises are present in almost every sector of the economy, such as banking, insurance, agriculture, craft, various commercial services, and health and social services etc. [20]

The International Centre of Research and Information on the Public, Social and Cooperative Economy (CIRIEC), on the other hand, while recognising the difficulties in arriving at accurate figures, stated that for the 2009/2010 period

> the social economy in Europe has over 14.5 million paid employees, equivalent to about 6.5 per cent of the working population of the EU-27 and about 7.4 per cent in the 15 'older' European Union Member States [and see also Illustration 10.3, which

has a different estimate of the number of people employed]. In countries such as Sweden, Belgium, Italy, France and the Netherlands it accounts for between 9 per cent and 11.5 per cent of the working population.[21]

It further adds that it 'increased more than proportionately between 2002–03 and 2009–10, increasing from 6 per cent to 6.5 per cent of total European paid employment and from 11 million to 14.5 million jobs',[22] diverging significantly from the commission's figures above.

CIRIEC also reported that for the 27 countries of the EU

over 207,000 cooperatives were economically active in 2009. They are well-established in every area of economic activity and are particularly prominent in agriculture, financial intermediation, retailing and housing and as workers' cooperatives in the industrial, building and service sectors . . . provide direct employment to 4.7 million people and have 108 million members. Health and social welfare mutuals provide assistance and cover to over 120 million people. Insurance mutuals have a 24% market share and further, 'associations employed 8.6 million people in 2010; they account for over 4% of GDP and their membership comprises 50 per cent of the citizens of the European Union.'[23]

France

In 2009, it was estimated[24] that in France:

- The social economy employs some 9 per cent of the workforce.
- There are some 160,000 associations. They employ 1.9 million people, which is 7 per cent of the working population. Half the jobs are in the health and care sector.
- The 8500 non-financial co-operatives have 3 million members and employ some 155,000 people. This includes the 1500 workers' co-operatives employing 25,000 people. The four co-operative banks employ a further 165,000 people.
- The health mutuals number over 5000 and employ some 83,000 people. Insurance mutuals number over 1800 and employ 45,000 people.
- There are 1200 foundations which employ 66,000 people.

These statistics, which are based on CIRIEC's sources, show considerable divergence from those produced by GHK[25] in 2005 such that the reliability of either's estimates must be questioned.

Spain

In 2013, it is estimated that in Spain the social economy represents 10 per cent of the GDP and includes 51,500 enterprises and organisations, which means a total of 2.5 million jobs. More than 10,700,000 people are linked to the social economy.[26]

US

The third sector was reported in 2012 to be the fastest-growing part of the US economy. While, since 2008, 'the overall number of employees in the US economy has been declining, employment in the non-profit sector continued to increase throughout the recession. In fact, the non-profit sector grew faster – in terms of employees and wages – than business or government'.[27] Non-profits accounted for '9.2 per cent of all wages and salaries paid in the US and the non-profit share of GDP was 5.5 per cent in 2010'.[28]

It was estimated that there were 2.3 million non-profit organisations in 2012, of which 1.6 million were registered with the Internal Revenue Service (IRS) of the US – equating to approximately one non-profit for every 200 citizens. The number of 'non-profit' organ-isations and the changes in those numbers over the 10 years to 2009 are shown in Table 10.5. In aggregate, the number of such organisations has increased by over 30 per cent in the period.

Canada

Because of its long tradition of relying on non-profit and voluntary organisations to address the needs and interests of its population, Canada has one of the largest and most vibrant social economy sectors in the world. Interest in it has increased in the past 10 years (although for considerably longer in Quebec), as demonstrated in the 2004 federal

Table 10.5 Number of non-profit organisations in the United States, 1999–2009

	1999		2009		
	Number of Orgs.	**Per Cent of All Orgs.**	**Number of Orgs.**	**Per Cent of All Orgs.**	**Per Cent Change**
All Non-profit Organisations	1,202,573	100.0	1,581,111	100.0	31.5
Public charities	631,902	52.5	1,006,670	63.7	59.3
Private foundations	77,978	6.5	120,617	7.6	54.7
Non-profit organisations	492,693	41.0	453,824	28.7	−7.9
Small community groups and partnerships, etc.	Unknown	NA	Unknown	NA	NA
Public Charities	631,902	52.5	1,006,670	63.7	59.3
Public charities registered with the IRS (including registered congregations)	631,902	52.5	1,006,670	63.7	59.3
Reporting public charities	246,733	20.5	315,662	20.0	27.9
Operating public charities	214,344	17.8	275,984	17.5	28.8
Supporting public charities	32,389	2.7	39,678	2.5	22.5
Non-reporting, or with less than $25,000 in gross receipts	385,169	32.0	691,008	43.7	79.4
Private Foundations	77,978	6.5	120,617	7.6	54.7
Private grant-making (non-operating) foundations	74,891	6.2	115,249	7.3	53.9
Private operating foundations	3,087	0.3	5,368	0.3	73.9
Non-profit Organisations	492,693	41.0	453,824	28.7	−7.9
Civic leagues, social welfare orgs, etc.	124,774	10.4	111,849	7.1	−10.4
Fraternal beneficiary societies	103,725	8.6	77,811	4.9	−25.0
Business leagues, chambers of commerce, etc.	70,718	5.9	72,801	4.6	2.9
Labour, agricultural, horticultural orgs	60,530	5.0	56,292	3.6	−7.0
Social and recreational clubs	56,429	4.7	57,255	3.6	1.5
Post or organisation of war veterans	34,608	2.9	34,593	2.2	−0.0
All other non-profit organisations	41,909	3.5	43,223	2.7	3.1

Source: Based on http://nccsdataweb.urban.org/PubApps/profile1.php?state=US (accessed 5 December 2012)

budget, which announced that social economy enterprises 'would be provided with access to existing small business programmes, along with new funding for financing and strategic planning and capacity building by community economic development organizations'.[29] In addition, the post of Parliamentary Secretary to the Minister of Social Development with a special emphasis on the social economy was created.

It was reported[30] in 2005 that non-profit and voluntary organisations accounted for 6.8 per cent of gross domestic product (GDP) (or 4.0 per cent ignoring hospitals, universities, and colleges). When the value of volunteer work is incorporated, they contributed 8.5 per cent of GDP. They employed 12 per cent of Canada's economically active population (or 9 per cent excluding the one-third of paid employees working for hospitals, universities, and colleges). The entire non-profit and voluntary sector engages nearly as many full-time equivalent workers as all branches of manufacturing in the country.

A further source[31] from 2005 showed that the social economy accounted for about 2.6 per cent of the total Canadian economy, which was larger than the contribution of aerospace (0.6 per cent), mining (1.0 per cent), or the pulp and paper industries (1.3 per cent) and about the same size as that of oil and gas extraction (2.5 per cent) (see Table 10.6).

Evaluations

Audit techniques, such as SROI (see Chapter 6), try to indicate to 'investors' in the social economy what social or other benefits those organisations have delivered as a result of their investments. Among the most significant contributors to the social economy have been governments, and their interest in the sector and their methods of involvement are described in Chapter 9. Governments, however, have generally sought to promote not just individual organisations but the overall sector, or at least sub-sectors within it such as social enterprises. Further, while governments might be pleased to see the general benefits which the sector delivers, they have usually contributed in order to achieve specific objectives such as the delivery of certain services or increases in employment in disadvantaged areas.

Audit techniques designed to identify the range of benefits delivered by individual organisations are not then particularly helpful to governments promoting an overall sector

Table 10.6 Some figures for the Canadian Economy

Sector:	Private Sector	Social Economy			Public Sector	
Organisation type:	For-profit business	Common interest SEEs	Public service SEEs	Other NGOs	Near government organisations	Government organisations
Number of Employees:	2 million, plus volunteers, in 2003					
		155 389 in 2004	740 000 in 1999			821 000 in 2004
Share of GDP:			2.5% in 1999, excluding volunteers		4.3% in 1999, excluding volunteers	
	87.4% in 1999			0.9% in 1999		5.8% in 1999

Source: Policy Research Initiative, *What We Need to Know About the Social Economy: A Guide for Policy Research*, http://www.envision.ca/pdf/SocialEconomy/ResearchGuide.pdf (Ottawa: Canadian government, 2005), p. 4

in order to achieve specific benefits. It is not just a question of whether governments get a social return on their investments, but whether, if there is a return, it is the return they wanted, and whether it is an adequate return for the investment of public money. They carry out evaluations at times, therefore, to indicate what they get for their money.

Issues around evaluation methodology

Evaluations are carried out to assess such initiatives to see what they have achieved and/or how they might be improved. Evaluations are not an easy or an exact science, however, if indeed they are a science and not an art.

Evaluation has been defined as 'the retrospective analysis of a project, programme, or policy to assess how successful or otherwise it has been, and what lessons can be learnt for the future'.[32] This definition indicates two aspects of evaluations: the assessment of success or otherwise, which looks primarily at the impact of a project, programme, or policy; and the lessons to be learnt, for instance to improve the delivery of a project, programme, or policy, which will look primarily at their processes. These two aspects of evaluations have also been described in the following ways:

1. *Improving and proving.* Evaluation, it has been said, has two primary aims:
   - an *improving* and *learning* aim to provide information that will help those involved to learn and so improve the design, operation, and outcomes of policy initiatives;
   - a *proving* aim to examine what difference the policy initiative has made to the individuals or firms or to the wider economic and social parameters it seeks to influence.[33]

2. *Formative and summative.* Formative evaluation is undertaken to provide information that will be used to improve a programme; summative evaluation is evaluation used to form a summary judgement about how a programme operated.[34] Overall, it is the impact, proving, and summative aspect of evaluations which indicates if programmes are achieving their purposes. However, conducting such evaluations is not easy:
   - Assessing whether a programme achieved its purposes is only possible where that purpose has been clearly stated and clear impact targets have been specified.
   - While the process of delivering a programme can be observed as it happens, it can then take some time before the subsequent impact will become apparent. Despite this, for reasons such as a requirement to justify further funding or because they have to be paid for in a limited budget period, there is often an incentive to commission evaluations before sufficient impact time has elapsed.
   - Assessing the real impact of a programme requires an understanding of what is going on and insight into the nature of the relevant cause and effect.

Other reasons why evaluations of public sector programmes might not be available or reliable have been indicated by Curran, who suggested that, at least in the field of small business policy, evaluations have been of two main kinds:

- evaluations sponsored by government funding departments and/or agencies delivering the policy, conducted by private sector for-profit bodies. Most small business support evaluation in the UK is probably of this type and often the results never enter the public domain.
- evaluations by independent (usually academic) researchers on a not-for-profit basis, sponsored by other than those funding or delivering the initiative. The results are normally made public with the aim of promoting constructive discussion.

The distinction between the two, according to Curran, is important.

> The first kind is much more likely to be favourable to the policy or programme than the second kind. Where those conducting the evaluation are dependent on the initiator or deliverer for their fees and future similar work, there will be pressures to be less critical. This is less likely if evaluation is by researchers not reliant on policy makers or deliverers for their funding and the results are open to peer scrutiny. One result of such a poor record is that generally small business initiatives receive more favourable recognition for promoting small businesses, employment and economic performance than they merit. [35]

An official view on policy evaluation is given in Illustration 10.4.

Illustration 10.4 An official view on policy evaluation

Assessing the impact of a policy is usually done through a policy evaluation. The UK government's guide to appraisal and evaluation (the *Green Book*) describes evaluation as 'the retrospective analysis of a project, programme, or policy to assess how successful or otherwise it has been, and what lessons can be learnt for the future. The terms "policy evaluation" and "post-project evaluation" are often used to describe evaluation in those two areas.' [36]

Evaluation, according to the *Green Book*,

> examines the outturn of a project or policy. When carried out it adds value by providing lessons from experience to help future project management or development of a specific policy. It may also contribute to the quality of wider policy debate . . . The evaluation itself should normally follow this sequence:
>
> i. Establish exactly what is to be evaluated and how the past outturns can be measured.
> ii. Choose alternative states of the world and/or alternative management decisions as counterfactuals. (The decision on exactly what should be compared with what needs clear thinking . . . The outturn of any complex activity will never be exactly as projected in advance. However the reasons for the outturn being in some respects better or worse than expected may be attributable to the 'state of the world'. Or it may be attributable to actions under the control of the responsible body.)
> iii. Compare the outturn with the target outturn, and with the effects of the chosen alternative states of the world and/or management decisions.
> iv. Present the results and recommendations.
> v. Disseminate and use the results and recommendations. [37]

The core of an evaluation should be the extent of the net benefit, or *additionality*, attributable to the intervention in question. Implicit in the foregoing, however, are two concepts that are often ignored in evaluation studies: the *deadweight* and *displacement* effects. They have the effect of reducing the net benefit of interventions. *Multiplier* effects have the opposite effect. They enhance the benefits and should also be considered. *Effectiveness*, *efficiency*, and *economy* are measures of different aspects of the process.

Additionality. This is the measure of the net benefit: the benefit which accrued as a result of the measure, whether intended or not, which would not otherwise have accrued.

Deadweight. This is a measure of 'what would have happened anyway' without the measure. Because of deadweight, even the direct effects alone of intervention are often not easy to ascertain. It may be possible to show that an enterprise has received assistance and has subsequently improved, but to what extent is that improvement due to other factors and would have happened anyway, even had there been no intervention?

Displacement. This is a measure of 'how much of the gain in one area is offset by losses elsewhere'. It may be that an enterprise directly benefits from intervention and increases its employment as a result. However, if the employment in another enterprise is reduced because the first enterprise wins the contract, the total employment between the two may not increase and therefore overall there may be no benefit. The increase in activity in one merely displaces activity in another, albeit the quality of the jobs may change. While, superficially, more solid enterprises may appear to be beneficial, this is so only if there is net social or economic benefit as opposed to redistributing existing benefits. (In addition, the benefits of a measure should exceed the cost of the measure.)

Multiplier effects. There can be additional benefits from the indirect or side effects of intervention. If an increase in activity in a directly affected enterprise results in an increase in activity in another enterprise, for instance because it is a subcontractor, that is a beneficial *multiplier* effect, which increases the extent of the additionality.

Effectiveness, efficiency, and economy. This is a trio of measures concerned with value for money. *Effectiveness* is the extent to which an intervention achieved its aims; *efficiency* measures the amount of direct output that the inputs achieved; and *economy* is concerned with the cost of those inputs.

Source: Based on S. Bridge and K. O'Neill, *Understanding Enterprise, Entrepreneurship and Small Business* (Basingstoke: Palgrave Macmillan, 2013), ch. 16

What is expected of the social economy?

Evaluations of the social economy need to start therefore with some idea of what was expected of the project, programme, or policy being evaluated, which will in turn be linked to what is expected of the sector itself, or of its components. At least three approaches to this aspect of the social economy have been suggested in earlier chapters:

The paradigm approach

In Chapter 3, in the section 'Paradigm differences', it is suggested that there are three broad choices for what people might expect of the social economy and in particular of social enterprises:

- Two of these choices see it as a source of benefits such as jobs and welfare provision:
  - One of them, in an economic/entrepreneurship approach, sees social enterprises as 'businesses' that can assist community regeneration. It puts an emphasis on their financial sustainability.
  - The other is a socio-economic policy approach, which puts less emphasis on self-sufficiency and sees the sector as 'patching up' the inadequacies of the welfare state.
- A third approach is a political/ideological approach, which envisages a social economy sector significantly strong to lever institutional change and to promote more democratic structures and citizen participation in decision-making.

Therefore, if a judgement is to be made about the effectiveness/impact of the sector, it is important to be clear about what ambitions are set for it. For instance, each of the following options offers a different framework within which to assess the impact of the social economy:

- Is it an attempt to produce an 'alternative business model' – a better business as the UK government would describe it?
- Is it a temporary or cut-rate mechanism for plastering over weaknesses in the welfare state?
- Is it to produce an improved model for better integration of service delivery to those in need?

- Is it a 'whole society' approach which ultimately aims to create a new political-cultural landscape in which democratic participation, citizenship, trust, integrity, and respect are more fully embedded?

A policy framework approach

A policy framework by which to understand the related objectives, approaches, themes, rationale, instruments, and measures for the UK government's approach to the social economy is described in Chapter 9. This suggests that, in attempting to assess the impact of the social economy in an economy/society as a whole, whether driven by government or other support bodies, an evaluation might consider one or more of the following:

- the impact of the social economy on the ultimate objectives of a more successful economy or a fairer society;
- the social economy's contribution to political drivers such as generating social inclusion and cohesion, improving public services, and improving economic competitiveness;
- the extent to which the specified success measures, such as greater awareness of the sector, more and better social enterprises, and fewer barriers to growth, have been attained;
- the achievement of the sector in terms of the performance indicators for each of the policy instruments such as new legal forms, greater financial support, more success in its tendering for government contracts, or more, louder, and coherent voices speaking for the sector;
- any specific indicators specified in policy documents. For instance, the UK government has chosen to consider change in the number and quality of social enterprises, greater awareness of the sector, and evidence of fewer barriers to growth.

An expected benefits approach

A third approach to assessing the impact of the social economy is to benchmark its performance against what many of its advocates surmise as its particular benefits to an economy or society at large. These benefits are described in Chapter 1 and summarised in Chapter 9. They include:

- the provision of goods, services, and social benefits which the public sector does not adequately provide;
- the provision of jobs for people who might not otherwise be employed;
- the fostering of enterprise (and economic competitiveness);
- a means for addressing some problems of the welfare state;
- the creation and retention of social surplus;
- the promotion of environmental sustainability, or ethical operations;
- the creation of social capital and social cohesion;
- other development help;
- a mechanism for a counterculture;
- the ability to reach parts that other initiatives cannot reach, in particular in tackling disadvantage.

In terms of assessing the impact of the sector, however, the problem is also made more difficult because:

- Not all of the benefits suggested apply to all social economy organisations. A clear perception is needed of what each segment of the sector is expected to deliver.

- There is recognition that the social economy not only complements some public sector provision where it adds value, but also leads the way in other aspects of meeting the needs of disadvantaged people, and it goes where public provision may follow subsequently. Thus, it has a 'pathfinder' role, and, through the learning gained by an organisation's initiation of new service delivery, new or improved public provision may develop. So what may appear initially as experimental and offering little tangible benefits may be the forerunner of considerable societal gain. Indeed, the gains may often differ from those originally anticipated (making it sometimes inappropriate to assess impact only against a predetermined objective).
- There are, on the other hand, areas where the social economy displays innovation without expectation that the public sector should then seek to complement or replace its services. There is no suggestion, for example, that credit unions, local enterprise agencies, or ethical retailers should be the forerunners of state provision (albeit many lessons may be learned which could affect the nature of other public sector provision).

The results of evaluations: how effective is government promotion of the social economy?

Broadly speaking, the different approaches summarised above encompass the different reasons governments have for wanting to promote the social economy. Chapter 9 looked at the different ways in which governments have sought to promote, support, and encourage the social economy, but to what extent have they got a return for their efforts? It has been suggested that sometimes the subsequently declared targets for government programmes are based on 'anything they happen to hit', but, on other occasions, clear 'SMART'[38] objectives are specified for government-funded projects, and evaluations are then carried out to establish what happened.

What have such evaluations revealed about the effectiveness of government policy in addressing the objectives set for it? In considering the effectiveness of UK government policy, Table 10.7 provides a useful starting point as it identifies the UK government's own suggested indicators for judging the success of its policy interventions. The performance indicators suggested in Table 10.7 are not SMART as they are neither expressed quantitatively nor bound by timescales. Given the relative lack of knowledge of the sector's starting point, however, it might be argued that attempts at quantification would

Table 10.7 The government's progress report

Issue	Independent review finding
Size of the sector	Respondents reported growth of the sector
Awareness of social enterprise	Increasing awareness of social enterprise, including high-profile examples of successful social enterprises
Business improvement and development	Availability of appropriate support has increased, and new and better tools have been developed to support the sector
Improving profile and credibility of social enterprise	Significant improvement, particularly in social enterprises' profile among policy makers
Underpinning evidence	The volume and quality of data and information on the sector have increased – in particular through the Department of Trade and Industry's Survey of Social Enterprise in the UK

Source: Office of the Third Sector/Cabinet Office, *Social enterprise action plan: Scaling new heights* (London: Cabinet Office, 2006), p. 21

be inappropriate. Indeed, without previous experience of the efficacy of the interventions and instruments used, quantified outputs could be regarded as meaningless, if not foolish.

Of importance also in any form of evaluation of policy impact is the relationship between success measures/performance indicators and ultimate policy drivers and objectives. In the case of the UK, the policy seeks to achieve, through the social economy in part, a fairer and more prosperous society, although there are different perspectives as to how, and to what extent, the social economy can advance these objectives (see Illustration 10.6). Is it by making 'better businesses' in the sector which can offer a more cost-effective alternative to the welfare system? Or is it by creating a fully integrated private–third–public sector continuum with the potential to create a different kind of economic system, or is it something else? Those are different means, and evaluations will need to know which one to consider.

In the UK a comprehensive review of the government's social enterprise strategy over 2002–2005 was carried out in 2005 by a firm of consultants on behalf of the (then) DTI. The findings of that review were summarised in *Scaling New Heights*, from which Table 10.7 is derived.

The review report itself reveals a cautious assessment of the progress made and it draws a distinction between 'progress in achieving the outcomes of the social enterprise strategy' and 'the contribution of the social enterprise strategy to the progress made', recognising that there are influences at work other than those led by government through its strategy. It concludes [39] that the social enterprise strategy has resulted in

- putting the sector 'on the map' among policy-makers;
- the development of consultative forums (e.g. the Social Enterprise Coalition) which are crucial for a cohesive approach to the sector;
- a common 'jump-off' policy for government departments, devolved administrations, and RDAs;
- better understanding of how social 'enterprise' can deliver social benefit;
- greater legitimisation of the sector in the eyes of other stakeholders arising from the leverage of additional funds.

However, it is not easy to find hard evidence in the report that the government's own success measures have been attained. The Cabinet Office itself acknowledges this, stating that it is 'difficult to know without baseline figures', but it adds that

- 'The *perception* is that social enterprise is growing.'
- 'There is *more* awareness of it and interest is growing.'
- 'Departments *are beginning* to look at how social enterprise might help them deliver their objectives'. [40] (emphasis added)

The report itself is cautious in its conclusions on the social enterprise strategy outcomes, frequently using qualifying terms. [41] For instance, it notes that

- 'The operating environment has become more conducive for the sector. Nevertheless, improvements in the enabling environment remain patchy ... reflecting differential prosecution of the SES objectives across governmental activity.'
- 'The review has identified a strong perception of growth and some concrete evidence of growth. The perceptions of growth may overstate the actual increase in activity because of pre-existing activity being redefined as social enterprise.'

It also notes that while the term 'social enterprise' has become 'a widespread part of the lexicon of government activity across and within, the United Kingdom, awareness does not necessarily imply understanding'. [42] In addition, Stevenson noted that despite 'a genuine recognition of their strong record in delivering services, the take-up of the social enterprise model across local and national government is patchy and fails to reflect the enthusiasm with which it is discussed'. [43]

In looking for concrete evidence of achievement against the success measures and per-formance indicators, there is much more evidence of initiatives having been taken than of proven results in the areas of growth, awareness (as understanding), and removal of growth barriers. In short, it is easier to identify and measure inputs and activities than results at this stage, and, to an extent, it may be argued this is because many of the interventions are only beginning to have track records.

That report was relatively positive, as far as it goes, and seems to suggest that the UK government might have made a reasonable start. Others, in looking at different initiatives or at different aspects of policy, have been less complimentary (and two such examples are summarised in Case 10.1). None of these reports, however, has looked at the longer-term impacts of the initiatives.

That may not be surprising because it does take time both for overall changes in a sec-tor to become apparent and for objective assessments of them to be made. It was, for instance, in the late 1970s and the 1980s that much government attention was paid to small businesses, yet it is only now that independent assessments of the overall effective-ness of that policy are becoming available. Unfortunately, the evidence in that case does not seem to be positive.

Ten years ago one book which included an introduction to such initiatives still con-cluded that 'there appears to be no strong body of evidence to say that intervention works, but also there is no clear evidence that it doesn't'. [44] Ten years later some of the same authors came to the stronger conclusion that 'Although there may be limited find-ings that cast doubt on the effectiveness of interventions, there appears to be significantly more reliable evidence for such a view than for the contrary belief that intervention has worked'. [45]

One example of a positive report [46] on an initiative in the social economy sector is that on Community Development Finance Institutions (CDFIs) in the UK. They are specialist enterprises, often operating on a not-for-profit basis, which deliver finance as well as other support services to (social) enterprises and individuals that cannot access funds from the mainstream banking sector. (For more on CDFIs, see Chapter 7.) The report concluded that the

> sector is now able to provide evidence of the scale and extent of its positive economic impacts in a robust and comprehensive manner. Given the known levels of public sector support, CDFIs are efficient delivery mechanisms for enterprise lending and the sector represents value for money.
>
> It should be noted, however, that the standard and common methodology for assess-ment of value for money had to be revised due to the lack of transparency of the sector in reporting income and expenditure figures. [47]

The report was not without its qualifications, however. (See Illustration 10.5.)

Illustration 10.5 Summary: CDFIs and economic and social impact

Robust, detailed and comprehensive evidence is now available of the economic impact of CDFI enterprise lending. This standard methodology has been applied at CDFI and sector level and draws on an expected standard range of CDFI monitoring data.

Despite poor monitoring data on income and expenditure against activities, given the known levels of public expenditure, CDFIs are efficient delivery mechanisms for enterprise lending and the sector represents value for money.

To demonstrate fully its value and cost effectiveness, the sector needs to develop its description and measurement of social benefits and impacts within a comprehensive and common framework.

More broadly, the use of logic models in this document illustrates how the sector and individual CDFIs can map their activities against funders' goals and as the basis of developing business cases, performance assessment and evidence of impact.

Potential actions

To map your individual CDFI and activities against a logic model and associated policy objectives;

To work with the CDFA and *Change Matters* to: develop common metrics and indicators for income, activity expenditure, and outputs; and, the development of a common framework to identify and assess social benefits and impact.

Source: GHK Consulting, *The National Evaluation of Community Development Finance Institutions (CDFIs): An Action-Orientated Summary for the Sector*, for the Department for Business, Innovation and Skills and the Cabinet Office URN 10/1019 (Birmingham: GHK, June 2010), p. 2

Conclusion

While it is clear that some social economy organisations have created jobs and some have launched social innovations, some have contributed to local regeneration and some do represent significant entrepreneurial ventures, the overall extent of that has not been quantified. Similarly, some social economy organisations clearly supplement the public sector social services and address what they perceive to be gaps in its provision, and some have sustained themselves for many years. Yet there are others which have found that they were unable to survive in such roles because they could not generate enough income, from whatever sources they could find, to sustain them. Have social economy organisations levered institutional change and promoted more democratic structures and citizen participation in decision-making? Given that political parties are social economy organisations, it might then be argued that they have done so, but that expectation has been laid specifically on social enterprises, and there again, there appears to be no clear body of evidence.

The chapter does not say much either about the effectiveness of government interventions to promote the social economy because, it seems, there is not much to say. This is, at least in part, because expectations around the potential of the sector have grown only relatively recently (but see Illustration 10.6), and so many of the interventions to support it are relatively new and may not have had time for their full impact to show. However, experience of other sectors where governments intervene to try to promote growth, such as that of small businesses, suggests that, despite the significant budgets devoted to this work, often there is little meaningful and reliable evaluation of its effects, and where there has been some overall evaluation, it is not indicating a significant impact.

Illustration 10.6 Do not have unreasonable expectations of the social economy

In the preface to their book *Placing the Social Economy*, Amin et al. state that

> Our evidence shows that it is naive and unreasonable to expect, as does UK, and increasingly EU policy, and increasingly also EU thinking, that the social economy can be a major source of jobs, entrepreneurship, local regeneration, and welfare provision. To do so, runs the risk of marked disappointment, a return to the vagaries of 'good acts' and 'good people' in combating social exclusion and meeting welfare needs, while

legitimating cuts in state expenditure or state welfare remit. We find, instead, that social enterprises – in the right places and with the relevant support – have a role to play that is complementary to provision via state and market. As such, they can achieve something genuinely different. The more ssuccessful social enterprises analysed in our research are those that open up new possibilities and networks for people who had previously been confined to the limited resources of poor places ... Therefore, our perspective is at odds with Third Way/New Labour thinking, which charges social enterprises with creating jobs, tackling social exclusion in the round, providing training, developing local services and local markets, and generally countering the effects of years of disinvestment and disengagement by public and private sectors alike. Furthermore, they are expected to become financially viable. Our findings demonstrate quite clearly that the social economy as it is currently constituted cannot deliver this range of outcomes. This is not only because of its own inherent limitations, but because of the different capacities of people and places to develop social economy activities – the poorest places having the least chance of doing so – and because these many problems cannot be tackled solely at the level of local communities. [48]

That does not mean intervention to support and promote the social economy is not effective, but just that it is not possible at this stage to conclude that the result of the various efforts is a stronger, bigger, better-organised and better-run, or more productive and contributing sector than would otherwise have been the case. Moreover, a full assessment of the impact of policies will require the sector to put a greater emphasis on measuring its social as well as its economic impacts (see Case 10.2).

Key Points of Chapter 10

- There is no single clear assessment of what social enterprises and the rest of the third sector achieves. Nevertheless, economic, social, local, environmental, cultural, arts, sporting, educational, political, moral, ethical, and personal impacts have all been attributed to it.
- Measurement of the impact of the social economy is at an early stage and there is little quantified evidence for the extent of these impacts.
- Many expectations of the social economy can be divided into three broad approaches: an economic/entrepreneurship approach seeking jobs and welfare provision with an emphasis on financial sustainability, a socio-economic approach also seeking jobs and welfare provision but primarily to compensate for welfare state inadequacies, and a political/ideological approach which seeks to lever institutional change.
- The third sector or social economy generally forms a significant part of economies but indications of its scale are partial and sometimes inconsistent.
- Despite significant recent government support for the social economy, or at least for parts of it, there is so far little evidence of what that intervention is achieving.

Case 10.1 | Examples of critical assessments of social economy initiatives

Community businesses in Glasgow

Hayton, who commented on the Glasgow Community Business scheme, defined a community business as 'a trading organisation which, through the sale of goods or services, aims to become self sustaining'. Nevertheless, he was critical of this experience of promoting community business because of the poor sustainability of the businesses started, the scheme's cost-effectiveness, the type of jobs created, their costs, and the extent to which the businesses were causing displacement. He also found that many of the enterprises established were not actually community businesses and classified them into the following four categories:

- community businesses owned and controlled by local residents with a remit to create jobs for local people by setting up commercially viable trading organisations;
- enterprises that were essentially conventional private sector companies with ownership and control vested in those who owned the company rather than the wider community;
- 'businesses' that were Urban Programme-funded projects that had been set up to run for the duration of the grant;
- 'businesses' whose objective was to create a service for a community rather than jobs. Effectively these were voluntary sector projects which, after an initial period of public subsidy, were able to survive as they relied upon unpaid labour. They had no intention of becoming commercially viable.

Hayton argued that the pressure on business performance indicators in the scheme emphasised business start-up at the expense of support to existing companies. The lack of a clear business approach to the management and development of community organisations is a theme running through Hayton's critique. His conclusion about the scheme was that

> the main outcomes were that many initiatives that were not community businesses were supported and there was a high failure rate as the emphasis was upon new starts rather than providing development support... Funding had... been provided at a far higher level than the support framework was capable of absorbing effectively. The consequence was a failure to deliver. Community business obtained short-term benefits by over-selling but these were at the expense of the concept's longer-term credibility.

As a result of this failure, it would appear that, at least in Glasgow, the term 'community business' became discredited to the detriment of the surviving organisations still known as community businesses.[49] Despite that, there are still many successful organisations which could be classified as community businesses.

Source: Based on K. Hayton, 'Scottish community business: An idea that has had its day', *Policy and Politics*, Vol. 28, No. 2 (2000), pp. 195–7

Regional Development Agency support for social enterprises
As indicated earlier in the chapter, much of the UK government's social enterprise strategy was, in England, implemented principally through the Regional Development Agencies (RDAs – which are now defunct and have been replaced by Local Enterprise Partnerships – LEPs). It is therefore instructive to examine the lessons to be learnt from the RDAs from their work in supporting the sector.

According to one observer, a major difficulty for the RDAs in seeking mainstream support for the sector was 'revealed as the struggle for *clarity*. Chief Executives and Directors of Strategy found it difficult to grasp what *social enterprise* and *social economy* meant.'[50] They therefore found it difficult to put a value on these sorts of activities as against other more easily measured components of their 'target-driven portfolio'.

The RDAs faced these issues at a difficult time for them, as they were facing significant organisational and strategic change. So, despite the impetus given by the publication of *Social Enterprise: a strategy for success*, confusion and complexity were dominant and the situation was compounded by:

- 'The DTI emphasis on trading social enterprise [*sic*] as the proper focus of attention – seeing social enterprises as relatively normal businesses operating in a marketplace.'
- A complementary range of initiatives relating to the creation and development of CDFIs and patient capital initiatives.
- A separate line of development arising from the legacy of EU programme-driven and other bottom-up and partnership polices, focusing on social enterprise as a tool for regeneration and inclusion with a focus on participation and engagement and with an emphasis on grant-driven development rather than market-driven development.
- A long-standing interest in what might be called the old co-operative movement, with an emphasis on democratic management but linked to the DTI social enterprise agenda.

Source: Based on C. Stutt Consulting, *Finance for the Social Economy in Northern Ireland* (2004), p. 38, www.colinstutt.com (accessed 7 October 2007)

Case 10.2 | Demonstrating impact

For Community Development Finance Institutions (CDFIs), social outcomes and impacts are important but this case suggests that they could be reported more effectively. The case is drawn from an evaluation of CDFIs and follows on from Illustration 10.5. It records the concerns expressed in the evaluation because the matters thus raised could be held to typify the issues facing initiatives in this and other social economy fields (albeit CDFI lending is not mainly to social enterprises).

According to the evaluation 'from a public policy perspective, the ability of CDFIs to demonstrate the **full range of their impacts** is crucial if the value and cost-effectiveness of the sector is to be understood and compared against other policy interventions'. Specifically the issues raised in the evaluation include:

'Defining, measuring and valuing the social outcomes and impacts of the CDFI sector

The CDFI sector has long highlighted the range of its social impacts. CDFIs generate various social impacts, including:

- employment creation and income generation in disadvantaged areas and under-represented groups;
- skills development and attitudinal impacts;
- local service provision;
- enhanced social capital;
- improved physical environment, etc.

The evaluation highlighted the **lack of consistent articulation and description of social outcomes at the level of individual CDFIs and the sector in its entirety.**

The evaluation supported the CDFA in trialling reporting of social outcomes as part of the *Inside Out* annual CDFI survey and, additionally, successfully sought reporting of social impacts in the business client survey.

A key finding from this work was that **few CDFIs measure these social benefits**. Previous evaluations of CDFIs have also identified the need for improvements in the social impacts evidence base. It should be noted, however, that a cost needs to be recognised in reporting against these impacts.

A major issue is that **there is no common framework for undertaking these measurements and benchmarking performance,** although the sector is actively seeking to develop such a framework, and is engaged with broader social value initiatives at government level.'

Source: GHK, *The National Evaluation of Community Development Finance Institutions (CDFIs): An Action-Orientated Summary for the Sector,* a report for the Dept of Business, Innovation and Skills and the Cabinet Office (Birmingham: GHK, June 2010), p. 20 (bolds in the original)

Questions, Exercises, Essay, and Discussion Topics

1. According to what criteria would you seek to assess the impact of the social economy?
2. How would you categorise the impacts of the third sector?
3. Why are the achievements of the social economy difficult to assess?
4. Can the overall impact of the social economy be assessed by gauging its size?
5. What do you think will be the impact of government support for the social economy and why?

Suggestions for further reading

GHK, *Social Enterprise: An International Literature Review*, a report submitted to SBS/SEnU (London: GHK, 2006).

J. Monzón and R. Chaves, *The Social Economy in the European Union* (Brussels: CIRIEC, 2012).

A.Westall and D. Chalkley (Eds), *Social Enterprise Futures* (The Smith Institute, London 2007), available on http://www.smith-institute.org.uk/file/SocialEnterpriseFutures.pdf (accessed 31 December 2012).

See the world's major co-operatives and mutual businesses at http://ica.coop/en/global-300, accessed 16 June 2013.

References

1. D. Smallbone, M. Evans, I. Ekanem and S. Butters, *Researching Social Enterprise,* Small Business Service Research Report RR004/01 (Sheffield: SBS, 2001), p. 32.
2. http://sroi.london.edu (accessed 4 April 2008).
3. J. Nicholls, S. Mackenzie and A. Somers, *Measuring Real Value: A DIY Guide to Social Return on Investment* (London: New Economics Foundation, 2007), p. 2.
4. Ibid., p. 5.
5. J. Monzón and R. Chaves, *The Social Economy in the European Union* (Brussels: CIRIEC, 2012), p. 45.
6. F. Lyon, S. Teasdale and R. Baldock, 'Approaches to measuring the scale of the social enterprise sector in the UK', Third Sector Research Centre, Working Paper 43 (Birmingham: University of Birmingham, 2010), p. 2.
7. Ibid., p. 15.

8. J. Kendall, *The Voluntary Sector* (London: Routledge, 2003), p. 22.

9. IFF Research, *A Survey of Social Enterprises across the UK* (London: Dept of Trade and Industry, 2005).

10. Office of the Third Sector/Cabinet Office, *Social enterprise action plan: Scaling new heights* (London: Cabinet Office 2006), p. 3.

11. HM Treasury/Cabinet Office, *The Future Role of the Third Sector in Social and Economic Regeneration: Final Report*, Cm 7189 (London: The Stationery Office, 2007).

12. F. Lyon, S. Teasdale and R. Baldock, 'Approaches to measuring the scale of the social enterprise sector in the UK', Third Sector Research Centre, Working Paper 43 (Birmingham: University of Birmingham, 2010), p. 6.

13. http://webarchive.nationalarchives.gov.uk/+/http://www.cabinetoffice.gov.uk/third_sector/social_enterprise.aspx (accessed 21 November 2012).

14. F. Lyon, S. Teasdale and R. Baldock, 'Approaches to measuring the scale of the social enterprise sector in the UK', Third Sector Research Centre, Working Paper 43 (Birmingham: University of Birmingham, 2010), p. 11.

15. Ibid.

16. R. Ridley-Duff and M. Bull, *Understanding Social Enterprise: Theory and Practice* (London: Sage Publications, 2011), p. 21.

17. http://www.startups.co.uk/social-enterprise-statistics.html (accessed 7 May 2012).

18. HM Treasury/Cabinet Office, *The Future Role of the Third Sector in Social and Economic Regeneration: Final Report*, Cm 7189 (London: The Stationery Office, 2007), p. 6.

19. J. Clark, D. Kane, K. Wilding and P. Bass, *UK Civil Society Almanac 2012* (London: NCVO, 2012), p. 7.

20. http://ec.europa.eu/enterprise/policies/sme/promoting-entrepreneurship/social-economy/ (accessed 24 November 2012).

21. J. Monzón and R. Chaves, *The Social Economy in the European Union* (Brussels: CIRIEC, 2012), p. 46.

22. Ibid., p. 46.

23. Ibid., p.16.

24. Ibid., p. 54.

25. GHK, *Social Enterprise: An International Literature Review*, a report for the Social Enterprise Unit (March 2006), p. 18.

26. www.socialeconomy.eu.org/spip.php?rubrique215 (accessed 20 April 2013).

27. http://nccsdataweb.urban.org/NCCS/extracts/nonprofitalmanacflyerpdf.pdf (accessed 5 December 2012).

28. http://nccs.urban.org/statistics/quickfacts.cfm (accessed 5 December 2012).

29. Policy Research Initiative, *What We Need to Know About the Social Economy: A Guide for Policy Research* (Ottawa: Canadian government, 2005), p. 1.

30. M. Hall, C. Barr, M. Easwaramoorthy, S. Sokolowski and L. Salamon, *The Canadian Nonprofit and Voluntary Sector in Comparative Perspective* (Toronto: Imagine Canada/Johns Hopkins University, 2005), p. iv.

31. Policy Research Initiative, *What We Need to Know About the Social Economy: A Guide for Policy Research* (Ottawa: Canadian government, 2005), p. 3.

32. HM Treasury, *Appraisal and Evaluation in Central Government: 'The Green Book'* (London: The Stationery Office, 1997), pp. 96–7.

33. R. Scott, Personal correspondence based on the work for Northern Ireland's Department of Economic Development.

34. A. Purdon, C. Lessof, K. Woodfield and C. Bryson, *Research Methods for Policy Evaluation*, Department of Work and Pensions Research Working Paper No. 2 (London: HMSO, 2001), p. iii.

35. J. Curran, 'What is small business policy in the UK for? Evaluation and assessing small business policies', *International Small Business Journal*, Vol. 18, No. 3 (2000), pp. 38–9.

36. HM Treasury, *Appraisal and Evaluation in Central Government: 'The Green Book'* (London: The Stationary Office, 1997), pp. 96–7.

37. Ibid., p. 12.

38. Specific, Measurable, Achievable, Relevant, and Time-bound.

39. GHK, *Review of the Social Enterprise Strategy*, a final report submitted by GHK (London: GHK, 2005), p. 54.

40. www.cabinetoffice.gov.uk/thirdsector, accessed 31 October 2007.

41. GHK, *Review of the Social Enterprise Strategy*, a final report submitted by GHK (London: GHK, 2005).

42. Ibid., p. 53.

43. A. Westall and D. Chalkley (Eds), *Social Enterprise Futures* (London: The Smith Institute, 2007), p. 3, http://www.smith-institute.org.uk/file/SocialEnterpriseFutures.pdf (accessed 31 December 2012).

44. S. Bridge, K. O'Neill and S. Cromie, *Understanding Enterprise, Entrepreneurship and Small Business*, 2nd ed. (Basingstoke: Palgrave Macmillan, 2003), p. 497.

45. S. Bridge and K. O'Neill, *Understanding Enterprise, Entrepreneurship and Small Business*, 4th ed. (Basingstoke: Palgrave Macmillan, 2013), p. 373.

46. GHK, *The National Evaluation of Community Development Finance Institutions (CDFIs): An Action-Orientated Summary for the Sector,* a report for the Dept of Business, Innovation and Skills and the Cabinet Office (Birmingham: GHK, June 2010).

47. Ibid., p. 19.

48. A. Amin, A. Cameron and R. Hudson, *Placing the Social Economy* (London: Routledge, 2002), p. x.

49. Ibid., p. 67.

50. Colin Stutt Consulting, *Finance for the Social Economy in Northern Ireland*, p. 38, www.colinstutt.com (accessed 7 October 2007).

Index

In this index "*c*" represents case studies, "*f*" represents figures, "*i*" represents illustrations and "*t*" represents tables.